D. B. BROMLEY

THE PSYCHOLOGY OF HUMAN AGEING

SECOND EDITION

PENGUIN BOOKS

Penguin Books Ltd, Harmondsworth, Middlesex, England
Penguin Books Inc., 7110 Ambassador Road, Baltimore, Maryland 21207, U.S.A.
Penguin Books Australia Ltd, Ringwood, Victoria, Australia
Penguin Books Canada Ltd, 41 Steelcase Road West,
Markham, Ontario, Canada
Penguin Books (N.Z.) Ltd, 182–190 Wairau Road,
Auckland 10, New Zealand

First published 1966
Reprinted 1969, 1971
Second edition 1974
Reprinted 1975

Made and printed in Great Britain
by C. Nicholls & Company Ltd
Set in Monotype Times

Contents

Preface

'We spend about one quarter of our lives growing up and three quarters growing old.' These were the opening words of the first edition of this book. The assertion is not as simple as it looks, as we shall see, but it is a forceful way of stating one general reason why human ageing is worth studying. The fundamental importance of the juvenile phase of the life-cycle cannot be denied, but it is debatable whether we should be devoting to it such an overwhelming proportion of our intellectual and material resources.

The study of human behaviour in adult life and old age is becoming increasingly important; work and interest in the theory and practice of social and behavioural gerontology should gradually enable us to achieve – for adults of all ages – benefits comparable with those that developmental psychology has achieved for children and adolescents. The biological, psychological and social effects of ageing create an intricate tangle of interactions which are interesting to the research scientist and challenging to the applied gerontologist. In spite of considerable achievements in the treatment of medical disorders in middle age and later life, we continue to underestimate the benefits that could be achieved if social and behavioural gerontology were *applied* to the problems of retarding and mitigating the adverse effects of 'normal' ageing. We all have a personal stake in the study of ageing because we all *expect* to survive beyond middle age and to grow old, and many of us do so; moreover, we all have dealings with older people, so the more we know about ageing the better we shall understand them and ourselves.

Like the first edition, this book should meet the needs of undergraduate students, for example, in psychology, sociology and medicine. It provides a firm foundation for postgraduate students in social or behavioural gerontology or in relevant professional work – clinical psychology or social work. But the book has been written with a wider audience in mind: it should interest professional people in health (general medical practice, psychiatry, geriatrics, nursing), industry, adult education, administration and government. I hope it will interest the general reader, who can expect to find a relatively straightforward account of all the more important aspects of adult life and old age, as well as explanations for many things that puzzle him. Diverse but related aspects of adult life and old age are approached scientifically, i.e. by reference to empirical observation and rational argument. This is important, because our attitudes towards human ageing are distorted by prejudices expressed, for example, in the way we sometimes use the adjective 'old' as a term of abuse.

In this revised edition I have retained whatever seemed true, relevant, and well expressed in the first edition; but – rather like a house which has become too small and unsuitable for continuing use – demolition work has been carried out wherever necessary, and hopefully a larger, more effective edifice has been constructed.

The book has been enlarged in the following respects. First, by a new chapter which redefines the concept and study of ageing; second, by a new chapter on the history of human ageing; third, by a new section on middle age and a new chapter on terminal behaviour (dying), which form part of a comprehensive account of the main adult stages of the human life-cycle; fourth, by an increased emphasis on social gerontology; fifth, by a complete reconstruction of the chapter on methodology; sixth, by new tables and diagrams. I have made only passing mention of bchavioural research on ageing in animals. Technical issues have not been evaded, but this has meant including some background information, since it is too much to expect all readers to be familiar with basic facts in all the relevant disciplines.

Sections remaining from the first edition have been extensively revised and up-dated, and bibliographical references revised accordingly. I have compiled the list of sources on the assumption that it is easier to trace backwards through the literature than forwards and so have selected mainly from recent publications. Numerous bibliographical notes are supplied for each chapter, and referred to in the text by consecutive numbers. The bibliographical notes not only list various sources for the information in the text, but also provide a literature guide to the psychology and science of human ageing.

Information about human ageing is difficult to present because the items have to be dealt with serially, although they are extensively cross-linked. The book, as it were, offers a comprehensive tour of social and behavioural gerontology; it is up to the reader to construct his own 'cognitive map' of this territory, and he may prefer to read the chapters in an order different from the one I have arranged. The more difficult chapter on methodology has been placed towards the end of the book because it is likely to be of interest mainly to research workers.

The complexities of human ageing are such that unqualified statements are often risky. Where they are used in this book, the intention is to simplify the presentation of the material and not to convey an impression of finality. Exact figures have been used sparingly because they are usually specific to the sample and the conditions of the investigation, and do not make much sense without detailed background information. Research workers are by no means unanimous in their views, and have to learn to live with rapid changes in the map of knowledge. If the reader wishes to make a *scientific* appraisal of human ageing, then he must accept the uncertainties and limitations of research. If the book contains any factual errors or misunderstandings, I should be glad to have my attention drawn to them.

Liverpool, 1973 D. B. BROMLEY

and accordingly I have curtailed the list of sources on the assumption that it is easier to trace backwards through the literature than forwards, and so have selected mainly from recent publications. Numerous bibliographical notes are supplied for each chapter and are referred to in the text by consecutive numbers. The bibliographical notes not only list various sources for the information in the text but also provide a literature guide to the psychology and sciences of human ageing.

Information about human ageing is difficult to present because the items have to be dealt with serially, although they are extensively cross-linked. The book, as it were, offers a comprehensive tour of social and behavioural gerontology. It is up to the reader to construct his own 'cognitive map' of this territory, and he may prefer to read the chapters in an order different from the one I have arranged. The more difficult chapter on methodology has been placed towards the end of the book because it is likely to be of greatest interest to research workers.

The complexities of human ageing are such that unqualified statements are often risky. Where they are used in this book, the intention is to simplify the presentation of the material and not to convey an impression of finality. Exact figures have been used sparingly because they are usually specific to the sample and the conditions of the investigation, and do not make much sense without detailed background information. Research workers are by no means unanimous in their views and have to learn to live with rapid changes in the map of knowledge. If the reader wishes to make a scientific appraisal of human ageing, then he must accept the uncertainties and limitations of research. If the book contains any factual errors or misunderstandings, I should be glad to have my attention drawn to them.

Liverpool, 1973 D. B. BROMLEY

Acknowledgements

I owe a great deal to the many people who have kindly volunteered to act as subjects in the psychological investigations that I have carried out. I realize more fully the long-term value of the constructive criticisms and ideas I got from friends and colleagues during the writing of the first edition of this book – in particular, the help from Robert Kellner, Sydney Tune, Stanley Berry and Dr D. W. K. Kay. I should like to take this opportunity to thank Dr M. Powell Lawton and Mr Art Waldman, of the Philadelphia Geriatric Center, who made it possible for me to spend a year in the United States of America and to meet many psychologists and gerontologists there whose work I now read with added pleasure. The University of Liverpool has been generous in providing resources for research and travel. The librarians in the University of Liverpool libraries and in the Medical Institution library have been extremely helpful over many years. The financial support for psychological research in ageing provided by a grant from the Medical Research Council has been greatly appreciated. My professional colleagues at Liverpool have been helpful during the writing of the revised edition of this book – in particular Professor L. S. Hearnshaw, Mrs Olive L. Keidan and Mr J. V. H. Eames in connection with the historical sections, Mr M. C. K. Tweedie, Dr Ann D. M. Davies and Mr M. G. Binks in connection with the methodology sections, and Dr W. J. Livesley in connection with the biological sections. Any factual errors and misunderstandings that remain are entirely my own. Professor H. W. Fairman provided the hieroglyph illustrations of old men shown in Chapter Two. I should like to thank several people for their secretarial services connected with this book and my research generally – in particular Mrs Dorothy Southern, Miss Pamela Yeomans, Miss Elspeth McTear, Mrs B.

June Fazakerley, and Mrs Jean Taylor. Miss Julia Vellacott and Mrs Carole McGlynn of Penguin Books have given invaluable assistance.

My main debt is to my wife Roma who has patiently put up with the heavy demands that research and writing have made upon my time at home, and who has made the domestic arrangements necessary for such work to be done.

Acknowledgements and sources regarding graphical and tabular material are given in the captions or bibliographical notes.

CHAPTER ONE

The Concept of Human Ageing

1. GERONTOLOGY AND ADULT AGEING

Gerontology is the scientific study of the processes of growing old. The term is derived from the Greek *gerōn*, *-ontos*, meaning an old man. This root is used to form related terms such as gerontocracy – government by the elderly – and geropsychology – the psychological and behavioural study of ageing. A closely related term is geriatrics, derived from the Greek *gēras*, meaning old age, and *iātros*, meaning physician; it refers to the medical care of the aged. The 'g' in geriatrics is soft; it is a matter of personal preference whether the 'g' in gerontology is hard or soft. The British usually put an 'e' in 'ageing', the Americans leave it out.

The scientific study of human ageing is a vast and sometimes terrifying and depressing subject. It reaches into the biological and medical sciences, the social and behavioural sciences, and even into technology and the natural sciences. Research in ageing makes calls on logic, statistical analysis and laboratory instrumentation. Beliefs and attitudes about later life find expression in the arts, in social welfare and government policy, and in philosophy. The fact that we are growing older makes itself felt in all sorts of personal ways in the ordinary affairs of everyday life.

Ageing is a complex sequence of changes. The organs and functions of the body are impaired. Some people suffer mild or severe psychological disorders brought on by degenerative disease or other causes. There are changes in sensory and motor capacities, in the central processing functions associated with intelligence, and in its physical basis – the nervous system. People's position in society changes; their beliefs, attitudes and personal qualities alter, as does their behaviour. The content and organization of one's experience changes.

Human ageing is a peculiar topic to study objectively. Apart from the emotionally disturbing effect of its personal relevance, there are wide differences *between* individual people, and severe methodological problems in research. The effects of ageing are complicated by interactions and feedback loops between many variables. Nevertheless, the biological, social and psychological problems of human ageing cannot be evaded, especially in advanced communities where a substantial proportion of members survive beyond the end of their active productive lives. These problems include occupational redundancy and retraining, social and economic provision for old age, leisure and retirement, and those associated with the social medicine of later life.

The scientific study of human ageing faces three main tasks: theoretical, methodological and applied. The theoretical task is to confirm and extend the conceptual systems which integrate and explain the observed facts of ageing. The methodological task is to develop suitable research procedures and to examine carefully the logic of arguments about the nature of ageing. The applied or practical task is to prevent or reduce the adverse effects of ageing.

A person's chronological age is closely associated with, but by no means a perfect index of, his physical and mental capacities, or his life expectation. Moreover, the outward and visible signs of ageing, which appear earlier in some individuals than in others, need not presage a more rapid decline of physical or mental capacities. These discrepancies have led research workers to think in terms of 'physiological age' and 'functional age', in their attempts to describe and explain time-related changes in adult life.[1-5]

It is a mistake to think of chronological age itself as anything more than a time marker. In abstract terms, 'adult ageing' is a series of time-related changes in a set of interconnected variables. These changes lead to greater deterioration, and culminate in death. This rather brutal statement may provoke the reader into protesting that adult life and old age also exhibit many features of growth or development. This is correct, and this is why we must try to distinguish between pairs of terms likc 'chronological age' and 'ageing', 'adult development' and 'juvenile development', 'adult ageing' and 'adult growth or development'. Life beyond the juvenile period is a combination of adult ageing and adult development, in which the cumulative effects of ageing eventually preponderate.

It is not generally realized that, even in early life and throughout the juvenile period, the processes of ageing – in the brutal sense mentioned above – are taking place. This is a matter for the biology of ageing and we shall not pursue it. For all practical purposes, in social and behavioural gerontology, human adult ageing begins as soon as a person completes his genetically regulated programme of growth, and for convenience we can locate this transition point at the intersection of late adolescence and early adult life, say between the ages of 16 and 20.

The concept of 'ageing' in the sense of 'deterioration' is, as yet, much less elaborate than the concept of 'development'. It is instructive, therefore, to examine the various meanings of the former with the help of a thesaurus and a dictionary. In this way we can form a concept of 'adult ageing' or 'age deterioration' which contrasts with the concept of 'development' and matches its complexities, as follows.

Adult ageing, age deterioration: to grow old, to develop the characteristics of old age; to pass into a post-developmental condition; to have passed beyond the stage of actualizing latent capacities or potentials (for development); to retreat from a more developed, complex, or more fully grown state; to degenerate, to regress, to retrogress, to become unmade; to bring to a less advanced or less organized state; to diminish, to become depleted, to become less available; to fall into disuse; to simplify; to withdraw, to involute, to retreat; to become closed in, constricted, tied down, enveloped; to wither, languish, lose vitality, shrivel; to become degraded, to decay.

This cluster of ideas is intended to do no more than jolt the reader into an awareness of how abstract and complicated the concept of 'adult ageing' really is. Clearly, ageing does not refer merely to the passage of time; it is not simply the opposite of development; it takes many forms, not all of which can yet be assimilated to a coherent conceptual framework. For example, like development, it exhibits changes in morphology (form, structure) as well as changes in function (activity, process).

2. OUTLINE OF THE HUMAN LIFE-PATH

The term 'life-cycle' is somewhat inappropriate when applied to human beings, because of the extended period of post-reproductive life. I prefer the term 'life-path', for reasons which are explained later. The life-path is the complex sequence of events which takes the individual from conception to death. For the purposes of description and explanation, however, and for reasons which are discussed elsewhere in the book (including our present ignorance of the relationships between development and ageing), it is convenient to maintain a distinction between the *juvenile* and *adult* phases of the life-path, and even to contrast them. Within each of these *phases,* it is possible to define a number of successive *stages,* which can be described in biological, psychological and environmental terms.

(a) *Juvenile Phase*

Briefly, the individual starts life at conception with the fertilization of an ovum. He goes through about seven weeks of embryonic development, and during the foetal stage gradually acquires the morphological properties necessary for life outside the womb which begins at roughly 38 weeks from conception. The average child rapidly develops competence in a variety of interrelated areas: perception, thinking and action. His behaviour and experience are shaped in all kinds of ways by the society to which he belongs.

It appears that a genetically regulated programme of biological development is being put into effect through morphological changes which influence, and are influenced by, the environmental and social conditions operating during the whole of the juvenile period. From a lifespan–developmental point of view, these changes lead to alterations in functional capacity and actual performance and so provide the foundations for subsequent phases of juvenile and adult development, and adult ageing.

Between the ages of about 11 and 16 years, there occur the biological, social and psychological changes known as puberty. Primary and secondary sexual characteristics appear, giving rise to reproductive capacity and to widespread changes in behaviour and inner experience, such as outlook and motivation. Early adolescence is a period of rapid development in other areas: secondary education is completed; some legal responsibilities and rights are acquired; stature increases and the child becomes more 'adult' in appearance and behaviour. The main programme of genetically regulated growth is nearing completion.

For our purpose, late adolescence, say 16 to 20 years, marks the transition from the juvenile to the adult segment of the life-path. The person reaches the end of his juvenile growth programme, although, as we shall see, he maintains some capacity for growth of different sorts throughout adult life and old age. The education and training typical of late adolescence is designed to fit him more specifically into an adult occupational role. A transition has to be made from the largely dependent juvenile status to the largely independent adult status. In urban industrial communities, the combination of biological and social changes often engenders unstable, short-lived, and sometimes deviant patterns of behaviour; anti-social behaviour reaches a peak, but there is also a surge of adventurism, creative activity and social concern.

This brief and simple description of the juvenile phase serves to remind us that adult life and old age are parts of an *historical* process. What we become depends in part on what we are now, which in turn depends on what we were in the past. However, we must not make the mistake of confusing an historical narrative with a causal analysis. The 'causes' of our behaviour do not act at a distance (in time), and they do not necessarily act directly. Study of the juvenile phase, therefore, may not be immediately relevant to the study of age changes in adult life and old age. What is first required is a description and analysis of the *proximate*, i.e. immediate or direct, causes of the effects of ageing and of the small number of major causes.

(b) *Adult Phase*

We shall deal with the complexities of adult ageing throughout the book. For the time being, all we need is a simple framework of ideas for understanding the main timetable of events in adult life and old age. As in the juvenile phase, the biological, social and psychological determinants of behaviour are closely interwoven. Compared with the juvenile phase, however, the biological processes in the adult phase are relatively slow – although cumulative in their effects – and do not show rapid transformations, except perhaps at the menopause or in association with disease or injury. The absence of well-defined indices of biological and behavioural competence means that division of the adult phase into segments or stages is to some extent arbitrary, and largely defined in terms of social characteristics. With the onset of old age, however, the emphasis shifts back as biological and behavioural competence diminish to levels below those required for the normal activities of adult life.

For convenience, then, we can distinguish seven stages or segments in the *adult* phase of the human life-path:

EARLY ADULTHOOD. This stage, say from 20 to 25, overlaps with that of late adolescence; it completes the transition from juvenile to adult status. Although circumstances vary between different cultures and historical periods, the average person in urban industrial society acquires a variety of adult social characteristics – legal maturity, voting rights and socio-economic responsibilities – for example, with regard to work, family maintenance, and privacy. He (and she) usually marries and raises a family. They continue to invest time, money and other resources in anticipation of future circumstances.

There are, of course, considerable differences between men

and women, between members of the various socio-economic strata, and, of course, between individuals, in the way this stage – and any other stage – of life is lived. Individuals become more fully 'engaged' in a variety of formal and informal social activities; the ensuing emotional and functional relationships bind people together into a complex system of interlocking social groups. Early adulthood may include further education and occupational training. Physical health and many athletic achievements are at their highest level. Intellectual vigour and experience have begun to produce achievements in science, literature, and the arts.

MIDDLE ADULTHOOD. This stage, say from 25 to 40, overlaps with the previous stage, and with the one that follows. In general, it consolidates the individual's public and occupational roles, and his family and private affairs. He accumulates material possessions and establishes relatively stable social relationships. Occupational and other sorts of progress continue, depending upon circumstances. Output – in the form of physical work, emotional investment, and intellectual creativity – is at a relatively high level, and the accumulation of experience eventually puts the individual into a privileged and commanding position, relative to his early adult status, giving him, for example, seniority and socio-economic security. The entry of the last child into school creates opportunities for women to become more fully engaged in occupational and social activities outside the home. Nevertheless, some deterioration in biological and psychological capacities takes place, in vision for example, and some aspects of intelligence also decline. Such deterioration is slight; it is not usually obvious in the ordinary activities of everyday life; but it can be detected by testing the individual's *maximum* performance capabilities.

LATE ADULTHOOD. This stage, say from 40 to 60, is characterized by further consolidation of the individual's public and occupational roles. Socio-economic differences and sex differences, however, complicate the description of 'middle age', which corresponds broadly to this period (see chapter Eight

Section 4). There are problems of progress in his career, and in the dispersal of children from the home. The menopause closes the reproductive life of women and provides an obvious biological marker for adult ageing, but seems to engender few social or psychological consequences. Changes in social circumstances, such as the departure of children, lead to some redistribution of activities and resources, but these events are usually anticipated and adapted to without great difficulty. Adverse changes in physical and mental health, and overall reductions in biological capacities, continue to accumulate and begin to limit the nature and scope of the individual's life, including his pace of work, his leisure, and his sexual activities. Many of these changes are needlessly accelerated by ignorance and unhealthy ways of life. Individuals vary in their willingness and ability to counteract, compensate for, or adapt to, the effects of ageing.

In middle age, as in some other stages of life, the individual may experience an increased awareness of himself; he may become more reflective – re-examine his past and present circumstances, reconsider his prospects and way of life. Although it may not be apparent to the casual observer, the middle-aged person can modify his values and attitudes, and readjust his impression of himself (his self-concept).

PRE-RETIREMENT. The period from say 60 to 65 clearly illustrates the interweaving of biological, social and psychological factors. The rate at which adverse changes take place – as judged for example by the proportion of people who become physically ill, emotionally disturbed, or functionally less competent – accelerates sharply from late adulthood. The decline in physical and mental capacities, including such obvious characteristics as appearance, sexual vigour, stamina and speed, further limits the nature and scope of the activities open to the individual. The effects are more noticeable in situations which push people close to the limits of their capacity, like heavy paced work or tasks requiring intelligence rather than experience. Many individuals, however, retain a relatively high level of biological and behavioural competence. It is usual for individuals at this age to occupy important positions in social affairs and at work because many of the skills they possess are the fruits of long experience. Towards the end of the pre-retirement stage – when people are near the end of their active working life – there is a tendency for them to 'disengage' from the main streams of social (mainly commercial and industrial) activity. In anticipation of their retirement, many people hand over responsibilities, shed work, and prepare themselves for the next stage – developing their leisure-time interests, for example, and curtailing their living costs.

RETIREMENT. For many people, this stage, from say 65 to 70, marks an important and rapid transition from an economically productive status to an economically non-productive and relatively dependent status. This raises all sorts of issues – sociological, ethical, psychological, as well as economic – some of which are dealt with in Chapters Four and Eight. Retirement means different things, depending upon the individual's sex, socio-economic status, and psychological make-up. In general, however, people disengage from their main occupation. This brings about a number of changes in their life – in daily activities, social contacts, and standards of living. On the other hand, it may or may not entail radical readjustments outside the occupational sphere. In time, of course, the cumulative adverse effects of adult ageing, and the greatly increased chances of disease and disability, lead a person to disengage from a variety of social commitments and interests, because he cannot cope with the physical and psychological demands – as seen by himself or others. Personal relationships with family and neighbourhood become more important. Some individuals, however, may still hold eminent positions in established social organizations, especially if the duties are largely concerned with ritual and ceremony.

OLD AGE. Old age, from say 70 until the terminal stage (see below), is defined by an individual's diminished ability to cope with the ordinary affairs of everyday life – because of a variety of late-life infirmities – without help. The chronological age just cited is even more arbitrary than the others. Individual differences are considerable, and elderly persons living with one another, such as husband and wife, usually provide mutual support. The average expectation of life at birth in advanced urban industrial societies is about 69 for men and 75 for women, with a further expectation of about 10 years for those who have reached these ages.

In old age, the individual is normally fully disengaged from the main streams of economic and community activity, though he may lead a more (or less) active social life with kin, friends and peers. His social status depends upon a whole variety of considerations, e.g. social attitudes, legal arrangements, and the nature and extent of his physical and mental capacities. Individuals do not necessarily become senile in their old age. Most die from natural causes without exhibiting this or other distressing psychological disorders.

TABLE 1. Death by selected causes

Main causes of death	*All persons: percentage of total deaths in 1969*
Cancer: digestive system	6·69
,, lung, bronchus, trachea	5·14
Cerebrovascular disease	13·97
Ischaemic heart disease	24·45
Pneumonia (except new-born)	6·82
Bronchitis	5·75
All accidents	3·30

Adapted from Table 57, p. 99, *Social Trends, No. 2*, 1971.

TERMINAL STAGE. In present-day society, the terminal stage is not recognized as a functional part of the human life-path. Dying is regarded in a very negative way: as a part of death rather than as a part of life. In strictly medical terms, it is the final stage in the breakdown of physiological functions necessary to sustain *life* – although we shall see that there are grounds for regarding it as a *functional* stage in the human life-path, which means adding psychological and social criteria to the definition of 'dying'.

Each individual dies either through some kind of terminal illness, whether manifest or not, defined as a 'natural cause', or through violence or other 'non-natural' cause. As shown in Table 1, the most frequent natural causes of death in later life are malignant neoplasms of various kinds, arteriosclerotic and degenerative heart disease, vascular lesions affecting the central nervous system, pneumonia and bronchitis. The most frequent causes of death by violence are motor vehicle accidents, falls and suicide. At present, the maximum length of human life is thought to be marginally above 110 years.

3. THE COGNITIVE BASIS OF THE IDEA OF AGEING

(a) *The Life-Path*

The process of functional ageing can be represented in abstract terms and in a schematic way by using the analogy of the 'path', illustrated in Figure 1. In the strategic planning and conduct of a complex operation, like building, it is possible to describe a sequence of events following a path from one state to another. Thus we can think of juvenile development and adult ageing (throughout the entire lifespan) as a complex sequence of events on a multiplicity of interconnected paths that start at conception and terminate at death.

A series of points represent states (whether biological, psychological or social) or transition points between one segment of the path and another. In contrast with the usual definition of a 'critical path', the analogy defines an ideal one which takes the optimum route through juvenile development and adult ageing. The analogy next defines a 'standard path' as one representing typical paths traversed by people who eventually die from natural causes in old age. A 'deviant path' is one which deviates substantially from a standard path (which in turn deviates from the optimum path).

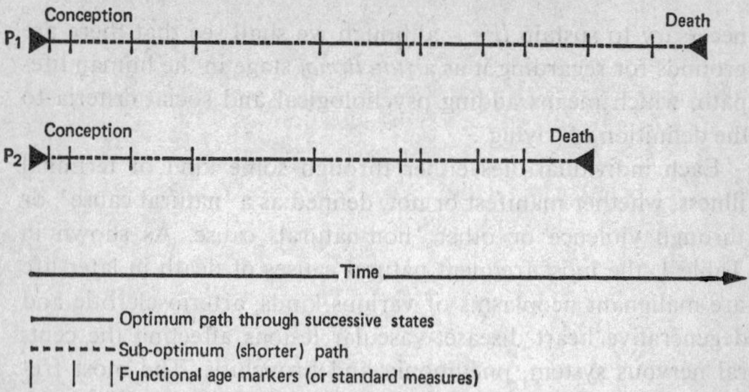

FIGURE 1 A simple schematic illustration of the concept of 'life-path', representing any biological, psychological or sociological sequence of events in the life of two persons: P_1 and P_2. See text for further explanation.

Figure 1 fails to represent the multi-dimensional nature of the human life-path, as well as its complexity and the interconnection between the different levels of organization of human life. For example, the concept of 'path' includes the notion that at a given time the sequence has reached one of several possible states, which must be followed by a transition to one of the possible states in the next set, as in the course of a disease or in the reaction to external stress.

The schematic representation of paths of development and ageing from conception to death requires symbols to represent transitional states, the optimum path between two or more states and deviant (shorter) paths between states. Length of life is represented by summing the durations of the states on the path actually traversed. Deviant paths take shorter partial paths and a shorter overall route from conception to death in comparison with standard paths. The optimum path at conception represents a theoretical maximum longevity. Chronological age measures the time taken to reach a particular state on the path between birth and death.

There are three advantages in representing the process of ageing in this way. First, it does not depend on the reality of the distinction between normal and pathological ageing (see

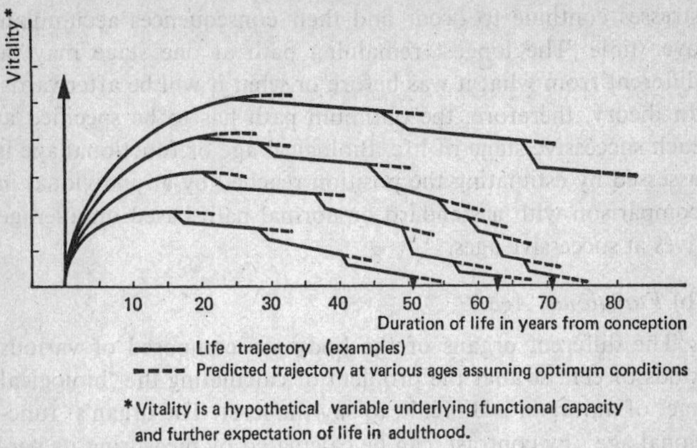

FIGURE 2 Semi-humorous image of 'life-trajectories' differing in duration because of the effects of ageing. The vertical arrow represents immortality – an escape, as it were, from biological gravitation. The individual is to be thought of as starting life on one trajectory, but as time goes by he drops into successively lower trajectories, one of which leads to his death at the point in time marked by an arrow-head.

Chapter Three). Second, chronological age is reduced to its proper role as a time marker. Third, the concept of 'path' can be applied to different levels of analysis, different component processes, and to shorter or longer sequences.

Initially, the optimum or ideal path varies from one person to another because of differences in genetic make-up, which predispose the individual to develop certain morphological features. Subsequently, it varies because of exposure to different environmental conditions, which provide constraints and opportunities for growth and change. Thus the optimum path in human development and ageing is a *potential* product of genetic and environmental interaction. Given the genetic and environmental possibilities, it specifies the path of *longest remaining functional effectiveness.* As soon as the individual starts to develop, however, he is obliged to deviate from this path because faults develop in his biological make-up and because environmental conditions are not ideal. Faults and stresses continue to occur and their consequences accumulate over time. The longest remaining path at one stage may be different from what it was before or what it will be afterwards. In theory, therefore, the optimum path has to be specified at each successive stage of life. Biological age or functional age is assessed by estimating the position reached by an individual in comparison with a standard or normal path based on average lives at successive ages.

(b) *Functional Age*

The different organs of the body are composed of various kinds of cell, so that the problem of calculating the 'biological age' of an organ is difficult, to say the least. The organ's 'functional age', by contrast, can be calculated by measuring its performance under standard conditions, and then comparing the result against norms based on representative samples. Whether one can apply the notion of 'functional age' to the person as a whole is a debatable point, since the person's functional effectiveness is determined not by the *average* effectiveness of all sub-systems in his biological make-up, but rather by the *least efficient* part of the system required to carry out the function. The notions of biological age and functional age, however, need to be further refined and validated if they are to lead to practical benefits.

Age changes in human behaviour can be thought of as the direct or indirect consequences of interrelated adverse changes in the anatomical structures and physiological processes of the body. Physiologists find markers for dividing up the person's development and ageing, not only by finding discontinuities in localized physiological processes and anatomical structures, but also and perhaps mainly by observing the emergence or achievement of new functional capacities (as development proceeds) and the disappearance or failure of such capacities (as ageing proceeds). The emphasis is on overall functional capacity, and the localized physiological and anatomical changes are seen to be relevant to development and ageing only in so far as they affect functional capacity. But functional markers may occur without obvious localized discontinuities in the physical basis of behaviour and psychological processes, otherwise the psychological markers are searched for in an analogous fashion.

The pathways of development and ageing, of course, refer to all processes at all levels of psychobiological organization – from the biochemistry of cells, through physiological changes in tissues and organs, to functional changes at a behavioural or sociological level.

It is obviously impossible to map all possible paths for all systems of the body at all levels of organization under all possible conditions. However, this should not discourage us from trying to map some paths for some systems under some conditions – namely, those which have theoretical promise. Some physiological processes, such as metabolic cycles and circulatory mechanisms, have been studied in terms of systems analysis, mathematical models and simulation. Such methods could be usefully employed to investigate optimum, normal and deviant paths in the social and behavioural aspects of human ageing.

(c) *Lifespan Development*

It is fashionable to approach the study of human ageing as a logical extension of developmental psychology – the study of infancy, childhood and adolescence. There is much to be said in favour of this current 'lifespan developmental' approach.[6–8] It attempts to study the human life-cycle in its entirety, to incorporate the juvenile and adult phases in one all-embracing framework of ideas, and to study the long-range relationships between development and ageing. As we shall see, however, the obvious merits of this approach tend to mask its limitations.

Juvenile growth can be described as an orderly, genetically regulated and directed programme of biological and behavioural development culminating in the young adult status. Adult ageing on the other hand can be described as an increasingly disorderly and undirected process of biological and behavioural disorganization and degeneration, culminating in death. Adult ageing lacks the coherence and logic of juvenile development; so, the convergence of juvenile paths of development towards the young adult status should not be confused with the subsequent divergence of adult paths of ageing, even though such paths all converge on and culminate in death. The impression of convergence is given by such facts as the average or maximum expectation of life; the fact of divergence is brought out by considering the variation between people in age at death.

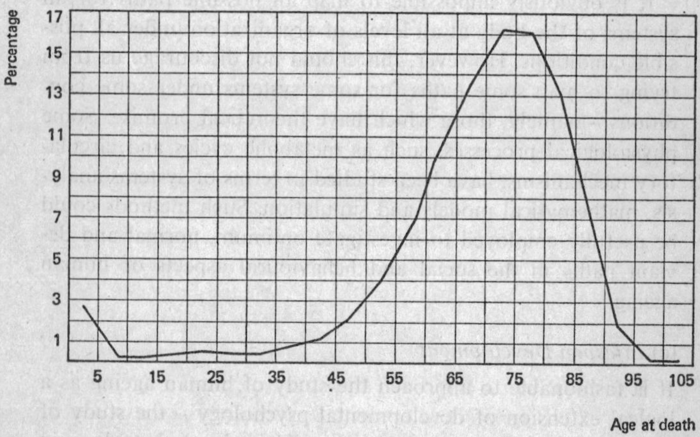

FIGURE 3 Percentage of cohort dying in each age interval. Based on life-tables for England and Wales, 1961–3. Source: H.M.S.O., London.

It should be noted, however, that although individual differences in function are said to increase with age, not all the empirical evidence supports this hypothesis; methodological complications, such as selective survival and psychological scaling, make it difficult to deal with this issue.

Although one should not underestimate the importance of studying the long-range consequences of developmental processes on adult ageing, it does not follow that theories and concepts of adult ageing must be simply logical extensions of those of development – as seems to be implied in the notion of a 'lifespan developmental' psychology. On the contrary, theories and concepts of adult ageing have to be formulated *independently* before the causal relationships between the two main phases in the life-path can be investigated.

(d) *Images of Ageing*

The historical survey (in the next chapter) of man's concern with the process of ageing will show that the transition to a strictly scientific, i.e. rational and empirical, view has been relatively recent. Nevertheless, a number of present-day scientific concepts relating to ageing had their beginnings in remote historical periods, and most of the imagery of ageing – in art, literature and daily life – derives, perhaps naturally, not from ultra-modern scientific concepts of ageing but from the more primitive, familiar, mystical views characteristic of medieval times and antiquity.[9,10] These 'images' of human ageing can be summarized fairly briefly. The first sees the human body as a container, like a furnace or cask; to begin with, it is full of an essential substance or spirit – innate heat, moisture, movement, life, spirit or vigour; this is gradually depleted or destroyed leading to cooling, drying, hardening, slowing, diminished energy, and greater vulnerability to damage or disease. From this first image derive the symbols of the inevitability of ageing – the candle burning out, the near empty well or cask, the dry withered leaf. The recent concept of ageing as a reflection of 'biological time' is thus related to the historical image of a fixed quantity of life which runs its course – hence the symbols of the emptying hour glass, sunset and the lengthening shadows, the four seasons and the end of the road. The second image of ageing represents a conflict within each person in which there is a growing imbalance between the positive forces of goodness, health, growth and repair, and the negative forces of evil, disease, damage and corruption. These latter forces eventually prevail. This image gives rise to various symbols – wormy and decaying substances, dilapidated buildings, worn and tattered clothing, rusty and broken tools or weapons. The third image of ageing is that of a process of renewal of life symbolized by the seed within the dry decaying shell, or by the insect or reptile shedding its outer skin, hence perhaps the idea of casting off our 'mortal coil' in life after death.

Part of the problem men had in former times in conceptualizing the process of ageing – a problem which can still be detected in modern works on ageing – was the confusion between ageing as a cause and ageing as an effect. The easy transition from one to the other made it difficult to identify the basic and contributory causes of ageing, hence 'ageing' became self-explanatory and almost a metaphysical concept, though not entirely closed to rational and empirical examination.

In recent years, scientific explanations for age-related changes in behaviour and its physical basis have been put forward; and related ideas such as normal versus pathological ageing (disease), intrinsic versus extrinsic ageing (stress, damage), and the cure for ageing, by means of an elixir or fifth essence (*quinta essentia*), have been persisting issues in the history of man's concern with human ageing.

CHAPTER TWO

The History of Human Ageing

PART I. MEDICAL AND PHILOSOPHICAL ASPECTS OF AGEING

1. INTRODUCTION

Old age and death are not inevitable. This was a belief and hope that prevailed among the physician–priests of Babylonia, Assyria and Egypt, and among the physicians of Greece, Rome and the Arab world. It was almost lost during the Dark Ages – preserved only by the alchemists in their search for an elixir of life. In more recent years it has been strengthened by scientific developments in the biology of ageing.

Scientific method – a system of rational and empirical methods for testing claims in order to eliminate errors in understanding – is of relatively recent origin, at least as regards its systematic and explicit use in the pursuit of knowledge. Much of what passes for knowledge, however, especially in the social and behavioural sciences, is neither scientific nor original, but the result of the systematization, elucidation and validation of ideas which have been in circulation for a long time at a commonsense level of understanding. Hence, it is useful and interesting to put one's subject of study into some kind of historical perspective.

Social and behavioural gerontology are of recent origin but, as we shall see, their historical roots are identical with some of those of medicine and philosophy. The history of social gerontology is further associated with political and economic developments from Elizabethan times to the present day (see Part II).

One valuable source of information about the pre-scientific era is a series of articles dealing with the medical history of old age written by F. D. Zeman and published in the *Journal of Mount Sinai Hospital* between 1942 and 1950. They include numerous quotations, illustrations and references; and they provide an unparalleled synopsis of the pre-scientific literature on ageing. These articles seem not to have been collected and reprinted in monograph form as proposed in footnotes to the title page of each article. The full list of references is given at the beginning of the bibliographical notes to this chapter at the end of the book.[1-15] Other people have made notable contributions, which are cited in the usual way.[16,17]

Some aspects of primitive men's attitudes towards old age are dealt with later, in connection with social anthropology (see Chapter Four, Section 6). For the moment, it is sufficient to say that primitive men probably made little distinction between human nature and the rest of nature. They would observe that some things changed while others remained unchanged, that some things could be controlled but others not. Physical disabilities brought about by accidents and diseases were prevalent, and action was taken to avoid or remedy such conditions. Physical health was valued, and human life was probably seen as something which persisted indefinitely unless brought to an end by an external agent – by killing, witchcraft or accident – rather than as something intrinsically limited. Before the advent of scientific knowledge, men's thinking about human nature was greatly influenced by superstition, animism and magic.

Among several primitive peoples, there is an awareness of the connection between the shedding of old skin and the apparent renewal of life in such creatures as snakes and lizards, and of the fact that some creatures go through a larval stage. The symbol of the serpent with its tail in its mouth represents eternity. The serpent and the worm figured prominently as symbols in primitive medicine. The serpent as an emblem of healing can be traced back to *c.* 2500 B.C. in Sumeria. The awareness that living things could be transformed from one form to another would reinforce the idea that human life and personal identity persist indefinitely. The Greek γήρας was thought of as a veil or skin over the body. Disease and death were thought of as bonds. It is of interest that both the Greek word γῆρας and the Latin word *senectus* refer both to old age and to the slough or skin cast by a snake.[18] In man's early history, it would be unusual for a person to survive into late life, except in fairly large settled communities; but an old person's dry wrinkled skin might have been sufficient for the analogy to be seen. Myths and legends regarding rejuvenation and the shedding of old skin are found in the folklore of early and primitive peoples. In modern societies, the condition of the skin is popularly regarded as an important manifestation of ageing.

2. SUMERIA AND ANCIENT EGYPT

The most remote traces of civilized concern for human health and welfare are found in Sumeria in the civilizations associated with Babylon and Nineveh, and with the king Hammurabi (*c.* 1950 B.C.). There is evidence of concern with hygiene and sanitation and with medicinal drugs. Some of the earliest clay tablets from Nineveh, dated about 700 B.C., but with text copied from *c.* 1500 B.C., prescribe treatment for greying hair and failing eyesight.

Until classical times, disease and death were thought of as caused by malignant supernatural agencies. Man's view of the world was based on beliefs in astrology and magic, hence his reliance on omens and divination, and on charms to ward off evil. Physical and mental disorders were attributed to possession by demons, and vile treatments were concocted to drive out these evil forces; the roles of physician and priest were closely related. Physical treatment was supplemented by psychological treatment in the form of rituals and incantations.

In the ancient world of Egypt and Greece, diseased and defective people were segregated from the larger community in the interests of hygiene and prophylaxis. Priest–physicians worshipped various gods, and practised the arts of healing on pilgrims and afflicted persons who visited their temples of medical learning.[19] The most famous name is that of Imhotep – vizier, architect and physician during the third Egyptian

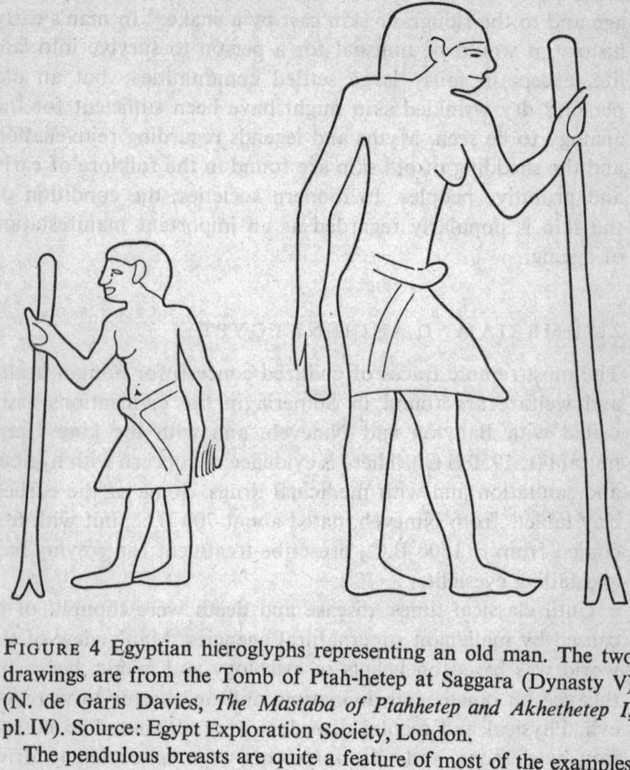

FIGURE 4 Egyptian hieroglyphs representing an old man. The two drawings are from the Tomb of Ptah-hetep at Saggara (Dynasty V) (N. de Garis Davies, *The Mastaba of Ptahhetep and Akhethetep I*, pl. IV). Source: Egypt Exploration Society, London.

The pendulous breasts are quite a feature of most of the examples of the sign in this tomb. They sometimes occur elsewhere but are not necessarily a regular feature in either Old Kingdom or later inscriptions. The Old Kingdom hieroglyphs are more carefully drawn. The head of the old man on the right is bald in front, but the rest of his hair is painted red!

The translation is of a polite greeting from a prince to a wise old man, 110 years old, who was a magician: among other things he could restore a head which had been cut off the body.

'He found him lying on a mat at the threshold of his house, a slave holding his head while rubbing it, while another massaged his feet. Then said the prince Hardedef: "Thy state is like that of one who dynasty (*c.* 2900 B.C.) – who was later deified. He is identified with the Greek god of medicine, Asklepios, whose emblem is the serpent. He proposed a variety of medical ideas including some relating to the treatment of the disorders of old age. There is a kind of historical continuity, in fact, between Egyptian medicine and present-day fads and fallacies regarding health and appearance, for example, constipation, wrinkles.

The earliest known medical papyrus on ageing was written *c.* 1600 B.C. and prescribes a treatment for transforming an old man into a youth. Thus, it is obvious that from the outset men were averse to the prospect of being old, and avidly searched for remedies to retard or reverse the process of ageing. It is interesting to observe that biological changes were regarded as critical – especially changes in external physical appearance, muscular weakness, and loss of sensory acuity. The Egyptian hieroglyph meaning 'old' or 'to grow old' represents a stooped human figure holding on to a staff for support. It first appears in inscriptions dated *c.* 2700 B.C. A subsequent papyrus *c.* 1550 B.C. refers to a number of common physical afflictions in old age and offers a variety of treatments, involving incantations and other magical and religious rites and the administration of various drugs and remedies.

Ancient Egyptian writings also expressed ambivalence towards ageing – this ambivalence has persisted throughout history to the present day. On the one hand there is the recognition that ageing is characterized by a highly undesirable physical degeneration; but at the same time there is the grudging recognition that later life has its own compensations and rewards, for example, status and experience, and that in any event one should be grateful if one survives to old age without suffering too many infirmities. The figure of 110 years was mentioned as the ultimate aspiration for length of life – a

---

lives before old age, – for old age is the time of dying, the time of encoffining, the time of burial – one who sleeps till day, free from sickness without hawking of the cough! This is the salutation befitting a revered person.' "

(Papyrus Westcar, 7, 14–20)

figure which concurs very well with present-day estimates of the upper limit of human longevity.

Attitudes towards old age were doubtless associated with family attitudes and relationships stressing love and loyalty between kin. The encouragement of respect and affection for parents and grandparents on the part of children has been a persistent feature in the socialization practices of human societies down the ages. The achievement of an advanced age was thought to warrant respect and honour from others – as evidenced by biblical sayings – especially if the older person had led a blameless life and possessed wisdom.

The books of the Old Testament are dated between 800 B.C. and 200 B.C. The Egyptian and Hebrew attitudes agree in taking pride in longevity and in family solidarity. The age at death attributed to mythical figures, like 950 years for Noah and 969 for Methuselah, obviously do not square with modern views even for the future of human longevity. Personages like Joseph and Moses are said to have lived to a great age – considerably more than today's expectation – but this is not surprising in a community without documents and valuing longevity. Claims to have lived beyond 110 years emanate from communities lacking adequate statistical records and having a reputation for longevity, or they prove to be exaggerated. The biblical estimate of 'three-score years and ten' is not very different from today's life expectation, although it must have been considerably in error as a statistical estimate of the expectation of life in those days. It probably discounted infant mortality and 'premature' death in adult life.

The Bible contains frequent reference to the physical and psychological characteristics of old age: menstruation ceases, sexual potency and desire are reduced, vision is impaired. Perhaps the story of King David and Abishag of Shunem is the first recorded treatment of hypothermia! Its success was noted in subsequent ages. The Bible also contains references to the diminished drives of the elderly and to their wish for a relatively quiet life among familiar people and surroundings. The command to honour one's parents is put powerfully, and fear of becoming dependent upon others must have been a strong incentive to inculcate appropriate attitudes in children. The ambivalence is apparent, however, in biblical stories of the way in which the views of the older generation might be rejected by younger people. Such rejection may have had to do with the unwillingness of younger productive members of a community to support the old dependents, and with the younger members' impatience with the outmoded views of their elders.

3. GREECE AND ROME

The Greeks' approach to medicine and human ageing derived in part from Egypt and Mesopotamia but was oriented towards reason and observation rather than towards the supernatural. It subsequently dominated the medicine practised by the Romans, and most of the medical practitioners in Roman territories were Greek.

Two Greek philosophers developed a framework of ideas for understanding man and nature, based on the four elements, as follows:

Empedocles *c.* 490–430 B.C.		Hippocrates *c.* 470–400 B.C.	
Cosmic Elements	*Their Properties*	*Corresponding Humours*	*Corresponding Temperaments*
Air	warm and moist	Blood	Sanguine
Earth	cold and dry	Black bile	Melancholic
Fire	warm and dry	Yellow bile	Choleric
Water	cold and moist	Phlegm	Phlegmatic

This provided a conceptual framework for understanding the physical world, medicine, human behaviour and the process of ageing, and had a profound and lasting effect on men's view of themselves and the world in which they lived.

Hippocrates made a substantial contribution to the understanding of physical health in late life. He recommended moderation in diet and physical exercise for longevity. He described a number of diseases and physical afflictions of late life, including cataract, loss of hearing, arthritis and insomnia. Ageing came to be viewed as a loss of innate heat and as a drying up of moisture, which might be remedied by food, wine, exercise and warm baths. This notion was to persist for many centuries, and was curiously appropriate.

Hippocrates was basically scientific in his approach and attempted to pursue descriptive medicine. His simple observations and remedies were incorporated into classical medicine, but not the spirit of his inquiries. In addition, this kind of rational and empirical work was minute in comparison with the widespread ignorance aggravated by superstitious beliefs in magic, demons, and popular remedies for common ailments. Physicians were not the specialists they are today, and in pre-Hippocratic times ill health was the concern of a variety of quasi-medical priests, magicians and faith healers. Treatment in the temples was based on a mixture of common sense, trial and error, magic, religion and suggestion. People with disorders which did not respond to physical remedies would naturally turn to religion or magic – a response not unknown even today. It is impossible to verify the nature and extent of the medical and pseudo-medical services and materials available to people in the ancient world. Professional medical practitioners probably pursued their work at various levels of rationality – medicine was not a narrow technical skill, but part of a comprehensive philosophy of life. Their knowledge and practices would diffuse through the community – being selected, distorted and added to in the process until they were indistinguishable from medical folklore.

The Greeks, like the Hebrews and Egyptians, emphasized filial love and the wisdom of age. But, in keeping with the ambivalence towards ageing mentioned above, they recognized the weaknesses and eccentricities of the aged. The literary portrayal of old men as sages or fools has also reflected this ambivalence. In *The Republic*, Plato refers to two of the less obvious but important features of late life, namely, the persistence of characteristics from earlier life, and the relief of having outgrown some of life's difficulties – frustrated ambition and unfulfilled sexual desire. The argument is that persons who are naturally well-adjusted and easy-going will cope reasonably well with old age, whereas persons lacking such dispositions are likely to be maladjusted in old age as in earlier periods of life. Plato's relatively positive and accepting view of old age differs somewhat from that of Aristotle who in his *Rhetoric* attributes a whole catalogue of negative characteristics to old people – what we would now call popular stereotypes. His method was to compare and contrast the assets and liabilities of youth with those of old age. He thought the prime of life lay between these extremes – the body is in its prime from 30 to 35 and the mind at about 49 years of age. Aristotle's view of old age was not completely negative, since he said that under certain conditions – being healthy and wealthy and growing old gradually – old age can be enjoyed. He also pointed out that people might live to a great age in spite of physical infirmities.

Aristotle's theory of ageing was that a living organism starts life with a kind of innate latent heat which is gradually dissipated in the process of living, and eventually disappears altogether. His theory foreshadowed the 'rate of living' theory of ageing propounded more recently by Pearl, and the discovery that basal metabolic rate decreases with age in adults. Aristotle observed that species differ in longevity. His observation that size and longevity are related has been partially supported by subsequent investigations.

By about the first century A.D. or earlier, Greek physicians were established in Rome. Early Roman medicine was simple folk-medicine using herbal remedies, incantations and charms; quacks, drug vendors and pseudo-oculists were common. Some attention was paid to what we would now call psychiatric disorders. Galen is probably the best known physician of this period. He prepared a comprehensive and systematic account of Greek and Roman medicine. His views were contentious but became the accepted medical dogma, and a main source for subsequent generations of writers on old age. In his *De*

Sanitate Tuendo, Galen dealt with such topical issues as exercise, diet, sleep and bowel function in old age, and drew attention to the problem of individual differences. Other writers described common social and behavioural characteristics of elderly people, and there was some recognition that ageing was a cumulative disease process.

Fairly high standards of hygiene were achieved in some areas of public and private life. Institutions akin to hospitals came into existence before Roman times, but Rome organized military and civil hospitals – *valetudinaria.*

Cicero (106–43 B.C.) in his *Cato the Elder on Old Age* (*De Senectute*) presents both a positive attitude towards old age and one typical of his day; it became a favourite source for later writers. He stressed the interrelationship of development and ageing, the reduction in desires, the capacity for continued psychological growth, the improvement in judgement based on experience, and the interaction of character and age. It is of interest to observe Cicero's recommendation to resist the process of ageing by physical exercise and diet, and intellectual activity. This emphasizes a fact of fundamental importance in social and behavioural gerontology, namely, that the social and behavioural aspects of ageing are secondary to, i.e. causally dependent upon, the apparently inevitable process of biological degeneration. But this is not to say that these secondary social and behavioural effects – disengagement, forgetfulness, and so on – may not further aggravate the underlying biological degeneration which initiated them. Cicero's reference to intellectual activity and learning in late life also illustrates an aspect of modern research in ageing – the attempt to measure the 'functional age' of an organ or a psychological capacity in terms of the extent to which it can grow in response to exercise and demand.

The notion that *life* rather than *years* is important is at least as old as the writings of Seneca (3 B.C.–65 A.D.) who stressed, among other things, the need to preserve the advantages of old age, and the increasing restriction on psychological and social growth imposed by each successive phase of life.

4. ISLAM AND THE MIDDLE AGES

With the decline of the Roman Empire in the West, there ensued a long period of intellectual stagnation vaguely referred to as the Dark Ages: *c.* 200 to 1200 A.D. Christianity attempted to destroy 'pagan' medicine and its temples, but in the process it assimilated some of its beliefs and practices (reference was made in the previous section to biblical writings on ageing).

Nascent scientific medicine, however, was in decline before Christianity was established – early Christianity had no place for science or systematic medicine. The institutions established to care for people unable to look after themselves – including the elderly infirm – were governed by monastic attitudes in which charity, prayer, and relief of suffering by simple home remedies were possible; but professional medical treatment was usually not available or even expressly forbidden. Earthly life was regarded as brief and of little significance in comparison with the eternal life that would follow (whatever form that took). The official preachings, of course, must have contrasted often with the actual practice of living, once again revealing the ambivalence felt towards the process of living and growing old. We still find a mixture of fatalism, 'Remember you must die', and hedonism, 'Enjoy the present opportunities'. By about the thirteenth century, there were almshouses and infirmaries, established in association with ecclesiastical institutions, which catered for orphans, the sick and the blind, and the infirm aged. Such institutions were often insanitary – dirty and overcrowded; they did not form a hospital system in the modern sense. In medieval England, there were about 1,000 such hospitals, about 200 of which were for lepers. Then when religious and political dissension led to the dissolution of the monasteries, their endowments were confiscated, and the hospitals could no longer be serviced and supported. In the sixteenth and seventeenth centuries, however, a number of almshouses were established through charitable efforts to help the poor (see Part II for the political and economic history of the aged).

In the Middle Ages the common man's ideas about disease and disability were as primitive as in the ancient world, and superstitious beliefs in magic, demons, elves and worms were widespread. People wore charms, were tricked by quacks, and suffered exorcism and vile forms of treatment. Some thought that sexual stimulation by young females would revivify the waning sexual capacities of old men and thus retard the process of ageing. The unspoken assumption underlying this and other attempts at rejuvenation, such as those claiming to improve the appearance of the skin or physical vigour, is that a temporary or apparent improvement in one of the more obvious physical signs of age signifies a general and permanent improvement, namely rejuvenation. Among the less attractive aspects of the history of man's concern with ageing is the medieval belief that drinking the blood of a child or milk from a young woman's breast would prolong life. Bathing in blood was also thought to have rejuvenating effects.

Writings from ancient India and China make reference to the problems of ageing.[20-22] Sexual beliefs and practices were prominent features of Taoism, and it was supposed that the essential spirits of the body, such as semen, could be preserved through unusual sexual practices. Taoism contains ideas similar to those in alchemy. In pre-scientific minds, a cognitive mechanism like 'sympathetic magic', i.e. concrete metaphorical thinking, leads to the formation of strong associations between ideas which have only a superficial resemblance – for example, the imperishability of gold and the imperishability of life; this helps to explain the tradition of alchemy within which the idea of the philosopher's stone and elixir of life was pursued. This imaginary substance would transmute base metal into gold; it would cure all diseases and provide an antidote to ageing – a pill of immortality.

The most notable of the Islamic physicians was Avicenna (980–1037) who defined the life-cycle, including old age, in terms of the classical qualities used by Galen. Avicenna remarked on the relationships between ageing and such things as climatic conditions, diet, fluid intake and urine excretion, exercise and bowel function. Maimonides (1136–1204) was another famous physician of this period who contributed views on old age stressing the value of wine and medical care, and warning of the dangers of sexual over-indulgence. His criticisms of Galen gained no support, and Galen's works became authoritative, and a hindrance to factual inquiry and innovation. A key figure during the late medieval period was Arnold of Villanova (1238–1311) who, among his other achievements, published a treatise on the preservation of youth and the retardation of old age. His approach was derived from the classical theory of elements, humours and temperaments. To counteract the adverse effects of the cold and dry humours in late life, the warm and moist humours must be encouraged by good food, wine, baths and so on. His recommendations provided a sensible regimen for the conservation of health and well-being in old age. He was an early editor of the *Regimen Sanitatis* of the medical school at Salerno, and engaged in the search for an elixir which gave rise to *aqua vitae* (alcohol).

Roger Bacon (*c.* 1214–94) was a scientist out of his time, though not free from beliefs in astrology and magic. He felt that failure to attend to physical health throughout life shortened the life of the individual and his offspring. Following an idea originated by Grossteste of Lincoln, he pointed out that the use of a lens could compensate for the impairment of vision in late life. His writings on the medicine of old age were based on classical and Islamic sources, and, as the title of one of his books, *The Cure of Old Age and the Preservation of Youth,* indicates, the preoccupation of medieval writers like those of former times was how to maintain youthful vigour against the ravages of age.[23] Possibly, for the reason we have already mentioned – the renewal of life in various forms in nature – it seems always to have been assumed that ageing (if not death itself) was not inevitable, and that some natural or supernatural remedy could in principle halt or even reverse the effects.

5. THE RENAISSANCE TO THE EIGHTEENTH CENTURY

In the fifteenth and sixteenth centuries the revival of learning known as the Renaissance brought to light the Greek and Roman learning on adult life and old age that had been preserved in Islam and Byzantium, and emerged from sources in Spain, Italy and Persia. The new learning provoked a reaction against the prevailing dogmas and authorities, and promoted a spirit of independent inquiry which was basically scientific and humanistic. A number of books on health and old age were translated into English and other vernacular languages and based partly on the classical doctrine of humours, astrology or other superstitions. Even the renowned humanist and Renaissance figure Erasmus, who recognized the inevitability of old age and death, nevertheless subscribed to a belief in the 'fifth essence' – derived from alchemy – by means of which he claimed a man could '... strip off senile weakness like a snake skin and be rejuvenated.'[24] Another source of medieval belief regarding ageing, derived from Greek sources, was the legend of the fountain of Juventa which would 'rejuvenate' those who bathed in its waters. The search for the fountain is said to have been the spur for a number of explorations, notably Ponce de Leon's discovery of Florida.

In the course of his historical researches, Zeman uncovered, in the *Gerontocomia* of Gabriele Zerbi of Verona (d. ?1505), an attempt to prescribe the proper management of old age.[25] It is based on Galenic medicine (via Avicenna) but appears to go beyond it in the sense that it incorporated Zerbi's own experience as a physician. The last two phases of the human life-cycle are defined and explained in astrological terms, and an attempt is made to establish criteria for the qualifications and duties of the 'gerontocomus' (geriatric specialist) and of the servants of the elderly. Even architectural and ergonomic factors are considered, together with recommendations regarding physical activity, leisure, recreation, sex, rest and nutrition – this last including such savoury concoctions as viper meat, distillate of human blood, and gold solutions.

Traditional remedies must have been regarded with scepticism by some, and the intractability of the disorders of old age reinforced the prevailing Aristotelian pessimism – with its varying reactions of anger, despair and resignation. Zeman cites Jerome Cardan (1501–76), 'Old age, when it comes, must make every man regret that he did not die in infancy'.[26] Ciceronian optimism, however, was also in evidence during the Renaissance: Cornaro (*c.* 1470–1566) advocated reduced food and drink, and the avoidance of emotional stresses; he emphasized the rewards of old age – to be enjoyed all the more when emotions are controlled by reason.

For Zeman, the works of Laurens (1558–1609), a French physician, represent the best late-Renaissance writings on old age. Laurens wrote in the tradition of Galen but without being constrained by it; of particular interest are his observations on the size and weight of the heart, his assertion of the intrinsic causes of death, and his recognition of individual differences in biological ageing.

Migration, trade, and the increasing urbanization of society, combined with ignorance and squalor, led to epidemics of various sorts and sizes, including bubonic plague and influenza. In the years 1348 to 1359 half the population of Europe is said to have died from plague. Towards the end of the fourteenth century, the prevalence of plague among the poor forced Parliament to pass Sanitation Acts in the interests of public health. Public sanitation and private hygiene had been prominent features of earlier civilizations, and belated recognition of their importance was to have significant repercussions eventually on infant mortality, longevity and the age structure of populations. Socio-medical and economic conditions lay behind significant legislation in Elizabethan times, such as the 'poor law', which was to have such profound effects on the health and welfare of the elderly that they can be traced right through to the British Welfare State of 1945. (See Part II.)

Throughout history, writings on the physical and psychological aspects of ageing have not been confined to medical literature. In the pre-scientific era there was not the kind of sharp separation that we have today between technical works and literature proper; an educated man was less of a specialist. Shakespeare, for example, drew extensively on traditional medical writings, including those dealing with old age, and amplified them with his own powers of observation and imagery. Francis Bacon's *History of Life and Death* published in 1658 dealt with ageing in relation to conduct, heredity and diet.[27] Bacon drew a number of sharp contrasts between the young and the elderly with regard to their respective abilities and personal qualities. He rejected many of the traditional myths regarding old age and offered an alternative account in terms of the differential rates of repair of the bodily tissues, whereby the parts which repair slowly induce decay in those parts which normally repair quickly; eventually, through a process akin to burning, the substance of the body is destroyed. Prominent among Bacon's other contributions to the study of ageing were his comments on family resemblances, physical attributes and diet.

An interesting episode in the year 1635 was the autopsy performed by William Harvey – who founded modern physiology and discovered the circulation of the blood – on Thomas Parr, who was supposed to have lived for nearly 153 years. Zeman quotes from Harvey's findings, and notes that Harvey appeared not to doubt Parr's longevity. The autopsy findings were published some years after Harvey's death, and they appear to have stimulated a series of autopsies on centenarians, thus leading to an interest in the pathology of late life, for example arteriosclerosis.

One or two independent minds in the fifteenth and sixteenth centuries had begun to explore the possibilities of instrumentation and quantitative methods in the study of medicine, including the medical problems of old age, although it was to be many years before such methods were taken up seriously or on any scale. In the seventeenth century, however, several works were produced dealing with the statistics of populations, births and deaths. In these areas, therefore, we see clear connections with modern laboratory studies and social surveys. Also in the seventeenth century advances were made in medical pathology —with obvious implications for the study of disorders associated with late life – such as diabetes and the coronary disease.

While these relatively modern thoughts were taking shape, however, much medical thought and practice continued in a context of magic, superstition, astrology, folklore and other encumbrances from the cultural traditions of those days. Thus, in spite of the efforts of men like Bacon and Paracelsus to break out of the sterile framework of classical medicine and develop a more rational and empirical method of inquiry, seventeenth-century scientific endeavour was unable to free itself from hermetics – magic and alchemy. Professional pharmacopoeias listed all sorts of curious substances for healing including, of course, cast-off snake skin. Physicians did not have the distinctive status they have today; they were still one of a number of contending medical and quasi-medical factions. A good deal of the credit for the establishment of modern medicine as a profession and science has been given to Sydenham (1624–89), a friend of John Locke, for his contribution to the clinical description of disease and his 'bedside' approach to patients.

The seventeenth century saw significant developments in science: the year 1645 saw the beginnings of what was to become the Royal Society; the microscope was invented; men moved closer to rational, empirical and experimental methods of inquiry into nature. By the middle of the eighteenth century, medicine was well on its way to the modern era. Boerhaave (1668–1738) practised clinical 'bedside' medicine, and carried out post-mortem work. Morgagni (1682–1738) studied morbid anatomy and its relation to disease. William and John Hunter (1718–83 and 1728–93) studied anatomy and pathology. Work of this sort laid the foundations for the study of the relationships between chronological age and the causes of death.

Gradual recognition of the merits of independent rational and empirical inquiry meant focusing more sharply on clinical and pathological aspects of human ageing – hence the emphasis on the detailed description of individual cases and on post-mortem findings. In this way, it was confirmed that old age is accompanied by a variety of general physical symptoms, including shortness of breath, sensory impairments, muscular weakness, as well as by a variety of specific diseases. Whereas the general prescription for good physical health in late life followed the traditional pattern – moderation in all things, proper diet, the avoidance of stress – the handling of specific diseases became progressively more technical. Zeman gives credit to von Fischer (1685–1772) for being the first physician to break with the medieval tradition and adopt an essentially modern approach to medicine. Discoveries by other physicians quickly followed and technical reports and treatises on medical problems and methods increased rapidly. Rapid developments were also taking place in the natural sciences.

According to Zeman, the first work in English on old age was *Medicina Gerocomia*, published in 1724 by Sir John Floyer, who was much influenced by Galenic medicine. The first American work was *Account of the State of the Body and Mind in Old Age*, published in 1793 by Benjamin Rush, who gave more attention than was usual to the problem of mental disease, though without recognizing specific mental diseases of old age.[28]

6. THE NINETEENTH CENTURY

Medical research developed rapidly in several European countries in the nineteenth century. Most of the major advances were not responses to the challenges posed by diseases of late life but responses to more fundamental issues like the prevention of infection, the improvement of surgical techniques, and the diminution of pain, though these naturally brought considerable benefit to people of all ages.

The discoveries of Lister, Pasteur and Metchnikov were to revolutionize public health by controlling epidemic diseases and infection. These discoveries had effects on the size and structure of populations, and therefore influenced economic and political events. They are thus related to the political reform movements which aimed to improve the condition of the poor and, with them, the elderly.

There was an increasing specialization not only in medicine but also in pure and applied science generally and it became natural to see the salient problems of old age as technical medical problems requiring the application of the same sorts of concepts and methods as were proving successful in the treatment of sick people at other ages. Geriatrics was not pursued with the same zeal as were other branches of medicine, but studies were made of the age distributions of diseases, the pathology of late life, and so on.

Mention should be made of Brown-Séquard who at the age of 72 attempted to rejuvenate himself by injections prepared from animal testicles. He was not successful, and his work created considerable adverse comment. Metchnikov proposed the theory that ageing was caused by the toxic effects of intestinal bacteria. The treatment quickly became popular but proved to have no significant effect. The event, however, illustrates the persistence of the hope that life might be prolonged – by some sort of elixir – well beyond its present upper limits; it appears that no one, so far, has demonstrated that this is a logical impossibility – like squaring the circle. Shortly afterwards, Steinach attempted to study the effects of tying the vas deferens so as to stimulate the proliferation of testicular hormone cells. Voronoff attempted to implant chimpanzee testicles in a man but did not achieve the hoped-for rejuvenation.

Medical research workers paid special attention to post-mortem findings, centenarians, morbidity, the circulatory system, and the response of the elderly to surgery. A notable contribution to the study of centenarians was made by Thoms, who wrote *The Longevity of Man: Its Facts and Fictions* in 1873 – a book which revealed the lack of evidence for many claims for longevity, including that of Parr.[29] His insistence on proper evidence and methods of inquiry questioned the prevailing assumption that the duration of human life could be increased two or three times. His work had the further consequence of stimulating greater medical interest in the disorders of old age.

In 1899 Magnus-Levy had demonstrated a decrease with age in basal metabolism; he was subsequently to confirm this finding by repeated measures of his own basal metabolism, and that of five other notable researchers, over a fifty-year period. Another important continental advance was the description of brain lesions now known as 'senile plaques'.

For many years, advances in European medicine set the pace for physicians in America. Zeman, however, cites some notable exceptions. For example, in 1890 Minot presented an address on ageing to the American Association for the Advancement of Science noting, in particular, changes with age in the relative sizes of cytoplasm and nucleus. An interesting link with subsequent work on adult intelligence and intellectual achievement can be found in the work of Beard, an American neurologist who was interested in the effects of ageing on the mental faculties, with particular reference to legal responsibility. He examined the apparent paucity of achievement beyond the age of 50 years. His notions – put forward in 1874 – were taken up again in 1905 by Osler when he compared the numerous contributions of men between the ages of 25 and 40 years with the negligible contributions of older men. The problems of adult intelligence and intellectual achievement were to become important issues in psychological research and remain so to this day (see Chapters Six and Seven).

The early hope of scientific medicine in the late nineteenth century and early twentieth century that a simple direct solution to the problem of ageing could be achieved through hormone treatment or by attention to dietary factors was not borne out. It became increasingly apparent that the processes of ageing were complicated and must be studied in a variety of ways, for example, by means of actuarial and mortality statistics, through the effects of radiation, by studying cancer and cell division, by investigating the effects of vitamins, drugs, hormones and diet, by examining the role of physical exercise, genetics, and so on – through the whole gamut of biological and medical possibilities.

While advances were being made in clinical medicine, surgery and pathology, some physicians were investigating the social aspects of medicine – in relation to housing, employment, hygiene, law, public health, insurance and so on. The movements leading towards social reform – including health and welfare provision for the elderly – were to increase in size and momentum, giving rise eventually to various political forms of the present-day welfare state.

PART II. THE POLITICAL AND ECONOMIC HISTORY OF THE AGED

1. MEDIEVAL, ELIZABETHAN AND VICTORIAN TIMES

Men have long been concerned to retard and alleviate the adverse effects of ageing, and all societies have recognized old age as a stage in life. In modern urban–industrial societies, the elderly are dealt with differently from other sections of the community, and the resources devoted to their health, recreation and welfare generally have a low priority. The physical and mental demands of modern industrial society have created a situation in which many older people are not able and not expected to fulfil a working role. In earlier times, it was the frail and the infirm who were distinguished as a needy social group. The 'able-bodied' elderly fulfilled a working role, circumstances permitting, and were not thought of as needing or deserving retirement in the modern sense. People occupying important social positions did not retire, they died in office. Retirement is of recent origin; it may be a passing phenomenon and give way eventually to social arrangements which make more sense logically and psychologically.

In remote times, charity and other social virtues were exercised in relation to the sick, the destitute, and the disabled; the needy included the elderly infirm lacking the support of family or friends. Giving relief to the needy was not necessarily an entirely disinterested act – it helped to assuage guilt, promoted social cohesion, and increased the likelihood of salvation.

In the third and fourth centuries, the Christian church in the Middle East established institutions for various categories of people in need; those for the aged were called 'gerontochia'. Such institutions were gradually established in western Europe, and were to be found in England in medieval times. There, the sick and elderly were cared for either by their feudal lord or in the monasteries, or they became destitute. An elderly person might enter into an agreement with his heir to be maintained with goods and services in return for his estate. Some rural workers could expect to be maintained in their retirement on the estate on which they had worked.[30] Almshouses in Britain date back at least as far as 1136 when the St Cross Hospital was established at Winchester. An almshouse was founded in 1437 in Ewelme, and named 'God's House'. Many were built in the sixteenth century but there were never enough to make much difference to the severe social and health problems of those days. The growth of the towns and of paid labour later created problems of unemployment and pauperism.

The religious disputes of the sixteenth century disrupted the growth of institutional care by the monasteries; and from the beginning of the seventeenth century, 'poorhouses' were set up by local parishes. These took in a variety of needy people – the blind, the physically and mentally sick, the disabled and so on; living conditions were desperately low, but they were society's only institutional response to the burden of age and incapacity until the reform movements of the nineteenth century.

Lack of sympathy for the needy and lack of understanding of the sociological and economic factors at work in society led, in England, to the development of laws dealing with the poor. Historical connections are not easy to establish and I shall merely outline what seem to me to be the main themes and events which have led up to our present position. My main source has been *The Coming of the Welfare State* (fourth edition) by M. Bruce.[31]

In 1598, during the reign of Elizabeth I, an Act for the relief of the poor was passed. It was precipitated by worsening economic conditions and poor harvests. It provided for 'the necessary relief of the lame, impotent, old, blind and such other being poor and not able to work'. The intention of the Act was to separate the incapable or aged poor from other destitute people; the former would lodge in 'abiding places' (poorhouses), the latter in workhouses. It was also intended to make able-bodied adults and children look for gainful employment, to restrict vagrancy, and to ease the overcrowding of towns. Social attitudes, however, and ignorance of economic, social and medical facts, meant that discrimination between individual cases was not adequate, and it became administratively convenient to house all kinds of destitute people in one type of institution. Naturally, living conditions in these 'workhouses' were often abysmal, and the threat of being reduced to such circumstances was a strong psychological inducement to seek employment until the Second World War. The 'work' provided, such as picking oakum – untwisting and unpicking old tarred ropes to provide material for sealing the seams of ships – was usually degrading, and the workhouse system actually aggravated economic conditions. The laws were strictly enforced and intended to deter the submerged sections of the community from making use of the little relief that was available.

The Elizabethan 'Poor Law', as it came to be called, was retained with little change until 1834 when, again in response to changing economic and social circumstances, it was reformed. Its severities were gradually mitigated, however, until in 1948 it officially ceased to have effect. Thus, in England in the seventeenth, eighteenth and nineteenth centuries, the aged were taken care of either by their family or employers, or supported by private charity, or – under the Poor Law – they received some parish relief or entered the poorhouse. Alternatively, they became destitute and begged. Vagrancy, however, was vigorously suppressed, and movement of the poor between parishes was severely limited, so as to prevent them from becoming a charge on a parish other than the one in which they were officially registered. Medical treatment was available at poor law dispensaries which were run on a voluntary basis in association with hospitals in some of the larger cities. It might be said that the elderly infirm were *relatively* well cared for until about 1870, by which time, as a consequence of widespread poverty and social disruption, they too had lost what little protection they had enjoyed.

In the second half of the nineteenth century, 'outdoor-relief' was regarded even less favourably than before, partly because of the increasing costs entailed by the Poor Law, and partly because of the prevailing social attitude which saw merit in fierce economic competition and low wage rates. The effect was to force more aged persons into poorhouses. The prevailing Ricardian economic theory argued that outdoor-relief had the effect of depressing wage rates, encouraging idleness, and diverting economic resources from more profitable endeavours. Even pensions – a relatively recent provision – were at first regarded as a disguised form of outdoor-relief, and further criticized as encroaching upon the individual's right to make provision for himself.

The Poor Law Amendment Act of 1834 was concerned with the 'able-bodied' poor.[32] The two basic principles of the Poor Law in Victorian times were as follows: first, to offer such unfavourable terms and conditions for poor relief that able-bodied persons at any age would be bound to accept any alternative except starvation; second, that poor law relief should provide living standards below those achieved by the poorest worker: this became known as the principle of 'less eligibility', that is that poor law relief should be less preferable than the lowest paid work.

2. LATE NINETEENTH AND EARLY TWENTIETH CENTURIES

From Elizabethan to Victorian times, the prevailing attitude among the wealthier and ruling classes, who were quite out of touch with the realities of life for the majority of the population, was that poor people were personally and morally responsible for their poverty and were therefore undeserving of support; they were even expected to suffer for the faults of their forebears. Thus the poor received little sympathy or help. Those who had no family to look after them when they became infirm and unfit for work, or unable to find work, had no alternative to the workhouse, unless they were fortunate enough to get a share of the relatively small resources of private charities.

Until the end of the nineteenth century, it seems to have been taken for granted that people got the old age they deserved: those who had led a good life were supposed to enjoy their last few years in peace and comfort; those who had not were supposed to end their days suffering and regretting the consequences of their misspent life. Christian teaching commanded children to honour, respect and love their parents; but it would require the skills of a professional social historian to discover to what extent such preaching was practised. The social structure and economic circumstances were regarded as fixed aspects of divine creation and not susceptible to alteration. Charity was regarded as a sufficient and proper way of dealing with people in need.

Even when these attitudes could be prevailed against, there was still the problem of the cost of making proper provision for old age, for example, by means of pensions. Booth's findings showed that the demand would be great. Surveys by public and private bodies showed clearly that, in the late nineteenth and early twentieth centuries, poverty was widespread (see also Part III, Section 2). It was associated with a variety of social ills – crime, disease, ignorance. In 1894, Charles Booth showed that the aged were particularly susceptible, and at this time nearly one third of the people over the age of 65 were receiving parish relief in England and Wales.[33] Moreover, increasing age brought a greater likelihood of becoming a pauper. Booth's findings confirmed and humanized the existing official figures, and they had a considerable influence on social and political affairs at least until old age pensions were introduced in 1908.

In 1895, a Royal Commission examined the problem of the aged poor and confirmed its seriousness, but failed to recommend major changes, partly in the hope that economic progress would eliminate want.[34] There was no general recognition that wage rates made it virtually impossible to provide for economic security throughout life, much less that the aged had a moral claim on society for support. After much public debate, and subsequent to the introduction of pension schemes in Germany, Denmark and New Zealand, pension rights were introduced in Britain in 1908 for people over the age of 70 who had been in regular employment but had little or no income. The difference between this measure and previous measures for dealing with the aged was that hitherto the cost and administration of relief had been the responsibility of the parish; relief was given only to people who were clearly destitute and 'deserving' of help. The cost of pensions, however, was to be met from general taxation. The introduction of pensions confirmed the rights of the aged, and recognized that individuals might not have been responsible for their own poverty; it confirmed that the Poor Law was no longer adequate to fulfil the obligations the community had towards its weaker members. The demand for pensions confirmed the extensive poverty associated with old age.

The origins of Friendly Societies date back to the fifteenth century. They were mutual aid bodies set up to raise funds for the relief of those members who were in need – the sick, the elderly and the bereaved. By the beginning of the nineteenth century, Friendly Societies were increasing rapidly in size and number. Their members paid regular subscriptions in advance – as a form of health insurance – to meet the cost of medical treatment and funeral expenses. People who were 'poor risks' initially, however, were excluded from membership. The extensive growth of the Friendly Societies during the nineteenth century made it possible for them to administer the funds of the National Health Insurance Scheme first introduced in 1911. They were supported by the trades unions, commercial interests, and Government alike. The introduction of compulsory health insurance met some resistance at first. The charitable organizations argued that a state pension would reduce voluntary donations. The Friendly Societies saw state intervention as a threat to their own activities, even though they were finding it increasingly difficult to cope with the claims of their older members. The administration of the state system, however, would have been impossible without their cooperation.

The financial basis of old age pensions was argued out in terms of whether pensions should be paid for out of taxation or funded by means of regular contributions during a person's working life. Pensions were still felt to be a disguised form of outdoor relief, which would inevitably lead to the demoralization of society, apart from being very costly. The costs were in fact initially greater than had been anticipated, and they continued to escalate. The effect of pensions on those elderly who managed to fulfil the requirements was, by the standards then prevailing, very satisfactory, though by modern standards poverty and hardship were still great and widespread.

Thus, the notion of an old age pension received as of right by a person who had led a productive and blameless life was not seriously discussed until the end of the nineteenth century. Even then, official opinion was that financial provision for old age was the responsibility of the individual; it was argued that as economic conditions progressively improved it would eventually be possible to do away with poverty and the need to relieve poverty. Although it fell to the central Government to make financial provision for basic pensions, this was not at the time intended to be the sole source of a person's income in late life. He was expected to make provision for it himself, out of his life's earnings, either by savings or insurance or by contributions to a Friendly Society. Some industrial and commercial firms organized their own occupational pension schemes and looked after the welfare of former employees in their retirement.

The political reforms of 1908 were partly a consequence of reforms in Germany. Bismarck had created a system of social insurance which, by 1889, included a pension scheme. This gave to the aged a measure of economic security as of right rather than as charity. Other countries evolved somewhat different systems of health insurance. In Denmark, state support for needy old people was introduced in 1891, and an applicant for relief did not have to demonstrate his inability to get support from his family as he did in Britain. The Danish pension system evolved in rather more prosperous and manageable circumstances than those prevailing in Britain during the Victorian era. It was not until the State Commissions on 'Old Age Survivors and Disability Insurance' started in 1910 that the United States began to move towards a social security scheme for the elderly. Most countries have accepted economic dependency in old age as the first legitimate form of dependency requiring government provision, but such provision has not received any priority in the allocation of resources.[35]

As medical science developed in the late nineteenth and early twentieth centuries, it became possible to treat sick people in hospitals rather than at home or in general purpose institutions for the needy. The growing numbers of physicians, specialists and medical auxiliaries created an increasingly complex pattern of private practice, research and teaching, in which hospitals played an essential part. Medical services were available mainly for those who could pay for them; public and private charities contributed to the medical care of the needy. The chronic sick, including a relatively large proportion of elderly people, benefited much less dramatically from medical advances and the professionalization of medicine than did children and young adults suffering from acute illnesses.

From about the middle of the nineteenth century improvements in medical care and public sanitation became more marked. The 'applied social science' of this period was concerned with issues such as public health, including epidemic diseases, sanitation, industrial pollution, water supplies, hygiene, purity in foodstuffs and medicines, and housing. Again, the main beneficiaries were infants and young people. Changes in the proportion of people surviving into late life were small in comparison with changes in infant mortality. It was not until shortly after the end of World War II that the British Government's policies took account of the growing fear that the expected increase in the proportion of the population surviving beyond retirement age would have serious effects on the economy. Subsequent improvements in child mortality associated with modern medicine have not been matched by equivalent improvements in further life expectation for people in middle or late life (see Chapter Three, Part II).

At a time when medicine was entering its modern phase of rapid scientific development, scientific discoveries in other branches of learning and innovations in social philosophy were radically changing man's view of himself and nature. The impact of social philosophy on the study of the welfare of the elderly in society, however, was at best small and indirect.

3. THE WELFARE STATE

Social policy for the aged has been affected by changes in social policy for the unemployed and other disadvantaged sections of the community, and for health. It has always been the product of a wide variety of interacting factors: on the one hand, social values and attitudes such as Christian charity, spontaneous feelings of sympathy and concern, economic individualism, liberalism, or socialism; on the other hand, ecological and historical factors such as industrialization, population size and structure, economic cycles, migration and war.

The welfare state in Britain is generally thought of as being created by the Labour Government of 1945. But, of course, its origins go back much further than that to the Elizabethan and Victorian Poor Laws and the social reforms at the beginning of the present century. When pensions were first introduced in Britain, they were financed out of general taxation, i.e. they were not 'saved up' in the form of contributions paid by the individual during his working life. By 1925, however, the idea of insurance against unemployment and sickness was extended to retirement. The main reason was that the cost of pensions had continued to rise and the proportion of retired people in the population had risen to about one in twelve.

In 1929 the functions of Boards of Guardians, whose members administered the Poor Laws, were taken over by the Public Assistance Committees of County and Borough Councils. Many hospitals were improved, but those which were left under the control of the Public Assistance authorities tended to house the aged and chronic sick in very poor standards of care and accommodation. Following the years of the Great Depression in the early 1930s, the British Government through the Unemployment Act of 1934 established an Unemployment Assistance Board. Its functions were to provide financial relief to those who would otherwise be a charge on local funds, to help with regard to occupational training and mobility, and even to advise on such welfare matters as housing, health, and useful activities. This was a long overdue step in the direction of helping older workers, especially those in depressed areas where employment prospects were poor.

An interesting departure from traditional social policy regarding the aged occurred in the 1940s, when, in reaction to the steadily increasing cost of living, pensions were supplemented by payments from the Assistance Board. In 1941, the Determination of Needs Act removed from family members some of the burden of caring for the elderly. Under the traditions of the Elizabethan Poor Law, a person in want had to be supported by parents, children and spouse. Memories of the depression years and of the threat of the 'workhouse' were fresh in the minds of older people in the early years of the welfare state. Many people, through ignorance or pride, did not take advantage of payments available through National Assistance to supplement inadequate pensions.

The Beveridge Report of 1942 was a basic document in the construction of the Labour Government's welfare state.[36] It recognized that social security in old age was an important and difficult problem, but warned against excessive provision for old age. The full extent of hardship among the elderly in the 1940s, and at other times when the cost of living has been rising, was not recognized then, and the problem still appears to be seriously underestimated.

The making of the welfare state in Britain in the 1940s included the difficult task of assimilating the country's medical resources into a National Health Service. Health education was extended, although it is difficult to assess its effect in making people healthier. The elderly as a whole need a substantial amount of medical, dental and nursing care, and the health service was expanded, improved and diversified partly in order to meet their needs. Hospital conditions were improved, and new patterns of residential and day care established. Home help was increased, and some of the burden lifted from members of the immediate family through temporary care, nurses' visits, and so on. More recently, schemes for 'sheltered housing' were put into effect. Even so, there are unmet medical needs among the elderly at large – for example, in connection with hearing, eyesight and mobility – which existing health services could not satisfy.

The Beveridge Report was much influenced by the prospect of changes in the age structure of the population. People in retirement were becoming proportionally, as well as absolutely, more numerous, they had legitimate claims for a greater share of the community's resources, and they made heavy demands on the health and welfare services. The elderly, however, were given no priority over any other sections of the community; pensions were kept low, as in subsequent years. At present, pensions are 'paid for' partly through contributions during the working life. Living standards in retirement may be supplemented by participation in occupational and private pension schemes, by social security payments, and by other community and charitable services. Organizations concerned with the welfare of the aged have had to struggle continually with successive governments even to maintain their meagre living standards.

The first report of the Royal Commission on Population was published in 1949 when the population of the United Kingdom was about 50 million, and the percentage of people of retirement age was about thirteen.[37-38] Today, the population numbers about 56 million, of which some 16 per cent are of retirement age. Pension costs, therefore, represent a sizeable fraction of the country's resources. Changes in the age structure of a population depend mainly upon the birth rate and life expectancy at birth; the social and economic issues associated with the age structure of populations are matters for continuing debate and investigation. Population forecasting, moreover, proved to be less accurate than was expected.

For reasons which would require a detailed social history to uncover, the welfare of people in need – the destitute, the mentally ill, the disabled, and the elderly infirm – has never been a major concern of modern societies. The welfare state formally recognizes the problem of old age, accepts responsibility for it, but provides minimal resources to meet it. Surveys of provision for the elderly and chronic sick in the post-war years revealed a depressing state of affairs. In 1948, the attitude of the British Government was that provisions for old age were best left to voluntary action. Local authorities were severely limited in what they were allowed to do for elderly people; they could provide residual care, but could not act positively to prevent distress or to raise living standards generally. Not until 1960 were local authorities empowered to visit the elderly in their own homes, to make inquiries, or provide services. Even today, the welfare of the aged in many public and private institutions leaves much to be desired.

4. SOCIAL SCIENCE AND SOCIAL HISTORY

We have surveyed the background of social gerontology in terms of the political and economic history of Britain from 1589 to about 1950. It could be objected that social gerontology is an empirical science, not political action, and that what is needed is a sociological account of the adult phases of the human life-path, as summarized in Chapter One. Age is obviously an important variable, but the *process* of ageing is a relatively recent focus for sociological inquiry. Human ageing has been of little concern to social scientists, except in so far as the 'aged' have formed a sizeable fraction of the poor; and except in so far as poverty has been studied in relation to the normal cycle of family responsibilities. Poverty, its scale and causes, has been a major concern of social scientists.

Social science includes political philosophy, and political action is a sort of applied social science – it reflects an underlying social theory, even though the theory is not stated scientifically and may lack empirical support. Bruce, however, takes the line that the evolution of the welfare state, and by implication the evolution of care for the aged, has been a piecemeal process created by a long and complicated series of historical events and socio-economic conditions. He maintains that the evolution of the welfare state has not been directly influenced by any political philosophy deliberately aiming for social reform.

Social gerontology, in so far as it could be said to have existed at all before World War I, was merely one facet of the wider concern that social scientists and political reformers had for disadvantaged sections of the community, particularly the very poor. Thus the early history of social and behavioural gerontology is indistinguishable from the early history of medicine and social philosophy. Modern social gerontology – expressed indirectly in new social attitudes and policies towards the aged as a distinct social group – began with the political reforms in Britain and elsewhere near the turn of the century. For all practical purposes, the history of *social gerontology* is the history of the 'poor law', the history of pensions, and the history of the welfare state. The beginnings of social gerontology are also located in political arithmetic, especially the social statistics of mortality compiled in the seventeenth century – see below.

The beginnings of *behavioural gerontology* are even more recent; they could be located perhaps in the work carried out by Galton in connection with the International Health Exhibition held in London towards the end of the nineteenth century.[39] An independent beginning occurred, however, when

American Army intelligence test data were analysed shortly after the end of the First World War. The appearance of Hall's book *Senescence* in 1922 made behavioural gerontology explicit in practice if not in name.[40]

Improvements in the health and welfare services, and improvements in pensions and housing have gradually improved living conditions for the aged. Nevertheless, people who have to rely solely upon an old age pension face the lowest standards of living of any section of the community. A national minimum income has not yet been achieved, neither have pensions been tied to changes in the costs and standards of living. In a welfare state, the community takes on the responsibility for the health, education and welfare of all its individual members, who in turn must provide, through taxation and in other ways, the goods and services needed to fulfil these responsibilities, including care of the elderly. Some of the economic problems associated with the increased proportion of elderly people in urban–industrial societies are dealt with briefly in Chapter Four, Section 1.

It is possible that biomedical discoveries will succeed in extending the human lifespan considerably, in which case radical changes will be called for in insurance schemes, retirement pensions and population policies. It is also possible that euthanasia, in one form or another, will become a more accepted method of dealing with some of the distressing aspects of old age, partly as response to the demand for a rational use of limited resources.

One effect of industrialization and welfare state policies has been the weakening of legal ties and obligations between generations within the same family and the strengthening of state control over the individual's fate in later life. In practice, the state takes control only when the elderly person would be worse off as a dependent member of his or her family; and many, probably most, old people depend in varying degrees upon both the state and their kin or friends. It is interesting to speculate on how the 'burden of age' will be carried in future years, when four-generation families will be more common;

lack of social interaction and shared circumstances would seem to lead to weaker bonds of affection between generations.

As areas of research and social action, poverty and old age attract few sociologists and fewer psychologists; the main effort is mounted by the voluntary and charitable organizations. Our present knowledge of the sociological and psychological aspects of ageing, however, is far in advance of our ability to apply this knowledge for the benefit of the aged. The limiting factor is the low priority given to old age by successive governments, which leads to a general lack of resources – materials, manpower, money.

In the United Kingdom, a National Old People's Welfare Committee was set up in 1944 to coordinate the activities of the main voluntary societies concerned with helping the elderly. Welfare committees were set up locally to coordinate voluntary effort such as home help, meals on wheels, legal advice, and so on. The NOPWC became part of the National Council of Social Service, but in 1970 it re-established itself as 'Age Concern', receiving roughly equal funds from charitable and Government sources. The Federation of National Old Age Pensions Associations has local bodies too and, as its name implies, it constitutes a pressure group devoted to raising pension levels. The National Corporation for the Care of Old People was established in 1947 by the Nuffield Foundation, following a survey of the elderly by Seebohm Rowntree. It is concerned with coordinating information and stimulating research into various aspects of human ageing.[41]

PART III. THE EMERGENCE OF SYSTEMATIC METHODS IN THE SCIENTIFIC STUDY OF AGEING

1. STATISTICS AND ACTUARIAL METHODS

In the seventeenth and early eighteenth centuries, old women acted as searchers in parishes to inquire into the diseases people had died of; their information provided the basis for 'bills of mortality'. Then, when the importance of social and medical statistics was recognized, relieving officers were appointed to collect the relevant information. Until that time, records of births, marriages and deaths were far from satisfactory for statistical and survey purposes. Nevertheless, attempts were made to construct life-tables and to examine the causes of death. For example, in 1662 John Graunt published his *Natural and Political Observations upon the Bills of Mortality*.[42] He was the first to represent the idea that a cohort of persons followed through life is systematically reduced by death at various ages; for example 3 per cent survived to age 60. This idea was more complicated than the notion of a crude death rate, and it led eventually to modern methods of analysing mortality and morbidity data and to other actuarial statistics.[42-47] Edmond Halley constructed a life-table based on deaths recorded for 1687–91 in Breslau.

Mathematics and statistics developed rapidly from about the middle of the seventeenth century. Life-tables and other actuarial methods were essential for life assurance and the effective running of the Friendly Societies; in the nineteenth century various life assurance offices were pooling their 'experience' in order to establish standardized life-tables. Naturally, the State was obliged to establish its own statistical resources. Mathematical methods for describing, analysing and forecasting age trends became increasingly useful for handling the accumulating data from official records, and for guiding commercial enterprise and government policy, for example in insurance, health and housing.

An important statistical development occurred in 1825 when Gompertz argued that the force of mortality increases logarithmically (in geometric progression):

$$R_m = R_o e^{\alpha t}$$

In 1867, Makeham added a constant:

$$R_m = A + R_o e^{\alpha t}$$

This fitted better with the data and took account of the fact that death is caused by both extrinsic (chance) factors and intrinsic (deterioration) factors.[48,49] If A is equal to zero, the Gompertz and Makeham equations are identical. Subsequently, attempts were made to express mortality rates more accurately, and over different segments of the life-cycle.[50] The hypothetical distinction between normal and pathological ageing can be expressed in statistical terms provided the various general causes of death – senescence, disease, accident – can be distinguished. Although the force of mortality can be expressed by means of a simple equation, it does not follow that the factors underlying the age trend are simple.

The Belgian mathematician and statistician Quetelet published *Sur l'Homme et le développement de ses Facultées* in 1835.[51] Quetelet compiled what would now be called social statistics on criminality, mortality and so on; he looked for regularities, the range of differences, and average values. He was anticipating modern studies of age and achievement by showing the relation between age and the productivity of dramatists. His other studies include growth curves and strength of grip for men and women. Quetelet's research findings, his awareness of the lack of data relating to age changes in biological, social and psychological capacities, and his realization that these changes must interact with one another, make him Birren's choice as the initiator of scientific investigation into the psychology of development and ageing.[52,53] As we have seen, however, the historical origins of statistical and mathematical gerontology lie not in nineteenth-century work, but in the seventeenth-century work on political arithmetic and life assurance associated with the names of Graunt, Huyghens and Halley.

Karl Pearson wrote *The Chances of Death* in 1892; he described the varying probabilities of dying at successive stages of life.[54] The work of Galton, a polymath, had considerable influence on the history of psychology generally – for example in connection with the study of imagery and sensory processes. He was influenced by Quetelet; he noted the effects of statistical regression and developed an index of correlation. He is counted as one of the pioneers of developmental psychology and the psychology of individual differences. Perhaps more pertinently, Galton demonstrated that late life is associated with a diminished capacity for detecting high frequency sounds. In 1884, at the International Health Exhibition in London, Galton set up an anthropometric laboratory in which nearly 10,000 children and adults were examined in a variety of ways.[55] The results of these investigations were made available subsequently; they appear not to have initiated any sort of systematic research in social and behavioural gerontology, but the norms for body measurements were of considerable value to the clothing industry.

Over the years, statistical investigations have established such facts as: women live on average longer than men; the expectation of life for children born today is considerably higher than it was a hundred years ago; the further expectation of life for people over the age of 65 years has increased relatively little during the last century; people in different occupations have different life expectations, for example doctors live longer than dentists. Another way of looking at mortality and morbidity tables is to consider what has been lost, such as years of life or working days. This requires an estimate of what would have happened to the person had he not succumbed to the risk. For example, a man who dies at the age of 40 might be said to have 'lost' 25 years of work and 35 years of life – if we assume that the limit of a 'normal' life is 75 for men.

In Britain nowadays life-tables and other sorts of statistical information relevant to health, welfare, age and so on, are regularly published by the General Register Office. More than one government department publishes statistical information, and various commercial and other organizations are concerned with the compilation of social statistics.[56-59] Statistics relating to morbidity and mortality are of considerable interest to research workers in biological and medical gerontology because they provide clues about the causes and possible prevention of illness and death. Social gerontologists make use of them too, especially in connection with the provision of health and welfare services for the aged. Behavioural gerontologists are less interested in them because they are often insufficiently detailed. For example, crude descriptive statistics relating chronological age to disease are of little help to a behavioural gerontologist who may be trying to relate physiological functions to life-history data and psychiatric symptoms in the pre-retirement period.

Both mortality rates and morbidity rates can be calculated in different ways, but in simple terms they represent the proportion of people at risk who succumb to the risk over a given period of time. For example, the rate of mortality (probability of dying) is equal to the proportion of deaths in the population at risk in a given period. The calculation of precise rates for specific risks, population and times requires fairly complicated statistical calculations and valid empirical data.[60]

2. SOCIAL SURVEY METHODS

Apart from the detailed Poor Law returns, which showed a preponderance of elderly people receiving relief, the first systematic social survey relevant to gerontology in Britain was begun in 1886 by Charles Booth and eventually published in seventeen volumes between 1889 and 1903.[61] Booth was primarily concerned with the living conditions of the working class in London and with the extensive poverty that existed. Old age was associated with poverty even before the industrial revolution; a survey by Booth published in 1894 confirmed the relationship.[62] Booth's survey method amounted to interviewing people who were well informed about the matters under investigation. His inquiries revealed more fully than any previous ones the destitution, starvation, crime, drunkenness, brutality and immorality characteristic of the London poor at the close of the nineteenth century. The material was tabulated and presented with documentary thoroughness, and Booth's efforts greatly influenced the social and economic policies of subsequent governments.

At the turn of the century, Rowntree published the first of a series of surveys of poverty and living standards.[63] This was a study of working-class families in York, and his interviewers elicited testimony direct from family members. Rowntree attempted to establish a poverty line more objectively and more precisely than Booth had. Further surveys of the living conditions of poor people were carried out in subsequent decades, and Bowley has been credited with introducing sampling methods into social survey work in 1912; he also took account of selection effects produced by refusals and omissions. From this time onwards, social survey techniques became increasingly rigorous and precise in terms of sampling, questionnaire design, and statistical analysis.

The Government Social Survey was established in Britain in 1941 to receive and coordinate various official surveys – for example, into ill health, nutrition and family expenditure. In the United States of America, particularly during World War II, social survey methods were developed intensively in connection with public opinion polling and advertising. Sample size and composition, for example, were extremely important as regards accuracy, cost and speed of operation. By 1950, social survey methods were well established and widely used in many countries.[64] Commercial interest in social survey methods followed developments in the U.S.A., and nowadays market research is used extensively in Britain in connection with consumer behaviour. The elderly, however, being relatively poor consumers, are not a prime target for advertisers and market researchers. Considerable use is made of 'panels' of consumers or subjects willing to participate in research investigations; for example, provision for such a panel (or register) was established by the Medical Research Council at Liverpool in 1956 and a panel was still being serviced and used for research in ageing in 1974.[65,66]

Nowadays, most surveys are carried out for research purposes, for example to discover the extent of psychiatric ill health among elderly residents in a community, to establish norms for intelligence and other measures of human performance, to examine social attitudes. Surveys of this kind are essentially mapping or descriptive exercises; other kinds of research require samples of subjects but do not set out to collect descriptive statistics for practical use and do not make inferences about tangible populations. Social surveys are methods of collecting quantifiable evidence to describe social conditions or to test sociological hypotheses, for example in disengagement theory; they are not a substitute for theory. Principles and methods similar to those used in social surveys have been used in longitudinal and cross-sectional studies of psychological development and ageing.

Not all sociological studies rely on rigorous survey techniques; some deal with social isolation and bereavement, for example, and rely more on the intensive clinical appraisal of model cases. The kinds of social survey we have referred to usually employ samples ranging in size from about 500 to 4,000, though smaller samples are not uncommon, especially in behavioural research. Population censuses are obviously large undertakings; they require extensive resources for planning, execution and analysis, and they take a long time to yield results. Hence they are carried out infrequently and use relatively crude measures and coarse categories.

Few surveys made shortly after the end of the Second World War were especially relevant to social and behavioural gerontology, but they included the following. In 1949, the Population Investigation Committee and the Scottish Council for Research in Education published a report on the secular trend in national intelligence based on a comparison of measures of intelligence of a group of 11-year-old children surveyed in 1932 and another group in 1947. The surveys confirmed previous investigations which had shown a small negative correlation between family size and intelligence. It was argued, therefore, that if there was a genetic basis to intelligence, and if parents of lower intelligence were breeding faster than parents of higher intelligence, then generation by generation the average intelligence of the nation must be decreasing. The expected secular decrease in mean I.Q. was not confirmed

– if anything an increase was observed; these findings have been debated at length. The relevance of the Scottish surveys for social and behavioural gerontology is that they illustrate the possibility that cross-sectional studies confound age and secular trend – see Chapter Eleven. These Scottish 'cohorts' are now aged 50 and 36 years respectively; they are suitable subjects for a study of adult intelligence – but how much of any observed difference between them could be attributed to the effects of *ageing*?[67] In 1947, the Nuffield Foundation published a survey on the living conditions of old people. This was followed up in 1948 by a socio-medical survey of a sample of elderly people in Wolverhampton.[68,69] In 1954, the National Council of Social Service published the results of a small survey of the social and economic circumstances of people over 70 years of age.[70] In 1954, the Ministry of Pensions and National Insurance, as it was then called, reported on the reasons given for retiring or continuing at work.[71] Hence, from about the year 1950, survey methods in social and behavioural gerontology were well established, and subsequent studies belong to the modern era. Techniques of sampling and assessment have not changed greatly and the methodological and practical problems are, relatively speaking, unchanged – except for computerization.

In 1970, the Social Science Research Council published an important review of longitudinal studies in the social and behavioural sciences and put forward proposals for establishing an institute for the study of human development and social change. Several gerontological surveys are described and discussed in this review.[72] The future may see developments in behavioural ecology methods (systematic observation of the behaviour of people in normal routine situations), and in the related techniques of surveillance and retrospective analysis.

3. PRESENT-DAY GERONTOLOGY

Studies in human ageing and ageing generally, in the early decades of the present century, gave rise to theories, methods, and results which are still matters for debate and continual investigation. The best sources of information on gerontology prior to 1950 are probably Cowdry's *Problems of Ageing: Biological and Medical Aspects*, Korenchevsky's *Physiological and Pathological Ageing*, and Comfort's *Ageing: the Biology of Senescence.*[73-75] Cowdry's book, in particular, has several chapters directly relevant to the psychology and sociology of human ageing; see also Pressey (1948).[76]

The scientific study of the *psychology* of human ageing has its origin in the work of Galton and Quetelet. It was not until early in the present century, however, that work began in earnest. The study of adult intelligence and intellectual attainments, for example, dates back to the works of Dorland in 1908 and subsequently.[77] Perhaps because of Galton's inquiries into hereditary genius in 1869 and human faculties in 1883, the topic of intellectual creativity was prominent at the turn of the century, and has been with us ever since. The big step forward came immediately after the end of World War I, when the debate about the average mental age of adults began with the publication of the results of the 'Alpha and Beta' tests applied to United States Army recruits. This debate triggered the adult intelligence testing movement, which dominated the study of human ageing until recently. The idea that 'intelligence' might decline during adult life was strongly resisted at the time, and a great deal of effort was subsequently invested in attempts to prove or disprove this idea. (For the main current issues in adult intelligence see Chapter Six.) One of the interesting features of this period was the unspoken assumption that the notion of adult intelligence could be assimilated to that of juvenile intelligence, and studied by means of the same concepts and methods. This brings us up to date, with the current issue of the extent to which a lifespan developmental approach to the study of human ageing helps (or hinders) the study of adult psychology.[78-80] The other main psychological theme in the early decades of the present century was the study of the effects of age on perceptual motor skills (see Chapter Five).

Progress in gerontology has been fairly rapid since 1950 for a number of reasons. Advances in medicine have emphasized the problems of physical and mental ill health in late maturity and old age. Individual discoveries about specific aspects of human ageing have stimulated more systematic research. Demographic and economic studies have raised concern about whether changes in the age structure of society would produce serious social and financial problems.

Scientific periodicals have begun to carry an increasing number of research reports on ageing: the *Journal of Gerontology* was established in 1945 by the Gerontological Society Inc., of the U.S.A. It publishes reports from biological sciences and clinical medicine, psychological and social sciences, and social welfare; it also carries articles on gerontological organizations in other countries and gives a valuable index to current periodical literature. In addition it publishes a house journal, *The Gerontologist.*[81,82] In Europe the scientific periodical *Gerontologia* was established in 1956.[83] Articles in a wide variety of other scientific journals continue to add to the literature of gerontology and geriatrics.[84,85]

The growing recognition of gerontology as a distinct discipline led to the appearance of it as a separate category in journals publishing abstracts of scientific reports and reviews of recent literature.[86-88] The Forest Park Foundation of the U.S.A. financed *A Classified Bibliography of Gerontology and Geriatrics,* which was published in 1951; large supplements appeared in 1957 and 1963. Dr N. W. Shock was responsible for the selection and classification of the references.[89-91] Easy access to nearly all the relevant literature saves professional and research workers an immense amount of time; a number of textbooks dealing with the social and psychological aspects of ageing have appeared in recent years – they are referred to in the bibliographical notes to this and other chapters.

The International Association of Gerontology was founded in 1950 on the occasion of the First International Congress of Gerontology in Liège, Belgium. Since that time, Congresses have been held regularly in different countries.[92,93] Several countries now have one or more research organizations dealing with the scientific problems of human ageing – as distinct from the numerous voluntary and welfare organizations which look after elderly and infirm people. In the United Kingdom, there are three societies: the British Society for Research on Ageing; the British Geriatrics Society; the British Society of Social and Behavioural Gerontology. It is expected that these societies, in cooperation with the National Council of Social Service, will eventually be coordinated to form a British Council for Ageing. The Medical Research Council, the Social Science Research Council, and the Department of Health and Social Security give some support and encouragement to research in ageing. The Medical Research Council, for example, has provided financial support for my own research work and that of my colleagues in ageing, and previously financed a Unit for Research on Occupational Aspects of Ageing. The welfare organization 'Age Concern' was formed in 1970; previously, voluntary effort had been coordinated by the National Council of Social Service. Private charities, such as the Nuffield Foundation, provide financial support for the welfare of the aged and for research in human ageing.[94]

CHAPTER THREE

Biological Aspects of Human Ageing

PART I. ANATOMICAL AND PHYSIOLOGICAL EFFECTS

The social and psychological aspects of adult life and old age cannot be understood without some knowledge of the underlying changes in human biology.[1-5] At the beginning of each of the following sections, a few elementary facts serve to introduce the material on the anatomy and physiology of ageing. Further information can be found in the literature referred to in the bibliographical notes to this and other chapters.

1. STRUCTURE OF THE BODY

(a) *Skeleton*

The skeleton gives shape and firmness to the body, provides attachments for the muscles, protects important organs such as the brain, heart and lungs and, together with the voluntary muscles, provides man with a leverage system for pushing, pulling and lifting. Full stature is reached by the late 'teens or early twenties. Afterwards there is little or no change in the length of the individual bones, though there may be a slight loss in overall stature, brought about by atrophy of the discs between the spinal vertebrae. This slight loss of stature may be exaggerated by a stooping posture due to muscular weakness, and, in some people, by atrophy in parts of the central nervous system. Some growth in adult life may occur in the soft parts of the body, such as the nose or the ears. As age advances, the chemical composition of bone changes, the bones become less dense, and this osteoporosis increases the risk of breakage late in life. Adverse changes of a more serious nature occur if there are gross deficiencies in diet, or in the presence of certain diseases. Movements of the joints become stiffer and more restricted, the incidence of diseases affecting these parts of the body increases with age, and the skeleton suffers from the cumulative effects of damage and disease.

The biological effects of ageing on the teeth are difficult to separate from the influence of diet, dental hygiene and repair. Teeth, in adult life, may be a cause of pain and discomfort. The gums recede, and the teeth become yellowish because of a thickening of secondary dentine. Loss of the teeth or changes in their appearance brings home the fact that one is ageing physically. Tooth decay is accelerated by the reduction in saliva. Resort to dentures means, at least temporarily, that one cannot eat or speak as well, and this may cause dismay and embarrassment.

(b) *Skin and Fatty Tissues*

The skin covers and protects the underlying structures. It consists of two layers: an outer or hard layer (cuticle), and an inner layer (dermis) which contains numerous glands and nerve endings. The glands secrete sweat, which consists of water, salt and excretory products. The evaporation of sweat from the surface of the skin cools it down and helps to regulate the temperature of the body.

Age changes in the surface of the body, especially in the face (wrinkles, loss of bloom, flabbiness), are obvious to the ageing person, and, with other age changes, such as thinning hair, baldness, greying, and varicose veins, may be upsetting for some individuals. The skin becomes paler and more blotchy; it takes on a parchment-like texture and loses some of its elasticity. The secondary consequences of biological ageing include changes in self-regard, confidence and social attitudes.

In the early and middle years of adult life, the average person in our civilization tends to put on deposits of surplus fat unless he readjusts his intake of food to his physical requirements. He becomes increasingly bulky until, much later in life, his subcutaneous fat begins to disappear, together with the muscles, leaving the now inelastic skin hanging in folds and wrinkles. The health and general appearance of the skin depends upon many factors. In old age it is the loss of subcutaneous fat that contributes most to its characteristic appearance. The tissues become less capable of holding water, so that under the microscope cellular structures have a thinner, denser appearance.

The regulation of food intake depends upon psychological factors such as habits and attitudes, and the utilization of food depends upon complex physiological processes. Some older people go short of essential foods such as proteins and vitamins, partly because they are short of money, partly from choice. Overfeeding, leading to excess weight, contributes to degenerative disorders in old age and tends to shorten life. In the rat such disorders can be inhibited by restricting the number of calories while maintaining an otherwise adequate diet. Calorie restriction during the period of development increases the life-expectation of laboratory rats. No one has yet recommended this procedure for human beings except where there is danger of gross overweight. Overfeeding results in increased metabolism and the inadequate elimination of waste products. Excess weight has adverse effects on the circulatory system, the kidneys and sugar metabolism, being associated with hypertension, arteriosclerosis, and diabetes. Weight reduction, however, can have beneficial results. The death rates for arteriosclerosis appear to have been reduced during World War II in some countries where reduced but adequate food rationing was in force.

(c) *Voluntary (Striped) Muscles*

The voluntary, or striped, muscles are those which lie along the arms, legs and other parts of the skeleton. They are attached to the bones either directly or by strong bonds of fibrous tissue called tendons. They contract by getting shorter and thicker, and thereby exert a force on the bone, which acts as a lever. As the muscle contracts, the muscle fibres shorten because of complex biochemical changes in the protein molecules of the fibres. Maximum muscular strength is normally reached at about the age of 25 or 30. After this age there is a gradual reduction in the speed and power of muscular contractions and a decreased capacity for sustained muscular effort. There is less elasticity in the muscle and an increase in fibrous material. There are, however, great individual differences in muscular efficiency, and exercise can improve muscles that have fallen into disuse. This is achieved by increasing the quantities of protein in the muscle fibres. Actually, the striped muscles may increase in bulk and in density up to about the age of 50 but after that the number of active muscle fibres and the amount of protein steadily decreases, and we get the typical wasted appearance of the very old person.

The cerebellum, underneath and towards the rear of the main cerebral hemispheres, is important in coordinating muscular activity. Changes in the cerebellum play only a small part in the loss of muscle tone which occurs in old age; the decline of posture and muscular coordination is more often affected by damage to the basal ganglia. There appears to be little change with age in the speed of reflexes or simple repetitive movements, although both speed and amplitude of movement may be affected by disease.

Muscular effort is limited by stiffer and more restricted movements at the joints, the lower working capacity of the heart and the lungs, and other factors. Prolonged muscular activity not approaching the limits of effort may be sustained for long periods by older men. The judicious use of rest pauses will improve the output of physical energy. Physical exercise greatly improves physiological capacities even late in life.

(d) *Involuntary* (*Smooth*) *Muscles*

The involuntary, or smooth, muscles are those in the walls of the stomach and the intestines, in the air tubes, and in most of the internal organs and blood vessels. They are not normally under conscious control – they operate automatically, under the direction of what is called the 'autonomic nervous system'. The effects of age on the smooth muscles appear small compared with other structures (except the smooth muscles of the blood vessels) and they seem to function fairly adequately even until late senescence. Although a few individuals suffer from increased frequency of micturition, any normal weakening of smooth muscle action, as for example in the bowels, is small compared with changes in the nervous system which controls such functions.

(e) *Connective Tissues*

Connective tissues are distributed widely throughout the body. They comprise collagen, elastin and reticulin, binding together various parts of the body and providing support. Some are involved in storing food, others in forming blood. Adipose tissue consists of closely packed cells containing large globules of fat.

As age increases, the amount of ground substance decreases and the density of the fibres increases, thus restricting the passage of nutrients and other substances through the tissues. The smooth surfaces of some joints become worn, and diseases of the joints are more common. The large molecules of collagen establish more cross-linkages throughout life, and so render the connective material less capable of stretching; this effect has had considerable theoretical interest for biologists. Collagen is found in the scar that forms over a wound; the scar tissue that forms late in life appears to be 'lightly bound' collagen, characteristic of the collagen normally found in the connective material of young people; it forms more slowly in older people, so that wounds heal less quickly, although other factors no doubt play a part. Collagen, like some other substances in the body, can become calcified with age, thus contributing to decreased flexibility of the joints.

2. VEGETATIVE FUNCTIONS OF THE BODY

(a) *Digestion*

The digestive system includes the mouth, salivary and other glands, oesophagus, stomach, pancreas and intestines. Food is digested (split up into simpler chemical substances which can be readily used by the body) mainly in the stomach and intestines by digestive juices secreted from various glands. The absorption of these substances takes place mostly in the small intestine, they pass into the blood by way of the capillaries or lymphatics and are carried by veins to the liver. Individual body cells are nourished by materials contained in the extracellular fluid, which oozes out of the capillaries and bathes the living tissues.

The body requires food in order to maintain its temperature, to produce energy, and to develop and renew its tissues. A well-balanced diet contains the correct proportions of proteins, carbohydrates, fats, mineral salts, vitamins and water, though people differ in their food requirements constitutionally and in the sort of work they do. Elderly people in reduced circumstances may not get an adequate diet (including vitamins and enough protein), and serious neglect may lead to a deficiency disease. A decrease in the secretion of saliva and gastric juice, including the digestive enzymes, results in less efficient digestion. On the whole the digestive system is relatively robust, and not seriously impaired by ageing, except for the increased risk of pathology common to all physiological systems.

The pancreas secretes sufficient quantities of the enzyme amylase to digest carbohydrates, although the output of ptyalin in the saliva is reduced. The pancreatic endocrine substance steapsin decreases as age advances, and this may help to account for the slower utilization of fat in older people. The liver and the gall bladder appear to be relatively unaffected by the normal processes of ageing, but these organs become more vulnerable to disease.

Digestion of a meal containing fat produces microscopic particles of fat, known as chylomicrons, in the bloodstream. Their numbers increase to a maximum and then return to a baseline level. As we grow older, the rate of absorption is much slower and the concentration of chylomicrons reaches higher levels. There may be some association between ageing and diseases connected with lipid metabolism.

The timing of the digestive processes is important and largely automatic, and some, such as salivation and the secretion of digestive juices, are set in motion before food actually reaches the mouth. There is also a psychological component in appetite and digestion, so that an old person's poorer appetite may lead to a poorer digestive response. Old people secrete less saliva and have less acute senses of smell and taste, and this may make extra attention to cooking and presentation important to secure an adequately varied diet. Mastication is less effective because of weaker facial muscles and poorer teeth, so the food should be of a kind which does not require extensive chewing. This may inadvertently lead to a poorer diet.

There are changes in the autonomic nervous system and the endocrine system at times of emotional arousal and these changes interfere with the digestive processes. Minor neurotic disorders can lead to stomach upsets, constipation or loss of appetite in some, and to overeating in others. There is no evidence that intestinal bacteria are seriously implicated in the biology of human ageing. In connection with this it has been suggested that certain kinds of food will delay the onset or rate of normal ageing. But there is no evidence for this belief, and provided the person's diet is varied and well balanced (containing the proper proportions of proteins, vitamins and so on) eating particular kinds of food will not retard the ageing process.

(b) *Removal of Wastes*

Some excretory products formed during cell activity are carried by the blood to the kidneys. A complex chemical process removes these products selectively from the blood and they drip as urine into the bladder. Waste materials from undigested food are expelled from the lower end of the alimentary canal.

The kidneys form urine by filtering water and dissolved substances from the blood and then reabsorbing some of these substances, for example glucose and some body salts. The organ as a whole atrophies gradually with the degeneration of its constituent parts such as tubules and glomeruli; there is, however, some compensatory growth of cell elements. The functional capacities of the kidneys – urea clearance, glomerular filtration and effective blood plasma flow – are not normally diminished to any great extent until late in life. There is, with ageing, a fairly steep rise in kidney disorders. These are usually linked with vascular conditions, and sometimes lead to brain disturbances and abnormal behaviour (see Chapters Four and Five).

Both urination and defecation are subject to a type of voluntary control through social learning, and regular habits have deep emotional significance for some people. Loss of control (incontinence) from various causes can be a source of embarrassment and a serious inconvenience in old age. Constipation at later ages may result from poor bowel function at earlier ages, lack of exercise, unsatisfactory diet (too little roughage or insufficient vitamins), as well as from damage and disease.

(c) *Metabolism*

A person's basal metabolic rate – the rate at which he uses oxygen while at rest – is measured by analysing a sample of the air he breathes out. The metabolic rate increases during exercise or excitement. Basal metabolic rate declines with age. This is partly accounted for by diminished thyroid secretion and other factors, but mainly by a decrease in the total number of cells and diminished activity in the major regions of the body such as the liver and muscles. The body's normal compensatory reactions to a fall in heat-production include the secretion of adrenalin, contraction of the surface blood vessels, and shivering. An older person reacts less quickly and less adequately to cold than a younger person. His voluntary muscular activity is less and his shivering reflex poorer. As he does not produce as much heat, he runs the risk of a serious fall in body temperature. Exposure to cold and poor living conditions can lead to hypothermia – abnormally low body temperature – which is a serious risk for old people.

High body temperature can be reduced by stopping or slowing down muscular effort, by sweating and by dilatation of the surface blood vessels to cool the blood. Older persons cannot cope as well as younger persons with heat and they cannot work as effectively in moderately high temperatures. Those who are fat in addition generate heat more quickly when active and lose it more slowly. The sweating reaction and the circulatory system become less efficient.[6,7] Age changes in temperature regulation have been observed in industrial workers, for instance in older miners, who sweat less when they are working and more when they are resting, because the sweating and circulatory mechanisms are sluggish and no longer capable of the same *range* of reaction. Temperature discrimination appears not to decline with age, which is surprising, since the general pattern of biological degeneration is towards poorer sensory discrimination. Younger animals (and younger human beings) quickly become acclimatized to changed physical surroundings – to higher or lower temperatures, to drier or more humid atmospheres; acclimatization is less efficient in later life.

Temperature affects longevity, at least in some lower organisms like fruit-flies; cold conditions appear to slow down metabolism and prolong life, while high temperatures have the opposite effects – but not because the 'rate of living' has changed. Living creatures, however, have evolved biological systems adapted to a narrow range of optimum conditions, as in the case of tropical fishes or those found in cooler waters. Departure from the optimum conditions in either direction tends to shorten life. Stress conditions such as heat and cold, and other 'extrinsic' factors such as diet, or exercise, or radiation have a particular relevance to gerontology in that they enable research workers to accelerate or retard ageing – by decreasing or increasing the average lifespan or by lowering or raising the level of age-related functional capacities. The normal expectation of human life is greater in temperate than in tropical or cold climates, though obviously factors other than temperature are at work.

The effects of age on protein metabolism in rats are that, broadly speaking, the proteins like collagen and elastin tend to increase with age; the central active constituents – like nucleii and mitochondria (intracellular structures) – decrease;

the water-soluble proteins increase in brain and muscle but decrease in liver cells.

Carbohydrate metabolism has been studied by the administration of glucose in a test of sugar tolerance – measuring the rate at which excess sugar is cleared from the blood. In older people, the blood sugar level continues to rise longer, to reach higher absolute levels, than in comparable younger people. The effect is more pronounced if a second dose of glucose is administered shortly after the first. The increase in frequency of diabetes through adult life confirms this effect. The impairment of glucose tolerance has been attributed to the reduced sensitivity of specific cells in the pancreas to changes in the level of blood sugar. This example illustrates the fact that some biological mechanisms of ageing are associated with the malfunction of specialized cells under specific conditions, which suggests that some control over the biochemistry of ageing is possible.[8]

As one grows older some minerals like sodium, calcium and potassium are taken up less readily, although these elements can still be stored. Solid metabolites such as pigments become deposited within and between cells, and cells may be unable to excrete them – a crude analogy is with the way a furnace becomes choked with clinkers making it difficult or impossible to maintain a fire. The metabolites have a toxic chemical effect and constitute a mechanical hindrance to the normal activities in the cell.

(d) *Cell Renewal*

The length of life of individual cells varies considerably depending upon the type of cell. For example, nerve cells do not multiply, many die only when the person dies, but others die much earlier. Red blood corpuscles are estimated to live about 120 days on average, whereas some leukocytes survive only a few days.

Some tissues of the body are replaced fairly rapidly by continuous cell division (mitosis); others are capable of renewal under certain conditions. In renewed tissues, age differences in the appearance of cells are usually slight. The rate of renewal of liver cells and skin cells decreases as age increases. Some tissues, however, including those of the nervous system, cannot be renewed.

In stained preparations the nucleus of an old cell is darker and its cytoplasm lighter than that of a young cell. This raises the possibility that the nucleic acid metabolism of the nerve cells is reduced as the cells become older. In the liver cells of senile rats the nucleus has been found to become enlarged, invaginated, split, or irregular in shape. Histological studies of nerve cells taken from senile patients at autopsy show various kinds of abnormality. Degenerative changes in ageing cells include: increased fat deposition in the cytoplasm, the conversion of the membrane to fibrous material, increased pigmentation, and – less often – enlargement of the cell together with the appearance of empty spaces within its substance.

Cell colonies descended from a parent cell are called 'clones'. Clones from mammalian cells *in vitro* die out after a limited number of doublings; the reproduction rate falls, the individual cells become less active and physically more deteriorated. Unicellular organisms reproduce themselves as clones, but the line needs to be invigorated periodically by fusion between two organisms.

(e) *Respiration*

The lungs receive air via the nose and mouth and trachea by the enlargement of the respiratory cage. The normal rate of breathing varies between about 15 and 18 times per minute in adults, but the rate and depth of breathing increase sharply during exercise, excitement or stress. Oxygen is absorbed into the bloodstream from the lungs, and carried to the tissues, that is to each individual cell in the body. There, chemical processes take place which supply the materials necessary to repair wear and tear and to produce heat and energy. Carbon dioxide, produced by the metabolism of the body, is absorbed into the blood and transported to the lungs, where it is exhaled.

Normal respiration is controlled by an automatic respiratory centre in the brain, which is sensitive to the amount of carbon dioxide in the blood, but voluntary control from higher brain centres is possible too, as for example in swimming. The brain is very sensitive to variations in oxygen supply. Moderate lack of oxygen produces varying degrees of inefficiency such as drowsiness, muscular weakness, poorer problem-solving and sensory-motor incoordination. Severe lack of oxygen produces confusion, loss of consciousness, damage to nerve cells and eventually death. Red blood cells and haemoglobin (which carries oxygen) appear to increase somewhat in later life. The general effect of ageing, however, is to reduce respiratory efficiency. Older people, moreover, do not have the same cardiac output (pumping action of the heart) as younger people. Their lungs contain a smaller volume of air; the residual volume after expiration is larger; delivery and diffusion of oxygen may be poorer because the oxygen has to diffuse through fibrous material to reach the cells. Poorer oxygenation may be crucial to performance.[9,10] Adverse age changes in the respiratory and cardiovascular systems can cause temporary impairment of nervous functions. Some attempts have been made to examine the effects of supplying oxygen to the brain by means of increased atmospheric pressure (in a hyperbaric chamber). Respiratory infections are more frequent among older people. The most common cause of respiratory failure is bronchitis. Physical and athletic performance falls off from about the late twenties; part of this fall can be attributed to a decline in respiratory efficiency.

(f) *Blood Circulation*

In the normal younger adult the heart beats at an average rate of about 72 beats per minute when at rest. The beat can be felt as a wave of increased pressure (pulse), for example in the radial artery at the front of the wrist. The heart rate changes if a person becomes excited, angry, afraid, or if he changes his posture or engages in physical exercise; the contractions become stronger and faster. The blood is pumped by contractions of the muscles of the heart, through the lungs, where it is oxygenated, to the heart and then throughout the body via the arteries, to the capillaries and back through the veins to the heart. The blood distributes oxygen and nutrient matter to all the tissues of the body, and carries away waste matter to be excreted; it carries carbon dioxide to the lungs to be expelled on expiration. A normal adult has a blood volume of ten or eleven pints. The blood pressure is maintained by the force of the cardiac contractions on the one hand and the resistance of the arterioles on the other. Blood pressure is maintained at a fairly constant (resting) level and adjusted to meet demand. Permanently raised blood pressure can damage the arteries. Low blood pressure can cause temporary impairment of the blood supply to the brain, as in fainting. Cerebral haemorrhage can occur if the blood vessels in the brain are damaged by disease or by cumulative normal degeneration. Raised blood pressure is sometimes associated with increased renin in some kidney disorders.

Relative to other organs, the heart changes little in weight with normal ageing. Its weight is related to body weight and to skeletal muscle. Growth in response to increased demand is characteristic not only of cardiac muscle, but also of striped muscle, lungs, and sweat glands. A mode of life that promotes a margin of physical capacity over and above normal requirements, for example by means of dietary regulation or physical exercise, could help to compensate for the normal degenerative effects of ageing by keeping the heart in good form.

After the age of about 55 the rhythm of the heart becomes slower and more irregular, although in extreme old age some individuals show a slight rise in heart rate. Arterial changes with age, if they occur in the brain, have markedly adverse effects. An impaired blood supply to the brain causes permanent structural damage through atrophy of the nerve cells; these effects are greatly increased in conditions of vascular disease. Areas of atrophy can occur without apparent local vascular impairment, but the brain can be selectively impaired by local deficiencies in blood supply (see also Chapter Ten).

The main arteries increase somewhat in diameter in older people, perhaps in response to the normal rise with age in blood pressure (which may itself be a reaction to the restrictions in blood flow imposed by thickening and calcification of the walls of the smaller arteries and by changes in the capillary system).

The tendency for thrombi to form inside the vessels (thrombosis) increases when the vessels are damaged; such damage is serious and becomes more common in old age. Deposits of fat may accumulate around the heart and the valves tend to become harder and less pliable. The working capacity of the heart decreases, which has the effect of diminishing physical performance.

Arteriosclerosis is a form of widespread degeneration in which fat is deposited in the cells and between them, and hard calcium salts are built up. Thus, the flexible cellular elements in the blood vessels are replaced by a firm homogeneous glossy substance. There is a thickening, hardening and lessening of elasticity in the walls of the blood vessels, especially the arteries. Coronary arteriosclerosis increases in frequency and severity as age increases from about 30 years, but many elderly people are not greatly affected by this condition. The ages from 50 to 70 years show the greatest mortality; selective mortality presumably eliminates a proportion of people predisposed to coronary arteriosclerosis, leaving the remainder to die from other causes at later ages.

Changes involving pigmentation, fibrous degeneration and atherosclerosis also become more common and more pronounced. Atherosclerosis is a form of arteriosclerosis in which materials containing lipids accumulate locally within or beneath the intima (innermost coat) of a blood vessel. It is a frequent cause of arterial occlusion and aneurysm, and seems to arise as a metabolic defect involving lipids and lipoproteins.

Arteries may become hardened by fibrosis without calcification; and arteries can lose their elasticity in the absence of arteriosclerosis. The process of arteriosclerosis may start quite early in life with the deposition of small particles within the arterial intima; as age increases, the particles – such as the lipid macromolecules which appear in the blood plasma following a fatty meal – gradually accumulate. Other factors play a part, however, since arteriosclerosis is not a universal characteristic in late life.

Changes in the circulatory system brought about by wear and tear may interact with arteriosclerotic processes to produce localized damage to those segments of the arterial system that are especially vulnerable to the action of heightened blood pressure. Arteriosclerotic changes are prominent factors in 'vicious circles' of impairment – as when narrowed arteries lead to raised blood pressure which may in turn aggravate the process of arteriosclerosis.

(g) *Homeostasis*

The term 'homeostasis' refers to a process whereby physiological mechanisms regulate and stabilize the 'internal environment'. They include the regulation of body temperature, the maintenance of appropriate calcium, and the control of the acid-base balance of the blood.

Most of the body's sugar is converted in the liver and stored as glycogen. The blood carries glucose for use in the muscles and in other organs of the body, especially the brain. Insulin, secreted by the pancreas, normally checks any undue rise in the level of blood sugar, while adrenalin and other hormones stimulate the release of glucose from the liver into the bloodstream. One of the failures of homeostasis is diabetes, a blood-sugar disorder, which increases in frequency with increasing age. The blood is slightly alkaline under normal conditions, but in strenuous exercise this alkaline reserve is diminished, and the recovery of the acid-base balance through respiratory and other functions is slower in older people. The homeostatic mechanisms must be flexible enough to cope with variations in demand. They must, for example, adjust to variations in physical effort, changes in temperature and food intake; they must operate appropriately during sleep, and following injury or infection.

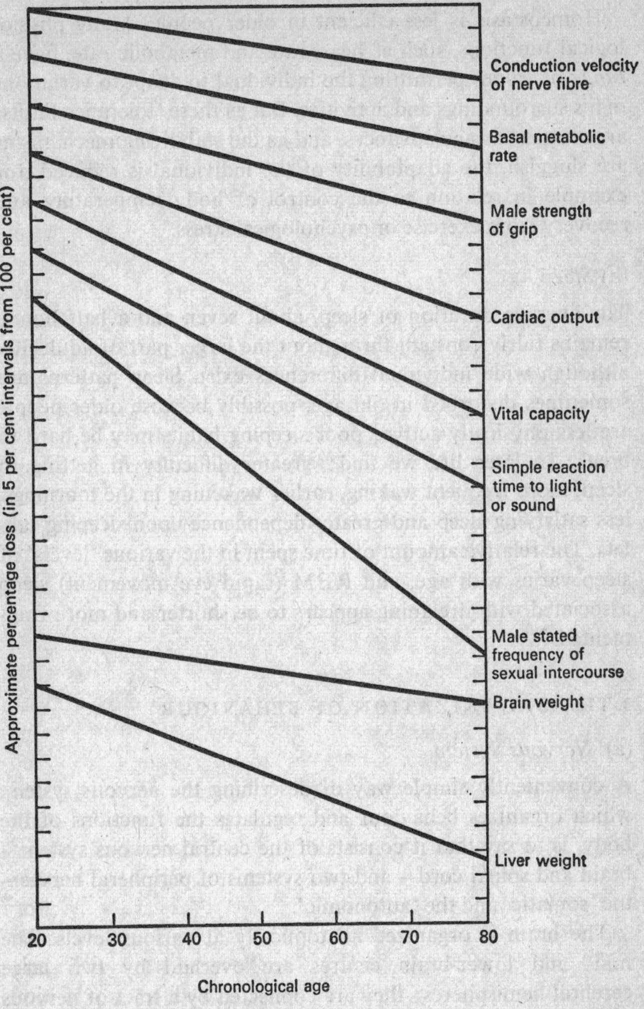

FIGURE 5 A simplified diagram illustrating relative age differences for several biological variables each expressed as a percentage loss of function from 100 per cent at the age of 20.

Homeostasis is less efficient in older people. Many physiological functions, such as heart rate and metabolic rate, have a *range* of values permitting the individual to adapt to variations in his surroundings and activities. But as these 'tolerance limits' are reduced as age advances, and as the stabilizing mechanisms are sluggish, the adaptability of the individual is reduced, for example in relation to the control of body temperature and recovery from exercise or psychological stress.

(h) *Sleep*

The average duration of sleep, about seven and a half hours, remains fairly constant throughout the larger part of adult life, although wide individual differences exist. Sleep patterns are sometimes disturbed in old age, possibly because older people are less physically active; poor sleeping habits may be hard to break. In later life we find: greater difficulty in getting to sleep, more frequent waking, earlier wakening in the mornings, less satisfying sleep and greater dependence upon sleeping tablets. The relative amount of time spent in the various 'levels' of sleep varies with age, and REM (rapid eye movement) sleep associated with dreaming appears to be shorter and more fragmented.[11-16]

3. THE ORGANIZATION OF BEHAVIOUR

(a) *Nervous System*

A conveniently simple way of describing the nervous system, which organizes behaviour and regulates the functions of the body, is to say that it consists of the central nervous system – brain and spinal cord – and two systems of peripheral nerves – the 'somatic' and the 'autonomic'.

The brain is organized anatomically at various levels. The mid- and lower-brain centres are overlaid by two large cerebral hemispheres; they are connected by a tract of nervous tissue called the corpus callosum. The cerebral hemispheres consist of several regions separated by fissures and cavities. Although there are several areas where functions are localized such as vision, hearing and motor control, other areas appear to have less specific functions, and the brain acts as a whole. The cerebral cortex provides the association areas necessary for higher mental functions such as intelligence, memory and imagination, and for the organization of experience and voluntary action, for example learning and emotional control. The individual nerve cells vary in size, shape and function; they are supported, nourished and protected by a massive and intricate system of glial cells which in turn depend upon the other organs and systems of the body such as the circulatory, respiratory and endocrine systems.

The early development of the brain brings about an increase in the size of the nerve cells, in supporting tissues, and in the cerebrovascular system. Nerve cells cannot multiply beyond the age of about one year. They are sensitive to variations in biological conditions such as lack of oxygen or interruption of the blood supply. The long-range effects – on age changes in adult behaviour and the brain – of undernourishment and other sorts of environmental deficit early in life have yet to be worked out. This is an obvious implication of the lifespan developmental approach to human ageing.[17,18,19] The effects of 'behavioural enrichment' on rats during their development seem to be to enlarge the brain and increase cortical thickness. Behavioural enrichment also appears to produce effects, though to a lesser degree, in the adult rat.[20] The implications of such effects for humans are obvious, unless they arise because of experimental artefacts, such as increased cranial capacity.

There are obvious problems in attempting to study the effect of ageing on the living brain, as there are with other organs of the body; so research emphasizes the pathological aspects of ageing rather than its normal physiological aspects. Moreover, data on pathological ageing relevant to brain function are frequently obtained from sources which are not typical of normal people. The age trends thus calculated do not necessarily reflect *normal* age trends. In addition, the biological uniqueness of the individual constitutes an obstacle for research into the effects of age on brain functions. The normal and pathological effects of ageing lead to a variety of changes in the anatomy and physiology of the nervous system, and consequently in the organization of behaviour and experience.

Brain weight decreases from about 1,400 grams in males in their twenties (1,250 grams in females) to about 1,250 grams in males in their eighties (1,125 grams in females). The decrease appears to accelerate in late life. Brain weight, however, is a crude measure of the number of intact nerve cells. During adult life, the water content of the brain appears to increase slightly for humans; the amino acid composition of cerebral proteins seems to be unaffected by ageing. Age changes in the relationships between behaviour and neurochemical processes in the brain are likely, for example a diminution in RNA response to avoidance training in older rats.[21] In rats, cerebral nucleoprotein remains roughly constant in the adult phase up to two years. It is no simple matter, however, to argue from age effects in animal behaviour to age effects in human behaviour (or brain function). In humans, brain RNA remains roughly constant during the adult phase, but diminishes in very late life, whereas DNA appears to increase. Remember, however, that cross-sectional differences in physiological measures based on pathological and non-representative samples of subjects do not necessarily reflect the normal changes with age of physiological processes *within* individuals. The acid-base balance (pH) of the brain declines slightly with age as it does for other organs. The mineral content of the brain varies with age. Some brain enzymes increase with age. Vitamin levels depend very much on diet, which is often inadequate in late life.

Advances in the study of ageing and brain function have been achieved by the use of special equipment such as the electroencephalogram (EEG), which magnifies and records the electrical activity of the brain.[22-24] The dominant EEG alpha frequency (8–12 cps), the delta (1–3 cps) and theta (4–7 cps) frequencies are slowed slightly and may be associated with longer reaction times to complex stimuli, otherwise the EEG records of normal healthy old people are similar to those of younger people. However, elderly patients with cerebral vascular disorders or disease show various EEG abnormalities. The EEG patterns react less sharply to sensory stimulation than do those of younger people, suggesting a lower level of arousal. On the other hand, older people seem to show more prolonged after-effects from neural (and mental) activity – a kind of 'inertia' which delays or interferes with subsequent activities. Injury, disease and atrophy of the brain can result in a variety of abnormal conditions, depending upon the degree and distribution of the damage.

There is diffuse cerebral atrophy in which some areas are particularly affected. The fissures in the brain become wider and deeper, the ventricles become larger and deformed; many nerve cells are lost, others suffer degenerative changes. In senile dementia, cerebral vascular disease, and in organic psychoses of old age the damage may be considerable (see also Chapter Ten). Degenerative changes take place in the cerebellum and the interior parts of the brain. There is an increase in neuroglial fibres (supporting structures) and patchy degeneration of the Schwann cells enclosing the nerve fibres. The spinal cord may show relatively more pronounced atrophy in its upper portion. Age changes in the brain are not necessarily intrinsic, and appear to arise mainly as consequences of adverse biological ageing elsewhere in the body.

Nerve cells die quickly from lack of oxygen. Parts of some fibres may be renewed but the nerve cell itself cannot be replaced. The capacity of a sectioned nerve fibre to regenerate diminishes in adult life. Individual nerve cells shrink and atrophy, the cytoplasm becomes paler, the nucleus shrinks and becomes displaced, Nissl granulation is reduced; the dead cell is replaced by neuroglia. In some instances the cyto-architecture of the cells is abnormal; senile plaques form; neurofibrillar degeneration and lipofuscin pigmentation lead eventually to a fragmentation of the network of neurofibrils and the blocking of cell activity by inert materials. The number of nerve cells is reduced – as shown by counting the number in a given area. For technical reasons, however, such counts are difficult to make and interpret, and there is lack of agreement about the nature and extent of nerve cell loss.[25-32]

The total number of nerve cells available is probably an important factor. Experiments with animals – at least animals with a relatively unspecialized cortex – have demonstrated the 'mass action' of the cortex. Neuropsychological studies of the human brain, however, need to take account of lesions in both the specific and non-specific areas of the cortex (see also Chapter Ten). The extent of cell loss is not the same for all areas of the cortex; this may help to account for the differential loss of capacities. The brain stem seems to be little affected by ageing.

Arteriosclerosis affects the brain by reducing the blood circulation, thereby reducing oxygenation, the distribution of nutrients and the elimination of waste products including carbon dioxide. Fibrous thickening of the arteries reduces their capacity. A loss of or reduction in blood supply leads to atrophy or death of nerve cells and surrounding tissues, although the relationship appears not to be explicable simply in terms of anatomical localization. A deteriorated blood vessel or a small aneurysm may leak; the bleeding within the brain damages or destroys localized areas, and produces a 'stroke'. The slow onset of cerebral arteriosclerosis permits the establishment of compensatory physiological responses such as the formation of passages between adjacent blood vessels; psychological compensation is also possible, for example the relearning of skills impaired by the disease.

The somatic nervous system comprises parts of the brain, the spinal cord and the peripheral (sensory and motor) fibres. The sensory receptors such as the eye, tongue, and pain receptors in the skin, are linked to the brain directly or via the spinal cord by sensory fibres, whereas the muscles receive their 'instructions' from the motor fibres. Nerve structures in the thalamus direct some of the incoming sensory information to various parts of the cortex and they have other functions, such as the perception of pain. The hypothalamus influences the pituitary gland, is concerned with temperature regulation and feeding and, as a higher centre for the coordination of the autonomic nervous system, plays a part in emotional behaviour. The spinal cord appears to reach a maximum weight of about 25 grams in the thirties, and then to decrease to about 20 grams in late life.

The effects of age on the somatic nervous system appear to be similar to those on other parts of the nervous system. The nerve fibre bundles appear atrophied – thickened in parts and uneven, with splitting and even disintegration. The blood circulation diminishes, connective tissue increases, and the essential active constituents of the nerve cells are reduced or lost altogether. Some slowing is apparent in the conduction velocity of the peripheral nerve fibres, and conduction-time across the synapse may increase, in which case the extra time accumulated over *many* synapses (as in central processes during a complex mental reaction) might be considerable.[33,34] The main portion of the reaction-time of a response to even a simple stimulus, moreover, is occupied not by the peripheral sensory or motor nerve impulses but by the central organizing processes of the cortex. This central decision time is proportionally greater in more complex forms of behaviour.

The autonomic nervous system (ANS) is largely outside voluntary control but the visceral responses it controls can be 'conditioned' – as in anticipatory anxiety or anger; they can also be deliberately modified by operant training and relaxation therapy. The ANS consists of a network of nerve clusters (ganglia) and connecting fibres. It carries a few sensory fibres, but is mainly a motor system controlling the involuntary muscles and glands and regulating the vital internal functions of the body. There are two sub-divisions: (a) the sympathetic division, comprising two chains of ganglia running alongside the spinal cord, connected by means of nerve fibres with the spinal cord and with the visceral organs, whose activity they help to regulate; (b) the parasympathetic division, consisting of two systems of nerve fibres named according to their anatomical positions – an upper (cranial) portion, and a lower (sacral) portion. The hypothalamus is the principal subcortical region for the integration of the ANS.

In conjunction with the endocrine system, the sympathetic division of the ANS facilitates the widespread simultaneous regulation of visceral responses, whereas the parasympathetic division is more selective and specific in its action. The two divisions of the autonomic system have, in some organs, a reciprocal relationship. The heart rate, for example, is accelerated by sympathetic innervation and slowed down by parasympathetic innervation. The overall effect is that of a self-regulating system capable of making adaptive responses and returning to a basic steady state.

The degree of preparedness produced by sympathetic excitation can vary between moderate states of tension and alertness to extremely powerful or disturbing emotional reactions. The action of the autonomic system, in maintaining homeostasis and the vegetative functions of the body, and in making the person ready to meet emergencies, fulfils a biological purpose. Its effects, however, may be excessive in relation to the requirements of civilized adult life. The mild states of tension and anxiety generated by slight deprivations, frustrations and conflicts can serve as the driving forces to sustain and direct a person's responses, but prolonged emotional tension or too frequent emotional upsets may not only be ineffective but also impair rational adjustment and lead to psychosomatic symptoms.

There are individual differences (and age changes) in temperamental qualities such as mood, emotional stability and intensity of feelings. As a person grows up, he learns when and how to express his feelings. He is not always successful, however, in handling his emotional problems and his reactions may very well include the kinds of compromise we find in minor neurotic disorders and in the more inadequate strategies of normal adjustment. The interaction of predisposition and stress lead to an increased likelihood of psychosomatic ailments and to neurotic or psychotic breakdown in later life (see Chapter Ten).

Few systematic studies relevant to behaviour have been made of the effects of age on the autonomic nervous system. Degenerative changes in late life in the autonomic and sensory ganglia are probably similar to changes elsewhere in the nervous system. Disturbances of the homeostatic mechanisms, for example vasomotor and endocrine secretion regulation, have serious implications for functional capacity and survival. Older subjects show weaker GSR reactions (sweat reactions to slight emotional tension). Conditioned reflexes are harder to establish in older animals (including man) and they are extinguished more quickly. Experimental neurosis in laboratory animals, induced by stress, leads to changes in physical condition and behaviour which, if well established and maintained without relief, show some resemblance to premature ageing, for example loss of functional efficiency, generalized weakness, apathy.

Measures of autonomic function are greatly affected by factors such as posture, state of mind and preceding activity; hence care is needed when making comparisons between age groups.[35-37] The effects of ageing on the ANS, however, seem slight in comparison with those arising from age changes in the central nervous system, the endocrine system and other bodily systems; however, this impression could be the result of lack of relevant data.

The normal effects of ageing on emotional responsiveness have been much neglected in behavioural gerontology. It could be argued that ageing has two main effects. Firstly, the reduction in the overall responsiveness of the autonomic nervous system and associated physiological functions such as endocrine secretion, and thus the physical basis of emotion, might well diminish the level of arousal, and make older people temperamentally 'flatter' and more phlegmatic. There is, however, evidence against this hypothesis.[38,39] Secondly, the gradual, cumulative, diffuse loss of cortex might 'disinhibit' or 'decontrol' emotional responsiveness, and the person's emotional reaction would become more primitive and more closely tied to the here-and-now situation, rather than modulated by cognitive controls. Thus, there might be less build-up of anticipatory emotion – hope, anxiety, aggression – and less prolongation of the after-effects of an emotional experience –

disappointment, pain, rage. This rather simple theory might account both for the emotional quiescence and apparent 'apathy' of many old people and for their capacity for intense but short-lived emotional reactions when provoked. It needs further elaboration to explain the general drift towards depression as age increases, perhaps by referring to the increasing frequency of depressing, frustrating and disappointing situations, including those arising internally as a consequence of reminiscence. (The psychopathology of emotion in adult life and old age is described in Chapter Ten, and normal emotional reactions are discussed in Chapters Four, Eight and Nine.)

(b) *The Senses*

Ageing has widespread adverse effects on sensory processes.[40,41]

VISION. After the age of about ten, the best viewing distance lengthens gradually until, by the age of 50, many people need to wear glasses with lenses to correct this long-sightedness. The lens of the eye 'ages' even from infancy, and becomes more opaque and less elastic in adult life. It continues to grow without shedding its older cells (which undergo chemical changes), and changes its shape.[42] It thus becomes less able to change focus, and senile changes in the ciliary muscles (controlling the shape of the lens) also help to reduce accommodation. Convergence of the lines of sight from both eyes is less efficient later on in life, probably because the exterior eye muscles become weaker, or possibly because cortical control is less effective. Age changes in the nervous system probably play a part in reducing the diameter of the pupil, thus restricting the amount of light entering the eye, and in slowing its reaction time to a decrease in illumination, thus impairing the older person's recovery from glare (though the response to brighter illumination appears unaffected). The iris fades and the cornea thickens, loses its lustre, and becomes less transparent. Age changes in the retina (the complex network of light sensitive elements and nerve cells at the back of the eye) bring about atrophy of the nerve cells and poorer blood supply, which contribute to poorer all-round visual performance. This means poorer performance in visual acuity, colour matching, dark adaptation, dark vision and contrast discrimination.[43-45] Critical flicker fusion and two-flash threshold decline little if at all until about the age of 50; some deterioration seems to take place at later ages.[46,47] Colour sensitivity shows a gradual loss of fine discrimination brought about by the yellowing of the lens, retinal changes and possibly other factors. In certain cases there are restrictions in the field of vision and arteriosclerosis may produce atrophy in the periphery, where the arterial blood supply is poorer.

Changes in visual perception clearly illustrate that ageing is a complex process; for there are not only various sorts of physical changes in the visual apparatus and the nervous system, but also concomitant changes in arousal and attention (which may help to account for age effects in the perception of illusions, and inter-sensory functions).[48-51] Levels of illumination and the visual characteristics of a display, for example size of print, rate of presentation, are obviously important in relation to work, driving and so on.[52] Degenerative changes in the eye accumulate with age, and diseases increase in frequency. There is a gradual loss of orbital fat, so that eventually the eyes appear shrunken, the blink reflex is slower and the eyelids hang loosely because of poorer muscle tone.

The visual capacities of elderly people can be improved not only by wearing glasses with normal lenses but also by the use of microscope lenses, stand magnifiers, and other optical devices for maximizing the use of residual capacity. Improvements in vision and other senses, such as hearing, can bring obvious psychological benefits, though such improvements may require special training in the use of these devices.[53]

HEARING. Loss of hearing during the adult years is usually gradual, and may not be noticed by the individual because most of the sounds which are relevant to his behaviour are well above threshold value. There are no obvious structural changes, except for atrophy of nervous tissue, especially at the basal turn of the inner ear. This helps to explain why hearing loss is greater for higher tones than for the lower tones. The very high tones are eventually lost completely, but moderately high tones can be registered if the sound is loud. There is some loss of hearing for speech (a mixture of high, medium and low tones), but it cannot be accounted for entirely in terms of the hearing loss for pure tones. Other factors such as intelligence, vocabulary and verbal context are involved.[54-58] Older people do not appear to compensate for their hearing loss by paying closer attention to the lip movements of the speaker. If anything, they are slightly poorer than younger people at lip-reading.[59] Cumulative damage can result from structural injury, disease and prolonged exposure to excessive noise, as for example in industrial deafness. Hearing loss is greater for men, probably because of their exposure to noisy occupational conditions, and greater for the left than for the right ear. Local arteriosclerosis (hardening and thickening of the small arteries) may produce limited hearing losses.

OTHER SENSES. Most age changes in sensory perception are in the direction of lowered efficiency.[60-63] There are degenerative changes in the olfactory and gustatory receptors: for example there is a decrease with age in sensitivity to sugar and salt, and a decrease in the number of taste buds in the tongue; the olfactory bulb (responsible for the perception of smell), at the base of the brain, atrophies; touch perception and the perception of movement and vibration also appear to decline with age. There is little experimental evidence that the perception of pain, heat and cold is weaker, but it seems reasonable to suppose that at least *some* deleterious effects of ageing occur because most sensory thresholds increase with age. However, the perception of temperature, for example, may be affected by deposits of fat and vascular changes. A threshold for pain from electrical stimulation of the teeth ranging from about 2 to 20 microamps has been observed, with little change over a wide age-range. If the sensory threshold for pain increases slightly with age but the tolerance level decreases, then older subjects may 'perceive' and report pain at lower stimulus intensities than younger subjects.[64-66] In all probability the vestibular senses (for posture and balance) are diminished in efficiency, and the situation is complicated by an increased susceptibility to dizziness brought about by vascular disturbances and perhaps by poorer patterns of sensory input from the muscles and joints. Poorer posture and balance contribute to certain types of accident in later life such as falls.

(c) *Vocalization*

Vocal changes with age are brought about in part by the hardening and decreased elasticity of the laryngeal cartilages, though these processes are usually complete by the age of 40. Later in life the laryngeal muscles atrophy, the vocal folds slacken, and changes occur in the pigmentation of the mucous membrane.[67,68]

The voice becomes more highly pitched as the person progresses from middle to old age, although in the thirties and forties vocal pitch appears to be lower than in adolescence and early adult life. In senescence the voice grows less powerful and restricted in range, becoming high and piping in many. Singing and public speaking, which make greater demands upon vocal capacity, deteriorate earlier than the normal speaking voice. Speech becomes slower, probably because of degenerative changes in the central nervous system rather than changes in peripheral mechanisms. Pauses are longer and more frequent. Slurring occurs in senile patients, and various kinds of speech disorder can arise from pathological changes in the brain.

'Inner speech' plays a part in thinking, so that the effects of age on verbal reasoning are likely to be the product of some interaction between degenerative changes in the verbal centres and degenerative changes in other parts of the brain concerned with intelligence. Relatively little, however, is known about the normal effects of age on the more subtle functions of language and communicative behaviour; on the whole they seem to be well preserved (see Chapter Six).

(d) *Endocrine Glands*

The endocrine system comprises the ductless glands, which secrete complex chemical substances called 'hormones' directly into the bloodstream. The hormones act as chemical messengers helping to direct the growth and functions of the body. The endocrine glands can be classified into three groups: first, those regulating specific aspects of metabolism, such as the islands of Langerhans, which secrete insulin, the hormone which regulates the utilization of sugar (inadequate insulin is one of the causes of diabetes), and the parathyroids which control the calcium content of the blood-serum; second, those working in conjunction with the autonomic nervous system, such as the adrenal medulla; third, those which appear to have more permanent effects on the development and integration of the body, such as the pituitary, thyroid, adrenal cortex and gonads.

PITUITARY. The pituitary gland is situated at the base of the brain and plays an important role in regulating the activities of other glands. The posterior pituitary helps in maintaining the water-balance of the body; the anterior pituitary regulates growth and the other endocrine organs. The pituitary appears to maintain its functions fairly well over the years.

THYROID AND PARATHYROID. The thyroid gland, situated at the front of the trachea, secretes thyroxin, an iodine compound; it stimulates and regulates metabolism. Insufficient secretion leads to an illness characterized by lethargy, chronic fatigue and lack of vitality, while excessive thyroid secretion leads to loss of weight, restlessness, excitability, insomnia and anxiety. Ageing eventually brings about a reduction in the size of the gland and the replacement of active cells by inactive connective tissue. It becomes less well supplied with blood and secretes less thyroxin. In normal people, however, it appears to remain fairly effective throughout the greater part of adult life.

Thyroid hormone affects metabolism, pulse rate and peripheral blood flow; so, age changes in thyroid function have repercussions on the normal activity of the cardiovascular system in adult life and old age. In old age, therefore, metabolic rate should diminish, thus increasing the risk of diminished body temperature in some circumstances.

The parathyroids regulate calcium-phosphorus metabolism; ageing appears to add to the large amount of interstitial fat in the parathyroids, and slightly to reduce essential tissue so that fewer cells are active.

ADRENALS. The adrenal glands, situated near the kidneys, consist of a medulla, which secretes adrenalin, and a cortex, which secretes a variety of chemical substances regulating carbohydrate metabolism and the salt balance of the body. These secretions help to mobilize the physical resources of the body during prolonged stresses, such as danger or hunger. Some hormones of the adrenal cortex have a masculinizing effect.

The absolute and relative loss of weight of the adrenals in adult life and old age is relatively slight, and the concentration in the blood of adrenocortical hormones seems more or less constant – although hormone output cannot be assessed directly. Adrenal insufficiency, therefore, has not been regarded as an important cause of physiological deterioration. Any deterioration – degenerative changes in cells, the replacement of active cell constituents with connective tissues, and arteriosclerosis – appears relatively late in life. There may be some compensatory growth in unaffected tissues, but with a risk of subsequent pathology. Abnormal adrenal insufficiency in older people may aggravate normal age changes, leading to muscular weakness and tiredness, or to complications in the pathologies of late life.

GONADS. The gonads – the ovaries or testes – produce reproductive cells, and secrete hormones which contribute to sexual development and behaviour. Hormone secretion rises sharply at puberty, and remains at a high normal level until it gradually falls off in middle and old age.

In women, degenerative changes in the ovaries and other organs in the body bring about a fairly abrupt cessation of the menstrual cycle around the age of 47, although there are large individual differences. This phase of life may be accompanied by irregularities in the menstrual cycle and by premenopausal sterility. Sometimes somatic disturbances, such as hot flushes, occur because of hormone imbalance, but in normal women the menopause appears not to have other serious symptoms (see Chapter Eight), although research reports are conflicting.[69] There is some atrophy of the vagina, uterus and breasts. Hormone replacement treatment seems to have some therapeutic value and lessens the severity of the hot flushes.

In men, degenerative changes in the testes and other organs of the body bring about more gradual changes in sexual function, though there are again wide individual differences. Structural changes take place in the testes and prostate gland, and fewer sperms are produced. The concept of a 'male climacteric' has not been adequately validated. Castration increases life-expectancy – with greater effect at earlier ages.[70]

Age changes in hormone secretion and hormone balance, and especially age changes in the hormones concerned with sexual functions, seem to be less critical in the biology of human ageing than had been supposed. The endocrine glands have specific but interrelated functions. They atrophy somewhat with age, but at different rates, so that the overall balance of male and female sex hormones (both of which occur in men and women) is altered and compensatory reactions take place. At the time of life known variously as the involutionary period, menopause or climacteric, pituitary gonadotropins (hormones which act upon the ovaries and the testes) are excreted in the urine in increased quantities; this can be regarded as evidence of a compensatory reaction to diminished ovarian and testicular function.

(e) *Sex*

Although sexual relationships between suitable partners can be maintained until quite late in life, there is normally a gradual reduction with age in the frequency of copulation and all types of sexual behaviour.[71-74] It is possible that the absence of an adequate stimulus (brought about perhaps by over-familiarity, reduced compatibility with the normal sexual partner, or lack of opportunity for sexual relations with more desirable partners) contributes to the reduction of sexual activity. Since a man is usually several years older than his wife, the reduction in frequency of sexual relations in marriage is more likely to be determined by his sexual capacity than by that of his wife.

PART II. CONCEPTUAL ISSUES

1. GENETIC AND ENVIRONMENTAL FACTORS

The relative importance and modes of interaction of genetic and environmental influences as they affect the process of human ageing are not clearly established; but the fact that species differ substantially in longevity means that genetic factors are important. The part played by evolutionary selection with regard to longevity, however, is not clear, and may be indirect. For example, many of the ailments which overtake us in middle and old age escape the selective pressure of evolution because they appear after the reproductive phase of life, for instance Huntington's chorea. Hence, any genetic predisposition to develop disorders like senile psychosis or hypertension tends not to be limited by differential rates of reproduction in a population, unlike haemophilia, for example, which is self-limiting. Furthermore, characteristics which make their appearance in late life – whether advantageous or disadvantageous to the individual – do so as a remote consequence of some 'counterpart' effect in the juvenile or reproductive period. Another aspect of this issue is the as yet unexplained difference in longevity for men and women, a sex difference also found in other species. Genetic influences are rarely simple; generally speaking, for complex functions anyway, genetic and environmental influences interact in ways which are difficult to explain.

Flies and mice have been selectively bred for longevity. A genetic influence on longevity has been confirmed by studies of twins. The difference between male monozygotic (identical) twins in age at death from natural causes is slightly less than that between male dizygotic (fraternal) twins; the effect is more pronounced for females.[75,76] Long-term genetic effects in late life are reflected in the close resemblance in physical condition and psychiatric breakdown of monozygotic twins.

In humans, grandparents and parents who live longer have grandchildren and children who also tend to live longer. The mother's longevity appears to be more closely correlated with offsprings' longevity than does the longevity of the father, although the father's longevity is also related to offspring's longevity – especially in sons. Expectation of life for an offspring is partly determined by the age of the mother. Within limits earlier-born offspring have a longer expectation of life than later-born offspring. The effect is caused mainly by neo-natal mortality, premature births, stillbirths and malformations, but a small differential advantage in longevity persists for earlier-born as compared with later-born children. It is difficult to disentangle the 'order of birth' variable from the 'maternal age' variable. The effects of maternal age on offspring need not be confined to obvious kinds of catastrophe but include varying *degrees* of minor influence. Some of the characteristics of later-born as compared with earlier-born children which are presently attributed to sibling relationships and parent–child relationships might arise from the deeper constitutional (but non-genetic, factors associated with the mother's biological age.

Genetic factors, disease processes, normal ageing and environmental conditions are all involved to a greater or lesser extent in the disorders of adult life and old age. Genetic susceptibility to bronchitis, for example, may not lead to bronchitis except in association with certain environmental factors such as smoking, air pollution and probably others. Smoking and excessive consumption of alcohol predispose to illness and shorten life, more so for some individuals than for others. Emotional stress, social isolation and dietary factors are suspected of playing a contributory role in certain disorders of adult life. When such connections can be demonstrated conclusively, then preventive and ameliorative measures can be developed. However, even if genetic make-up is a necessary and important cause of a mental or physical illness, it does not follow that the condition cannot be alleviated; certain metabolic disorders, such as phenylketonuria, have a genetic origin and yet respond to treatment.

Although many ailments of old age are incurable, modern medicine has revolutionized human society by increasing the average expectation of life by many years.[77] This has been achieved mainly by the successful treatment of diseases such as smallpox and diphtheria, and the control of tuberculosis and diabetes. The effect has been to increase vastly the expectation of life of young people, as shown in Table 2. The further expectation of life for older people, however, has changed very little over the period for which adequate records are

TABLE 2. Further expectation of life in years at various ages for males and females in 1901 and 1966

	Males		*Females*	
Year:	*1901*	*1966*	*1901*	*1966*
Further expectation of life:				
at birth	48·1	68·5	51·8	74·7
5 years	55·5	65·2	58·0	71·1
10 "	51·4	60·4	54·0	66·2
20 "	42·7	50·7	45·4	56·4
30 "	34·5	41·2	37·1	46·7
40 "	26·8	31·8	29·2	37·1
50 "	19·7	22·9	21·7	28·1
60 "	13·4	15·2	14·9	19·7
70 "	8·4	9·5	9·2	12·3
80 "	4·9	5·5	5·3	6·9

Adapted from Table 56, p. 98, *Social Trends, No. 2*, 1971

available; there may have been a decrease, even, because of the survival to later ages nowadays of people who are less robust. It appears that 110 years is about the upper limit of human longevity. In this country the *average* expectation of life is about 69 years for men and 75 years for women; and, short of a further biological and medical revolution, it seems unlikely that this average can be pushed much beyond the early eighties. People aged 80 today can expect to live on only a lit-

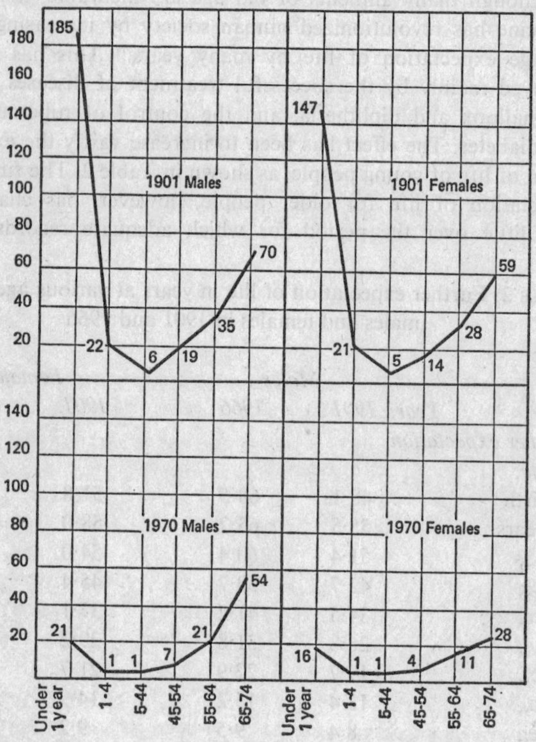

FIGURE 6 Death rates per 1,000 persons separately for men and women in 1901 and 1970, at six age levels. Adapted from Table 3, p. 48, *Social Trends, No. 2*, 1971.

tle longer than people aged 80 did in previous centuries, that is about five and a half years for men and seven for women. Although advances in medical knowledge have not extended what appears to be the natural maximum span of life, they have, through the employment of new surgical techniques and drugs, enabled more people to approach closer to this limit.

The great reduction in deaths from infection has made other causes of mortality – lung cancer and heart disease, for example – appear relatively more salient. The apparent increase in the prevalence of some diseases is partly explained by increased medical resources giving better detection. As advances in medical knowledge bring under control the dangerous diseases of infancy and childhood, more adult persons can expect to die from other diseases – those affecting the heart and blood vessels, respiratory diseases, cancer and brain disorders. Such diseases, unless they are brought under control, will increase as more people survive into adult life and old age.

In rats, physical exercise, within limits, appears to delay biological ageing.[78,79] In human adults, physical exercise leads to improvements in speed, stamina and strength, and in a variety of underlying physiological functions such as circulation and respiration.[80-87] Substantial improvements following physical training have been reported; this probably means that physiological measures derived from normal subjects of different ages reflect the effects of disuse and adaptation to non-demanding physical circumstances rather than the effects of ageing. The physiological functions of normal healthy adults improve rapidly in response to 'demand', even late in life. It is not clear that the physiological benefit has effects on ordinary behaviour or feelings of well-being, though this seems more likely than not. Physical training does not extend the 'normal' lifespan, except in the sense that it seems to increase the individual's powers of resistance to and recovery from physical ailments which might otherwise have been fatal, like coronary occlusion. It seems likely that central nervous functions play a part in the improvements following regular physical exercises. Many adults underrate their capacity for physical improvement and underrate the importance of exercise and diet in the maintenance of health and vigour. Exercise, in the present sense, means working against a load and over a period of time, so that the muscular effort required approaches a maximum, as in the use of a bicycle ergometer or treadmill.

2. NORMAL VERSUS PATHOLOGICAL AGEING

The biological changes associated with adult life are fairly gradual, although actual 'rates' of ageing are difficult to validate. Degenerative effects accumulate and the individual normally dies as the proximate result of the breakdown of a vital organic process. Different parts of the body begin to degenerate at different ages and deteriorate at different rates. Death can be medically defined by the cessation of circulation, respiration or brain function, but 'recoveries' are not unknown and the functions of the body do not all end abruptly at the same moment. In senescence, the functions of the body become gradually more unstable and uncoordinated. Senescence arises from the cumulative ill effects of damage and disease, or from degenerative processes inherent in ageing cells and tissues, or from an accumulation of, or deficiency in, biochemical substances. A combination of these and other causes is possible.[88]

Senescence is a general biological impairment which increases the likelihood of death or 'force of mortality' in later life as seen for example in the greater liability of older people to secondary infections and complications following an accident. Curves of mortality (graphs showing the increasing number of deaths at successively higher ages) can be described by mathematical expressions such as Gompertz or Makeham functions (see p. 68).[89,90] Mathematical and statistical techniques are used extensively in biological research in ageing, as in social and behavioural gerontology (see Chapter Eleven); the aim is not merely to describe observed phenomena but to test theories which purport to explain the effects of ageing.

By one definition, physical and mental diseases in old age

are pathological conditions relatively distinct from, although superimposed upon and interacting with, the normal patterns of biological ageing and psychological change. Alternatively, ageing can be regarded simply as an accumulation of pathological processes, which eventually kill off the individual by interfering with a vital function of the body. Certain kinds of disease tend to afflict the young; others, such as heart disease, some respiratory disorders, cancer and organic psychoses, tend to afflict older people. To die a 'natural death' in old age is to die from one or other of the non-violent causes entered on death certificates.

The distinction between normal and pathological ageing is convenient, but it may be misleading. Adult ageing in the sense of deterioration of function can be observed, and partly accounted for, in terms of pathological processes; but longevity in the absence of senescence is a hypothetical entity, like the philosopher's stone, and may remain so. Stripping away man's diseases to get at the 'intrinsic' causes of ageing may be rather like peeling an onion to get at its core!

V. Korenchevsky, in *Physiological and Pathological Ageing*, made much of the fact that some elderly human subjects (and animals) possess physiological capacities equal to or better than those characteristic of young subjects; he argued that this is evidence for the existence of primary (non-pathological) ageing. Similarly, some elderly subjects possess physiological capacities well below those of young subjects; he argued that this is evidence for the existence of secondary (pathological) ageing. The argument, however, is circular; pathological ageing is defined in terms of a substantial loss or negative deviation in functional capacity compared with a young/normal standard; normal ageing is defined by the absence of such deviation. However, there are individual differences in functional capacity and dangers in making inferences from cross-sectional studies (comparing different people at different ages). Thus, overlap between statistical distributions of physiological measures, or psychological measures, for young and old subjects is not sufficient to support the hypothesis that there are two kinds of ageing, as shown in Figure 7. Irregularities and discontinuities in statistical distributions are the usual indication that something is 'abnormal' – like the effects of a late-acting genetic factor, a threshold effect in some cumulative process, or a disease. Similarly a distribution of *difference* measures, i.e. a distribution of the differences between subjects at young and older ages has to be discontinuous or at least markedly different from normal in order to support the hypothesis that age effects in some subjects are 'pathological' rather than 'normal'.

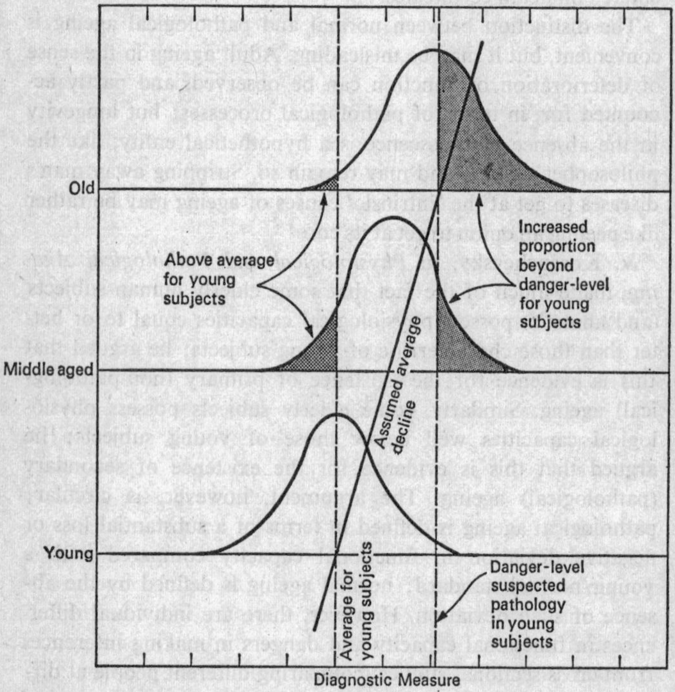

FIGURE 7 Hypothetical age effect on the distribution of measurements of a normative diagnostic variable.

Normal Versus Pathological Ageing

A wide range of individual differences among the elderly is not incompatible with the hypothesis that adult ageing is a summation of pathological conditions. Individuals differ widely at all ages, not only in the types and degrees of pathology that they exhibit, but also in all kinds of 'normal' physiological and psychological functions. Only hypothetical subjects are free from pathology and damage. Either they cannot exist or they cannot become senescent. In the latter case, they cannot die from disease or injury, so they endure indefinitely unless switched off or run down like some sort of biological clock. The issue of *normal* versus *pathological* ageing cannot be resolved unless these terms are defined independently of each other.

Severe sensory and motor impairments – blindness and other visual defects, deafness, paralyses, disablements – become more frequent as age advances. Much depends upon one's standards of comparison: an old person's blood pressure may be normal relative to that of his age group, but abnormal relative to that of a young healthy group. The discrepancy between an old person's vocabulary and abstract reasoning may be normal for his age and yet show that marked intellectual impairment has taken place since he was a young adult. A physical or mental condition that is common among old people may be regarded as normal, not pathological, whereas if it seriously disables a few older people it may be regarded as pathological. One might say, paradoxically, that there are lots of normal old people but no healthy ones. One serious consequence is that many disabilities are passively accepted as a necessary part of growing old, when in fact effective prevention, treatment, and prosthetic aid are available. The older person's self-assessment of his health differs from the assessment made by his physician; and the objective health needs of the elderly as a whole greatly exceed the resources allocated to meet demand.[91]

Biomedical advances can be expected to lead to: one, the prevention or alleviation of physical and mental disorders of adult life and old age; two, the prolongation of normal adult vigour, and an increase in average life expectancy; and possibly, three, an *extension* of the present limits of longevity.[92,93] Improvements in the treatment of physical and mental ill health, however, are not always followed up by corresponding improvements in rehabilitation and social welfare. Poverty, loneliness, squalor, undernourishment and unhappiness contribute to the general burden of ill health in old age and reduce the likelihood that medical and psychiatric treatment will produce lasting effects.

More people are surviving to experience the environmental hazards of adult life and to develop physical and mental disorders of late onset.[94] The pattern of physical and mental disease in old age could be altered by changes in medical and psychiatric care, and by social and economic changes in, for example, social attitudes and living standards. The costs involved in putting into effect preventive, ameliorative and remedial measures must be measured against the benefits derived from increased productivity, longer working lives, decreased rates of illness, and happier individuals. Old age is not entirely a consequence of biological degeneration; it is partly the product of political, economic and historical conditions. Old age is one of the stages in our conception of the human life-path; it is culturally defined by our beliefs about man and nature, and is subject to the prevailing system of attitudes and values. Human ageing is thus a biosocial phenomenon, and susceptible to some control.

3. THEORIES ABOUT THE CAUSES OF AGEING

The main aim in formulating theories of ageing is to conceptualize the *causal paths* taken by degenerative processes.[95,96] Some investigations are concerned only with certain segments of certain classes of degenerative pathways, for example the onset and course of a stroke, psychophysiological changes during the menopause, or adjustment to retirement. The main biological theories of ageing, naturally, attempt to portray the major pathways and constraints in the physical basis of ageing.

Even in a protected environment, there are bound to be adverse cumulative effects from disease and injury, which kill off individual members of a species. Where the environment contains dangers – in civilized communities these include traffic hazards, pollution and infectious organisms – even the luckiest person is bound, sooner or later, to sustain injuries and die. Individual members of a species, including human beings, die perhaps as part of the process of biological evolution – without individual variation there could be no selection, without population limitation there could be no reproduction and survival of individuals; genetic variation is built into living systems. The range of defects and hazards that living systems must contend with is considerable, but the fact that living things grow old and die is less impressive than the fact that they live at all.

Biological theories of ageing are too diverse and too technical to be dealt with at any length in a book on social and behavioural gerontology.[97–99] The fundamental mechanisms of biological ageing are not known for certain; and some of the conceptual issues, such as the distinction between normal and pathological ageing, or between functional and chronological age, have not yet been settled.

One theory is that cells, like tiny computers, are programmed by a genetic code which is effective up to about the age at which evolutionary forces cease to have any selective effects, i.e. towards the end of the normal period of reproduction. After this period of life, the programme carries on for a time, but it has not been evolved to cope with the further effects of ageing, which, as we have seen in relation to the non-renewal of nerve cells, may be severe. Nor will it cope indefinitely with the long-term consequences and accumulations of injuries and infections. This 'long-term' inadequacy of the genetic programme may mean that we grow old by default rather than by 'design' of nature.

Another theory is based on the fact that the production of antibodies by the 'immune system' declines during adult life and old age. Living organisms defend themselves from infection by forming antibodies which are capable of identifying and reacting against foreign or abnormal cells and proteins. The theory is that either (a) the immune system becomes less sensitive to differences between the body's own cells and substances and those that are foreign, or (b) the cells of the body undergo genetic variation (somatic mutation) and become liable to attack by the immune system, which identifies them as foreign and destroys them with specific antibodies. The antibodies produced by an aged immune system may be faulty; hence two sorts of error may occur – foreign elements are not identified, normal elements are identified as foreign and destroyed. These errors lead to pathological changes as well as to an aggravation of the normal degenerative processes. Some medical research in immunology is directed towards the prevention and treatment of auto-allergic diseases.

There could be a cumulative loss of chromosome fragments arising from errors in mitosis (cell division). Some types of error may be more likely than others, or more likely to occur under special conditions. Not all lymphocytes contain the normal number of chromosomes (23 pairs) and aneuploid cells (with a deviant number of chromosomes) appear to increase in frequency with age, and to be associated with adverse effects. The nerve cells depend upon other cells in the body, such as glial cells and blood cells; so they could be affected indirectly by somatic changes in the chromosomes of these cells, although nerve cells are fixed post-mitotic cells.

Molecular mechanisms within individual cells in the body are capable of repairing damage to DNA and of correcting errors in metabolism such as enzyme function or protein synthesis. These mechanisms, however, cannot meet every contingency, and so cells degenerate and die. The cumulative effect of these errors is to reduce the functional efficiency of the various organs and systems of the body and of the organism as a whole. The identification of specific repair mechanisms, however, would create possibilities for therapeutic intervention to retard the process of ageing, and constitute a theoretical advance. Measures designed to prevent or neutralize the adverse effects of free-radicals and toxic substances are being developed; some anti-oxidants, for example, appear to prolong life. But the biochemistry of living and dying is a technical matter outside the scope of this book.

Some physiological functions are associated with natural rhythms and periodicities – electrical activities in the brain, heart-beats, ovulation – reflecting clock-like biological mechanisms measuring 'life time' rather than 'physical time'. Genetic mechanisms may operate as switches, starting or stopping biological processes at various 'logical' points in juvenile development and adult ageing; the ages at which these genetic switches operate, however, may be affected by environmental factors which accelerate or retard development and ageing. Further research should throw light on the part played by 'biological clocks' in human ageing.

Experimental studies with animals show that the effects of ionizing radiation are cumulative and lead to the earlier deaths of exposed organisms from various causes. Radiation increases the incidence of some diseases which occur earlier in life, and this has the statistical effect of reducing the average age at death from diseases which occur later. The adverse effects of radiation are greater for older animals, perhaps because older animals have weaker powers of recovery and restoration. The effects of small doses for human beings, however, are difficult to assess. Irradiation effects are by no means simple and do not provide conclusive evidence for any biological theory of ageing, such as crosslinking of molecules, or auto-immunity.[100]

Experimental studies of longevity in animals and surveys of treatment effects in humans show that environmental factors – such as nutrition and drugs, radiation and toxic substances, temperature and stresses – can affect longevity and functional capacity. The advent of man-made substances and man-made conditions of life means that novel causes of ageing are evolving. The complexities of biochemistry and the uniqueness of the individual make it likely that, in addition to the causes and pathways of ageing which are common to large numbers of people, there may be some which affect only a few or perhaps only one person.

CHAPTER FOUR

Social Aspects of Human Ageing

Social gerontology is concerned with many of the issues briefly mentioned in the short historical introduction: government policy towards the aged and the poor, economic provision for retirement through insurance and pensions, health and welfare services, demography, family and kinship systems. The bulk of this sociological knowledge is concerned with *old people* rather than with *adult ageing*, although some studies of the family have taken account of adult phases of the life-cycle.

The first major attempts to formulate the nature and scope of social gerontology were the publication of *Handbook of Social Gerontology* (1960) and *Aging in Western Societies* (1960). Shortly afterwards, in quick succession, appeared *Social Welfare of the Aging* (1962), *Social and Psychological Aspects of Aging* (1962), and *Processes of Aging: Social and Psychological Perspectives, Volume II* (1963). More recently, Shanas and her associates have attempted the difficult task of comparing three industrial societies – the United States of America, Denmark and Britain – with regard to some of the social gerontological issues listed above.[1-6]

1. ECONOMIC AND INDUSTRIAL ASPECTS

Modern social gerontology studies the responses made by industrial societies to the challenge created by the existence of a substantial number of elderly dependent people who consume but do not produce goods and services within the prevailing social and economic conditions. For example, a modern industrial society can expect well over ten per cent of its members to survive beyond 65 years of age. Because of their relatively poor physical health, social isolation and poverty, these elderly people comprise a seriously disadvantaged section of the community and make legitimate, diverse, and (in sum) large claims on a socicty's resources.[7,8] The reasons why the aged are a segregated and disadvantaged section of the community include the following: a majority of them are women; on average, they command little wealth or income; they have lost many of the physical, social and psychological attributes valued by the rest of the community; they have withdrawn from central positions of power and authority; they are politically impotent, which springs partly from the lack of continuity in leadership.

Social gerontology is also related to a number of general sociological themes such as: social change and industrialization in relation to work roles, age and sex roles, family structure and solidarity. It has been discovered that nowadays people tend to marry at a slightly younger age, they have fewer children, the last child is born earlier in the mother's life, the mother is more likely to re-enter the work-force, and people are more likely to survive to a late age.

Societies differ in their population size and age-structure, and in the secular changes in their population. Industrialization brings a rapid increase in the proportion of younger dependent persons; this is followed in due course by an increase in the proportion of older dependent persons. These changes create political and economic problems, as well as social and psychological problems. These include: individual adjustment to changes in status during the life-cycle; the care of a small proportion of socially isolated and infirm aged people; the distribution of economic resources to elderly dependent members.

The problem of the *age-structure* of the population is less important nowadays than formerly. Industrialization, automation, and the achievement of a substantial degree of control over social and economic conditions means that the population is no longer so dependent on a young and physically vigorous labour force. For example, one finds widespread unemployment and under-employment, especially among women. Pressure of population *size* is the more serious problem.[9,10] Improvements in education and technology have vastly increased the capacity and output of workers of all kinds, resulting in shorter working hours and more 'service' occupations. Career structures have changed and new careers have come into existence. Social as well as biological factors, therefore, help to shape our fate in adult life and old age. Furthermore, improvements in health in the present century have added about ten years to the average *working* life. Finally, the age of retirement could be adjusted by government legislation.

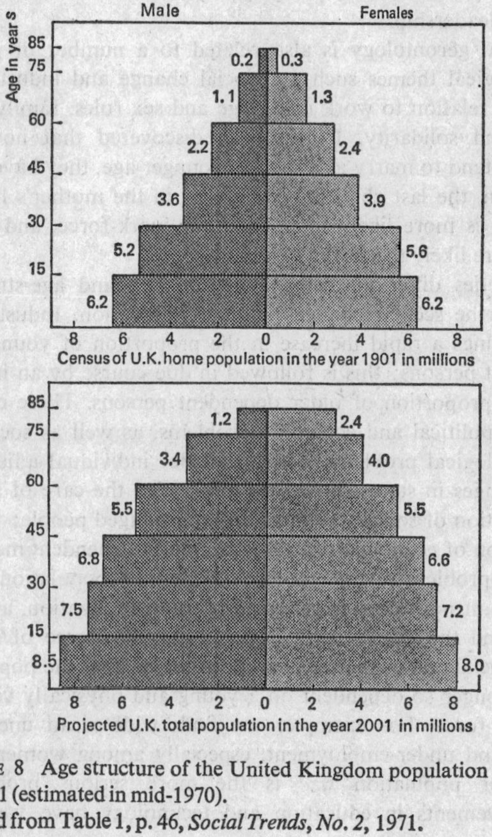

FIGURE 8 Age structure of the United Kingdom population in 1901 and 2001 (estimated in mid-1970).
Adapted from Table 1, p. 46, *Social Trends, No. 2*, 1971.

In Britain, less than a third of men and less than one tenth of women aged 65 years or more are in regular employment. Naturally, the numbers diminish at later ages. Whether a person continues in employment in late life depends upon such obvious conditions as employment opportunities, health, living costs, income and family circumstances. These and other factors form a predisposing set of conditions, and retirement is eventually precipitated by, for example, an illness, or compulsory retirement from a lifelong job. The substantial reduction in income on retirement, combined with lifelong low earnings for many, means that a common reason for wanting to work is to obtain more money. In Britain, however, about a quarter of all men retire a year or two before age 65; it has been argued that the *rate* of retirement at that time of life makes it unlikely that raising the age of retirement would make more than a marginal contribution to the economic well-being of the country.

The economic aspects of ageing are difficult to disentangle from the general economic and political circumstances of a community.[11,12] The basic problem is how to support, out of current and accumulated production, the non-productive members of a community – the children, the sick, the old and others. If the proportion of dependent to productive people is small, the problem is simple. But in Britain the output required to support the dependent members, by providing food, clothing, housing, health and welfare services, etc. for the children and the elderly, is large in relation to total output, and it is getting larger. This means lower standards of living, less capital for investment, and a slower rate of economic and industrial development. The problem can be dealt with in a variety of ways – by increased productivity (especially by means of automation and rationalization), by extending the working life (which will probably make only a marginal difference), or by reducing the amount spent on children and old people. Low spending on children's health and education is thought to be short-sighted and self-defeating, but spending on pensions and old people generally has traditionally been kept to a minimum. We do not have enough socio-technical stability to calculate expenditure nicely over the whole span of human life. Our present arrangements are an approximation to this ideal and are at least an improvement over the conditions endured by previous generations.

Since public funds must be used economically and political considerations cannot be disregarded, methods must be found whereby pensions are paid so as to secure justice and fair play for all members of the community. Paying benefits to one person to meet his needs may reduce the motivation of another person who is still able to work and earn, or bring about gross differences in standards of living between one person who can work and another who cannot. One solution is to make supplementary payments to retired or unemployed people to prevent their standards of living from falling too far. Many individual firms and insurance companies make provision for supplementary payments and benefits. The Department of Health and Social Security and various charities also make supplementary payments, but measures of this sort do not solve the main economic problem of making provision for old age. Taxation and incomes policies may eventually provide a more effective long-term solution, but part of the difficulty arises from errors in forecasting trends in the country's economy and population.

In view of the objective situation, it is surprising that almost half the men in retirement in Britain feel that they are at least as well off as they were shortly before they retired. Greater improvements will come when it is more widely recognized that security, leisure and reasonable standards of living during old age are rights achieved by an individual in return for his contribution, by way of his work and services, to the welfare of the community. Living standards depend to some extent on the efforts of earlier generations, and younger working people have a moral obligation to support the elderly.

Industrial progress sometimes creates redundancies among workers who are nowhere near the end of their normal active lives. In the past, industrial changes were often made with scant regard for the human problems they created. Nowadays arrangements such as unemployment benefits, severance pay, payment of removal costs, adequate notice of redundancy, the gradual running down of a work force, earlier retirement benefits and better facilities for retraining and re-employment make it easier for redundant workers to make a satisfactory readjustment.[13] Measures of this sort are more effective if adequate planning and coordination take place on a national and regional basis. Coordination and timing are difficult because many sections of the community are involved – the government, trade unions, local authorities, financial organizations and individual firms – as well as individual workers. The problem is to balance the need for industrial change and efficiency against the need to protect the older, more vulnerable, worker. In an expanding economy, advance notice combined with adequate, if temporary, financial security permits all but a few workers to find fresh employment. Even so, a man over the age of 60 is in a difficult position. For the individual, the circumstances and the effects are complex, and all manner of complications arise – health, disabilities, family commitments, his outlook, the opportunities open to him, the risks he is prepared to take, and so on. Industrial gerontology thus examines not only the larger social problems but also the occupational psychology of adult life with its attendant problems of selection, counselling, retraining, work study and the like.

Whatever differences there are between societies in the way they deal with ageing, certain common features can be discerned. Most people try to survive for as long as possible, often in spite of severe hardships. Old people disengage from the more central social activities, either because they find themselves unable to cope with the demands of their roles, or because others feel that changes should be made, so that the younger members of a community can pursue community interests vigorously and in new ways. Members of a community who have played an active part in local affairs often try to retain some measure of involvement in social organizations, as it is not easy for people to give up the status, rights and authority they acquired during their active years. Eventually, as physical and mental dilapidation increase, some sort of withdrawal from the mainstream of social interaction becomes necessary, and the individual's social life is largely confined to small primary groups, usually the family and friends. Failing this, the individual becomes isolated or enters into a dependent relationship in a home or an institution. His continued existence is then much less important to the larger community. An older person may leave a gap in the social network when he disengages or dies, but society is robust and soon replaces him. No one is indispensable. Society prepares in advance, for example, by keeping obituary notices up to date. In spite of their numbers, the aged are too heterogeneous to form an effective 'pressure group' in the larger society, and their tendency to disengage weakens their involvement in community affairs. In Britain, social movements among the elderly have emerged, concerned with welfare and pensions, and in America there are signs that the elderly are becoming politically more significant, although they are not under-represented in the accepted political sense.[14] The underprivileged (minority) position of the elderly is reflected in the small amount of broadcasting time, advertising, and newspaper space devoted to their interests as compared with people at other stages of life. Middle aged people, by contrast, are in a 'commanding' position.

2. HEALTH AND FUNCTIONAL CAPACITY

On reaching the age of 65, a man can expect to live for a further 13 years, a woman for 15 or 16 years. About 15 per cent become bedridden, housebound, or seriously incapacitated, either by general infirmity or by specific disabilities such as blindness, deafness, or vertigo; about 5 per cent exhibit psychiatric abnormalities, but not all are treated. The differences between individuals at all ages are so great that for most measures of functional capacity there is a considerable overlap even between widely spaced age groups. It is not surprising therefore to find that about one third of men at retirement age feel that they could continue in employment. In the United Kingdom, however, union and company policy, unemployment, the trend towards a shorter working life, and so on, make it impossible for more than a few people to continue paid work much beyond the normal age of retirement. About 5 per cent of all people over 65 are in institutions of one sort or another – nursing homes, residential homes, or hospitals, for example – because they are incapable of the degree of self-care required for life in the community. The percentage rises with age.

Old people vary, not only in their capacity for self-maintenance but also in their environmental circumstances – housing, finance, local facilities, social contacts and so on. Such variations contribute to differences in social adjustment. They present three interesting facets of social ageing.[15] First, people generally prefer to manage their own affairs, and prefer to receive financial support and welfare services for living at home (or somewhere like home) rather than go into a fully comprehensive residential institution. Second, the daily needs of many old people are met directly by close relatives or friends; the State provides only a small part of the total resources required even for the limited living standards that prevail. This sort of community support for the elderly infirm warrants improved State aid, such as the provision of meals, holidays, day care, domestic help and home nursing. The effect of health and welfare services on the care of the aged person by the family varies from one family to another, depending upon attitudes and circumstances; but there is no substantial evidence that State aid weakens family solidarity – rather the reverse. Third, health is partly subjective: in later life, we become 'adapted' to disability and ill-health; we may not recognize that, by normal standards, we need medical treatment.

The average old person in Britain consults his doctor about twice as frequently as a young adult. Screening tests for medical health play a valuable part in the treatment or prevention of some disorders in late life, but they do not reach everyone. Many people are grossly ignorant of medical matters and often fail to understand or follow medical advice. The effects of publicity and health education in relation to disorders in later life would almost certainly bring considerable benefits, as campaigns against smoking and obesity have shown; but the increased demands for medical and welfare services might prove impossible to meet.

The old person's subjective assessment of his health varies with his actual physical condition; but men, particularly, tend to overestimate their health, even relative to other old people. Physicians react to the symptoms of definite diseases, but the old person is more likely to pay attention to sensory and motor impairments and the disruption of his natural functions and activities. Physical incapacity and limited mobility have psychological and social repercussions, so that incapacitated old people tend to feel more lonely, depressed or anxious than those who are more mobile.

Scales for the measurement of functional capacity in late life have been developed. They range from simple questions about negotiating stairs, washing and dressing, and trimming toenails, to more elaborate tests, check-lists and rating scales. Dizziness, unsteadiness and restricted limb movements are frequently mentioned as reasons for inadequate self-care. Not all old people in residential care are severely incapacitated, and not all old people in the community are fully self-maintaining. Most of those who are more seriously incapacitated are single women or widows. Assessment of the needs and functional capacities of old people living in institutions or at home is essential for the effective administration of health and welfare services and of housing. There appears to be considerable ignorance and disagreement about the extent and kinds of old people's needs, so there is considerable scope for survey work and the compilation of statistical data.

The pattern of care for the elderly continues to move away from full-time institutional care towards sheltered housing and domiciliary care. The long-term social and economic consequences of such administrative policies are difficult to work out because of the effects of unanticipated factors. Some of the premises on which policies are based are explicit and open to examination whereas others are less clear. The term 'model' is used to refer to a system of ideas which purports to represent the internal logic and numerical relationships of some circumscribed process, for example pensions, housing, health and welfare services, medical diagnosis, on which policy is based.[16]

Social service occupations are providing an increasing number and variety of opportunities for women to enter full-time and part-time employment in areas which, one feels, are well-suited to their natural bent for family and neighbourhood affairs, and for human relations generally. Applied social gerontology, however, must be firmly based on scientific theory and method, and therefore needs an increasing number of research personnel and administrators.

3. THE AGE STRUCTURE OF FAMILIES

The age structure of the population of the United Kingdom has changed over the last century from one which was pyramidal in shape (large numbers of children and young people, fewer adults and very few old people) to one which is almost rectangular up to about the age of 55 and pyramidal for later ages. Improved life expectancy combined with smaller families might lead to a situation in which the kinship network becomes organized longitudinally and narrowly through several generations rather than laterally across several degrees of relationship. We thus have the prospect of conflicting loyalties and changing relationships between the two intermediate generations in the four-generation family – one family in five in Britain.

The changing age structure of the family creates new social and psychological problems of adjustment for individuals at all stages of the life-cycle, but people can adapt, in time, to novel 'family' arrangements, and laws can be changed to meet changing social conditions. The participation of non-family members in 'family' affairs is not uncommon. The increasing frequency of remarriage after divorce and the supposed increase in extra-marital sexual relations make it difficult to forecast the future of family life. The effects of class mobility, migration, education and cultural change further complicate the picture. Positive roles for the aged in family relationships are not well-documented for present-day society. Families and households vary, but typical family structures are probably not very different now from what they were in former times. Members of the extended family as well as friends and neighbours would provide support if needed, and the ties of duty, mutual obligation and affection, then as now, would persist over long periods of time even in the absence of social interaction.

In Britain, more than one fifth of the elderly live alone, and about one third live as married couples. Nearly half live with other people, usually a relative. The majority of old people live fairly close to a relative, and see their children fairly frequently. Social interaction with friends, neighbours and kin is usually sufficient to maintain stable patterns of communication. It is impossible to describe in full the social psychology of 'exchange' between older and younger generations in the same family or quasi-family. Such a description would entail an extensive exercise in behavioural ecology – mapping the kinds of daily activities they engage in. Sample surveys, however, have confirmed and refined commonsense impressions regarding the exchange of advice, gifts, money, emotional support, domestic help and other services, which create a system of reciprocal obligations and dependencies. The social psychology of human ageing – in the sense of experimental research into the details of social perception and interaction, conformity, attitudes and so on – has scarcely begun.[17-20]

Half the elderly appear to have almost daily contact with one or other of their children; less than a fifth, apparently, see neither children nor relatives for a week or more at a time. Class differences and physical distance affect frequency of contact. Investigations into the amount of social contact enjoyed by elderly people show that a small proportion appear to be socially isolated, whereas most elderly – men and women alike – do not *feel* isolated, even if their frequency of communication is low in comparison with younger people. On the other hand, some people feel lonely when the objective indices of social contact are high. From the point of view of social and psychological welfare, the degree and kind of affective experience associated with particular relationships is probably more important than mere frequency of social contact. Thus, such contacts experienced by the aged can range all the way from those which are brief, routine, superficial, instrumental and merely dutiful to those which are prolonged, spontaneous, deeply felt, rewarding or punishing, and based on personal involvement. The possible effects of ageing on emotional experience and responsiveness are referred to in Chapter Three, Section 3 (a).

Urban industrial life brings about occupational groupings in which social interactions and emotional relationships tend to grow out of the work situation. The family and other primary social groupings have to adapt to the demands of the work situation. When a man reaches the end of his working life, his social functions change abruptly, and he may feel useless and unwanted. The separation of generations within families, and the inadequate social and financial provisions for the elderly, make it difficult for parents and children to reunite after the parents have retired and the grandchildren have grown up. However, the difficulty can be social or psychological rather than economic, since parents and children do not share the same beliefs and feelings. Technological and social change, occupational differences between parents and children, education, housing, specialization of labour and social pressures are responsible for this 'emotional distance' between one generation and the next. Further improvements in life-expectancy and health, presumably, will bring about alterations in social and family life, as will changes such as re-employment, especially of married women later in life, and modified retirement practices.

Although the term 'generation' is commonly used, its meaning is often obscure, since adults in their forties say, do not constitute a functionally distinct age stratum, nor do they have clear cut relationships with adjacent 'generations' of people in their teens or in their seventies. Any reference to chronological age is relatively uninformative, because people are being born or dying continuously and the term 'generation' makes sense only when it is used to refer to people in a broadly defined age band, who can be *socially* identified either by their behaviour, or by the experiences they have had, or by their social attitudes: for example the generation 'in power', the 'veterans' of World War II, or the generation entering retirement.

The typical roles and statuses of the older members of a society can be expected to change with the changing socio-economic and cultural conditions of that society. The 'Victorian father' role, for example, contrasts with the modern role of father.

4. SOCIAL DISENGAGEMENT

(a) *Retirement*

Old age creates social as well as medical problems, but it is only recently that much attention has been paid to the cultural aspects of late maturity and old age. It is widely believed that many of the problems of adolescence are brought about by life-history events and inadequacies in surrounding circumstances; so some of the maladjustments and difficulties of old people may arise from analogous causes. Inadequate pensions, poor living conditions, occupational insecurity, harmful social attitudes, and the shortage of psychiatric counselling services are but a few of them.

One of the more obvious features of maturity and old age is social disengagement – a systematic reduction in certain kinds of social interaction. The theory of 'disengagement' has received considerable attention from psychologists and sociologists in gerontology. It is a kind of withdrawal from the mainstreams of social activity. It is normal in late maturity, and encouraged by comman social practices such as superannuation, limited terms of office, age limits, and many social norms and expectations affecting behaviour. The most obvious examples are people in retirement or semi-retirement.[21-24] Most people retire either because of ill health or because they reach a fixed retirement age. Some people continue to work, part-time or full-time, after their official 'retirement'. Their usual reasons are financial, although a proportion of retired people enjoy working, particularly if the working hours are short and the conditions congenial.

The ending of paid work, or a reduction in the time devoted to it, has a number of consequences. For example, the individual no longer interacts so much with his colleagues or workmates, and he takes part less frequently in the numerous social activities previously connected with his job. The elimination or reduction of occupational relationships tends to weaken ties of friendship. The retired person's relatives and children are likely to be widely scattered, especially in communities where people move around a great deal, and therefore provide fewer opportunities for visiting. The process looks like a sensible attempt on the part of the older person to distribute his reduced energies and resources over fewer but more personally relevant activities, to conserve effort, and to escape from demands which he cannot or does not wish to meet.

The old fashioned 'institution' for psychiatric patients and the elderly infirm unwittingly pushed the inmates' disengagement to its limit of absurdity by taking them out of society altogether, by providing only custodial care, and failing to give them help and opportunities to reorganize their lives (see Chapter Two, Section 2). This kind of treatment is less conspicuous nowadays because of the emphasis on rehabilitation and community care, for example day care in hospital, home help, clubs and outings organized by voluntary workers.

Individual differences in disengagement are common. Some elderly people stubbornly resist pressures put on them to reduce their commitments, to shed their responsibilities, and to do less work. They refuse to take good advice if it means giving up activities which have played a central part in their lives – a job, a small business, a cultural or scientific activity, a social or civic responsibility. Even more likely is resistance to the idea of giving up an independent life and a private home for residence in a nursing home. Some refuse to retire until forced to do so by ill health. Others die as they lived – active and involved with the world.

Although some individuals fight the process all the way, disengagement of some sort is bound to come, simply because old people have neither the physical nor the mental resources they had when they were young. Disengagement, therefore, provides a solution to some of the problems of adjustment in old age and signifies a practical reappraisal of one's position. In ideal circumstances, the process is graded to suit the declining biological and psychological capacities of the individual on the one hand, and the needs of society on the other. Normal disengagement seems to lessen the fear of death.

Disengagement is not an entirely negative process; though accompanied by selective withdrawals from certain social activities and occupational responsibilities, it may at the same time involve the commencement or renewal of other participant activities (engagements), especially those involving family, friends and neighbourhood. The net effect is a shrinkage in the older person's range of activities, and a diminution in the amount of contact he has with other people. Gradually the older person's life becomes separated from the lives of others; he tends to become less functionally associated with them, he is less emotionally involved, and he becomes more absorbed in his own problems and circumstances.

Since disengagement implies loss of membership from some of the small informal social groups which make up the fabric of society, the range and intensity of the social pressures brought to bear upon the person to secure his conformity to social norms are decreased. In extreme cases this can lead to isolation and personal eccentricity. Elderly individuals who have a history of difficult social relationships probably disengage more quickly and become more isolated than normal people. Elderly people who have been socially isolated for a considerable time find it difficult to settle into the community patterns of a nursing home or hospital.

The elderly person's most salient concern is often his physical health and, after that, his security and standards of living. A reduction in living standards and income consequent upon retirement, coupled perhaps with natural regrets on leaving close companions and familiar activities, may bring about a temporary depression or anxiety, but often it is the *prospect* of retirement rather than retirement itself which leads to morbid states of mind. Studies show that, given reasonable physical health and financial resources, the average retired man or woman soon becomes adapted to the changed circumstances and shows an improvement in physical health and outlook. It is not so much old age and retirement as the transition to old age and retirement that creates problems of adjustment.

Disengagement is fostered by the decreased physical mobility of the elderly person. Whether or not this is experienced as a frustration depends very much upon the elderly person's needs, habits and circumstances. An overall reduction in needs simplifies the elderly person's life and allows him to deploy his limited resources more effectively for the attainment of fewer but more personally important goals. This brings about a constriction in the range of his activities and outlook, and probably makes it more difficult for him to appreciate the needs and actions of younger people. Many social issues and events will have much less relevance for him when he has detached himself from the mainstreams of social life.

Recent psychological and social research has obliged us to alter our ideas about the nature of retirement. Retirement can no longer be thought of simply as a sudden enforced dislocation of a working man's life, almost inevitably resulting in feelings of rejection and physical or mental ill health. A substantial proportion of men retire or wish to retire a few years before the usual age of 65 years. After that age, an even larger proportion do not actively seek paid employment, although the generally low levels of income in late life constitute a strong inducement to work. There have been gradual but absolute improvements in the health and welfare of retired people and in their standards of living over many decades. Nevertheless, a high level of morale can be achieved only when their economic status compares favourably with that of working adults.

For many working men, the release from exacting physical labour over long hours in unsatisfactory conditions is followed not by frustration and idleness but by more enjoyable leisure-time activity, closer family relationships, and better physical health. When a man retires there are some forty or more hours in the week to be accounted for, the hours that he previously spent in connection with his work. It is surprising and at first puzzling, therefore, to learn that following retirement men do not feel very different from the way they did before, except for the obvious fact that they are not working. A great deal of the time spent at work, by definition, excludes 'personal time', and to that extent is not greatly missed. By contrast, much of the time spent in retirement is – or, perhaps, should be – 'personal time', that is time to do the important things one *wants* to do rather than the things one has to do. Hence, the extra hours available after retirement are easily absorbed by extra sleep, family and domestic activities, by more numerous and more prolonged leisure-time activities, and so on.

A large percentage of men in retirement say that there is nothing they miss. Work itself and money, especially in the United States of America, are missed by some; the people one worked with and the feeling of being useful are also missed, but to a lesser extent. Attitudes and patterns of adjustment change fairly rapidly during retirement, as one might expect. However, it is not age – the mere passage of time – that explains differences between individuals but rather the biological and psychological changes that take place *over* time. Men over the age of 65 who are working seem generally less lonely and better adjusted than retired men; but not necessarily *because* they are working. Physical health and personality factors underlie both morale and work capacity in later life. Retirement is rapidly becoming a normal and expected phase of the life-path, to be looked forward to, prepared for, and enjoyed. In response to social survey questions, a proportion of men in retirement say they have nothing to enjoy, but such a reply cannot be accepted at its face value because of the inadequacy of questionnaire methods as measures of behaviour. The measurement of 'life-satisfaction' is a current issue in social and behavioural gerontology.[25]

Paid employment plays a major part in a man's life, it acquires considerable emotional importance, and tends to define his main social role. The retiring person's problem is to find satisfactory ways of disengaging from employment without suffering economic hardships or emotional deprivations such as loneliness and boredom. Preparation for retirement is now a widely recognized need. It is catered for by many firms, voluntary organizations and centres for adult education. The financial and leisure problems of retirement can be met only by long-term planning. Many do not face up to the problem soon enough, and enter retirement inadequately prepared. Preparation means, among other things, putting money aside, buying and disposing of personal property and assets, attending to health needs, getting information and advice about leisure-time interests, and gradually changing the balance between disengagement and activity. Intelligence, education and social attitudes play a part in such preparations. People need to acquire new skills, new attitudes and interests, and new social relationships if they are to make the most of their retirement.

It is not unusual to find reasonably good morale among very old people living in the larger community, where survival to a ripe old age can be something to be proud of. Moreover, the very old are a highly selected sample, not at all representative of the cohort into which they were born. Their disengagement reaches a stable level, disrupted eventually by terminal illness and death. It is usual for retired persons to cope with their problems reasonably well, once the initial anxiety and unfamiliarity have worn off.

Even a modest living requires certain basic things – food, shelter, clothes, medical care, transport, emotional security, physical comfort, entertainment and recreation. Hence the ability to manage a budget sensibly is an important factor in good adjustment during retirement. At present, relatively little is known about the needs of retired people or the costs of meeting these needs. The fact that so much is heard about actual hardship in old age means that many retired people are not adequately adjusted. This problem, like many others, could be eased if extra money and resources were available.

In brief: income and assets provide for the material well-being of the retired person; some continuation of his earlier working activities or social relationships promotes a sense of belonging and participation; attention to physical comforts and health makes for more activity and security; and the proper use of leisure time provides a kind of dividend in feelings of achievement, usefulness and happiness.

(b) *Social Class and Sex Differences in Disengagement*

Disengagement works best for people who have maintained some continuity of activity throughout their lives – people with 'vocations' rather than people with 'jobs'. This is a matter of opportunities, economics and personal values. The professional man can often pursue some aspect of his life's work and maintain his professional contacts right up to the end of his life. Moreover, he has the time, money and opportunity to prepare for his retirement and to cultivate interests and activities which carry over into his later years. This continuity of activities, relationships and attitudes provides a stable pattern of adjustment which carries him smoothly from his busy adult working life to a more leisurely but satisfying retirement. Men in less favourable circumstances, however, spend a large part of their adult years in fairly routine jobs which earn them a living and a retirement pension but have little or no personal significance in the sense of providing activities and opportunities which extend beyond the job itself and beyond the normal working life. For some men in this situation retirement presents problems of adjustment, since it often occurs abruptly at the age of 65, and they have neither the continuity, which is important for good adjustment, nor the time, money and opportunity to prepare for a satisfactory retirement.

Greater provision for retirement benefits and courses in preparation for retirement would enable many more men to use and enjoy their declining years. In years to come, perhaps, a shorter working week, longer holidays, and a gradual retirement from paid work will give every individual ample opportunity to cultivate stable long-term interests and personal activities during his working life, which will carry over into retirement. Increased opportunity for such 'personal' outlets might do much to improve emotional stability and could lessen the stigma attached to retirement.

The woman's role is usually complementary to that of the man, and the problems of adjustment in later life for women can be met by a similar pattern of disengagement. Her task may be easier because, unless she is a single woman, she is not faced with the problem of adjusting to an abrupt retirement. A man depends on his job and his earning capacity for status, prestige, and authority in the home, and the transition from work to retirement may be difficult. His disengagement from work relationships is usually followed by a renewal of kinship ties, and he becomes involved in domestic chores such as shopping and baby-sitting. Working women are more closely bound than men to the kinship system; and women in general, on account of their continued domestic activities and established patterns of social interaction, especially with relatives and neighbours, have to cope with fewer demands for readjustment.

The departure of children from the home changes the environment of the middle-aged mother. Her husband's retirement calls for a further readjustment; and most married women become widows, which in turn creates problems of adjustment. Little work has been done on how these and other late-life problems of adjustment for women might be met more effectively – by education, preparation and counselling. In most cases she will look for support from the children, her own relatives and her husband's relatives, disengagement from kin being less likely than disengagement from other people.

Disengagement proceeds differently for most women as compared with men, and some of the stages – loss of children, disability, bereavement – may occur relatively early. Apart from possible sex differences in temperament and attitudes, a man's absorption in work and outside interests can weaken his emotional involvement with members of the family and provide him with powerful external supports, so that he may not react to family events with the same intensity as a woman. Women whose children have grown up, or women who have lost husbands, can often find other women of their age in similar circumstances, but a retired man or widower is less likely to have a large pool of possible acquaintances and may feel socially isolated unless he has family members to turn to. In extreme old age the range of activities for men and women alike becomes very restricted, so that their social roles are similar.

(c) *Criticisms of Disengagement Theory*

In its simplest and crudest form, the theory of disengagement states that the diminishing psychological and biological capacities of people in later life necessitate a severance of the relationships that they have with younger people in the central activities of society, and the replacement of these older individuals by younger people. In this way society renews itself and the elderly are free to die.

Criticisms of the theory of disengagement can be conveniently sorted into three kinds: practical, theoretical and empirical.[26-28] The practical criticism is that belief in the theory inclines one to adopt a policy of segregation or even indifference to the elderly, and to adopt the nihilistic attitude that old age has no value. The theoretical criticism is that disengagement 'theory' is not an axiomatic system in the scientific sense, but at best a 'proto-theory' – a collection of loosely related sets of arguments depending upon unspoken assumptions and doubtful premises. The empirical criticism, perhaps the most serious, is that the evidence which is called in support of the theory is inadequate or even untrue. For example, the time made available by retirement from full-time employment may be easily absorbed by alternative activities and social relationships. Although there are losses in social relationships following retirement or following the departure of children or the death of the spouse, yet other relationships with friends, neighbours or other kin are substituted and go some way to make good those losses. Furthermore, the activities and relationships of late life may be *more* important and absorbing because they are fewer in number and more 'personal' in nature.

Disengagement theory has been further criticized because it fails to mention that the disposition to disengage is a personality dimension as well as a characteristic of ageing. Moreover, contrary to expectation, engagement and activity are more likely to be sought after by older people, and accompanied by happiness and life-satisfaction. The theory under-emphasizes historical and cultural influences and over-emphasizes the universality and inevitability of the process of disengagement.

Thus, although patterns of promotion and retirement seem to confirm that industrial society has evolved mechanisms for replacing its obsolescent members, it does not follow that individuals lose their personal will to live. On the contrary, resistance to euthanasia has been strong and old people, as the most interested party, appear not to favour euthanasia as a social policy. Apart from a small proportion of infirm, deranged or socially isolated persons, the elderly continue to associate with others and to be useful and active in so far as their circumstances permit – not so much through central functional roles in the mainstreams of social organization and economic production, but rather in supportive roles and through *affective* relationships with kin and friends. A number of factors which might be regarded as indicative of disengagement, such as the proportion of people living alone, or infrequency of social contact, do not in fact increase sharply at the age of retirement, though they do increase steadily from middle age.

On the whole, it is more accurate to speak of 'industrial disengagement and increased socio-economic dependence' than of 'social disengagement'; in this way, the origins and circumstances of retirement are kept in focus, and the theory ties in more closely with empirical evidence and commonsense impressions.

The 'activity' or 're-engagement' approach to adult ageing has been contrasted with disengagement theory. The activity theory asserts that there is a natural inclination on the part of most elderly people to associate with others and to participate in group and community affairs. This natural tendency is often blocked and disrupted by present-day retirement practices. Hence arrangements should be made for retired people to find worthwhile activities suited to their age, personal qualities and health. Disengagement and re-engagement are counter-balancing tendencies. The former enables or obliges older people to relinquish certain social roles, namely those which they cannot adequately fulfil; the latter prevents the consequences of disengagement from going too far in the direction of isolation, apathy and inaction. For example, if retired people are not given care and affection and encouraged to use opportunities for enjoyment, they tend to become habit-bound and isolated and fail to make full use of their remaining capacities.

An older person who is inactive and isolated is likely at first to be bored and irritated, but this state of mind may pass as he becomes more passive, apathetic and inert. Stagnation leads to further falls in alertness and interest, and to a loss of mental and physical skills through disuse. Prodding an older person into action and overcoming his reluctance to participate in social activities *may* be an unwarranted intrusion into his private life, but a change of surroundings, stimulation and guidance will often help him to maintain an interest in life and derive enjoyment from the company of others.

5. ISOLATION AND DESOLATION

An interesting and useful distinction has been made between 'isolation' and 'desolation' in old age.[29] Old people may be isolated from people of their own age because of physical incapacity and disengagement; in addition, they may be isolated from younger adults because of cultural change and social mobility. However, through bereavement or other causes, some old people are bereft of any one person with whom they can enjoy close emotional contact. Infrequency of social contact can be referred to as 'isolation'. The grief and apathy following the sudden loss of a long-standing close relationship is far more serious and is referred to as 'desolation'. To be 'desolated' is to be left alone, neglected, forsaken by the person one deeply wants to be with; it is a kind of emotional deprivation; it is having no one in whom one can confide or upon whom one can rely absolutely. The loss is severe because the emotional investment or attachment was strong and deeply ingrained, and because there is unlikely to be any chance of forming a satisfactory substitute.[30]

Bereavement, however, usually triggers strong supportive reactions from other people. Reactions to bereavement, or to some other kind of deeply felt emotional loss, vary from one person to another because of differences in psychological make-up and in surrounding circumstances. The ability to re-establish normal patterns of behaviour also varies from person to person for the same general reasons. For example, the presence of an extensive network of sympathetic friends and family members obviously reduces the severity of the loss and hastens recovery, whereas physical incapacity and lack of mobility will probably hinder it. Partly on account of their greater life expectancy, more old women than old men are socially isolated – and desolated – and more of them are infirm.

Subjective feelings of loneliness are more closely associated with the severance of strong emotional ties than with solitariness. Both psychological desolation and loneliness are remediable. Hitherto such suffering has been regarded as natural and therefore acceptable, rather like the pains of illness or childbirth were once regarded. It is worth emphasizing, therefore, that psychological distress in the later years can be and should be alleviated to a far greater extent than is the case at present. At the present time, too little is known about psychosomatic disorders in late life to be able to specify in detail the physiological and psychological mechanisms underlying such conditions. However, depression and suicide appear to be correlated with physical illness; and psychological stress, such as that following bereavement, is associated with physical and mental ill health, and with an increased risk of death.

Suicide rates are higher for men than for women; the rate for women levels off in middle age but the rate for men continues to rise. There is a fall in the suicide rate at very late ages. At later ages, of course, survivors are successively selected samples of their original cohort; by definition they are healthy and lacking suicidal tendencies. A proportion of elderly people are incapable of conceiving, planning or carrying out such a deliberate act, and many others lack the means. For most elderly people, suicide is probably never seriously considered as a possible course of action.

One of the objectives of applied research into social isolation among the elderly is to identify and satisfy the needs of people who are not in a position to help themselves. Such research also helps to identify people who are 'at risk' in the community and who require regular visits from health and welfare workers. Some isolated old people are isolated partly by choice – they have a history of seclusion, shyness, independence or aggressiveness; others, of course, are socially isolated because of circumstances outside their control.

6. SIMPLE AND COMPLEX SOCIETIES

The study of older people in primitive societies provides some interesting comparisons for social gerontology.[31–35] The main differences between simpler communities – those with limited technical and cultural achievements – and more complex societies – the western countries for example – are that in the simpler communities fewer people survive to old age, and ageing as a biological process is less well understood. As the productive members of simple communities have few older non-productive people to support, the social problems of old age can be dealt with fairly easily, without recourse to elaborate institutional procedures: elderly people move into whatever social roles are available for people of limited physical abilities. Old age in a simple community is a considerable achievement in its own right, and a certain amount of prestige and respect may be attached to it, provided the burden of maintaining the old person is not felt to be irksome. In modern industrial societies, advances in medicine have created a social problem in the sense that many more people are surviving beyond the age when they are capable of performing useful work or even of maintaining themselves. This imposes burdens upon the productive members of that community and requires fairly elaborate social institutions to harmonize the lives of retired people with those of other members of the community. The social problems of old age are, in an important sense, twentieth-century problems.

In primitive communities, tasks such as fighting and hunting, which require high standards of strength, stamina and speed of response, are carried out by young men. Other tasks, such as settling disputes, entertaining, or offering advice, require the special skills and experience found among older members of the community. The few individuals who survive into old age find a considerable demand for their services in telling stories, looking after children, performing simple non-vigorous jobs, or manufacturing simple articles. The division of labour according to age may be closely regulated. In modern industrial societies, on the other hand, frequent technological changes make many kinds of production and service obsolete, and some workers become redundant before the end of their normal active life. Unless new employment is found, redundancy is hard to bear, since the individual may feel that he is being rejected by society, 'thrown on the scrap heap'. Older workers move into less popular, lower paid, menial jobs, and into work which is carried on in poorer conditions. Moreover, technological changes towards automation and the greater use of labour-saving devices are reducing the number of jobs available.

Most communities practise some sort of age-segregation, in the sense that certain kinds of activity like voting, bringing up children, holding office and retiring, are appropriate for people of a certain age. This system regulates the flow of replacement of individuals in social organizations. An interesting difference between simpler and more complex societies concerns the use of age limits and the principle of seniority. As experience is important in many public affairs, administrative authority tends to be exercised by older people. Some simpler societies have evolved what is called an 'age-set system' whereby all men born in a given period of time, say ten years, belong to the same age-set. The system usually takes effect from puberty after an elaborate initiation ceremony, and men stay in their age-set until they die. The system regulates the person's transition from childhood to adult life and binds individuals together in a complex network of functional and 'affective' relationships. Individuals within one age-set move through life together, passing from one social position to the next in a series of steps – for example, from junior to senior roles in hunting, farming or judicial affairs – each transition celebrated by rituals and ceremonies. In some communities the arrangements are more complex, since individuals in a higher age-set can sell their position to individuals in a lower one, and use their increased assets to buy a position in a still higher set. Each grade and social role is associated with appropriate norms of behaviour and social expectations, and integrated with other aspects of community life, so that the diverse activities thought necessary, like religion, fighting, hunting or migration, can be carried on effectively. The age-set system is a convenient, simple, social mechanism for securing continuity of community activities, authority and social control, and simple, well-defined social relationships.

In western societies, perhaps because they are large and complex, or because social mobility is important, the transition from earlier to later stages of life in the adult period is more varied and individuals are not grouped together in well-defined age-sets. The age-set system is applied to children: the transition from pre-school to school takes place for all children born within certain dates, and children in particular age-sets (approximately one year in range) tend to move through the school together. The age-set system in western society is much less rigid after full-time education ceases, but may be re-applied at the end of the working life in the form of a fixed retirement age. Many people derive considerable pleasure from the maintenance of personal relationships established in age-sets during their early years.

Adult roles have various *age-ranges,* and most social practices such as promotion and transfer are associated not with specific ages but with fairly broad periods of life. Calendar age is a relevant factor determining questions like seniority, promotion or pay, but it does not sharply define membership of an age-set. Society, as it were, recognizes the wide differences that exist between people of the same calendar age, in experience and ability as well as in physical fitness. Most husbands and wives are similar in age; friendship groups and social organizations often have a restricted age-range; and most promotions, appointments and retirements take place within certain age limits. These age-norms are natural social phenomena; and many reasons, not always good ones, are given in support of them. The introduction into simpler communities of western industrial and cultural influences has led to the breakdown of the age-set system. Technological and social changes reduce the economic adequacy of these communities. The younger members become more mobile, less amenable to social pressure and more inclined to marry without regard to family wishes. Gradually, as larger and more diversified communities become established, changes in social attitudes and values break up traditional social institutions, and weaken the power of the older, established members of a community. There may be a functional separation of generations in each family, which results eventually in geographical separation (dispersion or segregation in housing), and 'affective' separation (loss of positive emotional relationships).

Studies of the role of the aged in primitive communities, like other sub-specialities within social and behavioural gerontology, encounter methodological obstacles peculiar to themselves, including selection and bias in matters of method and observation. For example, the treatment of the aged does not necessarily directly reflect attitudes towards the elderly, for these attitudes are embedded in their cultural context; so in one culture the aged may be hated, but treated well because their departed spirits would otherwise be malevolent; in another culture, the aged may be revered, but killed or abandoned because their incapacity and dependence threaten the survival of a group leading a marginal existence.

In non-literate societies, older members provide a fund of information valuable in relation to, say, the weather, crop management, hunting and fishing skills, and modes of conduct and social organization. Their experience elicits esteem from younger members of the group. Experience, however, can become outmoded and incorrect. Hence socio-technical and other changes can lead to failure on the part of the older members to supply proper guidance, with a consequential loss of esteem. In primitive communities, belief in witchcraft may be important in determining how the aged are treated; illness in old age and death are associated with witchcraft and occult forces rather than with recognized diseases and other biological processes. In religion and magic, however, the elderly are more secure, since their knowledge and experience are 'untestable' in the practical or scientific sense, and are therefore fairly resistant to social change. Mystery, ritual and so on, provide the front necessary to sustain the illusion of power and, therefore, the esteem. In non-literate societies, too, knowledge has uses other than for immediate practical application. Knowledge of the community's history, for example, promotes solidarity, and story-telling provides entertainment. Thus, reminiscing by the elderly could be appreciated by younger members, and appropriately rewarded if it fulfilled such expressive functions.

Other roles for older persons in primitive communities include those based on experience, wealth and status, including judicial and ceremonial activities, consultancy and decision-making, and arbitration. These different activities all contribute to the shaping of the age-related system of values and attitudes in a culture. Esteem, of course, has to be translated into real terms – food, living space, sexual options, deference, protection, personal adornment and so on. Lack of esteem means lack of these benefits conferred by others.

CHAPTER FIVE

The Effects of Ageing on Work and Skills

1. JOB DESIGN AND TRAINING

The changing age structure of modern communities, the improving physical health of people over 40, and the increasing tendency for women to seek employment after raising a family, bring benefits but also create economic and social problems. These problems include redesigning work to suit older people, and training older people for new jobs. Retraining is needed not only for unskilled and semi-skilled industrial workers, but also for people in all sorts of occupations, including the professions.[1,2]

Work study and adult training can be used to help the expanding industries, and to devise remedial measures for disabled and incapacitated workers. Adult education and preparation for retirement could secure better adjustment and higher morale among older workers. The rate of technological and social change makes it likely that changes of job, education throughout life, adult retraining, and extended leisure or retirement will eventually become accepted as normal.

Information about age changes relevant to occupational performance needs to be made known to people in government, management and education whose job it is to make the most of our human and technical resources. The main obstacles to progress are prejudice against older workers, the lack of applied research on the specific occupational and training problems of older people, and traditional practices regarding promotion, pensions and retirement.

Working conditions and output can be improved by the application of work study (or 'ergonomics'). The scientific study of occupational performance in the second half of the working life – after the age of 40 – highlights deficiencies in the way a job is organized, so that improvements benefit workers of all ages. These improvements have to do with such things as posture, perception, movement and manipulation, the design of tools, muscular effort, time and motion factors, the use of mechanical power, lighting, layout of display and controls, fatigue and accident prevention. There is, however, relatively little information on age changes in the time and motion characteristics of occupational performance among older workers. As older people have less flexible postures and movements, their jobs should be arranged so that stooping, prolonged standing, difficult reaching and holding heavy objects are reduced to a minimum.[3-5]

The working environment, apart from being satisfactory with regard to general facilities such as toilets, canteen or companionship, should be safe. Equipment should be guarded, safety drills should be practised, and there should be a minimum risk of falling or tripping. Older workers should be protected against hazards arising from slowness of perception and response, from poor balance, and from working too near maximum capacity. Older machines and methods tend to be used by older workers, so that the introduction of new machines and methods usually means recruiting younger men and women. When the older techniques are abandoned altogether, there may be no occupational roles available for the redundant worker unless he can be transferred or retrained. Successful retraining has been achieved on a small scale in a range of occupations: driving buses and diesel trains, operating telephone switchboards, postal sorting, secretarial work, engineering production and maintenance work, machine sewing, and mending worsted cloth. However, the age factor in occupational performance and retraining is often less important than factors such as intelligence, motivation, attitude and education. Training older workers means more than simply teaching a skill; it means changing attitudes, dealing with anxieties and eliminating established habits. Job redesign and retraining methods must be examined carefully, because small differences in layout or procedure may create difficulties for older workers.[6,7]

Given sufficient foresight and planning, it should be possible to introduce changes in the skills required for work at all ages. Certain factors make the training of older workers more successful: if it is gradual; if the trainee can approach the task in his own way and at his own speed; if written instructions are available (but not essential); if the trainee can practise elements in the skill as he goes along; if he is an active participant rather than a passive listener; if (unobtrusively) he is prevented from making mistakes, especially in the early stages of learning; if he is guided on simple but important matters such as the proper way to hold a tool; if the connection between perception and action is direct; if he is given knowledge of results so that he has a sense of achievement and progress; if memorizing is kept to a minimum; if each element of the skill has a firm position in the total performance.

Training for a new skill requires more than one kind of readjustment. The older worker may have to adjust from solitary to team-work or vice versa. He has to adapt to unfamiliar problems, methods and surroundings, or overcome the 'mental strain' of learning after a long period of disuse. Sometimes he will say that he understands when he does not; only careful questioning and testing will reveal the nature of his inadequacies. Hence the need for research on programmed instruction and techniques of assessment.[8] Teachers have a great deal to learn about the special problems of educating and training older adults. These problems include the content and organization of adult courses, levels of difficulty, pace, the use of visual and other aids, the provision of background information, the management of anxiety and lack of confidence, and techniques of guidance and assessment.

In some firms special workshops for older operatives have been established. Elsewhere the cost is felt to be too high to justify either retraining or job redesign. Older workers who are not capable of normal rates of production-work are likely to be transferred, in time, to unpaced work, work based on custom or quality (craft skills or inspection), part-time work, and service jobs such as cleaning or time-keeping. Older trainees should be selected carefully because individuals differ widely in their willingness and ability to learn new skills and concepts. On the other hand, social justice implies equality of opportunity for retraining, and adequate financial protection for older workers who are unsuitable for transfer or retraining. Single crash courses are unlikely to suit older people; education and training are needed at intervals throughout a man's working life. Vocational advice and training are appropriate at all age levels.

Automation is creating more jobs which require mental skills (involving capacities adversely affected by ageing) but fewer jobs which require only simple manual skills. Thus the problem of training and transferring older workers will become worse unless alternative jobs can be created, for example in service industries.

2. ANALYSIS OF THE EFFECTS OF AGEING ON SKILLS

Much of the research work on the effects of ageing on skills was carried out by psychologists working under the direction of A. T. Welford. Welford's book, *Ageing and Human Skill* (1958), was the final report of the Nuffield Research Unit for Research into Problems of Ageing.[9] This research was inspired by the pioneering work on skilled performance initiated by Sir Frederic Bartlett at the Psychological Laboratory, Cambridge. More recently, research work associated with the University of Liverpool and the Medical Research Council has been published; this has been concerned with a wide range of topics relevant to the effects of ageing on occupational adjustment and functional capacity.[10,11]

In his experimental studies of the normal effects of ageing, Welford examined some of the more crucial mechanisms in skill by testing subjects to the limits of their performance on particular sorts of task. Deficiencies in their capacities were revealed by changes in the kinds and numbers of error, changes in the organization of behaviour, and changes in the amount and distribution of time required to cope with the task. In a typical experiment subjects view a display consisting of a moving set of parallel lines which wander about unpredictably, like the bends of an unfamiliar road. A driving wheel and an accelerator pedal are used to steer a pen-marker between the parallel lines. The amount of error in the trace can be reduced by slowing down the rate at which the visual display moves, increasing the 'distance ahead' that the subject is allowed to see and altering the sensitivity of the steering control. By varying these and other conditions of the task, the components of this visual–motor skill can be investigated.

Physiological degeneration in the central nervous system, the special senses, the muscles, and so on, leads to restrictions on a person's maximum level of performance. This decrease in potential does not become obvious, however, until either degeneration has progressed so far that his abilities fail to meet the demands of ordinary tasks, or severe demands are imposed by difficult tasks, so that the limitations brought about by even slight degeneration are clearly revealed as errors, omissions or delays in performance. A normal conversation, for example, imposes little or no strain on an older person because his abilities are more than adequate to cope with this ordinary task. However, if people speak faster or in a lowered voice, or if the topic shifts frequently, or elicits long technical sentences, then the older person loses track of what is being said, misunderstands things, and cannot contribute to the conversation as well as he could before. In normal everyday situations, older people appear to be in 'full possession of their faculties'; it is only when their capacities are tested to the limit that their impairment becomes apparent.

As age advances, the difference between *optimum* and *maximum* levels of performance decreases; older people therefore have reduced reserves. This can also be measured by examining age differences in the ability to perform two tasks concurrently such as driving *and* adding numbers.

Welford distinguished five possible effects of age changes in functional capacities, as follows. (1) Performance fails completely. (2) Performance does not fail completely, but efficiency is reduced. (3) Efficiency of adjustment is maintained *in spite* of the reduction in biological capacities – an older person can change his behaviour and his surroundings, and compensate for his deficiencies. (4) Older people show no loss in performance because the task is still well within their psychological and biological capacities; it is this sort of adjustment that leads people to deny that ageing has had any adverse effects. (5) The elderly over-compensate for their reduced potentialities and actually improve their performance; the physical and mental resources of adults tend to decline with age, but older people can be trained to use their resources more effectively, and 'exercise' frequently improves functional capacity.

A small change in the efficiency of a process involved in skilled performance has little overall effect, because the system is flexible, and the person's ability is normally well above the demands of the task. As age advances, however, many small deficiencies accumulate to produce poorer performance. These may be compensated for in all kinds of ways: wearing spectacles and hearing aids, improving working conditions, proper exercise and diet, retraining, changing the pace of the task and the distribution of effort, simplifying the performance, memory aids, drills and checks. Older people often fail to derive much benefit from written instructions, since they distract and divide their attention, thus increasing the risk of error or slowing them down. Too little interest is taken in ways of compensating for the adverse effects of ageing, especially as regards the skills required for the activities of daily living in old age.

Individuals differ in the way their performance deteriorates with age, partly because they also differ in the age of onset and in the rate of decline for different sorts of physiological function. Environmental circumstances, experience, attitudes, and compensatory adjustments also vary from person to person. For example, hearing deteriorates with age even under the best possible conditions, but it deteriorates more rapidly under conditions of excessive noise. The cumulatively adverse effects of alcohol, tobacco and sugar, of disease, stress and injury, and so on, can be expected not only to bring out differences between people but also to bring about a steady reduction in many kinds of skilled performance in later life, such as driving, sport, work.

The habits and attitudes we build up throughout life are not fixed mechanical patterns of adjustment, but flexible, adaptable strategies capable of dealing with a *range* of situations. Older people have acquired an extensive repertoire of behaviour patterns capable of dealing with many familiar situations, and capable of being applied in modified ways to variations on these situations. Ideas and responses acquired in one context and applied in another give rise to what is called 'transfer of training'. When an older person can bring his previous experience to bear on a new problem he feels more confident, he can organize his behaviour in familiar ways and make an effective response. This is known as 'positive transfer'. There are some situations, however, in which an older person cannot use his previous experience, in which case it becomes useless or 'redundant'; this may have serious consequences for occupational adjustment after the age of about 40. Previous training or experience can be worse than useless, a positive hindrance to the solution of a problem or the acquisition of new knowledge; this is known as 'negative transfer'. Routine adherence to certain kinds of military procedure can prevent an officer from reaching the right decision in a battle, for instance, or a designer steeped in one tradition may fail to appreciate an improvement in layout. Many situations can be dealt with partly or wholly in terms of past experience; so the older person's natural reaction to a novel situation is to apply whatever experience seems relevant. This initial reaction may increase his response time (as he considers possibilities and implications) but if he takes too long he may forget some relevant information and his response may be inappropriate. Some old people have become so well-practised in certain ways of thinking and acting that their reactions are inflexible and lacking in discrimination, as when statesmen apply outmoded values or scientists reject new ideas.

Welford points out that age teaches us both 'what to do' and 'what not to do'. Since we can often make a number of responses to a situation, knowing what we ought not to do helps to determine what we actually do in that situation. For example, as there are many ways of expressing an idea in words, our actual response is determined by the 'strength' of the alternative responses, and our appreciation of their relative advantages and disadvantages. Thus the choice depends upon our capacity to inhibit the less effective response tendencies; some experimental studies have shown for example that in certain circumstances older people are less capable of ignoring irrelevant information and ideas, and of suppressing irrelevant responses.

Considerable effort is needed to record and analyse occupational performance. Even the simplest movements have considerable complexity. A simple operation, such as moving a pencil across a sheet of paper and then back again, involves at least three components. One, the interval of time during which the subject perceives the signal to start and initiates his response. This can be as little as 150 milliseconds if he is warned to get ready. A rough approximation of its components gives 10 ms. for the auditory process, 100 ms. for the central process, 10 ms. for the motor process, and 30 ms. for muscle action. It is normally longer for vision than for hearing or touch, and it increases markedly if the subject has to discriminate between two or more signals for two or more responses. The kinds of reaction called for in a real-life driving situation involve complex choice-reactions to complex visual situations, often without warning. Two, from a standing start the pencil movement accelerates to a maximum velocity, achieves a uniform motion, decelerates, and then stops. For example, the acceleration occupies 38 per cent of the total movement time; a further 18 per cent is occupied by movement at a uniform velocity; a further 27 per cent for slowing down, and 17 per cent for the stop and change of direction. These figures are characteristic only of particular kinds of movement; other kinds of movement, involving searching, positioning and irregular paths, show different time and motion characteristics. Three, complex eye movements search and fixate, and help to guide the muscles of the hand and forearm.

One of the earliest systematic studies of the effects of age on simple movements was carried out in 1930 by W. R. Miles.[12] In its day, it was regarded as the most extensive psychological study of maturity and old age that had been carried out. Observations were made on 335 males and 528 females ranging in age from six to 95 years, with roughly equal numbers in each decade. The tasks included the following: releasing a key to start a clock; reaching and grasping a pencil from its position; positioning it in a hole and returning the hand to press the key again to stop the clock; lifting the forefinger of the dominant hand from a key and replacing it as quickly as possible; and cranking the handle of a light drill. All the movements were performed most quickly on average, by people in their late twenties and early thirties. Speed declined steadily throughout maturity and old age. The time required for the first task increased from about 1.2 seconds to 1.8 seconds; for the second task, from about 0.1 seconds to 0.35 seconds; and for the third task, using the dominant hand, cranking speed dropped from about 43 r.p.m. to 30 r.p.m. The evidence indicated a gradual increase in simple movement time after the age of about 30, despite wide individual differences in performance.

Decline in the speed of performance reduces working efficiency. The normal pace of working, however, is usually much less than the maximum possible. In Miles's investigations the subjects appeared to be highly motivated to do well and to be working close to their maximum. Productivity at work is not related in any simple way to ageing, partly because work output is a function of many variables, of which age is only one, and partly because decreasing speed can be compensated for by working nearer to capacity or by improved working methods. Each kind of performance tested by Miles showed a significant association with ageing, but a complex response in a task similar to the Wechsler-Bellevue Digit

Symbol Substitution Test showed a stronger association with age than the simple movement-response. The main effects of ageing impair the *central* decision processes more than the peripheral sensory and muscular processes, as shown in Welford's experiments.

Welford and his colleagues have made a considerable contribution to the theory and experimental investigation of skill and human ageing. The effects of ageing can be demonstrated in different ways, depending upon how performance is scored. Various indices are employed: time, output, effort, errors, wastage and so on. The instructions given to (or understood by) the subject, emphasizing one or the other of these aspects of performance, affect his behaviour. Care is needed in interpreting the results and generalizing the findings to apply to natural circumstances outside the laboratory.

In one experiment, subjects attempted to match the position of an object with the position of a pointer on an adjacent display. Older subjects were slower, making only about half as many attempts in a given period of time as did younger people, but they made fewer small errors. They were less able to understand the layout of the problem, conformed less well to the test instructions, and programmed their performance in smaller units of behaviour. The performance of older people on maze-tracing tasks is similar in these respects; attempts to simplify the task lead them into error and confusion.[13]

In another experiment, people were asked to trace numbers with a metal stylus. Older subjects required more time and made fewer errors. When the numbers were presented 'back to front', older people needed considerably more time than younger ones, and they showed less improvement on a second attempt. The sensory and muscular demands were much the same for the two experimental conditions. Welford also found that the time required for small movements increased only slightly with age, whereas choice-reaction time and the time required for changes of movement, such as from forwards to backwards, increased sharply, especially after the age of 50. He concluded, 'the main locus of slowing with age in sensory-motor performance lies not in the speed of movement but in the time taken by central processes initiating, shaping and monitoring movements.'

Small ballistic movements and rhythmic movements, such as tapping, involving a minimum of central organization, appear to be affected relatively little by ageing. Welford's evidence on the component times in a simple lever movement seemed to show that the acceleration and deceleration phases were not affected by ageing, whereas the time required for uniform motion increased by about 50 per cent between the ages of 20 and 70. The time required to stop and change direction also increased markedly. The decline with age in muscular response within the normal range is not large, and for brief movements, involving aiming and continuous control, the limitations on performance are brought about by slower central processes rather than by weaker muscular response.

The effects of ageing on the relationship between performance capacity and cautiousness were studied by comparing the behaviour of younger and older subjects on paced tasks. The time-characteristics of the performance were set by the task, and the person had to adjust his rate of work to these conditions or risk failure. Working on a mass-production assembly line means working at a set pace. If older people use more time to assess the situation but do not need as much as they take, their performance on a paced task ought not to suffer too drastically if the perception time is reduced. Tracking tasks, such as tracing a path on a moving band of paper by means of a remote-controlled pen, have been used to show that older people have less ability than younger people when the tracking speed is high, probably because the central processes are too slow. Increasing the distance ahead that can be viewed in a tracking task, like presenting a warning signal, helps the older person to cope more effectively, but it does not wholly compensate for his slower performance. The reason is that there are limits to the amount of advance information the older person can cope with: his short-term memory capacity is reduced as age advances. In daily life older people are at a serious disadvantage in fast traffic; at work they tend to move out of piece-work and into hourly-paid jobs.

The decline in speed of performance is one of the most outstanding behavioural characteristics of ageing.[14] This helps to explain age changes in intellectual efficiency, skilled performance, work output and research achievement. It also explains the existence of some misconceptions about the effects of ageing, since in situations where there are no serious time limits the effects on performance may not be apparent until late in life.

One part of a performance may be preceded in time by a relatively brief decision period and accompanied in time by perceptual and decision processes relevant to the next phase of the performance. If a control lever has to be moved through a central position to other positions according to a signal light on a display, the slowing down with age in choice-reaction is determined partly by *verifying* the preceding movement and partly by *choosing* the subsequent one. The effects of introducing a change into one part of the performance (such as a brief delay at the central position or choice-point) are spread over the whole performance. The ability to shift and divide one's attention decreases with age in situations demanding fast performance. In some conditions, older subjects are slower but more accurate than younger subjects. In other conditions pacing will, within limits, improve performance, but the effect is less for older than for younger subjects. The adverse effects of ageing appear sooner for paced than for unpaced tasks.

Under certain conditions and within a limited range of choices, age differences in decision time are constant over all degrees of choice. Older subjects take longer than the younger subjects under all conditions of choice (so that 'information-transmission' decreases with age), but they do not always appear to take *proportionately* longer for, say, an eight-choice as compared with a two-choice decision. However, even an eight-choice decision may be simple, for example sorting playing cards, but when decisions are more difficult, as judged by the failure rate, performance time increases more sharply for older people.[15,16]

3. OCCUPATIONAL ASPECTS

Little is known about age differences for various types of industrial work, although productivity declines overall to some degree. Many industrial operations are carried out at a reasonable pace, well within the working capacity of older operatives, though an absence of age differences in the overall time taken to complete a job might be accompanied by marked age differences in the time-distribution of the component parts of that job. Detailed time and motion studies, i.e. micromotion studies of skilled and semi-skilled work, should throw a great deal of light on age differences in performance, and on its overall organization. For example, without being aware of the process, older workers make a complex procedure simple by dropping out those parts which seem less essential. This is a normal process, but it can lead to serious errors and omissions if a critical element of behaviour is shed, for example failing to make a safety check at the appropriate time.

The pace of work is determined not only by the speed of industrial equipment, but also by incentives of one kind or another. Ageing is accompanied by a drift from one sort of work to another and older workers are more likely to be found on unpaced work. This is brought about in part by time-stress, but other factors are involved, including the extent to which the job involves what Welford calls 'continuous bodily movement and activity'. There is a slight tendency for younger men, up to the age of about 40, to be employed on light industrial operations, especially power-assisted work where speed is important. After this age a slightly higher proportion of older men are engaged on heavier work. Injury or illness, or an inability to keep up the pace of heavy work, leads older men to transfer to lighter work, but this usually means less skilled, lower-paid work. The same general trend applies to women workers.[17,18]

Some so-called 'heavy' industrial jobs do not approach the limits of human muscular strength and therefore do not impose excessive strains on older workers. But if heavy muscular work is combined with continuous effort and activity, and especially if it is paced, a proportion of older workers find the demands too great and make use of opportunities to find less exhausting work. Employment can of course be demanding in other than physical ways, but not much is known about the physical, intellectual and emotional demands of occupations such as general medical practice, teaching, nursing and other professions, so little can be said about the ability of older people to cope with intellectually or emotionally exhausting work. The kind of work that a teacher, doctor, engineer or executive finds congenial in his twenties may not necessarily be so satisfying or so well done thirty years later.[19]

Working conditions – including lighting, ventilation, heating, noise, fumes, and the way the work is arranged – play their part in the occupational adjustment of older workers. Although some older workers move into more congenial surroundings, many move into jobs where the working conditions are less satisfactory. The better workers escape from time-pressure into salaried positions; the poorer workers move to hourly rates. A few are 'carried' by responsible employers. Older workers sometimes experience difficulty in obtaining employment and have to accept less congenial work in order to increase the range of jobs open to them. Younger people, for various reasons, demand a higher standard of working environment.

Social changes arising from industrialization are contributing to the problems of gerontology in a number of ways.[20-23] First, there are the problems of redundancy and redeployment – sensitive issues for men in the second half of their working life or in occupations generally thought of as 'secure'. Second, there is the problem of shift-work; age changes in physical health and sleep patterns are relevant to this issue.[24] Third, there are the problems of vigilance and quality control at work: vigilance refers to the maintenance of attention in a monotonous task, quality control to the related problem of inspection; the effects of age on such things as arousal, and proneness to fatigue and distraction can be expected to affect work involving prolonged close attention.[25,26] Fourth, many women return to work from about the age of 30; the effects of ageing on their work performance and retraining are complicated by the long disuse of relevant skills. Although many sorts of performance decline with age, this decline could arise partly from disuse. Systematic training can produce improvements, although more slowly and to a lesser extent in older people.

It is clear that ageing affects human adjustment to modern conditions of employment; some of the sociological and 'personal' aspects of industrial gerontology were dealt with in Chapter Four. The attitudes of supervisors and managers towards 'older' workers vary, but it is commonly believed by them that older workers are slower though not necessarily less efficient, since their long experience and special methods of working often make up for reductions in speed and in sensory and motor capacities.[27] Managers are inclined to believe that older workers have poorer health and become tired more easily, that their eyesight and hearing get worse, and that they are more inclined to suffer from chest complaints and stomach troubles. Older workers are thought to learn more slowly, but to be more dependable, especially in semi-skilled work. The best years for adapting to new work methods or training for a new job are said to be between about 15 and 35 years.

Few efforts are made, however, to improve working conditions, production methods or training schemes to suit the needs of older workers. The usual way of dealing with the problem is to take chronological age and working capacity into account when work is being reorganized, when teams are being made up, or when replacements and vacancies occur. It is relatively rare for a man to be transferred because he is not up to the demands of a job – most men continue to do their work, or transfer only if a suitable opportunity arises. The arrangement is flexible and informal and goes on mostly without formal transfer procedures. When transfers take place, many firms recognize their obligations to older workers with long service, and attempt to fit them into the system as best they can, even if it means some loss of efficiency. The reasons often given for transferring older workers are that the work is too strenuous (especially if the man is over 50), involves long hours or night work, requires paced performance, or involves climbing, fine detail, concentrated attention or physical risks.

Older workers are thought to need less supervision and are seen as having a number of desirable occupational characteristics, including a sense of responsibility, settled habits and attitudes, reliability, conscientiousness, interest in the job and willingness to do a fair day's work. In addition, they are easy to manage, loyal and cooperative. They are said not to be argumentative or to lose their temper, though they are inclined to resist advice and instruction. Supervisors think of older workers as less likely to have accidents, because they are more careful and more experienced.

Several reasons have been put forward to explain the older worker's good reputation. One is that supervisors themselves are older men – half of them are promoted at or after the age of 40 and therefore appreciate the older worker's needs and problems. Another is that older workers are in a more vulnerable position than younger men, since they cannot find new jobs easily and are less mobile. It is thus in their interest to keep their job and work efficiently to keep the firm in business.

As there are considerable differences between one firm and another, and between one job and another, it is difficult to say anything definite about age and industrial productivity. Older workers are probably not comparable with younger men doing the same work: only those who are able and willing stay on and they become adapted to a particular job in a firm. Moreover, productivity is determined by many factors. Straightforward comparisons between older and younger workers show little change in output. Changes in training methods or production methods designed to help older workers would help to raise production at all age levels; so that, even if the productivity of older workers remains unchanged relative to younger workers, it is important to attend to the occupational problems of older workers, since one may expect to see (in relief, as it were) some of the factors which hold down the productivity of workers at all ages, such as illumination, work layout, hazards.

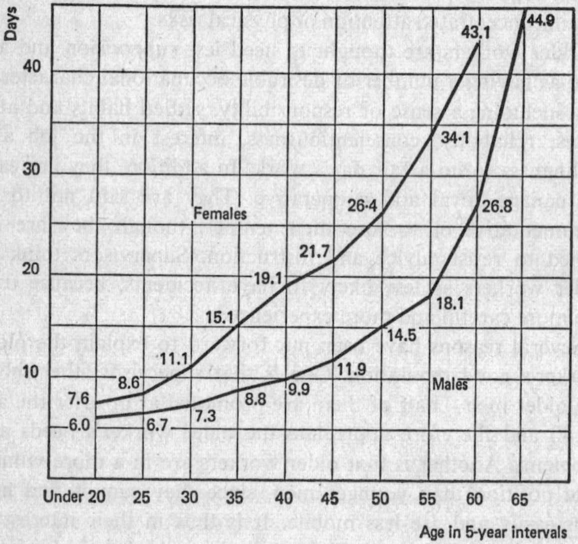

FIGURE 9 Incapacity for work from all causes except influenza in 1968/69 for men and women in Great Britain. Measured in days per person at risk.
Adapted from Table III, p. 15, *Social Trends, No. 2*, 1971.

The number of working days per year lost through incapacity in Britain rises from about 6 for men ($7\frac{1}{2}$ for women) under the age of 20, to about 10 for men (20 for women) at age 40, to about 45 for men (43 for women) near retirement. The generational trend is upwards, especially among younger workers, apparently because of the increase in the number of absences rather than in the the average length of absences, and because of changes in social attitudes and socio-economic conditions.[28]

Some problems of occupational adjustment and productivity arise as a consequence of a fixed age of retirement. Most supervisors say they prefer a variable retirement age because of the wide range of individual differences in ability and health at any given chronological age. Some prefer a fixed retirement age because it is simple, straightforward and 'fair'. The age of 60 to 65 is thought to be appropriate for retirement – it reflects the fact that most people are then becoming physically unfit for normal work, it ensures a steady evolution of methods by regular promotion and transfer, and allows a man some leisure-time after many years of work.

The provision for retraining and re-employment during the whole of one's active adult life would make it possible for education, work and leisure (including retirement) to be more effectively distributed throughout the lifespan. There are, however, obvious economic and administrative difficulties in making such arrangements.

4. ACCIDENTS

Every accident is the outcome of a number of factors, and the results of surveys of accidents need to be treated with considerable care and often with quite elaborate statistical safeguards. It would be incorrect to compare the accident rates for, say, bus drivers of different ages, since the younger and older groups are not comparable (conditions of service tend to eliminate the relatively unsafe driver), and their exposure to hazard might be unequal. It is difficult to make general statements about the association between age and accidents, and most studies limit their findings to particular kinds of work.[29,30] If younger and older groups are matched for accident rate, differences appear in the sorts of accident suffered. In some circumstances younger people have accidents because they lack experience, whereas older people have accidents because they are slow to respond.

Most accidents happen in the home – the main working environment of the housewife – where falls are an important class. The factors contributing to falls are numerous. They include: poor sense of balance, slowness in recovery after having been thrown off balance, negligence, unsafe equipment, dangerous postures, tripping over objects left lying about, inexperience, dizziness, failure to appreciate the danger (usually a younger person's mistake), failure to react quickly enough after the danger has been perceived, and failure to heed or to register warnings. Older people are slower to recover when thrown off balance and slower to move out of the way of a moving object.

Comparing the accident rates of older and younger workers in a factory, we sometimes find that the rate is lower for older workers, partly because selective factors eliminate accident-prone individuals from hazardous jobs – they die, they are sacked, they get injured or frightened and move to other occupations. Similarly, comparing the abilities of older and younger footballers is really comparing relatively new men, just making their mark, with rather older men, whose continuance in the game is proof of their better-than-average performance (otherwise they would have been dropped).

The number of older people driving is increasing, and drivers over the age of 60 (like those under 25) are more frequently blamed for road accidents, though they drive less and constitute a selected sample. Their more frequent faults are pulling out, inaccurate turning into or across a junction, failing to give right of way, and ignoring halt signs. The older driver's impaired skill can be accounted for by a variety of 'ageing' processes including impaired perceptual and motor functions, poorer vision in the dark, slower recovery from glare, poorer hearing, restricted attention and short-term memory (especially in complex shifting circumstances, for example, where both forward and rear vision are important), and slower reaction times. In fast traffic, the 'decision-load' approaches or exceeds their capacity to handle information. Older drivers should drive 'defensively'. They should avoid becoming involved in traffic which moves too fast and, if the pace of events is wholly or partly under their control, they should keep down their speed to match their capacities. Wide individual differences between drivers mean that age of itself is an inadequate index of driving skill; nevertheless, the relationship is there and becomes even more pronounced among older drivers who are fatigued, tense, intoxicated or lacking oxygen. Poor equipment and hazardous conditions tax a driver's skill to its limits, and so reveal deficiences not apparent under normal driving conditions.

5. MENTAL SKILLS

Some sorts of performance require very little in the way of sensory and motor capacities, but a great deal in the way of intellectual ability – playing chess is an obvious example. Several of the tasks referred to in the next chapter, for example Wechsler's Digit Symbol Substitution Test or the Block Design Test, are examples of what Welford has called 'mental skills'. Such skills enable the performer to attend selectively to a situation, to construe certain meanings by carrying out symbolic or imaginative transformations on perceptual data, and to apply internalized rules of procedure – schemata – in order to select or organize an appropriate response. Thus not only chess, but also driving a car, writing a computer programme, making business decisions, or navigating, entail some degree of mental activity. Occupational skills vary of course in their intellectual content. Some skills are so complex as to require not only the selection of personnel with the appropriate natural endowments but also long training and considerable reliance on external aids such as instruments, check-lists and reference manuals; commercial airline flying is an example of this kind of very high-grade mental skill, though many physical and psychological qualities in addition to intelligence are required of airline pilots, as for persons in other highly skilled occupations.

The experimental analysis of mental skills naturally begins

with relatively simple laboratory tasks. Welford described an experiment in which subjects tossed short loops of chain into a box several feet away. There were no age differences in performance, provided the connection between the perceptual display and the response was reasonably direct, but when the connection between the display and the response was made more indirect, by obscuring the target with a screen and obliging the subjects to view it in a mirror, the older subjects were less accurate and took longer to aim and throw. When a person has to 'translate' the situation, any complication in it slows him down and increases the number of mistakes. This holds for young people too, but the effect is more pronounced for older people. If the translation process conflicts with other pre-established rules of procedure, further complications are likely to arise; this is sometimes referred to as 'negative transfer' of training. It is not unusual to observe some 'rigidity' in the adjustment of older persons working under such conditions, in that they find it difficult to abandon the wrong procedure and adopt the right one. Common experience suggests that older people are less willing to abandon well-tried but inefficient practices in favour of new and more efficient ones.

In golf and other games, sensations from our organs of balance, and from our muscles and joints, are important in determining the response, but the subsequent evaluation, which psychologists call 'knowledge of results', may be visual or auditory. Knowledge of results sometimes has little effect upon the performance of older subjects, partly because they fail to register the errors visually, partly because they fail to make the proper translation from a visual cue to a kinaesthetic (movement-sense) correction. Some high-grade skills call for extensive coordinating translations between several sense modalities; such skills are difficult for older people to master or to maintain.

Welford described an experiment in which a row of lights was operated by a row of keys under three conditions of complexity. Errors probably arose from the subjects' natural attempts to simplify the task (so as to bring it within their range of competence), which resulted in inappropriate behaviour. The time required and the number of errors made increased sharply for the older subjects performing under the most difficult conditions. Welford has explained that each translation produces some decrease in performance with age, but several translations taken together produce a disproportionate fall in the performance of older people and, conversely, the *removal* of one complication may produce a great improvement – an important factor in training.

In another experiment a series of number-matrices were graded in difficulty. Each matrix consisted of numbers which had to be arranged so that the row-totals and column-totals were correct. Normal ageing produced a disproportionate increase in the number of errors on the more difficult matrices. Older subjects were unable to deal with a large amount of information arranged according to numerous criteria, since this involved shifting from one aspect of the task to another, with a consequent interference in the overall organization and continuity of behaviour. Older subjects were sometimes prepared to accept an inconsistent solution, illustrating perhaps a breakdown in their capacity for performance evaluation. At other times they abandoned the task as too difficult. Older people may accept an inadequate performance or an approximate result because it represents the best they can do. This sort of attitude is commonly observed in psychological studies of problem-solving behaviour. It is by no means characteristic only of aged people, but it is more characteristic of them. The ability to evaluate a performance is probably a function of the ability underlying the performance itself.

As age advances, the individual shifts from strategies which are intellectually demanding (but accurate and logically efficient) to strategies which are less demanding (but relatively inaccurate and inefficient). Experiments to determine the effects of age on inductive reasoning (abstraction and generalization) show that older persons are more likely than younger ones to become confused about the properties of the objects or events they are trying to classify. They more often fail to discover the distinguishing characteristics of a criterion class (predetermined by the experimenter), especially if the objects in the criterion class have properties shared by objects *not* in the criterion class.[31]

Older subjects take longer and want more information than the younger ones in order to achieve the same results. They experience greater difficulty in attaching meanings to cues and they lose track of data because of a reduction in short-term memory and mental speed. The disproportionate increase with age in time and errors on complex cognitive tasks as compared with simple ones may have something to do with the gradual but cumulative loss of brain cells and synaptic junctions. Loss of cells and dysfunction of cells in the nervous system lead to an increase in random neural activity and worsen the signal-to-noise ratio. Thus the organization of behaviour is reduced in scale, complexity and speed. Older persons can be compared with computers in which some components have become unreliable or have failed altogether. Such computers continue to function, in a limited way, if the problems are not too complicated or if longer, more 'round-about' programming is possible. The earliest indications of difficulty for older people are found in changes of tempo and accuracy; simple translation processes also occupy more time in old age, even when accuracy remains unimpaired.

For one experiment, subjects of different ages were presented with sets of statements and asked to work out their logical implications. The younger group confined their attention to the *form* of the argument and kept to the point when answering questions, whereas the older group missed the point and dealt with the *content* of the argument by making comments or bringing their experience to bear. Older subjects adopted a literal instead of a hypothetical approach.

Welford asked whether the poorer performance of older people is a result of actual interference with intelligence by the well-established habits and accumulation of experience, or a secondary effect of their inability to organize complex data in a logical manner. Solving problems by experience is not wrong in itself, but it may be inappropriate in particular instances.

6. MOTIVATION AND ATTITUDES

Adequate motivation and appropriate attitudes are needed if the reduced potentialities of the elderly are to be used to the full. Presenting an older person with an initially complex task, particularly an unfamiliar one, can provoke anxiety and a reluctance to put his abilities to the test. Mental skills, for example, can be acquired by working through a series of problems, starting from the most elementary and moving by stages to the more complex levels. Thus programmed instruction should be useful in retraining older workers, though the sort of programmed learning suitable for a younger adult is not necessarily suitable for an older person. Older people often prefer to work things out for themselves rather than follow a course of instruction, but this may have come about because ordinary courses of instruction are often unsuited to their needs, capacities and methods.

Subjects who are more highly motivated work faster and persist longer at a task. Small improvements in the performance of older people can be achieved by incentives and encouragement which presumably increase motivation. This improvement, however, is no greater than that which follows increased motivation in younger subjects. Hence the generally poorer performance of older people cannot usually be explained by their insufficient motivation. In fact, elderly subjects who volunteer to take part in psychological investigations are highly motivated to do well, and they are working closer to capacity than younger volunteers (see also Chapter Eleven, Section 4). In test situations or during training, older subjects are more careful and less confident. They try to minimize the risk of error and overestimate the risk; they guard against failure by combining low aspirations with strong attempts to succeed.

The older person's estimate of his own capacities is influenced by the attitudes and norms of the community in which he lives. These may not affect what a person *can* do, but they will affect what he is *likely* to do. The fact that older people try to take greater care does not mean that they succeed in making fewer errors than younger people. On the whole, speed and accuracy go together and, if anything, the association is closer among older people. Older people are more likely to abandon their attempt to solve a problem because they are slower and less able to master difficulties. They are more likely to settle for an approximate solution. This kind of behaviour need not arise from lack of motivation, since it is not difficult to demonstrate that even without time limits the mental output of older people does not reach that of younger people. Moreover, well-motivated and persistent older subjects add little to their overall performance by taking extra time.

Decreased motivation lowers performance; but if motivation and cognitive capacity are both reduced as age advances, which limits action most? Motivation and ability *interact* in some way to determine performance. Unfortunately, psychologists cannot measure motivation with anything like the objectivity and accuracy with which they can measure other aspects of human performance, and the problem of ascertaining the part played by age changes in motivation is likely to persist for some time.

Ideas and techniques in industrial society are changing rapidly, with computerization, automation and improved communications. Such innovations make demands on human adult intelligence which, according to Wechsler's figures, falls by about 24 points (of EQ) during adult life. The complexities of modern life present problems to people whose intelligence is below the average. The reduced intellectual efficiency of old people therefore handicaps them in relation to socio-technical innovations, and this may have something to do with their reputation for conservatism and rigidity. Research into the effects of age on skilled performance has obvious relevance to real-life industrial and professional work, as we have seen, and industrial gerontology is fairly firmly established. As yet, however, little research has been carried out into the effects of age on administrative and social skills which, after all, are supposed to be the fruits of experience.

CHAPTER SIX

The Effects of Ageing on Adult Intelligence

1. DIFFERENTIAL EFFECTS

(a) *Adult Intelligence*

The study of adult intelligence is concerned with intellectual abilities from the age of about 20 throughout the remainder of the human lifespan. It can be pursued in a variety of ways (some of which will be dealt with in detail) and its origin can be traced back to the First World War, when thousands of recruits to the U.S. Army were examined by methods based on the Binet test. The results, when published, startled both psychologists and the general public, for they showed that the average American young adult had a mental age of thirteen-and-a-half years, and that test scores decreased slightly with increasing age up to 30 and then more markedly up to 60.[1,2] The arguments provoked by these findings helped to stimulate research work on intelligence and mental testing and encouraged psychologists to explain and justify their ideas and methods. Not everyone is willing to accept the idea that intelligence subsequently decreases in adult life or even that it ceases to develop. Much of the confusion arises because intelligence can be defined in different ways, and because criticisms can be made of the methods used to investigate the effects of ageing.[3-6]

Psychologists measure a person's intelligence by administering a standardized test of mental ability and assessing his intellectual brightness *relative to other people of the same age.* Quite simply – if a man aged 50 takes a test called the Wechsler Adult Intelligence Scale (WAIS) and obtains a total score equal to the average score for persons aged about 50, his intelligence is average.[7,8] The term 'Intelligence Quotient' (IQ) is familiar now to many people, yet surprisingly few outside the field of professional psychology seem to understand its limitations. Briefly, an IQ test is designed so that, for example, items at mental age ten can be passed by an average ten-year-old, and those at mental age eleven by an average eleven-year-old. The items are said to measure 'Mental Age' (MA), since the ability to pass them depends upon intelligence and not merely upon Chronological Age (CA), although in normal children intelligence grows steadily with age. The IQ is defined as

$$\frac{MA}{CA} \times 100$$

For example, a boy's mental age (eleven years) is divided by his chronological age (ten years) and multiplied by 100 ($11/10 \times 100 = 110$) to obtain his IQ. Obviously a boy whose mental age is equal to his chronological age has an IQ of 100, whereas a boy whose mental age is less than his chronological age has an IQ lower than 100. The range of *normal* intelligence is from about 85 to 115 and includes about two thirds of the juvenile population. Thus the IQ is an index of a person's intelligence relative to other people, and a person with an IQ of 100 is of 'average' intelligence, brighter than half his age group, but duller than the other half; a person with an IQ of 130 is in the top five per cent of the population, whereas a person with an IQ of 60 is regarded as intellectually defective, since IQs as low as this or lower occur in the bottom one per cent of a juvenile age group.

It is convenient to think of intelligence as a natural biological endowment in respect of which people differ, so that its distribution in an age group is relatively 'normal' or bell-shaped. Like many other human attributes, such as height, growth of teeth, and physical prowess, it continues to mature (given the right environmental conditions) until about the age of 16 or 20. Up to the age of about 12 years, intellectual *capacity* (unspecialized intelligence) grows steadily, but then the rate of growth slows down and eventually ceases altogether. Individual differences in rate of growth and in the age at which maximum intellectual capacity is reached undoubtedly occur, just as they do for dentition, menstruation and height; but for the bulk of the population maximum intellectual capacity in the biological sense is probably reached somewhere between the ages of 16 and 20. The physical basis of intelligence is also reflected in the fact that people with above-average ability are physically healthier and tend to live longer.

Intellectual endowment should not be confused with intellectual performance reflected in scientific ability or in the social wisdom needed for dealing with people or for succeeding in business. Such attainments involve factors in addition to biological (or innate) intelligence: general experience, specialist knowledge, technical skill and personal qualities (to say nothing of good fortune, helpful connections and special aptitudes). Clearly, intelligence is only one attribute among many that go into the making of intellectual achievement or good social adjustment, and it can be distinguished from other attributes only with difficulty. For example, success in psychological tests calls for interest, attention, persistence and some familiarity with the sorts of problem presented in tests. It is, however, possible to design tests so that subjects are not penalized unduly because of extraneous factors, such as having been deprived of normal educational opportunities or being deaf or spastic. Psychologists aim to assess the *natural endowment* expressed in test performance. Time-binding (memory, imagination), relational thinking (abstraction, generalization), symbolism (language, imagery), together with cognitive speed and cognitive power are the main aspects of high-grade adult intelligence. In a sense, intelligence is the ability to organize and expand one's experience.

One way to consider the problem of measuring intelligence is to describe and comment upon some of the methods of the American psychologist, David Wechsler, who spent many years attempting to establish the effects of ageing on adult intelligence. In 1939, he published *The Measurement of Adult Intelligence* and in 1958 *The Measurement and Appraisal of Adult Intelligence.* Wechsler defines and measures adult intelligence in terms of a set of scores derived from a person's performance on eleven tests of intellectual ability. The individual tests are described, and discussed singly or in groups, as follows.

(b) *Verbal Ability*

VOCABULARY. This test measures the ability to define words from a list which becomes increasingly difficult as the words become less familiar. Persons who know the meaning of words such as 'picayune' or 'saturnine' tend to be more intelligent than those who do not.

INFORMATION. This test measures the ability to remember miscellaneous facts, i.e. general knowledge. Persons who know that paper is made from wood pulp and that the Wright brothers flew the first heavier-than-air machine tend to be more intelligent than those who do not.

COMPREHENSION. This test measures commonsense, or social understanding, by asking a person to explain familiar facts or state what his reactions would be to certain situations. Persons who know the functions of a court of law or who know the right thing to do in an emergency tend to be more intelligent than those who do not.

Vocabulary, Information and Comprehension are closely-related aspects of intellectual functioning in that persons who do well on one test tend to do well on the others. The three tests are closely associated with educational attainments, largely concerned with reproducing knowledge, and are unspeeded. Even so, in normal young adults they are indicative of general intelligence and correlate substantially with the non-verbal and speeded tests described later.

In spite of their common ground, the individual Wechsler tests call for somewhat distinct performances and make different sorts of demand upon the person's intellectual resources. The reader's understanding of age changes in adult intelligence will be facilitated if he considers each of the eleven sub-tests carefully as a *separate* measure of intelligence, for although each test takes a sample (or measures a part) of the person's mental abilities, the test performances are very differently affected by ageing. Vocabulary, Information and Comprehension show little if any decline in performance with increasing age after early maturity and there are many reasons for supposing that performance in them improves at least up to middle age (and possibly later for well-educated people with verbal interests). Several factors help to explain why performance 'holds up' with age.

First, the person does not have to think creatively; he has only to reproduce what he already knows. In this respect the three tests measure the person's verbal attainments. They are used to assess 'intelligence' because they are closely associated with mental development during childhood and adolescence (provided the person has had adequate educational opportunities and has not been socially underprivileged or emotionally disturbed). Up to the time of biological maturity, intellectual capacity and intellectual attainments develop at similar rates, but after maturity capacity tends to decrease in various ways even though attainments are maintained without undue impairment. The adult person's attainments show the *maximum* level reached by his intelligence and, as age advances, his capacity decreases, leaving some of his attainments as markers, showing the highest level reached. Vocabulary, Information and Comprehension are such markers, since the older person's ability to reproduce what he already knows reflects not his present level of intelligence but the high-water mark of his intellectual development.

Second, the person does not have to think quickly; he can ponder his replies, correct himself if necessary and work at his own speed. One of the clearest effects of ageing on intelligence is the slowing that occurs in the speed of intellectual activity. Commonsense, as well as innumerable experimental investigations and psychometric studies (using standardized mental tests), provide adequate evidence of this fact. Being able to think quickly is a sign of high intelligence and, contrary to common belief, the more intelligent person performs more quickly *and* more accurately than the less intelligent person on tests which measure the *rate* of intellectual output. As Vocabulary, Information and Comprehension tests make no demands for intellectual speed, they do not measure the person's present intelligence as effectively as do some others tests which will be described shortly.

Third, the person does not have to hold in mind a lot of information; he has to remember the question but he does not have to 'process' or reformulate it; so the demands upon his immediate memory (span of attention) are slight. Within limits, the capacity to hold in mind the information relevant to a problem is an important part of a person's intelligence; so, too, is the ability to shift attention from one aspect of the problem to another while retaining the information relevant to the problem as a whole. A decline with age in the capacity for dealing with complex problems – requiring the person to remember many details and to switch his attention from one part of the task to another – has been clearly demonstrated in studies of skill (see Chapter Five).

Thus, Vocabulary, Information and Comprehension tests measure intellectual attainments rather than intellectual ability, and the key to understanding the effects of ageing on adult intelligence is the fact that intellectual attainments are preserved (unless they fall into disuse), whereas the capacity to acquire new concepts, or to apply existing concepts quickly and accurately to complex situations, declines steadily throughout the years of maturity and may be accelerated in old age. Verbal ability (as opposed to verbal attainments) can be assessed in many other ways, however, and the study of the normal effects of adult ageing on complex language functions is of very recent origin.[9]

(c) *Short-Term Learning and Remembering*

DIGIT SPAN. Wechsler's test of Digit Span has two parts: digits forwards and digits backwards. In the first part of the test, the experimenter calls out in a regular unhurried voice a series of numbers, as 8, 7, 3, 5, 1. The subject attempts to reproduce the number series exactly. If he succeeds he goes on to a longer series. If he fails he has a second attempt with a different series the same length. If he fails again, he scores four, if this was the longest series he could remember correctly. In the second part of the test the experimenter calls out number series in the same way, starting with short groups of three and finishing with groups of eight, but the subject must now try to reproduce the numbers in the reverse order (the series 4, 5, 9, 1 would be reproduced as 1, 9, 5, 4). If he succeeds he goes on to a longer series, but if he fails he has a second attempt. The subject's score is the number of digits he can reproduce forwards plus the number he can reproduce backwards. A normal young adult should score about 13 (seven forwards and six backwards).

Wechsler claims that performance on this test (up to a maximum of nine forwards and eight backwards) reflects a person's general mental ability. Performance can be adversely affected by distraction and feelings of anxiety. Scores on this test are correlated with scores on tests of general intelligence which do not involve short-term memory to any great extent. Many other tests are better indicators of general intelligence – some people have a special aptitude for this sort of memorizing, and an outstandingly good memory span does not imply an outstandingly high level of general intelligence.

The effects of ageing on memory span for digits are not excessive, because the test is fairly straightforward: for men and women of above average intellectual ability, the mean score for digits forwards decreases slightly, whereas the mean score for digits backwards decreases more sharply. There appears to be no decline until after the age of about 45. Ageing has little effect on simple acts of short-term retention, but if the information has to be held *and* dealt with in some way (for example, by reversing the order of the items or by sorting the items into classes), the performance declines with age (see also Chapter Five).

Short-term memory sets up a temporary trace and involves a definite effort to remember – as in taking dictation or remembering a set of instructions. Long-term retention, on the other hand, provides a more durable record which usually requires little or no effort for its retrieval – as in exercising a well-practised skill like driving or remembering one's personal identity. Of course, the circumstances of recall, such as prompting or association, affect retrieval from long-term memory, as do circumstances affecting recognition. Similarly, factors like recency and rehearsal affect the kind and degree of forgetting in short-term memory. Learning involves a transfer process: information is scanned repeatedly in short-term memory so that a permanent record can be established in long-term memory, as in learning a poem. Similarly, skilled performance requires that information be scanned while an appropriate response is formed, as in typing or taking down morse code.

Nowadays, Wechsler's Digit Span Test is regarded as a relatively crude measure of short-term memory and as a rather insensitive measure of the effects of ageing on intellectual capacity.

OTHER METHODS OF STUDYING SHORT-TERM MEMORY. For research purposes, Digit Span has been superseded by more refined and recent techniques. In a test known as 'Paired Associates', the subject is presented with carefully contrived letter-groups, for example, UKJ – EDB (called 'trigrams'), and is required to learn a series of such associations. Under various conditions of initial learning, proactive and retroactive interference, time interval between items, and so on, the subject has to recall or recognize the associations. In 'Probe recognition', the subject is required to say whether a particular digit, word or syllable was or was not present in a series. In 'Dichotic Listening' the subject has to attend to two sources of information, such as digits or words, presented separately to each ear. Under various conditions of divided attention, length of list, time interval, similarity of stimuli, recall instructions, and so on, the subject is required to recall or recognize the stimuli previously presented, or to identify incidental stimulus characteristics, such as pitch or accent.

The study of the effects of ageing on short-term memory

constitutes a technical, vigorous and complicated area of contemporary research in behavioural gerontology.[10-23] The results so far confirm the generally deleterious effect of ageing on short-term memory under conditions of divided attention, but the contemporary debate is concerned with the *mechanisms* underlying this and other deficits in learning and memory. The basic problem is how to measure the effects of ageing on registration, retention and retrieval separately when all three are closely interlocked. Careful control of experimental conditions and refined methods of statistical analysis are used to investigate this problem. Short-term retention is affected by a number of factors, including initial level of learning, inhibitory processes such as fatigue, facilitation, cognitive context and strategy, rehearsal, sensory modality, interference and 'time'. Conflicting evidence makes it difficult to summarize the main findings briefly, and the issues raised encroach on topics dealt with in other chapters, such as psychogeriatric assessment, intelligence and skill.[24]

Further methods of measuring short-term learning and remembering include having the subject recognize or recall pictorial designs or words previously shown to him, having him learn a sequence of items by 'rote', and having him recall information which he had not intentionally tried to commit to memory. They all show a decline in performance with age – with a possible sex difference in favour of women on rote learning – but the rate of decline varies with the nature of the task. The various methods of measuring short-term memory are used partly for practical reasons, for example in diagnostic psychological testing, and partly for theoretical reasons, as in the investigation of theories about ageing and memory function.[25,26] The recall of recent experience is thought to be generally more susceptible to deterioration with age than is remote experience. Disuse naturally leads to some loss in long-term memory, which is recoverable on relearning.

Long-term memory is much less easily investigated than short-term memory, and it is difficult to control for such aspects as initial level of learning, practice, importance and so on. In certain conditions, there is a phenomenon of memory regression, in which an elderly patient shows impairment of short-term memory and memory for recent events, but has access to memories formed at a remote time like childhood, and confuses features of his present life with features from the past, for example mistaking his daughter for his sister. Long-term memory, however, is not as resistant to the effects of ageing as it sometimes appears to be.

(d) *Numerical Ability*

The ability to calculate and handle numerical relationships is a useful index of general intelligence. On the assumption that most people know how to add, subtract, multiply and divide simple numbers, and are familiar with coinage and simple fractions, Wechsler includes a series of problems in mental arithmetic as a sub-test.

ARITHMETIC. This test measures the ability to deal with simple numerical facts and relationships. For example, 'How much change would you expect from £1.00 after buying three plates at 28p each?'; 'A man bought a house for three-quarters of its original cost. He paid £6,000 for it. How much did it cost originally?' Marks are awarded for speed as well as accuracy. The subject has to remember the question and work out a solution, so the test involves short-term memory, but not to any great extent.

The decline with age shown by the Arithmetic Test is greater than for Digit Span, but far less than for some other tests to be described later. There are several reasons why this is so. One, mental arithmetic is a relatively simple cognitive skill, well-practised in childhood and used from time to time throughout adult life, so that it tends not to fall into disuse. Two, the Arithmetic Test is not a searching test of the ability to calculate: it is short, it does not sample the various arithmetical operations fully or systematically, and the time allowances are wide. Three, it requires little arithmetical reasoning or problem-solving (the problems call mainly for accuracy of computation).

This sort of skill, like reading or writing, does not involve the more complex functions of intelligence – finding relationships, working out implications, and so on. If we distinguish the 'mechanical' aspects of arithmetic from the more 'thoughtful' aspects, by using tests of numerical reasoning, we find little or no decline with age in the former (except that brought about coincidentally by a deterioration in memory span and speed of mental working). But there is some decline in the latter – the capacity for 'relational thinking' – since relational thinking lies at the heart of intelligence, and the ability to solve relational problems decreases with age. The rate of high-level accomplishment in mathematics reaches a peak in the early thirties and declines thereafter.

(e) *Abstraction and Generalization*

One of Wechsler's sub-tests uses the ability to discern abstract relationships as an index of general intelligence, by using a Similarities Test: for example, 'In what way are a diary and a log-book alike?', 'In what way are winds and clouds alike?' Questions of this sort measure the ability to think in abstract and general terms. A person who sees that a diary and a log-book are similar because they are both ways of keeping a record shows a capacity for orderly categorization at a high level of abstraction. A person who says that winds and clouds are both aspects of weather is more 'conceptually' competent than a person who says that the wind blows the clouds. The subject is given as much time as he needs; older people are not penalized by their slower performance. Responses are scored according to their level of abstractness: a person who consistently finds similarities by seeing both objects as members of a more inclusive class obtains a higher score than a person who can see only trivial or practical similarities. Performance on this test falls off somewhat as age advances.

The tendency for older people to become less capable of thinking in abstract terms is difficult to explain, because the notion of 'abstractness' itself is neither simple nor clear. Tests which purport to measure abstraction ability or conceptual thought measure high-grade intelligence or relational thinking.[27-29] Tests involving abstract classes and relationships (such as sorting tasks, proverb interpretation and series completion) reveal a decline in performance with increasing age, even when no time limits are set. Qualitative differences in the cognitive processes of older and younger subjects can be examined by analysing the sorts of errors they make.

Ask an old person to explain the proverb 'A burnt child dreads the fire', and the chances are greater than for a younger person that he will reply 'If a child is hurt by fire he will keep away from it' rather than 'Pain and disappointment make us wary'. The old person is more literal, more concrete, more concerned with tangible and immediate impressions, less able to detach himself from the particular example and consider the general class or principle, less able to ignore the individual fact in order to think in hypothetical terms. It is in these respects that the thinking of the older person becomes less abstract. The effect is not prominent except in extreme old age or senile conditions; old people may use proverbs and metaphors without grasping the abstract and general rules implied in them. They are also led astray more easily by the particular content of an analogy, and therefore perform less well on tests of analogies – which are a favoured way of measuring general intelligence.

These late-life changes in the *quality* of intellectual function have not yet been studied in sufficient detail to permit us to say that there is a systematic regression with age through successively more deteriorated levels of cognition. Although there is probably some similarity to juvenile stages of cognitive development, late-life changes probably represent a dissolution of the cognitive system rather than a systematic regression.

One of the best-known tests of relational thinking, Raven's Progressive Matrices Test, consists of a series of incomplete spatial patterns.[30,31] The subject has to identify the missing piece by working out the logical relationships running down and across the design, only one piece fitting the pattern correctly. The score is given by the number of problems correctly solved within a limited time. The normal effects of ageing on the ability to do the Progressive Matrices Test are pronounced, falling from about 45 to 25 items correct for the average adult between the ages of 20 and 70. Even if subjects are allowed sufficient time to attempt all the items, the effects of age are still substantial because older subjects cannot deal with the more complex relationships in the later items. Thus the noticeable effects of age revealed by Raven's Progressive Matrices contrast with the negligible effects of age on word-knowledge as measured by, say, the Crichton Vocabulary Scale.[32]

(f) *Non-Verbal Ability*

Five sub-tests in Wechsler's Adult Intelligence Scale, referred to as 'non-verbal' or 'performance' measures, are thought to be little affected by educational attainments. In spite of their apparent differences they are highly correlated. They sample various intellectual functions including short-term retention, mental speed, problem-solving, attention to detail, and the capacity to compare performance against appropriate standards.

Most of the time involved in an older person's mental reaction is occupied by 'central' processes (perception, thought, decision), whereas only a small part of it is occupied by sensory and motor processes (see also Chapter Five). This fact is relevant to understanding the effects of age on a simple coding performance – Wechsler's Digit Symbol Substitution Test.

DIGIT SYMBOL SUBSTITUTION. This test measures the ability to translate one set of symbols into another set. For example, digits could be coded as follows: 1 = [, 2 = $\wedge$, 3 = $\vdash$ and so on. The subject is presented with several rows of random numbers, and underneath each number he writes the symbol corresponding to it in the code. After a short practice period his performance is timed over ninety seconds. His score is the number of digits correctly coded. The results confirm other observations which show a marked decline with age in the speed of mental work.

Superficially there is nothing 'intellectual' about this task. It is a simple clerical operation, and part of the age decline is brought about by the older person's slower eye-movements and speed of writing. But other processes are slowed down too. Consider each step in the performance: attend to the first digit, store it in short-term memory, shift attention to the code, find the same digit, translate it into the equivalent symbol, store it in short-term memory, shift attention back to the first digit, retrieve symbol from store, write in the symbol; attend to the next digit, and so on. Obviously, to the longer actual movement times for eyes and hand we must add the longer fixation, shift and decision times. The older person's attention is more likely to be distracted so that he has to go back to the beginning of the cycle, or he may make mistakes. In either case his total output is reduced.

The fact that performance on the Digit Symbol Substitution Test is strongly associated with measures of general intelligence (in spite of its apparent lack of intellectual content) shows how important sheer mental speed is as an index of intelligence. Moreover, mental speed and short-term memory interlock, because information is spread over time and must be stored temporarily until ready for use. If the person works too slowly the backlog of information grows too large for his short-term memory to store and he begins to omit items and make mistakes. Writing down numbers in a game of Bingo, taking down dictation or morse code, and map-reading whilst travelling in a car are all examples of what psychologists call 'paced work', and performance in paced (and timed) work shows up the older person's intellectual deficiencies.

PICTURE ARRANGEMENT. This measures the ability to arrange a set of pictorial facts in a logical sequence. Sets of pictures, four or five in each set, of the type found in a humorous comic strip, are presented to the subject in a disorderly array. He studies the pictures and works out the relationships between them to find a meaningful order.

PICTURE COMPLETION. This measures the ability to detect omissions and errors. The pictures portray common objects, such as a house or a fish, a detail of which is missing, and the subject has to say what it is. This calls for fast systematic visual search, perhaps even conceptual analysis.

BLOCK DESIGN. This measures the ability to translate a small design (on a card) into a full-scale design (of coloured cubes).

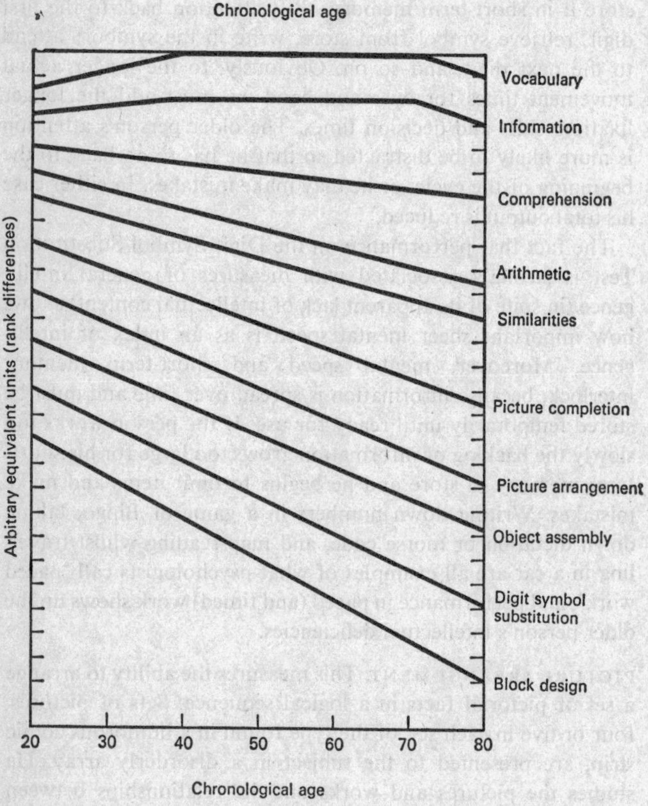

FIGURE 10 A simplified illustration of cross-sectional 'age differences' for the Wechsler-Bellevue Scale, expressed in equivalent units (rank differences).

As with the Matrices Test, there is probably an element of 'spatial reasoning' (a special aptitude for dealing with shapes and geometrical transformations). There is nothing unduly complicated about the designs, and given sufficient time a person of average intelligence can complete even the most difficult of them. But speed is important in the scoring, as it is for Picture Arrangement and some other sub-tests, so that few people complete all the designs quickly enough to obtain the maximum possible score.

OBJECT ASSEMBLY. This measures the ability to compose a picture from its separate pieces. The subject is presented with three jigsaw puzzles, and the speed and accuracy of his performance determines his score. Performance does not decline with age as rapidly as it does for the three tests just mentioned, but there is, nevertheless, a steady loss of efficiency. The test calls for intelligent guesswork, rapid rejection of inappropriate moves, sensitivity for spatial forms, and other aspects of general mental ability.

2. THE WECHSLER ADULT INTELLIGENCE SCALE

(a) *Standardization*

The WAIS is accepted and widely used as a measure of general intelligence.[33,34] A similar method, the Wechsler Intelligence Scale for Children (WISC), is used with younger groups. The problems and methods involved in the construction and standardization of Wechsler's tests of adult intelligence are too technical to be described and discussed in detail. It is sufficient to say that Wechsler took what he believed to be representative samples of people of different ages, and calculated the mean and the spread of scores obtained on each of the eleven subtests.

The original test, known as the Wechsler-Bellevue Scale Form 1, was standardized on approximately 1,000 adult men and women.[35,36] The revised test known as the WAIS was standardized on approximately 2,000 men and women ranging in age from 16 to over 75 years. Standards of performances were established to assess the mental abilities of a subject *relative* to those of other people. The highest total scores in the original test were obtained by the sample aged 20–24, whereas in the revised version the highest scores were obtained by the 25–29 age group. Moreover, the subsequent decline with age in total score was lower for the revised test than for the original version. Wechsler does not attempt to explain these discrepancies or to deal in detail with the age of onset and the relative rates of decline for the functions measured by different sub-tests. The technical problems of psychometric studies on this scale are too great for anything more definite to be said. For example, in the 15 years between the two tests, the apparent improvement in average performance could have arisen because of improvements in educational and living standards, better physical health, and greater familiarity with and easier adaptation to mental tests. Different tests and different samples might have given different results, but even Wechsler's revised figures show that peak performance for Digit Symbol Substitution, Block Design, Picture Arrangement and Object Assembly – the more exacting tests of intellectual efficiency – occurs in the 20–24 age group.

Wechsler's results and those of other workers agree in finding the peak of intellectual capacity (not to be confused with *attainment*) somewhere near the age of 20. It seems reasonable to say that this peak coincides with, and is probably an expression of, biological maturity. There has, however, been a swing of opinion away from the view that intelligence (general cognitive capacity) declines substantially in adult life. This has come about because the results of most longitudinal studies show little or no decline, or even gains, and because it has been recognized that secular trends and environmental differences may have been misinterpreted as age effects in cross-sectional studies. It is worth pointing out that the study of adult intelligence is grounded in the concepts and methods used in the study of juvenile intelligence. The question is whether such concepts and methods are the best ones for dealing with cognitive processes in adult life – perhaps an analysis in terms of 'mental skills' or the 'skills of experience', as in understanding people and events, would provide a more interesting and useful focus for research.

(b) *Intelligence Quotient (IQ) and Efficiency Quotient (EQ)*

The scoring of the WAIS is arranged so that for a young adult the average score on each sub-test is ten points. Since there are eleven sub-tests, the average score is 110 points, which is equal to an IQ of 100 (average intelligence). However, for persons aged 75 and over, the average total score is 69 points, which is, by definition, equal to an IQ of 100. Although a 75-year-old may be of average intelligence relative to other people aged 75, he is obviously less efficient intellectually than the average young adult, for whereas the old person gains a total score of 69 points, the young person gains 110. Moreover, whereas the younger person's scores are likely to be distributed fairly equally over the eleven sub-tests, the older person's scores are likely to be high on some and low on others, since some mental functions are adversely affected by ageing, whereas others are very little impaired.

There are two ways of expressing an adult person's intelligence: Intelligence Quotient (IQ) – intellectual ability *relative to that of his age group*; and Efficiency Quotient (EQ) – intellectual ability *relative to young adults* who are at the peak of their intellectual and biological efficiency. The average 75-year-old has an IQ of 100 but an EQ of 76. This EQ is obtained by finding what a score of 69 points would mean if it had been obtained by a young adult. If a 75-year-old man gains 130 points altogether, he is bright compared with other people aged 75, for on average they gain only about 69 points, and his IQ would be 136. A score of 130 points obtained by a young adult is equal to an IQ of 112; so the older person's EQ is 112, since this is a measure of his intellectual brightness relative to young adults who are at their best. The overall or average effects of ageing are assumed to be as follows: in the years between young adulthood and old age, intellectual efficiency falls from 100 to about 76. In the young adult, IQ and EQ are equivalent and mean the same thing, but for the older person the IQ stays more or less constant, by definition, while the EQ diminishes steadily. The young person with an above-average IQ (and EQ) of 115 who lives to the age of 75 can expect to have an EQ of about 90 at that age. A person of average ability at the age of 20 can expect to be of average ability at the age of 70; a person who is in the top 5 per cent of his age

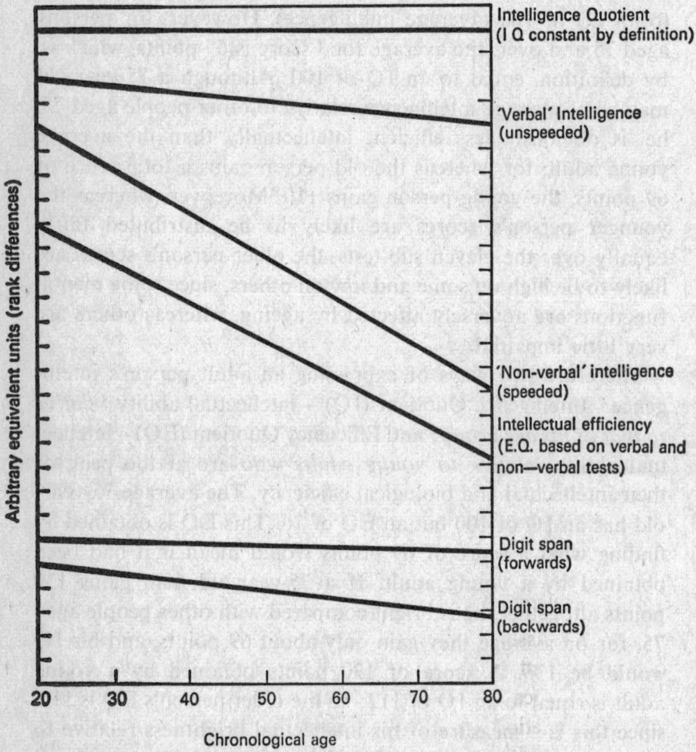

FIGURE 11 A further simplified illustration of age differences in Wechsler-Bellevue functions expressed in equivalent units.

group for intelligence can expect to stay in the top 5 per cent of his age group for the rest of his life, provided he does not suffer from mental disease or pathological brain damage. (The statistical data from which such assumptions are derived can be found in the WAIS *Manual* and in Wechsler's book *The Measurement and Appraisal of Adult Intelligence*.)

Longitudinal studies of juvenile intelligence show that measured IQ is by no means constant over the years. This affects the *theory* of intelligence, such as it is, and the interpretation of an individual's test performance, but it does not affect the practice of intelligence testing, which has a sort of actuarial basis. Longitudinal studies of adult intelligence also show that over a period of a few years some subjects improve with age, whereas some get worse and others stay about the same. We are not yet in a position to obtain *repeated measures* of intelligence at frequent intervals over long sections of adult life; so we can say little or nothing about variations within individuals, or about the causes and conditions of increases or decreases in measured intelligence in adult life. One could speculate that stress, physical or mental illness, or improvements in living conditions, might induce such fluctuations.

The Wechsler tests have sometimes been used in a short form, like using only the sub-tests: Comprehension, Vocabulary, Block Design and Object Assembly, or, alternatively, using a small sample of items. Short tests of intelligence are useful for screening purposes, but are clearly less reliable than full-scale tests, so they are unlikely to be of use as repeated measures.[37,38]

(c) *Intellectual Deterioration*

Wechsler classifies his sub-tests into two kinds: those that are more resistant to age effects and those that are less so. The former – Vocabulary, Information, Object Assembly and Picture Completion – he calls 'Hold' tests; the latter – Digit Span, Similarities, Digit Symbol Substitution and Block Design – he calls 'Don't Hold' tests. In one respect the estimated decrease with age of 24 points of EQ for the person of average intelligence, as mentioned above, is an *underestimate*, since the total number of points gained on the WAIS by older and younger people alike is compounded of scores on 'Hold' and 'Don't Hold' tests. If intellectual efficiency is measured only by the tests which show a decline with age (the so-called 'Don't Hold' tests), the decline with age is far higher than when it is averaged out for all eleven sub-tests. There is some disagreement about this aspect of Wechsler's work, because it is recognized that scores on the timed non-verbal tests fall off more rapidly with age than scores on even the least resistant verbal test (Similarities or Arithmetic). Wechsler argues that verbal and performance tests measure different intellectual functions. It is not unusual to find that a person's verbal IQ is different from his non-verbal IQ. The well-educated person who reads widely is likely to get a relatively high verbal IQ, whereas the quick, dextrous, practical person is likely to get a relatively high non-verbal IQ. The mental abilities involved in the untimed verbal tests are maintained quite well as age advances whereas the mental abilities involved in the timed performance tests are not.

Wechsler estimates the extent to which a person has deteriorated intellectually by comparing his scores in tests which show a decline with age with his scores in tests which show little or no decline. He includes both verbal and performance tests in each of the two categories 'Hold' and 'Don't Hold', so as not to over- or underestimate the extent to which the subject has deteriorated over the years. One objection to Wechsler's treatment of this problem is that the two performance scores in the 'Hold' category (Object Assembly and Picture Completion) do not hold up particularly well with age, and the two verbal scores in the 'Don't Hold' category (Digit Span and Similarities) are, relatively speaking, only slightly diminished by ageing. It is obviously unsatisfactory to find, for example, that the *performance* test (Object Assembly) which declines least, still declines more than the *verbal* test (Arithmetic) which declines most. The criticism could be met either by introducing time-limits into the verbal tests or by finding a number of non-verbal tests of intelligence which do not show a decline with age. Alternatively, one might include verbal tests of intelligence which show a steep fall in score with increasing age, such as Analogies or Verbal Reasoning.

Investigators have used the discrepancy between verbal IQ and performance IQ, or various combinations and weightings of the WAIS sub-tests, in attempts to find the optimum DQ for diagnosing specific psychiatric conditions, such as organic impairment, or neurosis.[39-42] The usual method of demonstrating normal intellectual deterioration is to measure the difference between declining and non-declining functions, as follows:

$$\text{Deterioration Quotient (DQ)} = \frac{\text{Hold score} - \text{Don't Hold score}}{\text{Hold score}} \times 100$$

A person aged 60 who scores 45 points on the four 'Hold' sub-tests and 28 points on the four 'Don't Hold' sub-tests shows an overall loss of 17 points – approximately 38 per cent of his 'Hold' score. This amount of deterioration is far in excess of that expected for an average 60-year-old – approximately 10 per cent; the discrepancy suggests intellectual deterioration over and above that of normal ageing. According to Wechsler's original figures, a normal person in his late thirties shows a 5 per cent loss of efficiency. By the age of 60 this normal loss has risen to about 18 per cent. The reader is reminded that when percentages are quoted in connection with psychometric (ordinal) measurements, they are purely for convenience. They do not signify an *absolute* amount of anything.

More recently Wechsler adopted a new method of calculating intellectual deterioration which shows zero if the person's scores have fallen normally with age, but the logic of the procedure is still the same. In practice people sometimes do better on the 'Don't Hold' than on the 'Hold' sub-tests, because some are verbally fluent and quick-witted, others are practical, careful and persistent. It follows that positive as well as negative discrepancies between the 'Hold' and 'Don't Hold' scores can occur. A negative discrepancy has no meaning; it is an error of measurement. Mental testing, especially in clinical psychology, where the Wechsler Adult Intelligence Scale is most often used, is a highly skilled business, and psychological assessment should be carried out only by experienced and properly trained psychologists.

The concept of 'intellectual deterioration' as a measurable process goes back some years. As long ago as 1930 intellectual deterioration was being measured by taking the difference between a person's estimated previous maximum mental level (when he was a young adult) and his present level of efficiency. Previous maximum mental level was measured by a vocabulary test which required only the reproduction of the meanings of words (there are other ways of measuring vocabulary). Present efficiency was measured by a variety of tests calling for new learning and fast mental work – decoding, immediate memory, maze tracing and rote learning. The discrepancy between the two sets of scores measured intellectual deterioration. During the growth period and up to early maturity, vocabulary and the ability to think and to learn increase together (provided the circumstances are appropriate). During middle and late maturity, vocabulary, which is resistant to the gradual and cumulative degenerative processes of ageing and relatively unaffected by some sorts of mental disease and brain injury, remains more or less constant, whereas the ability to think and to learn is gradually eroded by normal ageing or abruptly diminished by physical and mental disorders.

Wechsler thus distinguishes between the normal decline that occurs gradually as age advances, and the abnormal deterioration that occurs in conditions of mental disease and brain damage. There are similarities between these kinds of deterioration, and Wechsler defines senility (an extreme form of mental and physical dilapidation) as a normal long-term consequence of degenerative effects which accumulate during adult life. Some people never become senile, because they die prematurely – of cancer, accident, pneumonia or heart failure. Senility, however, is more usually thought of as a pathological (diseased) condition. Patients showing signs of senility or arteriosclerosis, in contrast to normal old people, are relatively more impaired on the Information and Comprehension tests of the WAIS, which suggests that the senile condition is not so much an exaggeration of normal old age as a disturbance of it.

After the age of about 45 an increasing proportion of normal subjects make abnormal or deficient responses on tests which are sensitive to brain damage – including tests of abstraction and generalization such as block-sorting or proverb-interpretation. Hence, normal ageing seems to be accompanied by a gradual but cumulative impairment of the physical basis of intelligence, although most normal people in old age do not appear to be mentally confused, and they manage the routine affairs of everyday life without evidence of intellectual deficit. It is only when they are examined closely by means of psychological tests that signs of intellectual deterioration can be detected in 'normal' elderly subjects. Primitive or abnormal forms of thought among elderly subjects are found among responses not only to tests of intellectual function but also to projective tests. The detailed analysis of errors and curiosities in performance is a further aspect of diagnostic and experimental testing in geriatric clinical psychology.[43,44] Diffuse damage to the brain could lead to cumulative adverse effects rather like a steady loss of population could disrupt a social organization, since the number of working units eventually falls below the minimum required to fulfil various functions. It could also decrease the 'signal to noise' ratio, and thus hinder cognitive organization at all levels.

Experiments with animals have shown that learning capacity is directly related to the *amount* of cortical tissue available, but the relationship may not be so direct in human beings on account of cortical localization. Brain-damaged subjects, however, learn less well than normal subjects, and have poorer short-term memory. It has not proved possible to demonstrate conclusively that the permanent cognitive structures are located in fixed specific parts of the brain, but at least *some* apparently specific and fixed memory traces seem to be located in the temporal lobes. Normal intellectual degeneration with age appears to be gradual and cumulative, though this might be an artefact of the methods used to investigate the effects of ageing. Substantial deterioration may appear in an individual over a relatively short period of time.

The theory of intellectual deterioration has a number of weaknesses. First, the various tests are by no means perfectly valid or reliable. That is to say, they do not necessarily measure what they are supposed to measure, as with former capacity in the case of adult vocabulary, and they do not always yield consistent results. Thus, a score which is derived from the difference between two or more imperfect scores is not likely to be a very reliable measure. Second, mental disease or focal brain damage can have *selective* effects on the various functions measured by tests of deterioration, for example, attaching meanings to words or objects, whereas the term 'intellectual deterioration' implies a diffuse or general impairment. Third, the actual deterioration score depends upon the functions contrasted as being 'more' or 'less' resistant. For example, if a person's score on the Mill Hill Vocabulary Scale is contrasted with his score on the Progressive Matrices Test, the index of deterioration is different from that obtained by contrasting his scores on Wechsler's 'Hold' and 'Don't Hold' sub-tests. The indices should, however, arrange persons in approximately the same *rank order* of intellectual deterioration.

3. CURRENT ISSUES IN THE STUDY OF ADULT INTELLIGENCE

(a) *Specialized and Unspecialized Intelligence*

The many quantitative and differential effects of ageing on mental abilities can be assimilated to a theoretical frame of reference which defines two basic aspects of intelligence. One refers to the unspecialized or fluid function of intelligence, sometimes called type A; it can be thought of as a natural endowment – innate general cognitive capacity – and is measured by tests which call for productive relational thinking and mental speed, but require no special knowledge or experience. The other refers to the specialized or crystallized function of intelligence, sometimes called type B; it can be thought of as an acquired characteristic – general knowledge and special experience – and is measured by tests which call for the reproduction of information or the exercise of a learned skill.[45]

Unspecialized intelligence is a hypothetical entity, a concept we need in order to make sense of individual differences and family resemblances in intellectual performance. It is estimated, as in the measurement of IQ, by reference to a person's mental performance relative to other people. Most intelligence tests, however, measure *effective* intelligence – cognitive competence – because the unspecialized function can only be expressed through actual performance, which entails some acquired knowledge and skills. Hence tests of 'intelligence' do not measure pure unspecialized intelligence directly. This could be done only by identifying and measuring the physiological or genetic basis of intelligence, and we appear to be a long way from such revolutionary discoveries.

If mental abilities are ranked according to their susceptibility to the normal effects of ageing, it becomes apparent that those which are more resistant (hold up with age) are relatively specialized, whereas those that are less resistant (don't hold) are relatively unspecialized. If mental abilities are then ranked according to their 'g' saturation (the extent to which they express the factor common to all intelligence tests) then the method of criterion analysis shows that the age factor and unspecialized intelligence are very highly, but negatively, correlated.[46] The wisdom of the older person is the wisdom of experience because as unspecialized mental ability declines with age, the older person relies more on what he has learned. The wisdom of the younger person is the wisdom of intelligence because, as specialized mental ability is lacking for want of experience, the younger person must rely on insight.

It is possible to think of unspecialized (fluid) intelligence as a sort of scaffolding within which the more enduring fabric of our experience is organized. In neurological terms, the physical basis of unspecialized intelligence might be the so-called association areas, since damage to such areas appears to have less serious consequences for adults than for children (who will be less able to organize their experience during the juvenile period of intensive development). People are genetically endowed with different potentialities for specialized and unspecialized intelligence. The existence of distinctive talents in, say, chess, mathematics, music and language, strongly suggests that there are areas of sub-specialization too. From conception onwards people are exposed to widely different environmental conditions which have cumulative effects and long-range consequences on their effective intelligence. It is not altogether surprising that they differ considerably from one another at any age and follow different pathways of growth and decline.

(b) *Component Mental Abilities*

The measurement of intelligence is full of conceptual and technical difficulties. General intelligence is best regarded not as one kind of human ability but as a collection or system of abilities, some of which can be measured relatively independently of one another. Under natural conditions, particularly, these abilities interact not only with each other but also with so-called 'non-intellectual factors', such as persistence or anxiety. The number and types of component abilities is a matter of debate and further research, but they include the following: fluid intelligence, comprising inductive reasoning, relational thinking, short-term learning and remembering, and speed of reasoning; crystallized intelligence, comprising verbal and educational level, mechanical and social knowledge; spatial reasoning and visualization; speed of perceptual and motor performance; accuracy and carefulness.

Psychometric methods cannot distinguish fluid from crystallized ability in an absolute sense, but the conceptual distinction is convenient. It is not that one is innate and the other acquired; each type of intelligence could be determined by both genetic and environmental conditions. This statement may be confusing at first glance; but the argument, admittedly speculative, is that the neurophysiological bases of the two types of intelligence are somewhat different and therefore liable to different genetic and environmental influences, even though they are closely interlocked in a functional sense.

One well-known test, Thurstone's 'Primary Mental Abilities', distinguishes five supposedly distinct mental abilities. As we have seen, the eleven sub-tests of the WAIS fall into clusters and overlap considerably in their function as measuring instruments, but the general intention is that they should take samples (in areas proved to be important) of the individual's mental abilities. The 'Primary Mental Abilities Test', however, is different. It is based on a complex statistical procedure, too technical to be dealt with here, which purports to show that intelligence can be regarded not as one general ability, but as several component abilities (different from those listed above). These primary abilities are: Verbal Meaning, or the ability to understand ideas expressed in words; Spatial Reasoning, or the ability to think about objects in two or three dimensions; Logical Reasoning, the ability to solve rational problems, to foresee, to plan, to deduce implications and to generalize from experience; Number Ability, the capacity to handle figures and deal with simple quantitative relationships; Word Fluency, the ability to produce ideas easily and quickly. The tests are all timed, but provision can be made for extra time so that a 'power' or 'accuracy' score as well as a 'speed' score can be obtained.

From what has already been said, it is not difficult to predict the effects of age on these primary mental abilities.[47,48] For subjects over the age of 50, allowed to complete the tests in their own time, the largest age decline is in Logical Reasoning, and the next largest in Spatial Reasoning. Both Number Ability and Verbal Meaning decline with age, but the decreases are small. Time limits reduce the range of scores for all subjects and obscure the differences between the tests as regards the effects of age. Nevertheless, when time limits are imposed, a consistent age decline occurs for all five measures (Word Fluency is always a time test).

Eight 'factorially pure' measures of mental ability – comprehension, verbal fluency, spatial relations, number, memory for names and faces, reasoning, dexterity and perception – applied to over 600 subjects aged between 16 and 89 years, yielded a score, based on all eight measures, which declined with age. The first four measures showed no decline until after the age of 40, whereas the second four showed a progressive decline throughout the age-range.

The work on component mental abilities has been made possible by the use of factor analysis as a method of accounting for the interrelations between tests. Attempts have been made to describe age changes in the structure and organization of intellectual functions. The attempt to identify distinct intellectual functions by means of factor analysis appears not to have contributed significantly to our understanding of the pathology of cognition, juvenile cognitive development, or adult intelligence. The so-called 'mental abilities' derived from factor analysis seem not to represent intellectual functions in the psychological or neurological sense. Hence, factorially-based Wechsler scores and profile analysis seem to have had little theoretical importance or practical use. Unfortunately, investigations of this sort are beset with methodological problems, so that it is not yet possible to say what the age changes are. One possibility would be for the factorial structure – of say the WAIS Tests or Primary Mental Abilities – to become less differentiated, i.e. for the general factor loadings to increase, and for the group factor and specific factor loadings to decrease. Alternatively, the structure could become more disorganized or, more likely, distorted in the direction of verbal attainments.

Factor-analytic studies of the WAIS generally identify two main factors, corresponding broadly to fluid and crystallized ability, and a minor memory factor. The effects of age on these and other factorial abilities are as described above.[49,50] There are other tests of cognitive ability which are supposed to measure the basic components of intelligence, such as those developed by Guildford. The ramifications of the study of human intelligence do not permit a simple statement of what is presently known. There are considerable differences, for example, in the concepts and methods used by psychometricians as compared with those following the developmental psychology of Piaget. It is difficult and probably unwise at this time to make definite statements about the effects of adult ageing on component mental abilities or on the cognitive stages identified in juvenile development.[51]

The distinction between convergent and divergent processes in cognition is a further aspect of the modern study of intelligence, and one also beset with conceptual and methodological complications. However, defined in terms of the rate and extent to which subjects can formulate original and rare ideas in response to relatively simple test materials, intellectual creativity declines with age even among bright subjects, men and women alike. Thus Lehman's findings regarding the decline with age in creative intellectual endeavour (described in a later chapter) can be accounted for in part by a decline with age in fluid intelligence – because psychometric measures of intellectual creativity correlate substantially with other estimates of fluid intelligence. Furthermore, the decline with age in creativity can be observed using untimed tests; the imposition of time limits amplifies the adverse effects of age.

In open-ended situations, that is, those calling for divergent or creative thought, older subjects gradually become less capable of thinking up new possibilities for relevant action; at least this is so if the situation calls for the application of intelligence rather than experience. Subjects were asked to sort a collection of test objects into classes. They could use shape, colour, or kind of marking as the basis for their responses. These were classified as either logical and appropriate, or as illogical and inappropriate. Older subjects could produce fewer of the former type of response. Sorting the various colours or shapes was rational and realistic, but making patterns, arranging the objects in rows and columns, or fitting them together like pieces of a jigsaw puzzle, was irrational and unrealistic. The second type of response reflects a low level of intelligence (the level of concrete operations and perceptual groupings), normally found in people with undeveloped or low grade intelligence, yet this sort of response occurs with greater frequency among older people. Similar shifts in the level of mental functioning, namely, towards a more concrete, practical, undifferentiated kind of thinking, have been demonstrated in patients suffering from certain mental diseases and brain injuries.

(c) *The Maintenance of Ability*

Little is known about the effects of mental or physical exercise on the maintenance of intelligence in adult life. It is reasonable to suppose that intellectual activity which is 'demanding' improves cognitive capacity by making good the adverse effects of disuse; some functions seem to be capable of growth in response to demand until relatively late in life. The evidence from animal studies has important implications. It suggests that the brain cortex – the physical basis for the organization of more complex forms of behaviour – responds to the demands of environmental stimulation by growth, not in the number of nerve cells, but presumably in size, organization and in supporting tissues and weight. The most pronounced effects are during juvenile development, but under appropriate conditions continued growth at a diminishing rate carries on into the adult phase. It is too early to evaluate this line of work; and it is not unusual in science to find that further investigations lead to less dramatic conclusions than initial studies suggest. Even so, it would come as no surprise to many psychologists if it were found that the main determinants of age changes in adult intelligence were to be found in early juvenile development.

Little is known about the differences between men and women in the way intelligence and personality are affected by ageing, but such evidence as there is suggests that the relative age changes are much the same for both sexes.[52-54] The problem of sex differences is complicated because women have a longer expectation of life (though not necessarily *biologically* younger than men of the same chronological age), but the average woman may be less intellectually active than the man and therefore more prone to the effects of disuse. Education is associated with the maintenance of ability in adult life, and this could produce a further differential effect of ageing between men and women. Furthermore, the limitation of psychometric scaling makes this kind of comparison difficult.

Psychological as well as physiological factors bring about age changes in mental ability. The poorer performance of some older people arises, in part, from diminished interest and motivation. However, after an initial reluctance arising from feelings of diffidence, older subjects usually become interested in a task, persist in it and try to do well (reluctance and lack of confidence are found among younger people too). But regardless of their willingness and efforts, older people perform less well than younger people. Emotional complications and self-defeating attitudes play a part in lowering the level of performance of some older people, but most systematic investigations are carried out on volunteers, so their grosser effects are screened out. The overall effects of ageing on intelligence, therefore, have probably been *underestimated.*

Most studies of the effects on intelligence and achievement of growing up and growing old have been carried out by comparing the performances of people of different ages and using the 'cross-sectional method' (see Chapter Eleven). The effect of averaging the performances of groups of people at each of several age levels produces a relatively smooth curve of development and decline; it tends to mask stepwise changes and fluctuations in the development and decline of performance for individual cases, which would be revealed if the *same* group of people were followed through part of the life span by using the 'longitudinal method'. Abrupt falls in intellectual ability might follow severe illness or mental distress or a period of intellectual stagnation, with partial recovery later. The longitudinal method, however, has its drawbacks, and there is considerable disagreement, currently, about the nature of adult changes in intelligence.[55-60] Compared with cross-sectional age differences, longitudinal age changes reveal substantially less overall effect of age on the WAIS sub-tests (performance on some verbal sub-tests improves), but the *relative* effects are much the same. Familiarity and practice almost certainly contribute to the improvements in score in follow-up studies.

There is, as yet, no adequate theory of adult intelligence. Such a theory would have to be coordinated with theories of intellectual development up to maturity, and describe age changes in the structure of abilities, accounting for alterations in the quantity and quality of intelligence in both normal and pathological conditions.

CHAPTER SEVEN

The Effects of Ageing on Intellectual, Social and Athletic Achievements

1. LEHMAN'S METHODS AND FINDINGS

(a) *Achievements in Science, Literature and the Arts*

In previous chapters, we examined the effects of ageing on intelligence and skilled performance as shown by various psychometric and laboratory methods. In general, these studies were concerned with investigating people's capabilities by measuring their behaviour in clinically or experimentally controlled conditions, rather than with describing what people actually accomplish in real life. In considering the effects of ageing on real-life achievements – in the arts and sciences, in business, politics, athletics and so on – we must distinguish between natural ability, which provides a kind of *potential* for achievement, and actual accomplishment, which obviously depends upon a variety of conditions, such as opportunity and health, in addition to such potential.

Historical documentation has provided a multitude of examples of human achievements. Tennyson published his *Ballads and Poems* in 1880 when he was 70 years old; he took his seat in the House of Lords when he was 74; in the same year his play *Becket* was published. Galileo published his dialogues on mechanics at the age of 74; his discovery of the diurnal and monthly oscillations of the moon was made when he was 73; his scientific creativity continued up to his death at the age of 78. However, Galileo achieved his insight into the movements of the pendulum at the early age of 17. Jane Austen wrote *Pride and Prejudice* when she was 21. Marconi had transmitted radio signals by the time he was 21. Obviously, intellectual achievements can occur throughout adult life, but citing examples and counter-examples is only the first step in the analysis of this problem, which requires a systematic method of compiling and analysing the relevant data.

The best work on this aspect of human ageing was begun by H. C. Lehman in 1928, and eventually published in *Age and Achievement* (1953), and in sundry other publications.[1-7] Lehman's method was simple but laborious. He tabulated the ages at which people had made significant contributions to art, science, music, literature, technology or medicine; or had achieved outstanding performances as entertainers, soldiers, sportsmen, statesmen, explorers or industrialists. The information was obtained from various sources: historical surveys, works of reference and encyclopedias; cross-references were used to obtain greater accuracy. Large samples of achievements enabled reliable comparisons to be made between different age groups. For example, one source book was Hilditch's *A Concise History of Chemistry* which contains the dates on which nearly 250 noted chemists first published their accounts of what later proved to be outstanding contributions to this science. Nearly one thousand contributions were tabulated. Lehman ascertained the date of birth of each chemist and worked out the *average rate* of output for each 5-year interval for the span of life covered (usually from the age of 15 to the age of 80). He found that the highest average rate of output of the chemists was ·165 (approximately $\frac{1}{6}$th) of a contribution per person per annum, found in the years between the ages of 30 and 34 inclusive, i.e., one contribution in six years by the best men in the field. Between the ages of 40 and 44, the annual rate of output had fallen to ·115 of a contribution per person per annum. Similar rates of output were calculated for each 5-year interval from the age of 15 to over 80. Using 'rate of output' makes allowance for the different numbers of people left alive in each age group. As it is convenient to make *direct* comparisons between rates of output in different fields, Lehman transformed the observed rates into percentages by taking the highest rate for any 5-year interval as 100 per cent and finding the proportionate percentages for each other 5-year interval. The highest rate of output for the chemists was in the 30–34 age group, i.e., ·165, which became 100 per cent; the 40–44 age group with an annual rate of output of ·115, became 70 per cent. Percentages were calculated for each 5-year age group and the results were tabulated or graphed.

We need not concern ourselves with the exact figures, but the general conclusions are as follows: one, in the years between the ages of 15 and 19 the *rate* of achievement in chemistry is low – about ·005 of a contribution per person per annum (3 per cent of the maximum rate); two, the rate rises steeply and steadily until it reaches a peak in the years between 30 and 34; three, after the age of about 34 the rate of output falls fairly steadily to ·078 (47 per cent) in the years between 45 and 49, and to nearly zero after the age of 70.

Lehman obtained age distributions for rates of output in many fields including: mathematics, practical inventions, chess, medical discoveries, philosophy, all kinds of music, art and literature. With few exceptions, these and other kinds of intellectual achievement show a relationship to chronological age similar to that described for chemistry.

The relative importance of the quality of a contribution was judged by the amount of space allocated to it, or by the number of times it was referred to. Lehman showed that recent achievements, especially those of people still alive, are difficult to evaluate, and to analyse in terms of age effects. An analysis of then contemporary American music composed between 1912 and 1932 showed an age relation quite different from the typical one. Productivity rose up to the age of 35, levelled off, and then remained fairly steady until the age of 70. Some of these works did not stand the test of time, since they were still in manuscript in 1932. There is less ambiguity about the merits of work produced by people long dead.

Lehman asked a number of competent colleagues to select the hundred most important contributions listed in Hilditch's *A Concise History of Chemistry*, and found that two thirds of them agreed on 52 of the contributions. The age distribution for this set of very high-quality contributions did not begin until the early twenties, but the rate of output increased rapidly to a maximum in the 25–29 age group. This early peak was followed by a sharp decline in the rate of output, which ceased altogether by the age of 60. Thus, the peak years for really outstanding performance in chemistry occur earlier in life than the peak years for achievements of lesser merit, and the association with chronological age is even more pronounced. Similar effects were observed in most other fields.

Studies using a large number of persons and many contributions show the effects of ageing on 'quantity' of output; studies using a small number of persons and a few very high-grade (highly original or outstanding) contributions show the effects of ageing on 'quality' of output. The total output of a sample of authors falls off with age relatively little, but when the authors' one best book (a measure of quality) is considered the rate of output falls fairly steeply after the middle thirties. In philosophy the age period 35–39 is the most productive, both in quantity and quality. The age trends observed by Lehman, based on relatively small numbers at each age level, fluctuate, but in spite of these sampling errors the general picture is consistent.

The peak years were not in the period 30–34 for every kind of intellectual achievement. The peak years for metaphysics, for example, were 40–49. The psychologists started making their contributions relatively late, in the period 25–29 years, reaching a peak at age 35–39, after which their output diminished gradually until it stopped at about the age of 80. The average number of contributions made by astronomers increased rather unevenly from the late teens to the early forties and then declined fairly steadily to the sixties and seventies. By contrast, a study of 45 authors producing over 600 poems showed an early peak at 25–29, followed by an abrupt decline to the ages of 35–39, then a gradual and uneven decline up to the age of 90.

Lehman was unable to find sufficient data for the construction of separate age curves for women, especially in science and technology, since so few women had contributed to these fields and many of them had not revealed their date of birth, which remained concealed even after death. One study, based on a few creative contributions made by women in science, showed an age relationship similar to that for men. Another study of children's classics, written by women, showed the usual peak years for output at 30–34.

There appear to be few or no differences between men and women in the rate at which their intellectual capacities diminish with age. Intelligence tests, unfortunately, are constructed in such a way that sex differences in performance are minimized. This does not mean that men and women are equal, on average, in native intelligence; rather, it is *assumed* that they are equal. There are some measures which suggest, however, that the two sexes are in fact comparable in intelligence, at least within the normal range. On the other hand, it is possible that rather more men than women may be endowed with extremely high general intelligence and special aptitudes of the sort frequently associated with creative intellectual achievement. Adverse social factors probably play a major part in limiting the contribution that women have made to various fields of human achievement. It will be many years before women have full equality of opportunity with men, and even then child-rearing and domestic constraints will undoubtedly restrict their intellectual achievements, especially in the period in which one would expect them to do their most creative work. Such evidence as there is suggests that the age relationship will be similar to that for men.

Literary achievements follow much the same age trend as other forms of achievement. However, best-sellers have (or used to have) a late-appearing maximum rate between the ages of 40 and 44, followed by a rapid drop. Poetry, by contrast, is typically a younger man's accomplishment, the peak years occurring between 23 and 35. As we might expect, the rate of output for poetry of very high merit falls off with age more rapidly than for poetry of lesser merit. Novels tend to be written later in life but, rather surprisingly, the rate of output for superior novels rises more slowly and reaches its maximum at age 40–44 (later than the rate for novels of lesser merit). The subsequent decline in performance is more pronounced for 'superior' novels. Comedies and tragedies show a peak at 35–39, but other prose selections show a peak at 40–44. Hymns and religious poetry written by women show a peak at age 35–39, with a more rapid decline in output for work of higher quality. There is a general tendency for 'great books' to be written by people under 40 years of age, but at every period of life, from the early twenties onward, one author or another has produced a masterpiece. Achievements in art and music showed broadly the same association with age as achievements in science, technology, medicine and philosophy. The age relation for output in music was much the same for people of different nationalities.

Some important discoveries, inventions and artistic achievements have been produced by very young men. Men who start to achieve early in life usually accumulate a larger number of attainments than men who start their creative work late. The average starting age of 135 chemists who produced only one major contribution was 36 years, as compared with 22 years for six chemists contributing over 20 major contributions. The less prolific workers also finished their creative life earlier. Total creative output, in chemistry at least, is brought about mainly by many persons making a few contributions each, rather than by a few persons making many contributions. The relationship between early creativity, recognition by others, and total eventual output also holds for English literature, physics, German literature, oil painting, composing grand opera, and philosophy. There is, therefore, a sort of triangular relation between eminence, productivity and early achievement. Relatively little is known, however, about the effects of juvenile development and experience on adult intellectual achievement.

Ageing affects not only the *rate* of intellectual achievement, but also the *kind* likely to be pursued. The creative achievements of older people are more likely to include published work previously presented by means of the spoken word –

lectures, personal memoirs and recollections. Older people write textbooks, which are often accumulations of specialized experience; they are frequently recognized for their achievements in the coordination of related areas of knowledge; they tend to complete work undertaken at a younger age or to revise earlier work; they excel at history; and, as one might expect, they write about old age.

A more detailed study of the *kinds* of achievement best suited to late life could be helpful, not only in unravelling the causes and conditions of age changes in intellectual output, but also in helping older research-workers to plan for their declining years.

(b) *Comment on Statistical and Methodological Issues in Lehman's Research*

Few people are so productive throughout their lives that their individual output shows the age relation clearly. But if the 1,086 patents taken out by Edison are arranged in chronological order, the highest number occurs at age 35 and the overall effect conforms to the general picture described above. The point on the age scale that divides output into two equal parts (early-appearing versus late-appearing) – the 'median' age – occurs *after* the age of 35, because the distribution of output, especially the distribution of high-quality output, is 'skewed'. Productivity is greater in the earlier part of the working life but continues right up to death, falling off in maturity and old age. The creative years are all the years between puberty and death. The age period around 35 years is merely the age at which the rate of achievement reaches a maximum. Lehman's findings most certainly do not imply that creative effort is worthless after the age of 35 or any later age. Individual differences apart, older adults have a great deal to contribute throughout their active lives as teachers, administrators, critics, historians and as creative thinkers in their own right.

Lehman's method constitutes an interesting departure from the usual run of gerontological investigations because it makes use of naturally occurring records, some of which can be cross-checked for consistency; in effect, it presents a lifespan account of human achievement by averaging the results for many subjects in overlapping longitudinal sets. Lehman examined secular trends in achievement but not specifically in relation to methodology. The methodological and statistical issues of research in ageing are taken up in Chapter Eleven.

The relationship between age and achievement varies because one type of performance, for example patenting electrical inventions, depends upon conditions different from those affecting another, such as painting pictures or making medical discoveries. It is difficult, therefore, to make exact comparisons for different *kinds* of achievement, and to achieve comparable levels of excellence in the different fields. Lehman's use of percentages was an attempt to overcome this difficulty. Despite the wealth of evidence and the careful arguments which characterize Lehman's research, objections have been raised about his methods and the interpretation of his results.[8-10] For example, some age trends based on the total output of long-lived creative people appear not to conform to those described by Lehman – possibly for a number of reasons not affecting Lehman's basic findings, including the fact that he took longevity into account. Variations on Lehman's method have been attempted.[11]

2. FACTORS AFFECTING AGE AND ACHIEVEMENT

Lehman suggested a number of contributory causes for the decline with age, after the early thirties, of achievement in the arts and sciences, although the exact role of each cause is not known. Some also play a part in the decline of intelligence and athletic achievement. Among these causes are: a decline in physical vigour and energy; a decline in sensory and motor capacities; physical and mental ill health; changes in motivation and attitudes; the encroachment of administrative and other kinds of duties; the negative transfer of obsolete ideas and methods. Factors other than those suggested by Lehman could be equally important, as follows: a decline in imagination; a decline in the speed of mental processes; a reduction in the amount of time devoted to creative work; loss of contact with creative people and new ideas; changes in interpersonal rivalry and cooperation; changes in the *nature* of scientific achievement, say from personal research to supervision of others; diminished incentives – pay, conditions, prestige and promotion – for creative work; failure to keep up with changes in scientific activity, as in the greater use of mathematics, computers and electronic instruments, and with new research methods and concepts; a disinclination to take professional risks.

There is nothing in Lehman's data to suggest that the best years for intellectual creativity *must* be in the early thirties. The lower limit of the trend towards earlier intellectual achievement probably lies somewhere near the age of 20, when intelligence, in the biological sense, has reached its maximum level of development; but as scientific achievement is always a product of both intelligence *and* experience, the maximum level of scientific ability must occur later.

Some of the factors mentioned above, contributing to a decline with age in intellectual achievements, operate because of age changes in the individual; others because of cultural or historical changes. Note the interlocking of social, psychological and biological influences. Case-studies and personal experience, as well as research investigations, have shown the relevance of some of these factors to the productivity of scientists, artists and writers; but we know very little about their *relative* importance for any class of people or any individual, or about the way they interact with each other to produce cumulative effects. There are probably counter-balancing forces – steady habits of work, the positive transfer of experience, improved opportunities and so on – which tend to maintain the quantity and quality of intellectual output after 30.

Lehman was unwilling to admit to a substantial decline with age in adult intelligence, arguing that adult intelligence is inextricably tied up with the motivation to think and to learn, and with the natural tendency to work from experience, which is greater for older people. The fixed attitudes, reduced physical stamina, poorer biological efficiency, and the less adequate environmental opportunities of older generations make it impossible, in his opinion, to compare their intelligence with that of younger generations. These factors obscure age differences in intelligence, but they are by no means as confusing as Lehman made out. Even highly motivated and persistent older subjects usually perform less efficiently on tests of intelligence than younger subjects (see Chapter Six). Furthermore, fixed (but now inappropriate) attitudes persisting into maturity and old age can be regarded as a sort of intellectual handicap which lowers the older person's effective intelligence. The biological, social, psychological and environmental causes of the relationship between age and intellectual achievement are not known – or rather, their relative importance, interaction and mode of operation are not known, but the general decline in intelligence and mental speed is an important contributory factor.

Creativity among established scientists sometimes finds indirect expression through the achievements of younger researchers working under their direction. In some cases but not in others, older scientists get the credit for work done by younger men. Delays in publication and the acceptance of new ideas means that, for younger people at least, the rates of output calculated by Lehman are two or three years *behind* the ages at which the actual intellectual work took place. Older people who have already made their mark professionally probably find it easier to publish, take out patents, or obtain facilities for further research.

One of the more serious effects of ageing is a fall in the rate at which a person can perform intellectual activities; so that even if the older person were capable of achieving high-grade performances, he would achieve fewer of them in a given period of time. The amount of time devoted to research can be an important factor governing the annual rate and total output of older workers because of a reduction in the speed at which they accomplish intellectual tasks. It is difficult to carry out adequate surveys which would throw light on this problem. The Robbins Report on Higher Education shows that professors in British universities appear to spend 27 per cent of their working time on research and private study, and 38 per cent of their time on administration and other work within the universities.[12] The percentages for non-professorial staff are something like 40 per cent and 20 per cent respectively, whereas for research staff they are 73 per cent and 11 per cent. The differences are large, but of course one would have to examine closely the actual number of hours worked, the nature of the research and a number of other circumstances before a true age decline in the time spent on creative work could be demonstrated.

Some creative work is done at unusual times and in unusual places; but the vagaries of creative imagination do not alter the fact that intelligence needs the raw materials of observation and experience in order to produce new intellectual constructions, and these assimilative and productive processes require time. The increased delay in creative conceptual processes can be demonstrated experimentally by timing performance on sorting tests. Three facts help to account for the decline with age in intellectual output: older men devote less time to creative work; they assimilate (and produce) new ideas more slowly; and their creative *capacity* is reduced.

One possible reason for the relatively rapid decline in quality of output is that 'superior quality' often means 'original', and an original contribution in art or science generally means a break-through into a new set of ideas, a new method, or a new set of facts. Such a break-through can be exploited not only by its originator but also by other workers. Exploring implications and *applying* new ideas, however, are usually regarded as requiring less ability than making original contributions. The often surprising and unpredictable process of scientific discovery seems to depend to a large extent upon chance and imagination rather than upon the more mundane, predictable and systematic (but typical) processes of scientific research. Sensitivity to problems and relations, and the ability to break through existing forms of thought and expression give the innovator in the arts and the sciences his rightful place in history. The ability to break through existing forms of thought probably depends upon unspecialized intelligence, whereas acquired specialist knowledge can be a hindrance. The systematic inquiries of the research-follower are made largely because he has acquired (not discovered) some specialized techniques of inquiry (or techniques of expression in art), namely, those that were developed by the innovator. The more familiar an idea or a method becomes, the less intellectual merit it has. Innovators, having produced new ideas, and having acquired something of a reputation because of them, are inclined and even encouraged to exploit them, rather than to produce more original ideas.

The effects of ageing on achievements of higher and lower merit cannot easily be explained by the factors which Lehman has chosen to emphasize. He says that the older person's waning interest and reduced efforts bring about a diminution in output, and that these factors are probably far more important than a decline in intellectual ability. But Lehman's own data clearly show that the *quantity* of work done by older scientists, philosophers, composers, writers and artists falls off more slowly than the *quality* of that work. If waning interest and reduced effort were the important factors, they should produce a decline in total output, with little or no difference between achievements of greater or lesser merit (unless the older person makes less effort to improve its standard).

The reduction with age in the quality of intellectual achievements could come about because the young innovator, having staked his claim to novel ideas and methods, spends his later years working out the more obvious implications and applications. The younger person hoping to work creatively must make new discoveries himself, unless he is merely to follow up the work of other men. This is a selective factor which directs younger men towards fresh fields of endeavour, since, as we have seen, 'quality' of achievement tends to be defined in terms of its originality.

Tests are being devised which, it is hoped, will distinguish between the more and the less imaginative subjects, even when these subjects have comparable scores on ordinary tests of unspecialized intelligence. The usual technique is to present the subject with a series of 'open-ended' problems, that is, problems which can be solved in different ways and at different levels of excellence or ingenuity.

The growth of 'team research' has led to increased interest in the dynamics of social interaction. We have seen that prolific thinkers produce ideas of superior quality; one explanation for this is that cross-fertilization occurs, in which ideas are combined to produce further ideas. A number of subjects acting together in a group can be expected to handle a problem better (find more and better solutions) than any member acting alone – for example, borough council members discussing town planning or a joint consultation committee discussing productivity. Team research must influence the effects of age on creative intellectual achievement, and the participation of older and younger people in a single research team (so combining imaginative fertility with wide experience) could be expected to have considerable advantages.

Experimental studies of creative intelligence, using open-ended tests, show that the effects of ageing are comparable with those observed by Lehman. Both the quantity and the quality of the responses decline with age, but the decline is more marked for the high-quality responses. The fact that creativity, as measured by open-ended tests, correlates highly, but not perfectly, with unspecialized intelligence gives further weight to the suggestion that much of the decline with age in creative intellectual achievement is accounted for by a decline in unspecialized intelligence, and a mental slowing down.

There is no reason to suppose that the age changes and the peak periods catalogued by Lehman are fixed and unalterable. Indeed, secular trends (discussed in Section 4), and the observed variations from one field of endeavour to another, suggest a complex network of causes and consequences, so that there is probably much that human beings could do to bring about improvements, once the critical influences are understood.

3. SOCIAL STATUS AND SPORT

(a) *Social Achievements*

In addition to studying the relation between chronological age and creativity in the arts and the sciences, Lehman studied many other kinds of human achievement. For example, he found that female film stars rise to fame at earlier ages and reach the peak of their fortunes earlier than do male film stars – 25 to 29 years, as compared with 30 to 34. The subsequent decline in the money-making achievements of female film stars is more rapid than for male stars. As with intellectual achievement, the decline with age after the peak years is more rapid for the higher levels of achievement. Film directors reach their peak between the ages of 35 and 39 and, with few exceptions, have ceased productive work by 55. Obviously, the decline with age in this sort of achievement is very rapid. It would be too simple, however, to argue that these results reflect a decline in the *ability* to act or to make films. The factors that bring about the rise and fall of actual achievement in any field are numerous and complex; biographies provide suitable case-studies to illustrate this point. In areas of achievement such as film acting, and to some extent in industrial and commercial leadership, the actual peak years for ability (whatever that means) are not known; so the age effects relate partly to status and reputation.

Age changes in the amount of money earned by people achieving very large incomes are quite different from those in intellectual achievement. The peak years for large earnings occur in the age period 53–58; but, taking into account the numbers of people alive in each age group, the largest *proportion* of people earning very large incomes is highest for the age period 60–64. A study of leadership and power in commerce and industry based on names and ages given in the 1938

American edition of *Who's Who in Commerce and Industry* shows that the biggest age group is 55–59; but, when account is taken of the number of people left alive at different ages, the highest proportion of leaders is in the age group 65–69 (although the proportions are high for all ages between 55 and 80). Further studies of the age factor in income, industrial leadership, commercial success and financial power show that the years of achievement occur relatively late in life, usually after the age of 60.

Lehman studied various kinds of social achievement: in government and politics, in military and judicial affairs, in learning and religion. Leadership and authority in these areas occurs relatively late in life, usually after the age of 40. For some reason, military leaders attain the peak of their profession between the ages of 40 and 44 as compared with naval leaders, whose most outstanding years are 55 to 59. Where exacting standards are set, as, for example, in plotting the age distribution of a small number of successful United States presidential candidates and comparing it with the age distribution for a larger number of unsuccessful candidates, the age of success starts later, in this example between 45 and 49; it has the same peak years, 55 to 59; and it terminates earlier, between the ages of 65 and 69. In other words, the effects of age on leadership are more pronounced for leaders of higher esteem than for leaders of lower esteem.

Lehman compared the age distributions for three kinds of achievement: founding a religious movement, being president of a religious organization, and being chief spiritual leader of the Roman Catholic Church. The age distribution for the religious innovators showed that a few were aged 20, but the vast majority were between 30 and 44; relatively few individuals over the age of 50 actually *founded* religious movements. The age distributions for the other two groups showed a steady increase in frequency from the age of 40 up to a peak period after the age of 80. Thus in religion, as in science, the arts, business and government, the years of creativity and innovation occur relatively early in life, between about 30 and 45, or earlier, but the years of consolidation, recognition and establishment occur later, from about 45 onwards. The influence of surrounding circumstances – opportunity, competition and so on – is perhaps even more obvious in relation to social achievement than in relation to achievement in the arts or sciences.

Leadership skills and opportunities occur fairly late in life, partly because of the balance of intelligence and experience (knowledge) required and partly because of cultural factors. The membership of older people on committees, councils and other bodies puts into their hands the machinery of social control. Their familiarity with this machinery – rules, procedures, rituals, ways and means, sources of information and the like – enables them to use their experience where a younger man's greater intelligence might avail him little. The study of smaller and simpler communities shows that even where longevity is not as great as it is in larger and more advanced communities, the elders tend to move into positions of authority, privilege and control.

One result of the decline with age in unspecialized intelligence and the increase with age in specialization and routinization of experience is that older people in responsible and influential social positions prefer older, familiar attitudes and methods, and resist the introduction of social reforms in, for example, penology, education and the armed forces, which they fail to appreciate.

(b) *Athletics and Sport*

Lehman found that the age of peak performance in athletics and sport was about 31 years. The biological effects of ageing on vigorous skills such as tennis, swimming, boxing and football appear earlier than on skills involving less physical effort but equal or greater coordination, such as billiards, golf and shooting. The peak years for championships in the more vigorous skills occur in the late twenties, whereas the peak years for the less physically exhausting sports occur in the early thirties. After the age of 31 there is a sharp fall in athletic and sporting achievement to the age of about 46. This rapid decline should not be interpreted as a sign that physical fitness declines early to a low level. Older men retain considerable capacity for muscular work, although their stamina, effort, coordination and speed in physical performance do not match those of younger men. As with other human capacities, the effects of age on physical prowess are most clearly revealed by testing to the limits.

4. SECULAR TRENDS

It is difficult to compare the merits of achievements occurring at different periods of history because of uncertainty regarding remote dates, changes in attitude towards publishing, and so on. The secular trend, in the age at which people achieve social eminence, is for later-born generations to attain status at older age levels as compared with earlier-born generations. This could be the effect of an increase in life expectation, plus the longer period of learning needed for leadership in modern societies. The opposite trend – in scientific achievement – might be produced by improvements in physical health and education, which lower the age of biological maturity and reduce the amount of time required to acquire the skills and knowledge needed to make original contributions to science. Despite the fact that there is much more knowledge, factual groupings and conceptual simplifications take place, so that knowledge becomes orderly and systematic, more specialized and easier to learn and remember – for example cell theory in molecula: biology. Improvements in education and in the techniques of acquiring knowledge – computers, libraries, scientific instruments, and so on – help to account for the secular trend in the age at which intellectual achievements occur most frequently. An increase in the average duration of life should make it possible to lengthen the range of the creative years, though without shifting the peak years for intellectual creativity. The age distribution for certain kinds of output is much the same for those who die early as for those who die late (where comparisons are made over the appropriate parts of the lifespan).

The historical shift in the age distribution of scientific achievements is considerable. In physics, for example, the rate of contribution of scientists born between 1785 and 1867 rose steadily from the age of 25 to a peak at the age of 35 and then declined steadily to 65; the rate of contribution for scientists born before 1785 rose steadily from the age of 25 to a peak at the age of 45 and then declined – sharply at first, then more steadily – to 75. Lehman published similar findings for many other areas of achievement. A comparison of early-born versus later-born individuals in chemistry, astronomy and oil-painting, however, failed to reveal similar findings. In some cases, the decline in output was sharper for the later-born contributors. Lehman suggested that the delay between achievement and recognition became shorter because of improvements in publishing and patenting, and this may help to explain why later-born persons seem to make their contributions at earlier ages than those born earlier. Social changes, furthermore, have taken art and science out of the hands of the amateurs and the privileged leisured classes and handed them over to full-time professionals.

The average age for peak performance in any one field sport is slightly higher for recently documented achievements than for those of earlier years. Lehman puts this down to the greater financial motivation in modern commercialized sport, and to improvements in physical health in recent years. It would not be surprising, however, to find that this trend has been reversed. In sport, and in the arts and sciences, the secular trends vary considerably from one field of endeavour to another; and it may prove possible, by carefully examining such variations, to reach more positive conclusions about the causes and conditions of age changes in performance, and to eliminate methodological artefacts.

The relation between age and leadership has been shown to contrast with that between age and intellectual creativity in the arts and sciences, and with physical accomplishment in sport. According to Lehman's data, the peak years for established leadership status occur between the ages of 50 and 70, whereas those for intellectual and sporting attainments occur between 20 and 40. Moreover, whereas social leaders appear on average to be older than their predecessors in similar positions, creative artists and scientists appear to be doing their best work at earlier ages. The distribution of achievements throughout the lifespan covers a wider range of years for earlier-born as compared with later-born generations. This effect could arise for a number of reasons, such as greater competitiveness, improvements in publication, financial incentives. Secular trends in health, education, and possibly intelligence further complicate the issue.

CHAPTER EIGHT

Personality and Adjustment in Middle Age and Old Age

A person's 'personality' is defined by the consistencies and regularities running through the behaviour episodes making up his life-history or some major phase of his life-history. These consistencies and regularities include any general fact that identifies the person and distinguishes him from other people of a similar sort. In normal usage, personality characteristics refer to the psychological and behavioural characteristics of the individual rather than to his biological and sociological characteristics (unless these are relevant to understanding his actions and states of mind).

1. APPROACHES TO THE STUDY OF PERSONALITY

The psychometric approach to the study of personality has traditionally focused on one issue, namely, traits. Traits are supposed to be stable psychophysiological dispositions within the person inclining him to react in 'characteristic' ways in given situations, as, for example, timidity, sociability, emotional control. This approach employs standardized tests, like questionnaires, to measure operationally-defined characteristics and uses the information thus obtained for the purposes of selection and counselling, and formulating theories.

The psychodynamic approach has focused on the feelings of the individual, for example on the causes and consequences of anxiety, guilt, depression, and on the forms of thought (beliefs, values, attitudes) through which the individual tries to establish some sort of working relationship with his environment. This approach employs clinical case-study methods to assess intuitively defined characteristics and uses the information for practical purposes, especially for the therapeutic treatment of deviants and maladjusted people.

The distinction between the psychometric and the psychodynamic approaches is not sharp; theorists and practitioners borrow concepts and methods from both. Biographical analysis, for example, combines useful features from both approaches and seems to be particularly appropriate for the study of personality and adjustment in adult life and old age.[1]

People with broadly similar endowments brought up in similar ways develop comparable modes of adjustment, in the sense that they can be compared with reference to common standards or scales of measurement. In this way, by surveying, for example, spending habits, sexual behaviour, interests and personality traits, we can make comparisons between men and women, between people from different social classes, and between different generations of people. We can also study changes *within* the same subjects as they grow older or respond to different environmental factors, such as stress.

So-called 'objective' methods for assessing personality and adjustment have been used extensively in gerontological research to measure changes with age in marital happiness, leisure-time interests, introversion, depression and so on. Unfortunately, little or no attention has been paid to the extent to which standard measures of personality and adjustment are valid and reliable for different adult ages. In the absence of relevant evidence, an observed change or difference in score could be interpreted as a shift in the meaning or validity of the test score rather than a genuine change in a psychological attribute.

The methodological problems of studying ageing are difficult enough without the further complications that arise in connection with the methods and concepts of personality study. Nevertheless, psychologists use psychometric methods in their attempts to study the effects of ageing on the 'dimensions' of personality and adjustment.[2-5] A wide variety of methods can be applied, as follows. Rating scales and self-ratings used in conjunction with flexible interviews yield quantitative data about personal qualities, motivation and complex attitudes. Probing questionnaires enable the investigator to examine in detail such activities as: spending habits, leisure-time activities, social contacts and television viewing. Non-directive interviews explore the older person's private world of wishes, personal feelings and social attitudes, and they assess his self-concept. Standardized verbal scales measure the older person's traits, morale, interests, values, beliefs and opinions. Projective methods (interpreting ink-blots, completing sentences or building a story around a picture) are thought to reveal, indirectly, motives and attitudes, and ways of dealing with the world. Projective tests are open to a number of objections on scientific grounds, but it is claimed that they show changes with age in the achievement needs of older people, and growing tendencies towards inactivity, submission and introspection.[6-8] Affiliative needs appear to become deeper and more selective. Older subjects express less emotional involvement in the activities they describe, less worry, and less assertiveness. Their lives and surroundings become simpler.

Biographical analysis includes a range of methods, for example the content analysis of diaries and autobiographies, life-history interviews and inventories. The aim is to identify common features in the lives of people who, for example, become maladjusted or live exceptionally long lives. The attempt to 'average out' patterns of behaviour and experience for people in general is obviously not very productive of new insights; what is required is the biographical analysis of specific and well-defined groups, such as unmarried female teachers or army officers. Biographical diversity is to be expected even within these relatively narrow groups, but the age trends should average out more clearly, and the results would be of general interest in sociology and psychology. Biographical analysis cannot achieve the impossible – it cannot provide a comprehensive life-history account of the average man (or woman). At best it can deal in detail with only one segment (a series of episodes) in a person's life, or deal superficially with his life-history as a whole. It would be interesting to examine those events which the person himself regards as making up his life-history. What is it that gives them psychological significance and fixes them in his memory?

The reasons usually offered for using these methods rather than relying upon common experience are, firstly, that they are quick and convenient; secondly, they increase the range of observation; thirdly, they improve objectivity and quantification, and so help to provide more systematic evidence about ageing. They can be used in all kinds of research: drug trials, attitudes of supervisors to older workers, age changes in interests, attitudes to retirement, age changes in confidence, anxiety and other aspects of personality and adjustment, and capacity for self-care. Capacity for self-care, however, is a topic which illustrates that methods which give quick and convenient, but indirect, measures of behaviour and experience in adult life and old age may be invalid; they may lead the investigator to draw the wrong conclusion, in that responses to a questionnaire may not correspond with the results from direct observations of subjects in their normal surroundings. Similarly, subjects may over-estimate or under-estimate their physical health, depending upon the specific questions asked and the standard of comparison used. An elderly man may claim to be able to wash and dress without difficulty, to do his shopping, and to take care when crossing roads, though actual observation may reveal that he is much less competent than he claims. Similarly, he may say that he has very few visitors, when he has more than the average. Verbal reports from subjects of all ages need corroboration. A further disadvantage of such questionnaires and verbal scales is that they need to be 're-calibrated', as it were, to suit the particular cultural conditions of the samples being investigated. It is important, therefore, to test the validity of methods of assessing personal adjustment, especially in relation to life-satisfaction and the activities of daily living, so that benefits go to those who are most in need of them.[9]

Older people responding to an attitude scale use the more extreme response categories, possibly because they prefer a simple (unambiguous) situation. They are probably more prone to 'response styles' than younger subjects or, more likely, prone to different response styles. For example, under certain conditions they use the 'Don't Know' category less often than younger people. In addition, they more often omit items, possibly because they are afraid of making mistakes, or are unable to think of satisfactory solutions, or because of a loss of attention.

There is surprisingly little systematic evidence of the attitudes and beliefs held *by* adults of different ages, or of those held *about* adults of different ages. It is not known whether the determinants and processes of attitude formation change with age. Attitudes, beliefs and values, however, are expressed in all kinds of direct and indirect ways in everyday behaviour, for example in consumer behaviour, voting and the expression of opinion.[10-12] Some ambivalence towards the aged is common. We feel love and affection and a sense of responsibility for our parents, grandparents and elderly relatives (and by association, other elderly people), although hostile attitudes with their roots in early parent–child relationships may persist throughout life. Younger people may resent the burdens imposed by the elderly, and the authority and wealth that the latter are slow to relinquish.

Whether a person thinks of himself as young, middle-aged or old depends upon many things – not merely his calendar age, but also his physical health and outward appearance, the way he is treated by other people, and the prevailing social norms and attitudes regarding age differences. Realizing that one has become older can be amusing as well as depressing and is a common experience in early middle age.

Young adults and middle-aged people, in the United States at least, agree in most of their beliefs about the elderly. More young adults, however, believe that older people live for some time after they retire and are frequently at a loose end, whereas about half the middle-aged adults believe that people die soon after retirement. Younger people believe that older people need less sleep, whereas only about a half of the middle-aged subjects share this belief. Many younger men (but not younger women) resent the power that old people have in business and in politics. Very few elderly persons think of old age as the most satisfactory period of their life. Most of them choose early childhood as the happiest period, and old age as the least happy. Negative attitudes towards old age are frequent, but less marked among elderly people who are financially secure, in good health, and capable of leading a relatively independent life.

The stages and facets of adult life described in Chapter One correspond broadly to those known to common sense and confirmed by biographical analysis. These include, for example, the transition from school to work, from the single state to marriage. Subsequently, there are transitions through occupational and family stages of adult development. The years of investment, expansion and effort give way to the 'harvest' years of middle age, and to its later phases of reassessment and reorganization. Retirement naturally ushers in changes in some facets of life, but rarely induces serious discontinuities. Old age and terminal behaviour complete the series – physiological factors dominate the situation and life is reduced to its more basic dimensions. The study of personality in adult life and old age has been conceived as a developmental study of these stages and transitions in the life-cycle.[13-15]

2. MOTIVATION AND FRUSTRATION IN ADULT LIFE

Motivation in general (drive) appears to decrease in old age, probably because of decreased energy and poorer arousal mechanisms; some kinds of motivation, including sexuality, fall off fairly steadily. It is common experience that old people have less intense enthusiasms, and frequently need strong incentives, support and encouragement to embark on a new course of action. Age changes in motivation, however, are very much a matter of continuity and development, depending upon temperamental qualities and experiences in life.

Human interests are varied and closely associated with historical changes (for example, television viewing and motoring) which make cross-sectional comparisons difficult. Moreover, age changes in leisure-time interests are obscured by situational influences such as local opportunities and cost. The general trends can be predicted from what is already known about the effects of age on physical health, speed of performance and intelligence, namely, a trend away from participa-

TABLE 3

Percentage of leisure periods for activities cited as the chief pursuit

Activity	*Males Age 46–60 married without children under 15*	*Age 61+ retired*	*Females Age 46–60 married without children under 15*	*Age 61+ married*	*Age 61+ widowed*
Television	24	21	23	29	25
Reading	4	8	8	10	13
Crafts and hobbies	3	4	15	14	12
Decorating/car maintenance	9	2	2	—	1
Gardening	15	18	9	9	5
Social activities	3	5	9	6	14
Drinking	1	2	1	—	1
Cinema and theatre	—	—	—	—	—
Non-physical recreation and spectator	9	6	6	6	5
Physical recreation	8	3	2	1	—
Excursions	9	4	10	6	2
Parks and walks	5	11	4	8	5
Other	7	10	5	8	10
Not known	3	6	6	3	7

Adapted from Table 22, p. 65, *Social Trends, No. 2,* 1971

tion to spectatorship, a trend towards less energetic and less hazardous activities, and a trend towards self-paced and passive interests, such as gardening, reading, television viewing and simple amusements.[16]

A person's long-range aims and the established patterns of social interaction at home, at work or elsewhere provide a framework within which he plays his part in life. Thus the stability, coherence and consistency characteristic of the well-adjusted person arises not only from *within*, from stable dispositions of personality and temperament, but also from *without*, from the controlling, stabilizing and directing influences of his physical and social environment – his family and domestic circumstances, his work, his interpersonal relationships, money, material possessions and geographical position. He is, in part, a 'creature of circumstance'. When he retires some of this external physical and social framework is removed, and he has to change his ways; if he has not prepared for retirement, adjustment is more difficult.

Motivation and affect are difficult to investigate because of the problem of making inferences about inner experience, capacity or disposition from observable behaviour. Methods of studying motivation and affect are broadly the same as those found in the study of personality and adjustment (of which motivation and affect are part) and include physiological procedures.

Under conditions of frustration and emotional stress, a person's motivational state becomes strongly focused on the immediate future, concerned with protecting his self-interests and mobilizing his inner resources. During early adult life, presumably, as in juvenile development, motivation towards expansion of the ego predominates, although the stresses of adult development in a competitive achieving society produce a certain amount of frustration. In middle age, some kind of equilibrium seems to be established for most people. In later life, however, motivation towards withdrawal, avoidance and substitution predominates, because the person's physical and psychological resources cannot sustain the demands being made upon them. A serious sort of frustration is that engendered by any persistent, stressful, no-solution situation which first elicits violent reactions such as anger or undirected frenzy, and eventually leads to despair, apathetic resignation or stereotyped pathological responses. This might be a useful paradigm for the study of abnormal behaviour in later life.

Frustration during late maturity and old age can arise for a number of reasons including: adverse physiological changes and restrictions on activity; occupational redundancy; failure of occupational aspirations, with a consequent limitation of living standards; failure to keep pace with cultural, social and scientific developments, leading to the feeling of being out of date and out of touch; loss of youthful vigour and freedom, coupled with the uninviting prospect of growing old, usually reinforced by prevailing social attitudes; loss of valued or stabilizing emotional relationships through bereavement; loss of employment or the departure of children; the 'no-solution' problem of being caught in a web of unsatisfactory circumstances from which escape seems impossible, such as family ties, physical disability or lack of money.

Critical episodes at any time of life can bring about new attitudes and new adjustments. Some events are experienced by the person as traumatic, for example going bankrupt, being divorced, or becoming deaf. Such episodes mark brief periods of conflict, frustration and unhappiness, and may result in considerable reorganization of the person's motives and actions. While leaving a scar, they need not undermine (and may even strengthen) the person's emotional stability. Other formative experiences can be very gratifying, for example, falling in love, coming into money, or achieving success in cultural or scientific work. In old age, being well-adjusted means being emotionally stable and resourceful in adapting to changed circumstances like bereavement, retirement, ill health or loss of employment. Except in conditions of senescent mental disorder the basic structure of the personality appears to be maintained, perhaps simplified and more clearly delineated, throughout late maturity and old age.

Physical changes in the nervous system and endocrine system are bound to have repercussions on motivational states and affective expression – for example, on sexual behaviour and temperament. Age changes in motivation can be expected to have pervasive effects on other aspects of the process of adjustment: attitudes, decision processes and learning. Such changes are not wholly endogenous; latent desires can be activated if the environment contains incentives, that is opportunities for their fulfilment. Similarly, motivation may diminish if opportunities for satisfaction are persistently curtailed. Exogenous, i.e. environmental, conditions and reinforcement contingencies thus 'shape' the motivational characteristics of older people, for example by decreasing opportunities for sex and physical adventure, and by increasing opportunities for family activities and sleep.

The combined effects of endogenous and exogenous factors lead to behaviour which is difficult to interpret in terms of motivation. In fact, motivational concepts are logically suspect. Hence any description of age changes in motivation is difficult to substantiate, especially if the behavioural evidence is indirect, in the form of responses to projective tests or questionnaires. The question is whether motivational interpretations of age changes can or should be de-emphasized in favour of more strictly behavioural concepts – stimulus conditions and reinforcement history. For example, the so-called 'crisis points' in adult life could be understood not as intrinsic phases in motivational development but as the fortuitous effects of a way of life.

The existence of powerful situational constraints on behaviour, and of powerful conditioning influences, provides a challenge to the view that 'personality' factors are the prime determinants of individual adjustment. The failure to identify and accurately measure the basic dimensions of personality, at least to anything like the same extent as other determinants of behaviour, reduces the value of standardized tests in the assessment of the effects of ageing. This point of view must not be taken as a rejection of the psychometric approach to personality and ageing, but rather as a caution against uncritical acceptance of its claims.

3. THE SELF-CONCEPT

Although most personality characteristics appear not to be as consistent across situations as some investigators had supposed, characteristics relating to the self-concept are fairly consistent in young adults. But is it reasonable to believe that they are fairly stable in relation to ageing? We are on such close and familiar terms with ourselves that we are not likely to register age changes in our self-concept, just as we scarcely register changes in our physical appearance. Our appearance, however, is an external fact and can be compared against photographic records, whereas only people who diligently keep personal diaries can observe age changes in the self.

The view that one's impression of oneself stays very much the same throughout adult life is not unreasonable if we accept that the major formative experiences take place in the early years, with adult development making only marginal modifications. On the other hand, the experiences of adult life are cumulative, and for some people a number of them are intense. Biological changes and personal experiences in adult life are bound to have some effects on personality and adjustment, but any effects have yet to be adequately described and analysed. Any effects on the *self-concept* are also uncertain.[17]

The self-concept is difficult to investigate. The methods employed in research include: adjective check-lists, self-ratings, projective tests, and the content-analysis of self-descriptions. The apparent increase with age in anxiety, introversion and neuroticism, and the apparent decrease in risk-taking and confidence, point to some sort of age change in the self-concept.[18,19] Presumably we form a more unfavourable impression of ourselves as we grow older. The negative value placed on later ages supports this idea. Aspirations normally exceed achievements, and as long as the individual feels that he still has time, resources and opportunities, he can ignore the discrepancy. Eventually, however, he must realize that the discrepancy is there to stay, and he may blame his 'failure' on himself.

The psychodynamic approach to normal ageing is essentially a psychology of 'ego functions'. That is to say, it is concerned with changes in self-awareness, self–other relationships, strategies of adjustment, and the control and expression of feelings. In some psychiatric disorders of late onset, patients exhibit a variety of neurotic and psychotic symptoms, some of which lend themselves to psychoanalytic interpretation (e.g. melancholia). One psychodynamic account of ageing suggests that after several juvenile stages of ego development, the young adult either develops an affective and functional relationship of intimacy (usually with a marital partner) or suffers a sense of personal isolation; in middle age the person either becomes generative, i.e. behaviourally and psychologically expanded and future-oriented, or suffers a sense of personal stagnation; the elderly person, finally, either achieves a sense of integrity, i.e. realism, or begins to despair.[20]

Throughout normal adult life, people are faced with the problem of adjusting their values and attitudes to their changing circumstances and to their changing physical and psychological capacities. These readjustments affect every facet of behaviour and experience – sexual relationships, parenthood, work, leisure, social attitudes, self-regard and so on. The inner experience of old age has been given some expression in literature, but has so far received little scientific attention.[21-22]

4. MIDDLE AGE

(a) *The Concept of Middle Age*

One of the difficulties with the term 'middle age' is that it is ambiguous. It does not refer to any well-defined phase in the human life-cycle and it means different things to different people – depending upon whether they are younger or older, male or female. Nevertheless, middle age is a convenient fiction in so far as it points to an important aspect of adult psychology which has received little attention from gerontologists until very recently.[23]

We have seen that the so-called 'normal adult' period extends from the late teens to retirement age or beyond – though this span of 40 or more years does not, of course, constitute an entirely unchanging phase of the lifespan. During this period, the biological effects of ageing are gradual and cumulative but relatively unobtrusive. There are compensatory changes in physiological and behavioural processes and the individual generally has adequate time and opportunity to adapt to his changing capacities and circumstances.

There are no reliable biological or behavioural markers for middle age, except perhaps the menopause; but this is not a satisfactory marker, because it is quite variable in terms of chronological age. Post-menopausal women, however, appear to lose some of the protection they enjoyed against coronary artery disease as a consequence of changes in hormone balance. Contrary to popular belief, the menopause is not associated with uniform behavioural consequences such as emotional upsets. The existence of the so-called 'male climacteric' is doubtful, although the notion has been invoked as an explanation for marked changes in the mid-life behaviour of some men. The age of 40 is popularly thought of as the transition point into middle age; this corresponds with the age at which the average working man in Britain enters the second half of his working life. Among women, child-bearing is usually complete and the biological changes associated with the menopause are beginning, the average age of women at the menopause being about 47. The mid-point of the adult portion of the human life-cycle is between 45 and 50 for men and between 50 and 55 for women. At this age the average man or woman can expect to live for about another 25 years. This mid-adult age, however, is merely a statistical fact of no particular biological or behavioural significance.

In the popular imagination middle age is associated with comfortable, settled, domestic and occupational routines. Middle-aged people are popularly thought of as fairly sedate and conservative, a little past the excitements and discoveries of youth. In professional work, people are usually middle-aged before they become 'established'. Hence, middle-aged people are in a stronger position financially and as regards authority and influence than other age groups.

Thus, middle age does not refer to the earlier stage of life when people in competitive achieving societies are making their way through successive occupational levels and establishing a network of family members and lasting friendships. Nor does it refer to the later stage of life when they are preparing to disengage from their main occupational role. So, in some respects, middle age is a high point in the life-cycle. Lying roughly between the ages of 40 and 60, it finds the individual in a fairly good state of health; his psychological capacities are relatively unimpaired, and he has accumulated considerable experience which he can use to advantage at work, or in public or domestic affairs. He is as well off, secure and privileged as he is ever likely to be. The physical vigour of youth may have passed or the supposed tranquillity of old age not yet arrived, but over all 'middle' age compares favourably with other ages, and is indeed sometimes referred to as the 'prime' of life.

(b) *Physical Health in the Middle Years*

The apparent stability of the middle years is, however, something of an illusion brought about by psychological adaptation. For example, familiarity with our own behaviour and physical appearance, and that of close kin and friends, means that we do not register the slow but inexorable effects of ageing – only when people renew acquaintance after a period of separation do age changes appear so noticeable. Although there is a surprising lack of evidence on the issue, it is likely that the adverse biological and behavioural consequences of ageing consist in part of stepwise changes consequent upon illness, accidents and stresses affecting a critical function, and of threshold effects resulting from the building up of many small intrinsic changes.

The biological hazards of the middle years are different

from those at other ages. Ill health arises from a variety of interrelated causes, and one remedy does not usually result in a substantial improvement in health. The death rate is two or three times higher in the second half of middle age than in the first half, i.e. between about 20 and 45. The main causes of death are cancer, heart disease, strokes and respiratory disease. Coronary heart disease is associated with unhealthy living habits, such as smoking, drinking, lack of physical exercise, and inappropriate diet. The proportion of people who are ill rises gradually to about the age of 45 or 50 and then accelerates fairly sharply. The full extent of psychiatric ill health in middle age has yet to be determined but the most common psychiatric ailment is depression. Neurotic and psychosomatic disorders also increase in frequency. Suicide accounts for a very small proportion of deaths in middle age, but suicide and attempted suicide increase in middle age and are more common amongst men.

Cross-cultural comparisons reveal substantial differences in death-rates and causes of death in middle age, even between advanced societies. In recent years, the life expectancy of women in middle age appears to have been improving more than that of men, in spite of the fact that the death rate for men is already about twice that of women. The picture is complicated by regional and secular variations within different countries.

Physical and mental ill health in the middle years imposes demands on the hospital services and on the general medical and welfare services; it leads to absence from work, low productivity and economic loss, as well as to difficulties in personal adjustment and interpersonal relationships. Much of this ill health could be prevented or reduced by earlier treatment, health education and medical screening. Various forms of treatment have been developed, including surgery, drugs, prosthetic aids and, more recently, behaviour modification for psychiatric disorders.

For some people, serious physical or mental ill health forces an abrupt and major readjustment in their way of life, and the acceptance of restrictions that they would have previously thought intolerable. For the majority, however, the biological changes of middle age are gradual. They are adapted to without radical alteration in the individual's self-image or daily activities. Nevertheless, the effects are cumulative, and the individual is eventually obliged to accept the fact that he is no longer 'young'. This may be brought home to him through reductions in work capacity, loss of sexual powers, incidental experiences in daily life, and comparisons with other people regarding physical appearance, career status, and so on. This realization is usually intermittent and partial at first, but conviction and acceptance of the fact come gradually through experience.[24]

People in middle age are often concerned with their health, whereas young adults take their physical condition for granted and are relatively free of minor ailments. The cumulative effects of normal ageing and the increased prevalence of definite physical and mental disorders in the middle-aged create a heightened awareness of their state of health regarding weight, digestion, sleep, aches and pains, and the like. Absence from work because of sickness rises sharply from about the age of 45; frequency of consultation with a physician increases to about six times a year on average. Many middle-aged people, however, are grossly ignorant of matters relating to human biology, and their attempts to improve their appearance and physical fitness or to alleviate minor medical conditions are often unsuccessful. The maintenance of physical fitness, in the strong sense, requires more dedication and resources than many middle-aged persons can muster.

The gradual realization that one is growing older leads to a number of behavioural changes at home and work, in leisure activities and social interests. Many people avoid activities inappropriate to their 'middle-aged' status. This status is, however, not clearly defined by chronological age but rather by self-assessment and social pressures, so that middle-aged people can quite easily take part in activities appropriate for either younger or older people. Age segregation is indeed much less marked than in adolescence or late life, and one of the joys of middle age is the realization that one can often *make* the social rules instead of feeling constrained by those already in existence.

(c) *Socio-economic Factors in Adjustment to the Middle Years*

In Britain, men in manual work achieve their highest earnings in their forties as compared with the fifties for men in non-manual work. Women in manual work reach their peak in their late twenties as compared with women in non-manual work, who have fairly constant earnings over their working life. These differences point to the possibility that the psychological and behavioural features of middle age depend to some extent upon socio-economic class.

Income and living standards tend to improve with age. The 'trajectory' of socio-economic status, however, varies between the two broad social classes. The average working-class man has passed his peak earning capacity by the age of 40, whereas the middle-class man does not do so until 50. Although non-manual earnings start at a lower level at the beginning of the working life, they soon overtake manual earnings and exceed them substantially after the age of 30. Partly as a consequence of their higher earnings and initial financial assets, and partly as a result of their education and values, middle-class people are more likely to acquire material and financial assets, and to find time and opportunities for constructive leisure and social advancement. Working-class people are much less likely to have these advantages, and therefore view middle age differently. Retirement and preparation for retirement are also viewed differently. Working-class men do not have the time and resources to prepare adequately for retirement. Hence they face a more serious reduction in their social and economic status and in the activities of daily living when they retire than do men in the professional and managerial occupations. Middle-class people do not have the same degree of insecurity in the pre-retirement period, and they can maintain a substantial degree of continuity throughout their later years. This probably contributes to the stability of their self-image, social interaction, and mental health.[25]

If this line of reasoning is sound, socio-economic factors should contribute to an earlier feeling of being middle-aged in working-class people, as compared with middle-class people. The working man may feel that he is 'too old at forty': he reconciles himself to such security and status as he has managed to achieve and settles down to a comfortable routine. The professional man, on the other hand, feels that 'life begins at forty': he has probably achieved a high standard of living and family security, and he can now afford to relax more and enjoy his leisure.

(d) *Sex Differences in Middle Age*

The adult developmental status of married women is closely tied to the following sequence of events: first employment, marriage, birth of first and subsequent children, entry into school of the last child and re-entry into paid employment, departure from home of last child, birth of grandchildren, retirement from paid employment, husband's retirement, husband's death. There appears to be little information on the adult development of single women following a career in full-time paid employment. Divorced women usually marry again. The middle age of a married woman is largely shaped by her marital circumstances, her family and neighbourhood roles. It starts with the release from responsibility for the daytime care and control of her children. This is a gradual rather than an abrupt process, and is affected by such factors as the number and ages of the children, their schooling and employment, and so on. It coincides broadly with the onset of middle age for her husband. Much of the married woman's domestic life continues unchanged in middle age because social and family activities easily fill the time formerly occupied in looking after her own children. More married women are returning to paid employment after 30, when their last child has entered school. Nowadays the average age distribution of life-history events differs considerably from that of former days; in particular, a woman's age at the marriage of her last child has decreased from about 55 to 45 since the end of the nineteenth century.

Marital relationships appear to deteriorate on average from early adult life to middle age. The currently increasing role of divorce – representing perhaps the tip of the iceberg of marital disharmony – supports this idea. Marriage partners feel less satisfied with the relationship, are less happy, and less likely to agree. Moreover, sexual activity decreases with age and, in the United States at least, people report less sharing of interests and activities in the later years of marriage.[26] The effects of age on sexual behaviour are dealt with briefly in Chapter Three, Section 3.

Some women are predisposed to physical and psychological disorders precipitated by age changes and the emotional stresses of adult life. The incidence of emotional maladjustment is higher for women than for men, although the suicide rate is lower.[27] Substantial differences between men and women in death rates for selected causes suggest that some high-risk disorders in men could be avoided, such as lung cancer and heart disease.

Whereas men become more concerned with their own health and anxious to maintain their functional efficiency (at work and play), women become more concerned with their husband's health. That is to say, men engage in what is called 'body monitoring' whereas women engage more in 'rehearsal for widowhood', in the sense that they engage in fantasies of what they would do if their husband fell ill, died or became mentally disturbed, and may press for assurances that they will be provided for in the event of bereavement.

A further aspect of sex differences in middle age concerns the fact that men and women hold different values. In women, the physical and psychological attributes of sexual attractiveness are highly valued in the late teens and early twenties. These are soon supplemented and then largely replaced by the socially valued attributes associated with being a wife and mother. In men, the physical and psychological attributes of masculinity can be sustained almost indefinitely, not because there is no loss in virility, physique and appearance but because masculine virtues – vigour, competence, strength, courage – can find direct expression in sexual and parental activities, and metaphorical or symbolic expression in work and leisure activities.

(e) *Some Advantages of Middle Age*

People who achieve socio-economic security and maintain good health can find middle age very rewarding. About three quarters of the total intellectual output of scientists and writers is distributed over the age-range 30 to 59. Half the discoveries and developments in medicine and psychology are made after the age of 40. The years between 30 and 59 account for about 70 or 80 per cent of the total time spent in important posts in political, military and industrial institutions. Social positions held in high regard involving ritual and ceremonial functions, for example in religion, government or law, are rarely occupied before middle age, although many elderly people hold such positions. Personal authority and esteem are likely to reach their maximum in middle age even in more ordinary walks of life.

The accumulated experience and stabilized attitudes of middle age make it easier to respond effectively to the normal demands of the environment – even physical performance, as in driving or athletics, is modified by experience. By the time they reach middle age most people are established in a 'psychological niche'; that is to say, they have become adapted to a limited environment and their adjustment to the activities of daily living has been reduced to a regular routine. This can improve life considerably, through feelings of security and fulfilment for example, and the avoidance of stress and anxiety. One disadvantage in all this is that the behavioural niche may become a rut. Experience provides the perspective and patience needed to make sound judgements and to work out the implications of decisions and actions. Thus we are relieved of the burden of having to think afresh each time we are faced with a problem, and we feel more confidence in decisions based on experience. The middle-aged person often has a wide range of social contacts and is thus in a good position to collect information and solve problems, as in business or scientific research.

(f) *The Inner Experience of Middle Age*

We have seen that some middle-aged people achieve a high degree of security, and their outward forms of behaviour become stable and regular to the point of routine. Their thoughts, feelings and desires have also been shaped by experience to become conformist, square and unadventurous. One is led to wonder whether or to what extent flexible and creative states of mind can be maintained within such a secure and regular framework of behaviour. For other people, middle age is a time of achievement and gratification. Far from leading a humdrum existence, their circumstances call for enterprise, self-reliance and determination.

One can draw an analogy between the course of a person's life and the log of a journey. In this analogy, middle age represents a critical choice-point at which the individual tries to review his progress so far and make decisions about the rest of the journey. In a sense, the individual constructs a private version of his own life-history, and during middle age, as at other ages, he tries to integrate the various strands in it so as to make a coherent narrative. His life-review is not necessarily attuned to reality, because his recollections are likely to be selected and distorted in order to minimize any feelings of anxiety, guilt and regret.

The middle-aged person's subjective account of his life so far is not just a matter of adding the latest instalment to the series told at earlier ages. It is rather a matter of enlarging the story and revising it in the light of recent events and experiences. Self-justification no doubt plays an important part in reshaping the story, but the process is also purposive, in the sense that the individual is trying to make sense of the past so that he can understand the present, and plan for the future more effectively. Biographical and autobiographical analysis already have an established place in social and behavioural gerontology and are among the more promising methods for studying the inner experience of adult life and old age.

Middle age constitutes a kind of vantage point in the geography of personal experience. Retrospectively, the terrain looks different from the way it appeared during the journey, and we see that we might have traversed it differently. Prospectively, the terrain looks limited and somewhat bleak, especially in the distance. We may decide therefore that the best strategy is to simplify the rest of the journey by being much more selective and realistic in our choice of objectives, and by mobilizing and conserving our resources to maximize the likelihood of success. This view of the future differs from that of the young person who has not yet discovered his capacities and limitations and finds it difficult to formulate long-range strategies in view of life's uncertainties. At fifty, however, our personal future seems to be shrinking rapidly, and we begin to look at the sand in the upper half of the hour-glass. The realization that one has only a further expectation of 23 years (28 for women) – or worse, perhaps only 15 or 20 productive years – has different effects on different people. Some concentrate their minds on important unfinished business and set about reappraising their activities and aims in life. Others feel depressed and demoralized. Most, no doubt, fall somewhere between these two extremes – uncertain of their self-assessment, not disposed to schedule their time rigorously, and inclined either not to think about the problem or to compromise and adapt to prevailing circumstances.

Perhaps the most important aspect of the inner experience of middle age is the intermittent realization that the circumstances and events of our life so far have had cumulative and long-term consequences which have created a set of constraints and limited opportunities which form the inescapable matrix out of which our future actions are born. If we have been fortunate and have managed our lives well we may feel very satisfied with the outcome so far; if not, then the growing realization that our freedom of action is becoming severely restricted may precipitate adverse reactions ranging from momentary flashes of regret and anger to psychologically disabling feelings of depression and hopelessness. As middle age continues, the individual becomes increasingly aware that the chances of breaking out of the web of circumstances in which (perhaps erroneously) he feels enmeshed are rapidly diminishing. For some individuals this constitutes a kind of mid-life crisis which results in severe maladjustment or suicide (as a response to a no-solution situation), or in radical deviations in behaviour – marital break-up, emigration, change of occupation. For others, the only way out is a radical change in fortune.

In the process of comparing ourselves with others, we identify with people who have lived through the same historical episodes – military service, political events, socio-technical changes – and who have been conditioned by them in the same way. Hence the tendency to distinguish different 'generations' of people – the post-war generation, the 'beat' generation, and so on.[28,29] This identification strengthens the assertion that middle age is a state of mind. If, in our own private view of ourselves in comparison with other people, we define ourselves as middle-aged, and act accordingly, then we are, in a real sense, middle-aged. Naturally, there are differences between individuals in the terms of reference used for such comparisons. For example, the 50-year-old stockbroker may have much the same picture of middle age as a 50-year-old lawyer or architect, but this picture may differ from that of the dock-worker, artist, or politician of the same age.

Middle-aged people also compare themselves with others in respect of health, circumstances, appearance, career grade and so on. In association with the process of life-review, such self–other comparisons may increase or decrease their feelings of self-esteem, making them feel happier and more confident or disappointed and guilty. Inadequate self-assessment means that the person has a false picture of his resources and prospects; he may grossly overrate himself and fail to appreciate the limited freedom he has to control his own fate; he may forget that he has to live with the consequences of his actions. By contrast, the person who underrates himself never discovers what he could have become.

In middle age, as at other ages, self-assessment and self–other comparisons are usually related to social values. Adults prefer to look younger than they are, to be healthier and more vigorous than average for their age, to achieve acclaim or seniority while they are still relatively young. In these and in other ways they maintain a check on their adult developmental status. Although each of us has his own unique frame of reference for making such comparisons, the basic criteria we use are broadly similar to those that other people use, since we share with them a similar cultural background – norms, attitudes and values.

A prominent feature of middle age, then, is the inner experience, the state of mind. The foregoing account, however, may be in error to the extent that it over-intellectualizes the process of mid-life adjustment. There are many men and women who are not by education or inclination disposed to the kind of reflective thought just described. For these people, middle age is not so much an experience as a way of life.

5. OLD AGE

(a) *Outline of the Research Methods and Findings of Reichard, Livson and Petersen*

Some interesting findings and ideas have been described in *Aging and personality: A Study of Eighty-Seven Older Men* by Suzanne Reichard, Florine Livson and P. G. Petersen.[30] The study was carried out in the U.S.A., but the findings appear to be applicable to old people in Britain. The methods used were intensive interviews, ratings and psychological tests. The subjects were men between the ages of 55 and 84, half of them retired and half still in full- or part-time employment. They were volunteer subjects and probably better adjusted than most older men. The methods and concepts are promising and could lead to important advances in the difficult field of personality research and ageing.

The retired men were less active in recreations, compared with those still in employment, but more active in domestic jobs, household maintenance, social visiting and the pursuit of productive hobbies. They showed as much, if not more, political interest, especially in relation to pensions and earnings. They stressed the disadvantages of retirement and the advantages of working for a living, whereas the individuals still at work stressed the value of leisure in retirement and tended to underestimate the advantages of working and earning. Many of the employed subjects were anxious about their impending retirement, but few of those retired were upset at not working for a living. They complained only about their reduced financial circumstances. The normal, reasonably well-adjusted, older person is fairly realistic in his appraisal of facts, accepts himself for what he is, tends to see his wife as an equal partner in a joint enterprise, and is fairly tolerant in his assessments of the worth of his close relatives.

There were no great differences in physical health between the retired and the working subjects. The older retired subjects were more easily fatigued and physically weaker, though they claimed to be in rather better health than they had been while working. They were not excessively concerned about their health or too ready to deny their health problems. They were on the whole less anxious than the younger men, and saw their advanced age as an achievement in its own right and something to be proud of. Anxiety about death was less in the older group. The retired group were less passive and dependent in their relations with older people, and more responsible; they were also less defensive, less suspicious, and less erratic in their social relationships. They gave the impression of being more open and trusting, more secure and stable, less hostile to women, more sociable. The men nearing retirement appeared somewhat more inadequate, resentful, depressed, pessimistic, apathetic or contemptuous of themselves.

From these comparisons it appeared that a critical period

for adjustment is shortly before retirement. During this time, men become increasingly agitated about its consequences and problems. The effects of ageing, however, and the problems of retirement affect people in different ways and at different times. The problem is not so much 'being old' as 'becoming old'.

As very bright children grow into adult life they are likely to be physically healthier, richer, and better adjusted than average-intelligence adults, and less likely to need psychiatric attention or to commit suicide.[31] Healthier and brighter older people have a number of characteristics indicative of better personal adjustment. These include an inclination to see the advantages of old age and retirement (in terms of accumulated experience and skill, and freedom from worries and responsibilities), a better retention of the capacity for original thinking, ingenuity when faced with practical problems, and involvement with other people in matters of mutual interest. On the other hand, these same older, brighter, healthier persons are somewhat more obsessive, restless, and inclined to complain about their work, their wives or their children. These negative characteristics may arise because such people are still relatively fully 'engaged' with life activities and with other people, and so are likely to experience the disappointments and frustrations which can be avoided by the more fully 'disengaged' old person.

Subjects with fairly obvious intellectual impairment, but within the normal range of deterioration, more often reported a history of disease and poor health in their later years. They had disengaged earlier and more fully. They complained relatively little about their financial status or about the work they had to do. As might be expected, they were less articulate than their healthier and brighter peers and more inclined to find satisfaction in the fact that they had reached a ripe old age.

As most circumstances in everyday life do not tax normal elderly people to their full capacity they give the impression that their faculties and personal qualities are relatively unimpaired. Intelligence is only one factor among many that influence a person's adjustment to his environment. Equally important are characteristics such as freedom from morbid emotional predispositions, relevant experience (including familiarity with particular circumstances), energy, resourcefulness and social skill. Measured intelligence may thus give little direct indication of overall adjustment to retirement and old age. Note that the measurement of *functional capacity* requires either a comprehensive itemized schedule, testing whether the old person can perform specified tasks, or a shorter scaled series in which the response to an item carries implications for a range of behaviours not explicitly tested.

Examination of the data collected by means of intensive interviews, rating scales and case-histories showed the following tendencies: the better-adjusted men were more often married and had their wives living with them; they were financially better off (an adequate income and good material assets help to bring security and confidence); they had constructive, rather than defensive, attitudes towards retirement; they undertook more useful activities, had a more realistic picture of themselves and old people in general, travelled more and had more cultural interests; their emotional relationships with other people were warmer and more stable; they were healthier (or less worried about their health problems), showed more consistency in their employment history, more readily accepted the facts of ageing and death, and showed relatively little depression, anxiety or other neurotic symptoms, such as seclusion or dependency. On the other hand these better-adjusted men were inclined to express stereotyped ideas and attitudes. That is to say, they tended to think in clichés, and to conform to standard ways of thinking and behaving.

In everyday life proverbs, clichés and other kinds of popular wisdom help us to think quickly in concrete terms; for example, it is easier to talk about accelerators and brakes than about complex and abstract economic ideas. Proverb interpretation has been used in the clinical assessment of cognitive capacity, though not without criticism.[32]

(b) *Five Strategies of Adjustment in Old Age*

In the Reichard study, a type of multivariate analysis known as 'cluster analysis' was applied to 115 ratings of the personal characteristics of 40 well-adjusted and 30 poorly-adjusted subjects. It revealed five fairly distinct 'types' of person – or rather, five fairly distinct ways of 'coming to terms' with the problems of old age. The personal characteristics listed below describe these five types. Approximately one third of the subjects, however, could not be neatly labelled. The descriptions reflect American rather than British modes of adjustment and circumstance. Each 'type' is a kind of composite photograph and the descriptions suffer from the 'fortune-teller effect' which makes it possible for individuals to read different meanings into a general statement.

CONSTRUCTIVENESS. The first strategy, characteristic of fourteen *mature* (constructive) men, approaches the ideal standard of adjustment for elderly males in a modern civilized community. It is basically that of an intelligent, well-integrated (not neurotic or anxious) individual who enjoys life and establishes warm, affectionate personal relationships with other people. This individual is humorous, tolerant, flexible, and aware of his achievements, failings and prospects. He has had a happy childhood, suffered relatively little emotional stress in adult life, and had a stable occupational history. He is free from financial worries, happily married, and his life history shows continuity and development rather than discontinuity or lack of sustained progress. He is fairly satisfied with his achievements, self-assertive without being aggressive, capable of expressing his feelings appropriately, and neither inhibited nor uncontrolled. He is not prejudiced against minority groups, and is tolerant of faults in other people. He has accepted the facts of old age, including retirement and eventual death, the prospect of which he deals with calmly and undespairingly. He has a constructive (future-oriented), optimistic attitude towards life. He is self-sufficient within the limits set by his physical condition and circumstances. He has a strong character, acts in a responsible way, and forgoes immediate satisfactions in the interests of superior long-term benefits; he can plan, save, and tolerate temporary deprivations and frustrations. He retains a capacity for enjoyment of food and drink, work and recreation, and may still be sexually active. His interests are well developed and show a continuity with the earlier part of his life. His friendships are close and he appears to have overcome any feelings of hostility he may have had towards people who injured him in some way in the past. His self-esteem is high and he can count on the support of people around him. He looks back on life with approval and few regrets, and forward with anticipation to what is yet to come.

DEPENDENCY. The second strategy, characteristic of six *dependent* (rocking chair) men, is also socially acceptable, but tends towards passivity and dependence rather than activity and self-sufficiency. It is basically that of a fairly well-integrated individual who tends to rely on others to provide for his material well-being and give him emotional support. He is unambitious, glad to retire and be free of work with its responsibilities and efforts, and derives no enjoyment from such work as he may have to do. He eats and drinks a little too much, gambles and tends to live beyond his means. He tires easily and enjoys relaxing in the privacy of his home. His wife is the dominant partner. His giving way to her frequently and without resentment may continue a pattern of adjustment in relation to women which evolved out of his experiences with a dominant mother.

Many individuals of this sort marry late and raise only small families. Their relationships with other people show a mixture of passive tolerance and unwillingness to get involved in relationships which threaten to disturb their security and comfort. They have fairly good insight into their own personal qualities and actions, and manage to combine feelings of general satisfaction with the world (they are not disappointed or hostile) with tendencies towards being unrealistic, over-optimistic and impractical.

DEFENSIVENESS. The third strategy, characteristic of seven *defensive* (armoured) men, represents a less acceptable mode of adjustment in old age, because many of its characteristics are reminiscent of minor neurotic faults found among younger people. However, it works, even if the cost to the individual and to those around him seems to be high in relation to the benefits it secures. The 'armoured' type of person was found among the older members of the panel of subjects investigated, with an average age of 73 years. Although a heterogeneous group, they could be described as emotionally over-controlled, habit-bound, conventional and compulsively active. They had a stable occupational history and had been well adjusted at work. They were actively engaged in social organizations, had planned well in advance to meet the financial problems of old age and, although they worked hard, they seemed to work more for extrinsic (defensive) reasons than because they found their work interesting. They were self-sufficient, and would refuse help in order to prove to themselves that they were not dependent upon others. They were difficult to interview, becoming anxious and evasive when discussing social and family relationships. They usually expressed only stereotyped conventional beliefs, telling the interviewer what they thought was normal and socially desirable rather than venturing a personal view. These defensive old men seemed afraid of the threatened dependency and relative inactivity of old age, putting off retirement and keeping a busy schedule of activities which prevented them from facing the facts of old age. Many of them over-idealized their fathers and appeared to have an overdeveloped sense of duty, especially with regard to work and self-sufficiency. They disliked having nothing to do, had strong drives for achievement, and were more concerned with life's external problems than with their own motives, feelings and values. They could see few advantages in old age, and were envious of young people, even though they were satisfied with their own lives and achievements. They would come to terms with old age only when forced to do so. In the meantime the prospect of old age and eventual death was ignored and avoided by keeping busy.

HOSTILITY. The fourth strategy was characteristic of sixteen *angry* (hostile) men, who tended to blame circumstances or other people for their own failures. They were aggressive and complaining in their dealings with other people, and were both competitive and suspicious. These morbid emotional leanings were, however, not accompanied by depressive tendencies. Partly on account of their reduced standard of living and lower income, they thought of old age in terms of starvation and poverty. Like the older 'armoured' men, their views were oversimplified, and they were prejudiced against minority groups. They were habit-bound and inflexible in their attitudes and values, and held unrealistic notions about themselves and the world. Often their suspicions verged on feelings of paranoia, thus encouraging withdrawn modes of adjustment. They expressed a strong aversion to the prospect of ageing, and saw in it little other than a deplorable deterioration of physical and mental powers, culminating in death. Their defensive reaction to this uninviting prospect (like the reaction of the 'armoured' men) was to plunge themselves into active work and to defer the evil day of retirement for as long as possible. Unfortunately many of these men lacked the capacity for making realistic and constructive adjustments in their retirement. They had little insight into their own motives and attitudes, rejected all thought of becoming inactive and dependent upon other people (possibly because of their lack of trust in others), and found ready excuses to back up their inadequate and unrealistic patterns of behaviour.

Unlike the three types of older person already described, the 'angry' men often had an unstable occupational history. They were moving into a lower stratum of the socio-economic system, and were often in conflict with other people. Like the 'armoured' men, however, the 'angry' men tried to counteract the effects of ageing by keeping active, refusing to relax, sticking closely to a fairly fixed routine, and adhering rigidly to rules and discipline. Their life-histories revealed patterns of minor incompetence and neurosis; and now, in their old age, they often showed anxiety, pessimism, depression, feelings of failure, poor financial planning, lack of ambition, lack of drive or persistence, avoidance of self-examination, lack of realism, distrust of others, and a desire not to become dependent upon other people. Their prejudices were easily aroused; congruently, they had been submissive in their relationships with their fathers, and had grown up receiving and giving little affection. In late maturity they became neurotically dependent upon their wives or children and saw them as demanding persons with perfectionist standards. The 'angry' men's reaction was a kind of baleful resentment. They envied young people and were hostile towards them. They could see nothing good in old age, they had not become reconciled to it, and they were afraid of death.

SELF-HATE. The fifth strategy, characteristic of four *self-hating* men, differed from the fourth in the way the aggression had been dealt with. The 'self-hating' men had turned their hostility upon themselves, were critical and contemptuous of the lives they had led, had been unambitious, and had no desire to live their lives over again. They had moved steadily downwards in terms of socio-economic standards, were passive, somewhat depressed, and lacking in initiative, unable to make proper financial provision or to accept responsibility. Often these men had been unhappily married (or felt no warmth or affection for their wives). They were able to accept the facts of ageing, but were unable to make the best of things by adopting an optimistic, constructive attitude. They had few hobbies, were unpractical and tended to exaggerate their physical and psychological inadequacies. They were pessimistic and did not believe that an individual has much influence on the course of his life, feeling themselves rather to be victims of circumstance.

They had ambivalent feelings towards their father and

mother, were not interested in other people, derived no satisfaction from heterosexual relationships, and felt generally lonely and useless. The 'self-haters' were well aware of the facts of ageing; they felt they had had quite enough and they were not envious of young people. Their main feelings were those of regret, self-recrimination and depression. Death appeared not to worry them, since they saw it as a merciful release from a very unsatisfactory existence.

The five strategies of adjustment are not distinct or exclusive categories; and within each there are differences between individuals. The less well-adjusted elderly men appeared to have been somewhat maladjusted *throughout* their lives, although some of the 'mature' individuals reported brief spells of maladjustment.

Additional personality types with somewhat different clusters of behavioural characteristics (strategies of adjustment) have been suggested by further research.[33] Since these strategies are usually variations on a basic theme which has characterized the person's behaviour over many years, biographical analysis seems to be a useful method of investigation. Some of the precursors of psychological disorders in late life might be identified through research of this kind.

6. SUCCESSFUL AND UNSUCCESSFUL AGEING

People who manage to survive to old age are likely to have evolved strategies of personal adjustment which enable them to avoid emotionally disturbing situations. But, of course, survival is possible with psychologically unsatisfactory forms of adjustment. Anxiety increases steadily with age especially among women. Anxiety arising from what social psychologists call 'cross-pressures', typical of adolescence, probably diminishes with age, because the older we get the more likely we are to have ironed out difficulties and contradictions in our circumstances and relationships with others, and because we 'disengage' from those sectors of society that we find difficult.

Older people differ widely, but many become more cautious and less confident. Measured age changes in confidence and cautiousness are slight. Cautiousness becomes more prominent with age, in that older people are less discriminating with regard to the particular hazards of different situations. By contrast, younger people are confident in some situations but not in others. Rigidity, the inability to modify an habitual response, is not a simple or single personality trait and, unlike 'confidence', does not show a definite relationship with age.[34] Naturally, habitual ways of thinking and behaving increase with age, partly because the long familiarity with a stable environment has 'shaped' behaviour in this direction. The slower pace of behaviour brings about, directly or indirectly, changes in personal adjustment, achievement and occupational performance. Intelligence, too, is an important determinant of personal adjustment so that age changes in intelligence bring about changes in 'personality'.[35] The tendency to use over-simplified (stereotyped) forms of thought, such as clichés, seems to follow as a consequence of the reduction in intelligence. There are further age changes in basic processes such as arousal, temporal integration and energy level, which could also bring about changes in measured personality traits. It is difficult to tease out cause from effect, and proximate cause from remote cause, in this welter of interacting influences.

Personal adjustment is rated high if the individual is effective in overcoming frustrations, resolving conflicts, and achieving socially acceptable satisfactions and achievements. Good adjustment expresses itself in happiness, confidence, sociability, self-esteem and productive activity. Personal adjustment is rated low if the individual cannot overcome frustrations, resolve conflicts, or achieve satisfying results by means of socially acceptable forms of behaviour. Poor adjustment is expressed in hostility, unhappiness, fear of people, morbid anxiety, dependence, guilt, depression, feelings of inferiority, apathy, withdrawal or incompetence. But good personal adjustment for the individual depends upon good personal adjustment among the people with whom he interacts, since maladjustment in some creates conditions which foster maladjustment in others. Vicious circles of obstruction, resentment, retaliation, anger and guilt may be set up by family discord, difficulties at one's place of work, and so on. As judged by the usual criteria, neurosis increases in frequency as age advances, especially among women (see Chapter Ten). Symptoms of mental and physical disorder, however, are obscured by the complexities of the ageing process, and may go unnoticed.

In retirement, allowances are made for the elderly person's physical and mental inadequacies, and he is less often relied upon by others to do things which might tax his resources. He is allowed to potter about in his own way, doing things which are important to him (and useful in their own right), but not critical in the sense of being essential or urgent tasks involving the real interests of other people. Personal adequacy is reflected by the person's social adjustment – the affective relationships he has with those people with whom he is in close and frequent contact. Elderly people achieve successful adjustment in different ways. One person is happy to retire to a small house and garden away from everything and everyone (except perhaps a spouse, close friend or relative), whereas another finds happiness in a three-generation house in a crowded neighbourhood. This is another reason why social relationships and inner satisfaction, rather than work capacity or material circumstances, are the appropriate indices of personal adjustment in old age.

In spite of their individual differences, people who grow up and grow old in the same community frequently acquire roughly comparable modes of adjustment and can be assessed against accepted values and common standards. Successful adjustment depends upon adequate standards of living, financial and emotional security, good physical health, regular and fairly frequent social interaction, useful activity and the pursuit of personal interests. The successfully adjusted elderly person shows enthusiasm for doing things, resolution in pursuing his aims (which are realistic), fortitude in the face of adversity, insight into his own character, and a prevailing mood of happiness or contentment. Optimum adjustment calls for continual *changes* in behaviour and circumstances throughout life.

An elderly person can be sick, and yet make an adequate adjustment to his environment. Illness affects people in different ways depending upon their personal qualities and surrounding circumstances. Optimism, for example, helps one elderly person to make a good recovery from a heart attack, whereas another, predisposed to depression or passivity, becomes dependent and hypochondriacal. Experiences which make us feel that we are growing in wisdom or competence induce feelings of happiness and optimism. Conversely, experiences which make us feel that we are making no progress or even slipping below earlier achievements and standards induce feelings of anxiety, guilt and depression. In fact, in so far as it can be measured at all, overall happiness decreases steadily throughout life from the late twenties.

In late maturity and old age, the 'coming to terms' aspect of personal adjustment becomes more prominent, because time and opportunities are running out. People come to terms with life in old age in various ways: there is no standard or best mode of adjustment. The later years of life need not be static and unchanging, but personal adjustment should evolve smoothly and logically out of earlier patterns of behaviour. If a sense of *continuity* and *identity* can be maintained, in spite of the physiological, social and psychological changes, the process of re-engagement can proceed successfully; this is essential for adjustment since it secures a more effective deployment of the elderly person's reduced resources. Normal ageing is gradual, by psychological standards at least; and, with foresight, planning and social support, much can be done to ease the problems of adjustment and to improve the general level of achievement and happiness.

A person can 'come to terms' with his environment, although his behaviour may not square with community ideals, statistical norms, or particular psychological notions about what is good or bad for old people. The socially accepted criteria of adequate adjustment in old age include the following: congruency between inner mental states and external circumstances; a degree of continuity between past and present patterns of adjustment; acceptance of old age and death; a degree of euphoria arising out of security and relief from responsibilities; and, most important, security and adequate financial circumstances. The bulk of well-adjusted old people lead lives which are fairly tranquil and concerned mainly with routine personal activities. In the final stages of life the most that can be reasonably expected is fortitude in the face of illness, reconciliation with people, and some consideration of what consequences one's death will have for others.

CHAPTER NINE

The Terminal Stage: Dying and Death

1. THE CONCEPT OF DYING

Dying and death are taboo topics; most of us regard them as morbid and best ignored or avoided, hence they are unfamiliar issues for thought and discussion in daily life. Until recently, they have rarely been studied as psychological or social phenomena. Dying and death, however, to put it paradoxically, are facts of life, with a special relevance to ageing.[1-11] Normal aversion to these issues can be lessened by using more neutral phrases like 'terminal stage' and 'terminal behaviour' and by adopting a disinterested scientific approach.

The 'terminal stage' can be defined as a persistent awareness of the prospect of death from natural causes in late life. Thus we are not concerned with dying and death in children, or through violence, or even with premature and unanticipated death in adult life. For reasons which will become obvious later, it is convenient to regard dying as a distinct stage in the human life-path, ending in biological death. In some instances, this stage begins with the onset of an illness which is known to be fatal; the illness continues its course with or without the person realizing or responding to the prospect of death. In other instances, the terminal stage emerges gradually as the person becomes aware of and behaves in response to his greatly foreshortened, residual, expectation of life.

At least three facets of dying can be distinguished: biological, social and psychological (or behavioural). The biological facet reveals the physiological and medical processes, i.e. normal physical degradation and disease. The psychological (or behavioural) facet reveals the thoughts, feelings, needs and actions of the dying person. The social facet reveals the social, institutional and cultural processes associated with dying, death and bereavement.

The biological moment of death can be defined by a number of medical criteria such as the cessation of breathing, loss of heart beat, or disappearance of electrical activity in the brain.[12] The different parts of the body do not all die at the same time; it is well known that some organs can be recovered shortly after death and used in transplant operations. Also, some individuals who were thought dead according to normal criteria have been known to recover or have been resuscitated by artificial means. Finally, some individuals have been kept alive, rather like animal preparations, by massive medical and technological support, without any apparent psychological life or voluntary action on their part.

The social moment of death has a number of effects, the most explicit of which are probably those having legal significance, such as the redistribution of power and wealth. The death of an adult has social repercussions analogous to those associated with birth and marriage; it requires some reorganization of the social fabric and tends to be the occasion of social rituals designed to acknowledge the event, hence the associated funeral rites, mourning and commemorations. Naturally, such rituals and the whole social psychology of bereavement vary from one culture to another and from one historical period to another; there are social class differences and individual differences which are relevant to sociology and anthropology.[13-15]

Some of the anxiety and confusion felt in response to a person's dying arises from contradictions and omissions in our system of values and attitudes. The socialization process does not deal adequately with the business of dying, although young children are very matter-of-fact about death if given opportunities to talk about it. Anxiety about death is probably an adolescent experience first of all; this anxiety reappears in modified forms in middle age, in later life, and finally in the terminal stage. The inadequacy of religious frames of reference for dealing with personal death is a relatively recent consequence of the secularization of society; there are also shortcomings in the various non-religious alternatives. In a sense, what matters to the individual is not the *fact* of death but the *meaning* of death.

The idea of death can be symbolized in a variety of ways and used to form potent figures of speech remote from its literal meaning. Our present-day aversion to the topic appears to stand in marked contrast to the almost obsessive preoccupation with it in the Middle Ages. Psychoanalytic theory gave a prominent place to Thanatos, the death instinct, but this concept appears to have little or no relevance to modern psychology. It should be noted, however, that the term 'thanatology' has been coined to refer to the scientific study of death and dying, especially the study of its social and behavioural aspects.

By definition, the further expectation of life of an old person is short, i.e. his 'chances of death' are high, even if the actual cause of death and the time left to live are uncertain. An old person reaches the terminal stage when he realizes that he could die 'at any time' from natural causes, and when his behaviour is influenced by the meaning of that realization. There are ample conventions for disposing of the body and the estate of the deceased; but there are few norms for *conduct* in the terminal stage itself. Moreover, cultural changes have taken place so rapidly nowadays that few people are able any longer to derive benefit from the limited comfort and guidance offered by traditional beliefs and practices. A wide range of differences between individuals is tolerated: we feel no particular surprise if one person suffers severe and prolonged emotional upset at the prospect of dying whereas another person exhibits a calm, even humorous, acceptance of it. Similarly, responses to bereavement encompass stoical acceptance, nervous collapse, or other, less extreme reactions. The absence of social prescriptions for bereavement behaviour and terminal behaviour makes it difficult for us to anticipate how other people will react, and this uncertainty adds to the difficulty of finding appropriate forms of conduct.

In some primitive communities, the elderly infirm are put to death or abandoned, and expected to accept their fate. In other communities, however, especially those which emphasize filial piety and the continuity of personal identity after death, the elderly are cared for lovingly during the terminal stage, regarded as active but invisible agents or spirits after they have died, and are appealed to for help or placated by gifts.

In Britain, historical changes in the social customs associated with bereavement have resulted in substantial differences in behaviour in comparison with the years before the First World War. Part of the reason, presumably, is that there have been changes in the age distribution of mortality, especially infant mortality. There is also less emphasis on religion, and the stigma of dying a pauper has been removed. Improvements in, and the greater availability of hospital care, drugs and other medical services have further reduced unexpected deaths in the 'prime' of life and hence the need for financial support of those bereaved.

Part of the difficulty of coping with the terminal stage arises from the failure of current religious and philosophical beliefs to provide a satisfactory way of coming to terms with personal mortality. It remains to be seen whether a humanistic approach to these problems will achieve a more satisfactory solution. The secular society has yet to evolve a role and status for people in the terminal stage. This is not likely to be achieved in the near future, since even the retirement period has not yet been properly incorporated into the socio-economic systems of modern cultures. In the absence of a positive philosophy which finds *value* in terminal behaviour, we can expect to see the evolution of voluntary and obligatory euthanasia to prevent the prolongation of lives no longer worth living.[16,17] This would be one alternative to present-day segregation and negative social evaluation. Advances in human biology, however, would provide another alternative if it proved possible to keep the terminal stage tolerably short, i.e. free from prolonged physical debility and psychological distress, as in Aldous Huxley's *Brave New World*.

Further consideration of the historical and anthropological issues associated with dying would take us too far afield, but there are undoubtedly systematic differences associated with sex, socio-economic class, cultural background. The ritual aspects of death have diminished steadily over recent generations, but social prescriptions for the conduct of old people who are dying from natural causes seem never to have been well-formulated. Among the public at large, there are diverse views about the nature of death – and not simply because of religious differences. For example, relatively few adults believe in heaven or hell, in a literal or biblical sense, but a large number believe in some kind of personal existence after death. Some even suppose that there will be continuity of personal relationships with others. Belief in the existence of the spirits of departed people is common, even in modern societies. Euphemisms have been coined to refer to the taboo topic: passed away, last sleep, gone to rest. The terminal stage is regarded with considerable aversion and thought to have no intrinsic worth. Death itself is regarded as so abhorrent that the psychological and social processes which make life *human* may be lost in the technicalities of medical care.

2. SOCIO MEDICAL ASPECTS

In modern societies, dying is regarded as a problem to be dealt with almost exclusively within a medical framework, because of our preoccupation with the 'causes' of death. The terminal stage, however, can be studied in a wider context which includes the social and behavioural sciences, and even literature and the arts.

The terminal stage begins with the onset of a progressively worsening physical condition which runs a fatal course within a relatively short time. In many instances, the course of the illness, its duration, severity and eventual outcome are uncertain. Moreover, the elderly person is usually suffering from a multiplicity of biological defects and diseases, and it is not always possible to predict the particular terminal 'path' that will be taken by a given individual. For a terminal patient who had expected to live for many more years, a physician usually carries the burden of telling him and his family that he is dying. Otherwise, he is likely to engage in self-diagnosis, or be unduly defensive or optimistic, and never reach a realistic assessment of his 'chances' of dying.

The physician's problem is not merely that of stating an opinion, but rather of 'communicating with the patient' so that he can fully appreciate his circumstances and take appropriate action.[18,19] If, for any reason, the physician thinks it wise to withhold his opinion that the patient is dying, he must still help him to make sense of his puzzling environment – the medical treatment, family concern, bodily changes, and so on. The physician, therefore, is largely responsible for deciding what information and opinions are appropriate to a particular case, and how and when these are transmitted to the patient, his family or friends.

Physicians and nurses are trained to sustain life and health, and are therefore strongly inclined to resist the idea that the patient cannot survive longer. They are over-optimistic about the effects of medical treatment, especially in response to inquiries from the patient and his family. They may neglect the psychological and social aspects of dying – especially if the patient is allowed to return home. They may even feel defeated and angry if the patient dies in spite of their efforts to keep him alive. Doctors and nurses are largely untrained in the social and psychological aspects of physical illness. They have more than average concern for human welfare, but this is insufficient in a situation which calls for interpersonal sensitivity and awareness of the wider psychological and social framework of the patient's condition: for example his emotional reactions to surgical disfigurement or disability, his disrupted domestic circumstances, the depressing effect of the hospital environment, and his failure to understand his predicament.

One of the less satisfactory aspects of the hospital care of patients is the tendency for them to be treated as objects rather than as persons. The consequence is that they feel intimidated or worse – the victim of events over which they have no control. Hence there are strong grounds for the argument that the terminal environment should be 'humanized' – as it is in a modern 'hospice' for the dying – even if that means less emphasis on the prolongation of life. The psychological care of elderly patients who are expected to die shortly is obviously a difficult task, and there is some evidence that nursing staff, who often constitute the only constant source of emotional support and information for the patient, find themselves unwilling or unable to cope with this aspect of their work – in contrast with their efficient management of the technical aspects of life-support.[20,21] Selection and training of staff, however, can be expected to lead gradually to improvements in the psychological management of terminal cases.

The medical and hospital management of the dying person is obviously a central issue in the study of terminal behaviour but it is not the only issue; hence the need for personnel with aptitude and training in psychological and social skills who can develop ways of helping people to make the transition to the terminal stage and help relatives and friends to prepare for their bereavement. The hospital care of terminal patients is an exacting task requiring rare personal qualities and proper training. Talks and discussions alone are insufficient; practical experience in the management of actual deaths, management of the effects of a death on other patients, attendance at autopsies, and even role-playing are the sorts of training required in order to overcome the initial aversion to work of this sort. The 'psychological autopsy' (see later) provides an ideal method – a way of studying dying in the context of the total situation.

Non-medical ways of improving adjustment during the terminal stage include, for example, psychological counselling for the patient and for his family and friends.[22,23] Improvements in the socio-technical environment, especially as regards communication, relocation and the side-effects of treatment, also affect adjustment. A rational and comprehensive cost-benefit analysis of terminal care based on humanistic values would probably give increased weight to non-medical intervention in fatal illnesses. The duty of the medical and nursing staff is to prolong life, but not under any conditions or at all costs. These costs include: resources withheld from other patients, the prolongation of financial and emotional stress for the family, the cumulative delay and disruption of the social system, and the prolongation of the patient's distress.

At present, then, decisions about medical treatment have serious implications for the social and psychological aspects of terminal illness. But the responsibility for decisions could be *shared* not only with the patient but also with his close relatives and friends. Such decisions might include, for example, those relating to the diverse costs and benefits of treatment, the social arrangements for personal care and attention, and those affecting the understanding and the emotional reactions of all concerned. Decisions about non-medical management cannot be avoided by doing nothing, since inaction is a kind of action, and decisions and their consequences go by default. For example, failure to communicate with the patient fully and in good time means that he suffers a prolonged period of uncertainty and anxiety; he cannot avoid trying to make sense of what is happening to him, and in the absence of proper information he probably misconstrues the situation; he picks up scraps of medical information and misinformation; he mistrusts people and is unable to cooperate fully; he is puzzled and distressed by the behaviour of others and by the treatment or clinical environment that he is required to endure.

The social and psychological aspects of terminal behaviour are difficult to deal with in practice because there is often a great deal of uncertainty about the patient's prospects. Among elderly people, the course of an illness can affect and be affected by a number of concurrent physical ailments. Possibly for this reason, physicians and nurses are reluctant to tell an elderly patient that he is dying or that there is a high risk of death. Presumably it is felt that this error of omission is preferable to the mistake of having told a patient who recovers that he is unlikely to live much longer. When asked if they themselves would want to know if there was a strong likelihood that they would die, most physicians and nurses say that they would, and so do most ordinary people. Nevertheless, there is considerable reluctance to discuss this possibility with the person most concerned, at least until it has become a largely foregone conclusion. This is perhaps another illustration of the fact that dying and death are taboo topics.

The fear is that if he were aware of the imminence of his death or the degree of risk, the patient would somehow 'give up the struggle' to survive and thereby shorten his life-expectation even further. There appears to be little or no reliable evidence on this aspect of popular wisdom. There are no scientific data other than clinical impressions and anecdotes to support the idea that an effort of will, or a psychological attitude like determination, or the general will to live has any causal effect on survival. Phrases like 'the will to live' or 'giving up the struggle' or 'fighting an illness' are figures of speech and may have little or no basis in reality.[24] The analogy with psychological factors in physical effort – endurance in athletics or concentration in mental skills – is probably not altogether apt because such 'psychological effort' can be translated into voluntary action, whereas a person who is seriously ill has no control over his physiological processes. Moreover, even in athletics and other relevant areas of performance, the psychological elements – grit, courage, tenacity – are not well understood. The added stress and shock of becoming aware that he is dying might have some sort of adverse threshold effect on a patient's precarious physiological condition, but there appears to be no firm evidence of this. However, the prevalence of figures of speech in common language and the possibility of death by voodoo and hexing in primitive communities suggests that the physiological repercussions of psychological stress could be fatal, especially to someone in a poor state of physical health; hence the question must be left open for the present.[25]

3. POST-MORTEM PSYCHOLOGY

One of the more interesting approaches to the study of dying and bereavement has been the attempt to develop a method of 'psychological autopsy' which makes a post-mortem examination of the psychological and social factors surrounding the death of an individual.[26] By analogy with a medical autopsy, the aim is to uncover the circumstances and events relevant to the occasion and manner of a person's death. As might be expected, rational and systematic inquiries reveal that the psychological and social factors in terminal adjustment are sometimes different from what one expected, and less simple than one supposed. The method, pioneered in research into suicidal behaviour, can be used for research and training purposes. Ideally, it reveals faults and inadequacies in the life circumstances of the deceased person; these then provide leads for the improved management of subsequent terminal cases. In addition, it sensitizes medical, nursing and social personnel to some of the less obvious aspects of terminal care; it reasserts the importance of the community in caring for its dying members; it makes explicit some of the assumptions, prejudices and norms underlying attitudes and practices in relation to dying and bereavement.

Psychological autopsies reveal a number of interesting findings. Even among geriatric patients, a high proportion have some degree of awareness of the terminal situation. Useful psychological and social information may not be entered into the patient's records. The technicalities of physical medicine may dehumanize the patient's terminal environment. Patients are frequently discouraged from talking about their impending death; this leads to some confusion about the state of mind of the terminal patient. Some have premonitions of death, but these are not always borne out; dying and death may feature in the contents of a patient's hallucinations and delusions. Attitudes towards death vary from glad acceptance through apathetic indifference to severe anxiety. Calm acceptance appears to be the characteristic response of patients with good adjustment. Even among geriatric patients, the terminal stage provides opportunities for the expression of socially meritorious conduct and even for psychological 'growth'. Psychological autopsies have shown that behavioural and psychological changes can appear *in advance* of the final deterioration in medical condition; typically, changes are in the direction of withdrawal, inactivity, decreased interest and responsiveness, and mental depletion. Psychological and social intervention at this stage might not help much in reviving flagging biological processes, but they could improve the quality of life in the final stage. Many elderly people and people in terminal care accept the negative evaluation placed upon them by society. They regard the terminal situation as nothing more than an antechamber to death. A more positive philosophy would regard the terminal situation as the last opportunity that the individual has to express his best qualities, make amends for his errors, fulfil his obligations, assert his rights, and respond with all his resources to the challenges presented by that situation.

4. ADJUSTMENT TO THE PROSPECT OF DEATH

Old people who are not mentally impaired cannot help becoming aware that their lifetime is almost at an end. Many of their friends and kin have died, and they realize that they are much more liable to fatal illness or accident. Thus the idea of death is not unfamiliar, and for some at least the prospect is not as forbidding as it was in their earlier years – they have run out of important reasons for living. Other old people, however, become anxious, depressed and maladjusted; for example, they feel angry at the injustice or waste of their life, they fear the unknown, or they become frantic, apathetic or confused in the face of a painful situation outside their control.

It is not unusual for old people to accept their impending death in a fairly unemotional matter-of-fact way.[27,28] The normal reaction of friends and kin is to oppose this attitude and to persuade the old person, perhaps quite wrongly, that he (or she) has many more years of life still left to enjoy. We have a strong drive and an ingrained habit of fighting and avoiding the risk of death, and of encouraging others to be like ourselves. In opposing the old person's acceptance of the prospect of death, however, we reveal a misunderstanding of the change that has taken place in the *meaning* of death for a person who has become adapted to the terminal stage. Our reaction is a consequence of the fact that death and dying are taboo topics. There are strong social prohibitions against suicide, and against killing others whether by neglect or deliberately – witness the sanctions against euthanasia, and until recently, against abortion. But the question is whether it is right to resist changes in the old person's attitude.

A rational and empirical examination of the terminal stage obliges us to question conventional wisdom. The assumptions underlying social attitudes towards dying and death can be examined to see whether other sorts of belief and action provide more satisfactory alternatives to those currently available. There is little to gain by refusing to accept or discuss a person's impending death, particularly if that person is becoming justifiably reconciled to it. Rather like sexual and excretory functions in former times, the topic of death elicits embarrassment and defensive attitudes; the conventional response is to deny or avoid the issue, and to rationalize one's rejection of it as giving comfort and support to the old person. Our inability to discuss the prospect of death with an old person reinforces the idea that the terminal stage has no value and must be rejected. The reason is quite natural – dying and death are often associated with pain, fear, ugliness and hopelessness, but we do old people a disservice by blocking their attempt to come to terms with death.

People differ considerably in their reaction to the prospect of dying. Moreover, circumstances alter cases, and a person's terminal behaviour depends partly upon his residual capacities and psychological disposition, and partly upon the circumstances in which he finds himself. His interpretation of the situation plays an important part in his efforts to cope with life's last challenge. Again, we are referring only to natural death in old age. Given that there is little objective information on normal behaviour in the terminal stage, we must assume that adjustment to the prospect of dying, like other sorts of adjustment, is 'characteristic' of the person, in the sense that we can recognize the operation of long-standing personal qualities which have been the central organizing factors underlying the person's adjustment to a wide variety of other situations earlier in life. For example, people who have been inclined to depression and apathy in the face of stress can be expected to react in this characteristic way; others who have been typically stubborn and independent, or optimistic and self-denying, can be expected to react in their different ways.

Although social prescriptions for the conduct of people who are dying, or who have been bereaved, are not very well defined in modern society, yet they are not entirely absent. Hence dying and bereaved persons frequently behave as they are 'expected' to behave, and this depends upon the norms governing their particular social position. Reactions to bereavement naturally vary with the particular circumstances and qualities of an individual.[29-32] The usual reaction to the loss of a loved relative or friend is a sense of grief. The intensity and quality of the grief, however, depend upon the nature of the loss – the momentary sadness felt at the death of a distant friend is different from the spasmodic surges of grief following the death of an aged parent, and different again from the prolonged and deep sense of desolation consequent upon the death of a loved one.

The grief associated with bereavement is not necessarily a clearly delineated feeling. There may be a good deal of ambivalence and variation over time; for example, sorrow and disappointment may be mixed with anger, guilt and anxiety. Bereavement constitutes a stress situation and can precipitate psychiatric disorder, psychosomatic illness or suicide. Many widows, for example, experience feelings of guilt about their role in the events leading up to the death of their husband; and widowhood reduces life expectancy. The psychological and social aspects of widowhood have been the subject of systematic studies. The reorganization called for following the death of a spouse introduces an added source of stress, with regard to emotional deprivation and living arrangements, and this increases the risk of death of the bereaved person.[33-36]

There are good reasons for supposing that preparation and psychological support help to alleviate such distress and interpersonal conflict.

In old people the awareness of dying has developed slowly. There has been time to adapt to the prevailing circumstances, and time to learn appropriate strategies of adjustment. Without such adaptation, the awareness of dying evokes feelings of dread associated with a sense of isolation, loss or rejection. Stress reactions and neurotic maladjustment arising from such feelings can be ameliorated by the administration of drugs and by psychotherapy.

5. PREPARATION FOR THE TERMINAL STAGE

Making an adequate adjustment to the terminal stage includes handing over responsibilities, making arrangements for dependents, effecting reconciliations, and either attending to unfinished business or enjoying residual opportunities for work, companionship, or leisure activities. The main problems of terminal adjustment, however, are likely to be psychologically demanding: coping with pain, anxiety, frustration, discomfort and depression; establishing a tolerable level of sedation; and managing the activities of daily living.

How are we to prepare ourselves for this eventuality? Many people survive into late life and die a natural death, so the question is relevant for most people. To ignore or reject it is to deny any sort of value to the terminal stage, and by implication to deny that the dying *person* has any value. Most old people have probably become reconciled to the prospect of dying, even if they have been discouraged from openly expressing this attitude. Those who retain sufficient insight and awareness feel that the disadvantages of living have begun to outweigh the advantages. Among younger adults, of course, such awareness and reconciliation is less likely and the problems of adjustment to dying are correspondingly more difficult.

Most of us have few or no opportunities to observe the behaviour of people who are dying or to appreciate at first-hand their thoughts, feelings and wishes. Even in late life, a person who is dying, in the medical sense, is generally segregated from others, partly out of respect for the patient's privacy, partly because dying is disturbing to others. Usually, only a few people – physicians, nurses, close kin or friends – are allowed to share the occasion, which has probably been regarded as avoidable for as long as possible. Thus the actual duration of the terminal stage varies, depending upon whether one adopts a narrow short-term medical definition of dying or a broad long-term psychological definition, i.e. it depends upon the *meaning* of dying.

The prospect of death is itself sufficient to provoke anxiety, but anxiety-provoking situations not infrequently contain stimulus elements which elicit other emotional reactions, such as anger, depression, guilt. Such reactions have their origins in the life-history of the individual; hence the individual's response in the terminal situation is conditioned by these prior experiences. In the case of late-life attitudes towards his own death, the individual frequently has adequate time and opportunity to become adapted to the certainty of his demise, although some will avoid facing up to this eventuality for as long as possible. Where the surrounding social conditions provide opportunities for close emotional support and clarification of one's ideas through, for example, a confidant, a therapist, a social worker or a religious guide, and where these influences have been sustained over a long period, the individual can become adapted to the situation and may acquire effective strategies for adjustment which will help him to cope with the more stressful conditions later in the terminal stage.

There are at least four reasons for the apparent decline with age in late life of anxiety about death. First, through a gradual process of learning the older person has reorganized his thoughts, feelings and motives to bring them into line with the now familiar fact of personal mortality. Second, he may be out of touch or out of sympathy with the modern world; hence his personal involvement and future time perspective are much reduced. Third, the ratio of the costs to the benefits of staying alive becomes increasingly adverse and the net value of his personal existence diminishes. Fourth, the process of disengagement diminishes the external pressures or incentives to stay alive. Other people, however, are often unwilling to accept the aged person's estimate of the terminal condition and in so doing they diminish the value of the terminal stage itself.

Western societies have been so preoccupied with growth and change that personal development and achievement have been over-valued, with a corresponding neglect of old age and terminal behaviour. There are some social philosophies, however, which try to give a more balanced view. Although it may seem paradoxical, what is needed is a more constructive attitude towards – or philosophy of – dying and death.

Looked at in terms of social learning, the fact that we are largely shielded from dying and death means that we are rarely exposed to relevant learning situations or 'behavioural models'. Even literature and the arts generally make little reference to terminal behaviour as we have defined it, i.e. to the behaviour of normal people dying from natural causes in late life. Perhaps the only aspect of human behaviour in response to the prospect of death which has been dealt with adequately in fiction, biography and journalism is that which concerns relatively young, vigorous people fighting in defence of legitimate rights during war or other social upheaval. Soldiers, revolutionaries and martyrs should know how to die, their behaviour – whether in fiction or in real life – exemplifies the prevailing social ethos and provides a variety of 'behavioural models' for young people to emulate. Their behaviour becomes legendary and heroic as it is assimilated into the history and cultural framework of a community. But natural death in old age in modern life lacks the dramatic and heroic qualities found in works of fiction and history. It is not surprising, therefore, that most of us – lacking either first-hand or second-hand experience of the normal terminal stage – do not have the concepts and skills necessary for dealing effectively with the social and psychological problems of dying and bereavement.

We find ourselves at a loss: we do not know how best to console the person who is dying; we are unable to understand or manage our own reactions; we find the behaviour of other people unpredictable and disturbing. The dying person himself, particularly if his awareness of dying has come abruptly or prematurely, may have little idea of what he can do in the circumstances. He has little or no background experience, he has no behavioural models to emulate, there may be no one to whom he can turn for advice and guidance. If it were not for the process of adaptation, referred to above, the normal terminal stage would be a painful no-solution situation instigating frustration reactions such as panic or apathetic resignation.

A more constructive attitude towards the terminal stage requires some reassessment of its value. One might regard it as analogous to the ending of a story – surely not the least important part. Moreover, the normal terminal stage is not devoid of opportunities for the manifestation of meritorious conduct, even if the circumstances and the responses are a far cry from those portrayed in fiction and biography. The terminal stage has its own values and rewards, its own peculiar merits, style and forms of experience. Although the average old person's death is not linked with important ethical issues like that of the soldier, revolutionary or adventurer, it nevertheless offers opportunities for the expression of courage, audacity, determination, humour and so on. It is the behavioural expressions of these and other relevant qualities that constitute the appropriate 'models' for vicarious social learning.

The problem is that socially desirable reactions to the stress of the terminal condition are not likely to appear without some preparation. And, as we have seen, such preparation is not systematically provided in the normal course of events. It is not surprising that the absence of opportunities to observe and critically examine the process leads us to adopt some curious attitudes and practices which have already caught the interest of anthropologists, sociologists and psychologists.

The unique circumstances and psychological make-up of each individual make it difficult to prescribe exactly what a dying person would have to say or do in order to exhibit socially meritorious conduct. It is unlikely that a person who is not already strongly predisposed to behave sensibly, calmly and bravely will do so in his last weeks or months. One solution to this problem is to deal with the issue as and when it arises by means of short-term support and counselling. Another is to make long-term preparations by cultivating throughout life the kinds of attitudes and values that can deal effectively with bereavement and personal death. Psychological help for people in their final phase of life is relatively rare, and more could be done to encourage adaptive and socially desirable behaviour, to discourage maladaptive and regressive forms, and to help discover what options are still open to the terminal case.

We need to familiarize ourselves with the psychological and behavioural aspects of dying while we are still alive and well. Through first-hand observation, through literature and the arts, through open discussion and scientific inquiry, we can become acquainted with the facts and values of dying. This includes consideration of the more desirable (as well as the less desirable) forms of conduct that are possible. Unfortunately, there is as yet little scientific evidence relevant to understanding problems of personal adjustment during the terminal stage, that is, little firm evidence exists about the typical behavioural capacities, attitudes, and emotional resources of terminal cases.

A certain amount of sociological research has been carried out in connection with bereavement in general and widowhood in particular. The situation faced by women widowed in late life is eased somewhat by their realistic anticipation of this eventuality and by the companionship of other women of comparable age who have also been widowed – this provides opportunities for mutual support and consolation, the sharing of advice and help, and so on. Widowers are usually in a less favourable situation.

Terminal behaviour is adaptive in so far as it is directed towards *mastering* the terminal situation. Clearly, religious and magical practices associated with dying have been designed to prepare the deceased person for the anticipated circumstances that death would bring, in particular an afterlife. Unfortunately, as we have seen, those of us who are alive and well are inclined to frustrate the dying person's attempts to prepare for and achieve psychological mastery of the terminal situation; we hinder his attempts to come to terms with death by denying that he is dying. During the terminal stage the person becomes greatly dependent upon others, and there is obviously a great deal that the community can do to support and guide him. The most obvious help is adequate medical and nursing care; but such help loses much of its worth if it is not firmly embedded in a coherent cultural system in which relevant ethical considerations operate. Ideally, such a system would enable the terminal-stage person to engage in satisfying social relationships, to maintain or enlarge his behavioural competence, to effect emotional readjustments, and to achieve mastery of the terminal situation in a manner which is personally and socially acceptable.

It would be absurd if our natural concern with the psychological and social aspects of the terminal stage led us to disregard the physical process of dying. It is obvious that medical care and treatment are salient aspects of the terminal stage. In addition to specific diseases and physical disabilities, the terminal case is likely to suffer from a variety of general ailments such as aches and pains, digestive disorders and disturbed sleep. Medication, including pain-killing drugs and nursing care, are regarded as the first line of support; but these efforts may be wasted if they are not backed up by a second line of support in the form of psychological and social care. The goal is not the maximum prolongation of biological life, but the maximum prolongation of *human life*. Most of us cannot expect to die as we would have wished, and in any event the 'preferred form of death' varies throughout life. The problem of determining the extent to which the individual should be allowed to control his own fate during the terminal stage probably does not arise in most cases; but when it does, it raises some awkward ethical, medical and social issues. The way the individual prefers to end his days may conflict with the interests of others. The problem with psychological support – professional or otherwise – for the dying person is that the form it takes depends upon debatable ethical considerations, apart from uncertainty regarding its supposed beneficial effects. The kinds of psychological support proposed are fairly commonsense measures intended to provide the patient with a confidant, and with opportunities to enjoy an attractive milieu, to understand what is going on, to give him some semblance of personal control, to cope with his feelings, and to make the most of his residual resources and opportunities. In this way, it is possible to ameliorate some of the defects of present-day methods of dealing with terminal cases.

The psychological and social study of terminal behaviour is not simply a matter of easing the stresses on this or that individual. It is also a matter of changing society itself – its norms, its values, its laws – and of finding a positive value for terminal behaviour in a basically secular society. The study of dying presents us with a paradox, 'Dying is a kind of living'. The practical question is, 'How can we help the dying person to live by helping him to die?' Some of the side effects of dying – pain, ugliness, incontinence, insomnia – may be more disturbing and depressing than the prospect of dying. Hence the need for good medical and nursing care, and for a realistic, humane appraisal of the total situation.

The stresses experienced by the terminal person can hardly be coped with effectively in the absence of preparation and psychological support. Preparation consists on the one hand of a willingness on the part of the individual to develop the sorts of attitudes, beliefs and values that make sense in the terminal situation, and on the other of a willingness on the part of society to readjust its norms and institutions so that the terminal person has a recognized and valued place in the system. Nowadays, more people are living longer, and we can all expect to spend a rather longer time dying. This is one good reason for attempting to incorporate the terminal stage as a *natural* final stage in the normal life-path. If it is to be lived at all, it should be lived because it has some intrinsic worth. Attitudes of aversion and deceit, denial and segregation, are likely to be overcome only through the *acceptance* of a positive philosophy of dying.

To be educated for dying as well as for living does not mean that we need become morbidly preoccupied with death. The realization that each of us will die gives us a common interest; it helps to focus our attention and energies on the present and the near future, and on the absurdities of some of our present values and social practices.

CHAPTER TEN

The Psychopathology of Human Ageing

1. ADULT LIFE

This section deals with the relationships between chronological age and psychiatric disorders in general. The next section deals in more detail with the major disorders of late life. It is not yet possible to specify with any accuracy the complex organic changes and processes involved in many psychiatric ailments. Some abnormal mental conditions are caused by damage to the brain or by metabolic or endocrine disorders which may or may not be inherited or related to age changes. Psychological stresses can precipitate mental illness in persons who are predisposed. This has led to the practice, in psychiatry, of distinguishing two broad categories: organic disorders and functional disorders.[1-3] An organic ailment can be traced, directly or indirectly, to a definite disease, injury or malfunction, particularly in the brain – for instance, a tumour or toxic state. A functional ailment is one for which no definite disease, injury or malfunction of the body can be found. A functional ailment might therefore arise either because of an organic condition which cannot be detected by existing methods, or through the acquisition of maladaptive patterns of behaviour such as hysterical paralyses, paranoid ideas or phobias (there is some disagreement about the aetiology of such conditions). Although the inadequacy of the distinction between organic and functional mental illnesses is widely recognized in psychiatry, it nevertheless provides a convenient diagnostic framework. Of patients over 60 admitted to mental hospitals probably about half have functional disorders, for example, affective psychoses or paraphrenia; nearly half have some organic brain disease, such as senile psychosis or arteriosclerosis; and a small proportion have acute confusion.

(a) *Acute and Chronic Brain Disorders*

One broad class of mental disorders is caused by or associated with malfunction of the brain tissues. Within this broad class there are two subsidiary classes: *acute* and *chronic.*

The *acute* disorders (which reach a critical condition relatively quickly) include those brought about by: infections in the brain or elsewhere in the body, drugs or poisons including alcohol, head injury, cardiovascular defects, faulty metabolism, growth or nutrition, and neoplastic, e.g. cancerous, conditions. In acute brain disorders there is a temporary, fluctuating impairment of the brain and of behaviour during which the patient is confused about his identity, his whereabouts and his relations with other people. His mind wanders, and he may have hallucinations and brief mild delusions; he may be moody, aggressive, and his sleeping and eating habits are often disturbed. A common acute brain disorder in old people is delirium caused by infections or toxic states; delirium can also be caused by impaired blood flow to the brain in heart or chest disease, for instance, or by cerebral embolism (obstruction of a blood vessel).

The *chronic* disorders are relatively long-standing and usually progressive and they include: brain disorders associated with cerebral arteriosclerosis or other cardiovascular disturbances, senile and presenile brain disorders, and epilepsy. Other conditions causing permanent and sometimes progressive brain damage are infections such as syphilis, and toxic states such as those brought about by the prolonged use of alcohol or drugs. Head injuries can also cause cerebral damage leading to psychiatric illness. In chronic brain disorders the damage to the tissues is relatively diffuse, and the adverse effects on behaviour are permanent if the disorder is progressive, although the progress of the disease may be slow. Some disorders are variable and not progressive. The psychological effects appear in the gradual erosion of the patient's memory, his poor retention of recent learning and experience, impaired judgement and problem solving, and the gradual loss of normal habits of adjustment. The most frequent conditions in old people are brought about as a result of cerebral arteriosclerosis and other cardiovascular disorders, and senile brain disease. Syphilitic infection and the excessive, prolonged use of alcohol are rarer causes. In old people living alone malnutrition may be an important precipitating cause of psychiatric illness.

(b) *Functional Psychoses*

In functional psychoses the disturbance is such that the individual can no longer deal appropriately and realistically with his environment; his perceptions, thoughts and actions are often bizarre and disorganized, and his relationships with other people are grossly impaired.

AFFECTIVE PSYCHOSIS. The term 'affect' is used in psychology and psychiatry to refer to feeling and mood. In affective psychosis the feelings, emotions and moods of the patient are severely disturbed, provoking changes in his behaviour. In *mania* he feels greatly elated or irritable, and becomes overactive, over-talkative, and carried away by a flight of fanciful ideas and extravagant action. In *depression* he feels hopeless and full of despair, his thoughts and reactions are often painfully slow, he may become anxious without good reason or, more rarely, irrationally agitated.[4] In *manic-depressive* psychosis some patients have alternate episodes of depression and mania. Patients may suffer from perceptual distortions, delusions and hallucinations. Such disorders sometimes ease for a time and then recur. Depressions are commonly divided into two categories: psychotic or endogenous (caused by factors within the person), and reactive or exogenous (attributable to stresses imposed on the person). There is usually a history of depressive episodes in the former. It is often difficult to determine whether a depression in old age is endogenous, or a reaction to external stress or a symptom of an organic cerebral condition. This is an important problem because it has a bearing on the choice of treatment. Electroconvulsive therapy

(ECT) often alleviates a 'functional' depression but may aggravate an organic condition.

Affective disorders are found throughout adult life. In late maturity and old age depression predominates, sometimes accompanied by severe agitation. The distinction between a psychotic depression and the depressed phase of a manic-depressive psychosis is usually made because some patients have a history of manic episodes, whereas others do not.

INVOLUTIONAL MELANCHOLIA. This term is sometimes used to refer to a type of affective psychosis which occurs in late middle age. The most frequent symptoms are severe depression with intense feelings of guilt, delusions, anxiety, agitation, hypochondria and insomnia. The term also refers to the depressed state of manic-depressive psychosis.

SCHIZOPHRENIA. Next to the mental disorders of senescence, schizophrenia is probably the largest, most intractable and least understood group of mental disorders. Older people may develop schizophrenia, but usually it begins as an illness of late adolescence or early adult life.[5] The disorder is characterized by a disorganization of the personality. The patient becomes psychologically 'detached' from the real world, suffers from various disorders of thought or feeling and, in severe cases, appears to be incapable of more than brief occasional periods of lucidity when he can make contact with other people. Schizophrenia is often sustained for many years. Many elderly psychotic patients, originally diagnosed as schizophrenic, continue to survive in mental hospitals until late maturity and old age. In old age their symptoms change towards those characteristic of the mental disorders of senescence, and the differences between the various clinical types of schizophrenia become less marked.

At one time long-stay mental patients frequently became 'institutionalized', that is, apathetic, habit-bound and intellectually deteriorated. Patients with schizophrenia, senile psychosis or other serious mental illnesses were unlikely to improve under routine hospital conditions. Nowadays, efforts are made to keep such patients active and interested in things and to return them, whenever possible, to community care. Even so, the adverse effects of institutional routines are clearly observable in geriatric wards and homes for the elderly.[6] These effects are compounded by physical infirmity which limits mobility, and by an apparent decrease in activities requiring psychological effort.

PARANOIA. Although paranoid symptoms sometimes dominate a schizophrenic condition, many psychiatrists distinguish a separate kind of psychiatric disorder known as *paranoia.* Paranoid patients are relatively rare. They have delusions of grandeur or persecution but tend not to hallucinate. Abilities are well preserved, and the more intelligent patients build up a comprehensive and detailed system of delusional ideas, often centred on one or more actual events in their life. Although the delusional system occupies an important place in their life they may be able to conduct most of their affairs normally. Paranoid delusions occur in mental illness in middle life and later, and the milder conditions may be difficult to distinguish from socially acceptable degrees of suspicion and eccentricity.

(c) *Neuroses and Psychosomatic Disorders*

Neurosis is a psychiatric condition giving rise to prolonged and exaggerated reactions, such as anxiety, depression and bodily discomfort (which all of us experience sometimes, even in normal health). Neurotic symptoms can be psychological, somatic, social or behavioural, or a combination of these. Neuroses differ from psychoses in so far as gross personality breakdown or bizarre delusions and hallucinations are absent. The typical neurotic patient has a history of psychological maladjustment which often dates back to childhood and manifests itself in periodic states of anxiety, phobia and depression, and less frequently in dissociation and other 'hysterical' symptoms.

Conspicuous neurosis and psychosomatic illness rarely appear for the first time in old age, but minor neurotic ill health and physiological disorders of psychological origin can arise in middle age or later, and may be maintained into later life, sometimes complicating the clinical picture when symptoms based on degenerative changes begin to appear.[7-10] The prevalence of neurotic maladjustment among the elderly living in the community has been estimated to be about 10 to 15 per cent. Old people who are markedly neurotic are likely to have shown severe maladjustment or neurosis earlier in life. Neurotic conditions starting only late in life are usually linked with stress such as physical illness or bereavement. Unmarried or divorced people, and those who experience neurotic breakdown in middle age, are also somewhat more inclined to neurotic disorders late in life. These vary in intensity. Mild forms of obsessional behaviour, morbid and irrational fears, and worry about personal health are more common in late life, especially among anxious introverted people; but these do not amount to an incapacitating neurotic breakdown. Other kinds of maladjustment, not usually regarded as psychological ailments, such as withdrawal, suspicion, tiredness, poor standards of conduct and bad temper, are probably also more common, if only because our physical and psychological resources are reduced as age advances. Conspicuous changes of this sort, however, may foreshadow a more serious psychiatric disorder. Hysterical conversion symptoms – loss of sensation or loss of movement in a part of the body, loss of memory, and so on – are uncommon; such symptoms are difficult to distinguish from those associated with functional psychosis or brain damage. However, neurotic symptoms do not appear to be the precursors of dementia, i.e. loss of judgement and intellectual powers.

The clinical description of neurosis is based on the symptoms presented by younger adults rather than on abnormal behaviour in the elderly, who are likely to show a different kind of 'neurotic' behaviour. A considerable amount of psychiatric experience may be required in order to judge the relative contributions of predisposition, environmental stress and ageing.

Psychosomatic disorders are *physical illnesses* precipitated or aggravated by psychological factors.[11] One interpretation is that psychosomatic symptoms, such as asthma, some skin disorders, migraine or peptic ulcers, are physiological complications brought on or made worse by stress and emotionally disturbing conflicts. Another view is that psychological strains merely aggravate an existing illness, or act as the precipitating factor for a type of illness to which the individual is constitutionally predisposed. Organic changes associated with prolonged frustration and conflict may not appear for some considerable time, or not at all if the person is not constitutionally predisposed to a psychosomatic disorder. There is considerable variation between individuals. Psychosomatic disorders are different from the various bodily symptoms which we all experience at times of strain (such as 'butterflies' in the stomach, cramps, palpitations or excessive perspiration). Such symptoms are common and can be severe in neurotic individuals. The constitutional factor is important because some people who have a crippling psychiatric illness do not develop a psychosomatic disorder, whereas others who apparently have no neurotic symptoms (and may even be outstanding in their achievements) can suffer from severe psychosomatic illness.

Malfunction in an elderly person is likely to be treated *as if* the condition were an inevitable consequence of old age, but the discerning general practitioner or psychiatrist may see, from the patient's medical history, and from other evidence, that some assurance and psychiatric support is called for in addition to physical treatment. The situation as regards minor physical ailments in late maturity and old age is complicated by the natural increase in the older person's concern about his physical condition, and this may lead to hypochondriacal preoccupations.

(d) *Other Kinds of Abnormal Behaviour in Adult Life*

Several 'special manifestations' of psychiatric illness which are associated with age cannot be dealt with in detail. They can occur in the absence of psychiatric illness and could be referred to just as conveniently elsewhere. They are briefly mentioned in the interests of completeness to illustrate the scope of social and behavioural gerontology.

CRIME. This occurs mostly in the 15 to 40 age group. Crimes such as assault or indecency committed by elderly people for the first time may follow from natural degenerative processes outside the individual's control, but can occur without demonstrable intellectual deterioration. Certain crimes, such as forgery or embezzlement, are more often committed by older persons. Crimes associated with poverty and mental disorder (vagrancy, chronic drunkenness) increase with age.[12–14]

SEXUAL DEVIATION. This may be symptomatic of one or other of the disorders already mentioned, as, for example, schizophrenia. Sexual potency, interests and activity normally decline gradually in late maturity and old age, but the onset of degenerative changes and the loss of normal sexual outlets can lead to a temporary loss of self-control, giving rise to sexual misdemeanours.

DRUG ADDICTION AND ALCOHOLISM. These are frequently consequences of personality disorder, but as it often takes many years for the full effects to develop, the chronic and severe cases are likely to be mature adults. Drug addiction leading to psychiatric complications is a rare cause of mental illness; milder forms of habituation are common, for example regular medication with sedatives and sleeping tablets among adults. There are, however, cultural differences and secular changes in the use of drugs, including alcohol and nicotine. The gerontological implications are not clear.

STRESS REACTIONS. Exposure to severe or prolonged stress during, for example, a painful illness, battle or civilian disaster, may elicit, in normal adults, symptoms similar to those described for the neuroses and psychoses. The symptoms – acute anxiety, phobias and hallucinations – are a consequence of the emotional shock but the precise mechanism, as in many psychiatric disturbances, is not known. If the person is rested and treated, and circumstances return to normal, his symptoms disappear at a rate commensurate with his predisposition to break down. Adult life and old age bring painful and prolonged emotional stresses – illness, accident, bereavement, unemployment or retirement, and impaired health.[15-19] The reaction to stress in old age is likely to be both more intense and longer for individuals with a history of neurotic or psychotic breakdown.

SOCIAL ISOLATION AND SUICIDE. Social isolation contributes its effect in a variety of psychiatric disturbances, as, for instance, in depression. Studies of suicide have shown that the highest rates occur in areas where family and neighbourhood ties are few. Even the relatively high rate of minor neurotic ill health among older women might be explained in part by the contributory effect of a reduction in family and social interaction. On the other hand, it is likely that the personal dispositions which lead to social down-grading and an inability to enter into new social relationships also predispose to mental ill health and suicide. Unfortunately, the extensive literature on empirical studies of suicide seems to have provided little support for many widely-held theories.[20-22] In Britain, suicide caused 0.73 per cent of deaths in 1969. Mental illness is probably involved in about one third of all suicides. Among women in 1969 the death rate from suicide and self-inflicted injury per 100,000 rose from 6 at age 15–34, to 13 at 45–64; whereas for men the corresponding rates were 8 and 18. Thus at all adult ages men are more likely than women are to kill themselves, and suicide occurs more frequently in late maturity. Some normal or relatively normal individuals seek a way out of an intolerable social situation or medical condition; others suffer from mental illness in which severe depression plays a part. It may happen to patients who are undergoing treatment, and to patients who are still in the early stages of an untreated psychosis or a severe neurotic depression. Depression is common in both sexes, probably more frequent among women. Suicide is more likely among individuals predisposed to affective disorder and among the relatives of such individuals. Thus suicide and affective illness are associated. Physiological, social or psychological factors play a part in bringing about a suicide. Some individuals are aware of their serious physical condition; others are lonely and see no point in living. Sometimes social attitudes and personal values delay the act; at other times a crisis or an opportunity precipitates the event. Official statistics underestimate the number of suicides because coroners are likely to be biased towards a verdict of 'accidental death', thus sparing the dead person's relatives the social stigma associated with suicide.

Psychological research into the problem of suicide can be carried on by analysing suicide notes, reconstructing the dead person's history, studying the precipitating factors (in so far as they can be discovered), and by studying evidence supplied by persons who made unsuccessful attempts to kill themselves. Some people take an overdose of drugs or injure themselves in other ways to draw attention to their desperate plight without really wishing to end their life. But many older people who attempt suicide are suffering from severe depression, and it is more difficult in these cases to separate out those patients who attempt suicide as a threat or demonstration from those who fail in a serious attempt because of technical incompetence or the vigilance of other people. Threatened suicide, contrary perhaps to popular belief, often precedes actual suicide. Both suicide and mental illness are found with greater frequency in the lower socio-economic classes, and especially in urban areas which are run down and socially disorganized. It is probable that at least half of the suicides in later life are committed by people who have some sort of psychiatric illness, and that proper social care and psychiatric treatment, especially if made available early, would drastically reduce the number. Physical illness is a frequent contributory factor in suicide.

(e) *Some Methodological Difficulties in Studying the Psychopathology of Human Ageing*

Age trends in mental illness are difficult to assess, for several reasons. First, mental illnesses vary in severity. The statistics compiled from hospital returns by the Registrar General refer to patients with relatively severe disorders; statistics compiled by insurance companies refer to patients with only moderately severe symptoms; and statistics based on records kept by general medical practitioners may include relatively mild cases of mental illness. The age trends for similar psychiatric conditions which vary in severity are not identical, although the broad trends, already indicated, are not in dispute.[23] Second, there is some lack of uniformity in the diagnosis and labelling of mental disease; doctors vary in their ability to diagnose mental illness, and to keep detailed records. Some people are reluctant to admit to conditions which might categorize them as 'mental' patients. Third, there are age, sex and social class differences in behaviour, which complicate the assessment of the prevalence of mental illness. Fourth, differences between investigators in the way they compile and interpret their observations influence the results – for example diagnostic criteria, source of data, duration of the study and type of community sampled. Fifth, there are secular changes associated with developments and fashions in theory and treatment, and with the effects of social attitudes, migration, demographic changes and so on.

In the course of one year, approximately one adult in five sees his doctor about symptoms which are obviously emotional in origin (or, at least, with somatic symptoms lacking apparent organic pathology). If we consider only those persons who consult their doctor for some reason, then in one year about one third of them attend with symptoms of this kind. About half these patients have somatic symptoms only; half have symptoms which are overtly emotional. In many cases the symptoms are mild and presumably do not greatly affect the patient's domestic and occupational adjustments. However, it must be remembered that we do not have reliable standards of *normal* mental health – whether a person is regarded as abnormal or not depends not only on the observer's judgement but also on other factors, such as the tolerance of his family and local social norms.

In one medical practice the proportion of women patients with neurotic ill health (consulting a doctor at least once in a two-year period) was about 30 per cent for women in their twenties rising to about 50 percent for women in their sixties.[24] Only about 15 per cent of men patients in their twenties consulted a doctor because of neurotic ill health, rising to 25 per cent for men in their sixties. For a large part of the adult lifespan neurotic ill health is twice as prevalent in women as it is in men. This is partly because of factors like the relative ease with which a woman can consult her doctor, or the accepted social role that she has in worrying about the children and other family matters. Many women are not resistant to the idea that they need a doctor's help in coping with emotional disorders. Women in different domestic circumstances have different attendance rates, so that, whatever the explanation for the apparent sex difference in neurotic ill health, it is not likely to be a simple one. The complexity of the sex difference in the occurrence of psychiatric ill health is shown, for example, by a greater prevalence of mild neurotic ill health for women and yet a higher suicide rate for men.

The estimated prevalence of neurotic illness at each age level depends partly upon the diagnostic criteria used. If only incapacitating neuroses are considered, the maximum prevalence is in the age group 25 to 45; but according to some investigations, if both mild and severe conditions are considered, maximum prevalence is reached at the age of 55 to 65. After the age of 65 further comparisons are difficult because of the selective effects of survival, and the diagnostic difficulty of distinguishing between minor neurotic symptoms and minor somatic ailments such as stiffness or pain in the joints, which are common in old age. Even if we knew the exact prevalence rates in old age, it would be difficult to compare them with prevalence rates at other ages because of the changed social circumstances and physical health of the elderly.

Neurotic conditions often have no definite time of onset or recovery, so little can be said about their duration. The mildest neurotic conditions can be expected to last for about two to four months. People who experience a more severe illness, like a neurotic breakdown which makes them unfit for work, have a longer expectancy of illness – 60 per cent recover within two years, 90 per cent recover within five years. After recovery, patients appear to have a greater risk of further breakdown. Neurotic conditions often recur over a number of years. Sometimes a moderate to severe neurosis coexists with a physical illness. The psychological consequences of ordinary physical illnesses seem not to have been studied in any great detail, but research may reveal age differences. Neurotic patients consult their doctors about twice as often as do non-neurotic patients, partly because some neurotic patients have both neurotic and physical ailments.

2. OLD AGE

(a) *The Prevalence of Psychiatric Disorders in Late Life*

In old age the risk of mental illness reaches a peak. Much of it is associated directly or indirectly with pathological processes in brain tissues, and in the cerebral blood vessels. Psychiatric illness in old age is a serious problem in social medicine which will worsen as the proportion of elderly persons in the population increases, but no part of adult life is free from susceptibility to mental illness.

Accurate estimates of the prevalence of psychiatric illness are difficult to make for many reasons, and actual figures must be treated with some caution, but roughly speaking about 5 per cent of people over the age of 65 suffer some sort of psychosis.[25,26] From 5 to 15 per cent suffer less serious mental disorder, and approximately 10 to 15 per cent suffer from neuroses or character disorders. In this country patients over the age of 60 make up at least 25 per cent of admissions to hospitals, and, if account is taken of private facilities and home-care, the percentage requiring psychiatric treatment is certainly much higher. Of these patients, at least 10 per cent, probably substantially more, appear to have some brain damage, though only about 5 per cent are seriously affected.

About 5 or 10 per cent have some sort of psychotic disorder, mainly depressive; the contrasting condition – manic or hypomanic state – is much less frequent and probably accounts for 5 or 10 per cent of affective disorders in late life. About 10 per cent have fairly conspicuous symptoms of neurosis. Almost half the patients with dementia have cerebrovascular disease, and about a third have other cerebral deterioration. In about one fifth, both are present. Paraphrenia accounts for nearly 10 per cent of first admissions of women aged 65 and over. In the community at large, therefore, about three quarters are normal by psychiatric standards even at late ages.

(b) *Pathological Changes in the Senile Brain*

Some aspects of age changes in the brain were dealt with in Chapter Three. Post-mortem studies show various pathologies in the brains of old people with dementia.[27-29] These include thickening and hardening of the main cerebral blood vessels, and damage and occlusion in the fine network of cerebral blood vessels. Changes in the blood vessels seem partly independent of changes in the nerve cells and glial tissues. The latter changes include: gliosis – an increase in the supporting tissue (neuroglia) of the brain and spinal cord; the loss of many nerve cells and adverse changes in the structure of others; wider and deeper fissures on the surface of the brain, and larger ventricles (fluid-filled spaces within the brain); the disruption of cortical lamination (patterned layers of brain tissue); the appearance of senile plaques – small irregular shaped areas of degeneration in the brain, which show up as dark blobs when revealed by the staining techniques of microscopy; neurofibrillary changes in which the fibrils within the neuron become thickened, tangled and severed.

Vascular and primary nerve cell changes are both common, so they may appear together. Damage to the brain may be either focal (occurring in one or more small local areas) or diffuse (spread throughout the brain tissues). Such changes, which become apparent at post-mortem, are strongly associated with the organic psychoses, but they occur quite frequently, though usually in less marked degree, in patients diagnosed as functional psychotics, and, indeed, in old people who have shown no mental abnormality during life and are assumed to have a normal brain.

The degree of overlap of symptoms between different psychiatric categories is large, and a good deal of variation exists between patients within any one category. The severity of degenerative changes in the brain is correlated with the severity of the symptoms displayed by the patient when alive, the association being more pronounced for psychoses with definite organic origins, i.e. showing the characteristic 'organic' mental symptoms associated with the term 'dementia'. As it is difficult to assess the severity of symptoms in 'normal' people and borderline psychiatric cases – since they do not come under systematic observation – we do not know to what extent severity of degeneration in the brain is associated with normal intellectual impairment and personality change in old age. Such degenerative changes can, however, be observed at post-mortem in people without a history of mental illness or brain damage. This could mean that some people can tolerate a degree of degenerative change in the brain, in much the same way, presumably, as they can tolerate other sorts of anatomical and physiological defect. On the other hand, there may be certain areas in the brain where a small amount of damage can precipitate conspicuous symptoms and signs of psychosis. Damage to the mamillary bodies and their connections, for example, seems to be associated with memory disturbance, though psychotic symptoms such as delusions and hallucinations do not appear to be regularly associated with damage to particular areas of the brain.

The brain is an extremely complex physiological system. Disturbances and damage originating in one part can be expected to have repercussions throughout the system. Given our present limited understanding of the physiology of the brain, theories about the way the brain ages, based on pathological and physiological data regarding lesions, post-mortem studies, EEG records, etc., are at best tentative. But recent technical developments such as the echoencephalograph, chronic implants, and regional blood-flow tracing promise greatly to improve our understanding of the physical basis of age changes in behaviour.

The particular sequence and pattern of symptoms shown by a patient with brain damage depends to some extent on the kind of personality the patient had before the onset of the disease, and on the particular kinds and amounts of brain damage. Moreover, since each person has his own biochemical individuality, the complexity of the problem can be easily imagined. Certain clinical symptoms such as dementia, failure of memory and disorientation in time and place, are, however, very characteristic of patients with definite brain damage irrespective of personality or aetiology.

(c) *Classification of the Disorders of Late Life*

The classification of psychiatric disorders in later maturity and old age is by no means settled, but broadly speaking the illnesses are as follows: senile psychosis; psychosis with cerebral arteriosclerosis; affective psychosis; late paraphrenia; and in middle age, presenile dementia. The International Classification of Diseases (I.C.D.) gives a detailed coding of diagnoses of psychiatric disorders in adult life and old age. The seventh revision of the I.C.D., for example, distinguishes 19 diagnoses under senile psychosis and under arteriosclerotic psychosis, depending on the other conditions with which these disorders are associated.

Psychiatric illness is presumed to arise through the interaction of predisposing factors (the product of genetic characteristics and basic life experiences) and precipitating factors (such as physical illness or emotional stress).[30-32]

SENILE PSYCHOSIS. Senile psychosis appears from about age 70 onwards. It is more common in women than in men, and its onset is gradual.[33-35] Intellectual deterioration is relatively slow but progressive; the patient loses interest and becomes less responsive; he loses the finer shades of feeling and emotion. As his physical and mental resources diminish, he is confined more and more to his own thoughts and restricted to his home surroundings. Memory impairment is one of the more obvious early signs of an impending senile psychosis, and the recall of recent events is more markedly affected than the recall of events in the patient's early life. Memory disorders are sometimes associated with disturbances of affect. The patient has less energy and becomes easily upset; he sleeps fitfully and potters about aimlessly.

The senile psychotic may wander about at all hours, and shout and scream in imaginary arguments. Loss of conscious control and a coarsening of social feelings can lead to anti-social conduct. The main distinction between senile dementia and normal ageing lies in the far greater extent and rapidity of the deterioration and the higher mortality in senile dementia. The pathological changes in senile psychosis are diffuse.

In the earlier stages the prevailing mood is typically one of shallow depression sometimes involving transient paranoid ideas and morbid, misplaced fears of retribution for non-existent sins and crimes. The patient's short-lived delusions are feeble attempts to find some pattern of meaning for his disordered thoughts, perceptions and feelings. In the late stage he may no longer recognize familiar people who have been away for a few moments; he may accuse people of theft or interference, and become confused about the identities of people he has known. In these respects senile dementia and cerebral arteriosclerotic psychosis are similar.

Physical stress or social disorganization may bring on a delirium in which the patient becomes restless, difficult to manage and susceptible to auditory and visual hallucinations. Many cases first come to the attention of the hospital authorities because of the disturbance caused by the delirium. Some patients show paranoid suspicions which lead them to issue threats or assault other people. They usually regain some conscious control of their behaviour after the delirium, but most of them are left with a more marked dementia.

Within about six months of the onset of the disease, though

the rate of progress is variable, the senile psychotic has usually become physically enfeebled, mentally slow, emotionally dull and apathetic, and easily tired. His grasp of circumstances and events becomes rapidly worse, and he attempts to fill in the gaps in his memory with guesswork and fantasy. For a time he may try to disguise his real condition by covering up and excusing his mistakes, and by putting on a cheerful, friendly attitude. As the illness progresses he can recall less of his past life, and even outstanding events are forgotten although sometimes preserved as isolated memories. As the patient loses his grasp he becomes confused and deluded about his present environment, and about the people around him. His reduced mental capacities make his thoughts vague and incomplete. He finds it difficult to follow a train of thought and cannot cope with unfamiliar circumstances. As with normal old people, he may reveal his failing powers by trying too hard, or making excuses, or doing the wrong thing. Eventually the disease encroaches on lifelong habits, and the patient cannot think properly, speak coherently or write effectively. He tends to talk around the issue, wander off the point, repeat himself and use empty phrases. His speech becomes incomprehensible inappropriate, and finally a meaningless babble. His social and emotional behaviour deteriorate with similar severity and rapidity. His mood is usually vague, flat, dull and apathetic, and his emotional reactions are slow and weak.

Where elderly individuals have had to fend for themselves, their senile condition brings about a decline into filthy conditions and appalling neglect, until the attention of the authorities is drawn to the problem. Many senile cases are already in a fairly advanced stage of the disease when admitted to a mental hospital, and mortality is high. Death may follow an infection, or simply bring to an end an existence in which the patient is unconscious, or unable to feed himself, incontinent, with falling blood pressure, and suffering loss of body weight and decreasing temperature.

The causes of senile psychosis are not yet fully understood, though general nursing care and medical measures can mitigate symptoms. Functional capacity is sometimes diminished by disuse and can be restored to a limited extent. Genetic factors undoubtedly play a part, but the exact mode of inheritance has not been determined; nor is it known to what extent neurophysiological defects, biochemical factors or other factors play a part.[36] It is probable that neuropathological changes – presumably biochemical in origin – are an indispensable condition of 'true' senile dementia, though there is a wide range of individual susceptibility.

Given adequate medical advice and family resources, a person in the early stages of senile dementia may be looked after at home, unless or until he becomes unmanageable. Patients do not need to be confined to bed unless they are exhausted or ill; a modicum of activity, social interaction and recreation should be beneficial. Nutrition, cleanliness, toilet habits and the avoidance of accidents will be the main home nursing problems. When psychiatric and medical problems arise, professional advice should be sought, and hospitalization may become necessary.

PSYCHOSIS WITH CEREBRAL ARTERIOSCLEROSIS. Senile changes, and the psychological symptoms that accompany them, can be compared with those associated with cerebral arteriosclerosis. The two conditions, however, are not independent either as regards the behaviour they produce or their physical basis. They are frequently combined, as in the condition referred to as 'chronic brain syndrome'. Arteriosclerotic psychosis develops more rapidly. It fluctuates in severity, and may clear up temporarily; the personality tends not to deteriorate so rapidly. In addition there are certain signs and symptoms characteristic of cerebral vascular disease. Changes in the retina are consequence of localized damage and are not seen in uncomplicated senile dementia.

Psychosis with cerebral arteriosclerosis usually begins in late maturity as the result of disturbances in the circulation of the blood through the brain. The degenerative sclerotic process may affect the main and the small arteries of the brain, and the smallest blood vessels and capillaries can be restricted or blocked. These changes include many widespread small areas of infarction (an 'infarct' is an area of tissue which has died from lack of adequate blood supply) or haemorrhage, areas of softening and changes in the texture and appearance of the cortex. Patients frequently have high blood pressure or a history of cardiovascular disturbances.

Like other elderly psychiatric patients, patients with cerebral arteriosclerosis often come to the attention of the psychiatrist or geriatrician only when the disease has made considerable progress or when the patient has suffered an acute delirium or a 'stroke' (a sudden loss of sensation and movement resulting from brain haemorrhage or thrombosis). This is probably the best-known manifestation of cerebral arteriosclerosis, though a similar process, affecting other parts of the brain, may cause less conspicuous lesions. Both may be associated with cerebral dysfunction if the lesions are sufficiently large. The 'stroke', resulting in a localized neurological defect (such as hemiplegia – a consequence of a vascular lesion interrupting the motor pathways) and associated with mental confusion or unconsciousness, is a common occurrence and a frequent 'presenting' symptom. On examination it often turns out that the patient's memory has been failing for some time, that he has been restless, emotionally disturbed, and that his mind may have been wandering for some months before his delirious episode. He may have had headaches, giddiness, blackouts and palpitations. Within a short time his memory impairment becomes more marked, his concentration suffers and he becomes slow to grasp the meaning of a situation, especially an unfamiliar one. Gradually the deterioration encroaches upon habitual performances, making him work inefficiently, narrowing his range of interests and initiative, and altering his emotional reactions. The general effect of the disease is to destroy the more complex and subtle features of the personality, though judgements based on experience, and the more salient personality traits, may remain relatively intact. This contrasts somewhat with senile dementia, which has an unremittingly progressive destructive effect on the central organizing dispositions of the personality.

The patient with cerebral arteriosclerosis reacts to his condition by becoming morose and pessimistic; his emotional control is weakened so that if he becomes tearful he is likely to weep bitterly, or if he becomes amused he is likely to laugh uproariously. The symptom is thought to arise partly as a consequence of lesions in neural motor pathways controlling emotional expression.

A confusional state is a state of acute mental imbalance and excitement which usually occurs during the course of cerebral arteriosclerosis, though it may also occur in other physical illnesses. The delirium puts patients out of touch with reality and makes them appear seriously demented. This sometimes happens in the early stages of the disease. Patients tend to recover from the episode quickly and leave hospital for a time. This cycle of events can repeat itself several times, until the cumulative brain damage and dementia make institutional care necessary. In a number of patients the deterioration is gradual and mental confusion may not occur. In the clouded state, patients are confused and inaccessible for a matter of hours, days or even weeks, and 'clouding of consciousness' can become a frequent and seriously disabling symptom. Confusion may be apparent, or greatly accentuated, at night. Patients fail to appreciate their real situation; they wander about the house or the streets, turn on the gas, switch on the lights, start fires, talk incoherently and resist attempts to get them back to bed. Each successive delirious episode, even if it occurs several months after the previous one, leaves a patient more deteriorated; but with proper encouragement patients may, for a little while at least, partially recover and appear reasonably competent.

Mental disturbances often cannot be traced to any particular cause. In old people a delirium is often brought on by a physical illness, such as pneumonia, anaemia, heart failure or severe bronchitis. It can be associated with post-operative complications or metabolic deficiencies, hospitalization, avitaminosis or a high temperature. Old people are much more likely than young people to become delirious because of a physical illness, which again illustrates the older person's greater susceptibility to pathological processes. Distinguishing between these transient confusional states on the one hand, and those associated with senile psychosis and psychosis with cerebral arteriosclerosis on the other, is a diagnostic problem for the physician, the patient's confused mental state making his diagnostic problem more difficult. But in practice, unless there is evidence to the contrary, it is assumed that the condition is caused by the physical illness, which is treated energetically. It can often be shown that the physical illness preceded, and can account for, the onset of the delirium. Intensive vitamin treatment has been given by some physicians, but there is no conclusive evidence that this aids recovery, except where the patient has suffered from obvious vitamin deficiency.

Feelings of depression occur frequently in cerebral arteriosclerosis, but they are not usually as severe as those found in affective psychosis in later life. The patient's mood is shallow and shifts easily from one extreme to the other. Suicidal tendencies may be pronounced in a delirious episode, but disappear abruptly when the patient's mood shifts. It sometimes happens, too, that a psychotic patient with cerebral arteriosclerosis is also predisposed to an affective disorder, in which case there has usually been a history of episodes of depression (or mania) earlier in life, unconnected with vascular disease. With patients of this kind it may prove necessary, as a last resort, to use electroconvulsive therapy to alleviate the depression and reduce the risk of suicide, but this is not normally used in the treatment of psychosis with cerebral arteriosclerosis; rather, antidepressant drugs are the treatment of choice.

In cerebral arteriosclerosis the onset of serious lesions in the brain is indicated by partial paralyses, tremors, speech disorders, and, less often, by sensory defects (temporary or permanent), or, more rarely, by convulsions. These are caused by the clotting of blood in the arteries of the brain (cerebral thrombosis). In cerebral haemorrhage the outcome depends on the brain tissue destroyed by the bleeding; in severe brain haemorrhage the patient becomes comatose and dies. Certain neurological signs may herald the onset of the disease before the psychological abnormalities become apparent. For example, the pupils contract and dilate slowly in response to changes in illumination, the muscular contractions elicited by tapping the tendons may be unequal, and stroking the sole of the foot elicits an upward rather than a downward reflex action of the big toe.

Patients retain some degree of personal cohesion until the late stages. Death need not be caused directly by arteriosclerosis – common causes are pneumonia and heart failure. The immediate prospects for the psychotic with cerebral arteriosclerosis are better than those of the patient with senile dementia, but the deterioration in his behaviour eventually becomes as severe as that of the latter patient. There is no treatment that can retard the progress of cerebral arteriosclerosis, unless it is associated with high blood pressure, when treatment will perhaps slow down the rate of deterioration.

Various disorders of perception and understanding may follow a 'stroke' – a hemiplegic patient, for example, may appear to be demented (mentally deteriorated) but actually be aphasic (unable to use or understand language) and so present a problem of rehabilitation. Many patients can be cared for at home or in hostels, where the general atmosphere and social amenities may be better than in a hospital, and where proper rehabilitation includes visits by social workers, supervised nutrition, participation in small groups and recreation.

Hypertension (abnormally prolonged high blood pressure) usually appears for no apparent reason, but sometimes as a consequence of kidney disorders. Ageing brings about an increase in blood pressure, and hypertension can lead to impairment of brain functions by damaging the blood vessels. Very severe hypertension can cause serious symptoms such as fits, unconsciousness or transient muscular weaknesses.

High blood pressure makes the walls of the arteries thicker and stronger, but other factors are probably involved as well. People who are overweight are more likely to suffer from hypertension and from other diseases of the heart and blood vessels. Hypertension can lead to structural alterations in the kidneys, which can, in turn, lead to a constriction of the blood vessels. In a few patients whose hypertension is caused by a diseased kidney, the disease may be cured by the surgical removal of the diseased kidney. High blood pressure can sometimes be controlled with the aid of drugs and visceral training without, of course, reversing structural changes that may have occurred in the brain.

Prolonged or periodic emotional stress of considerable severity can lead to a rise in blood pressure. Some individuals are more prone than others to strong cardiac reactions when emotionally upset, and such people may be prone to hypertension. Patients are usually advised by their physician to take a rest, have longer periods of sleep and find a more settled environment, in the belief that this will alleviate the condition, or at least delay the onset of its more serious consequences. For those who are reasonably intelligent and cooperative, a lot can be done to improve physical health, emotional outlook and life activities. The earliest symptoms are similar to those of mild neurotic disorders – headaches, fatigue, sleeplessness.

AFFECTIVE PSYCHOSES. Depression is a common complaint in elderly patients.[37] There are several reasons why this is so. Firstly, the various stresses of old age such as retirement, bereavement or physical illness are likely to provoke feelings of frustration, failure, disappointment, grief or resignation. Also, more people are surviving into later life to suffer from depressive psychotic illnesses and other functional psychiatric disorders. Moreover, the degenerative processes of old age, and the organic disturbances of the brain, intensify and sustain depression. Withdrawal and depression in response to any physical illness also become more likely as age increases. 'Depressive reaction' is diagnosed if the emotional disorder is disproportionate to the stress, or fails to clear up when the patient's circumstances improve. In *psychotic* depressives the history need not reveal a precipitating factor, but there is often a history of previous breakdowns.

The diagnosis and clinical description of psychiatric disorders in adult life and old age are difficult because of the multiplicity of factors involved, the range of differences between individuals, and the differential effects of age, sex and social class on aetiology and symptoms.

Patients who get severe depression for the first time late in life appear to be constitutionally different from those who suffer from depressive psychosis at an earlier age. Some of the depressions of old age occur in patients who have suffered from a depressive psychosis for a large part of their adult lives, to which the symptoms of senescence are then added. Elderly depressives become anxious, guilty and restless; they can become markedly worse within a few weeks – increasingly restless, hopeless, miserable and unable to sleep or to eat properly. The risk of suicide increases with depression. Patients who are severely depressed may attempt to kill themselves not merely because they have nothing to live for but also because of their delusions.

These dramatic symptoms can be contrasted with a simpler type of depressive reaction which differs only in degree from the normal reactions of older people to bereavement, illness and other kinds of stress. Patients in this category become very much slower in their thoughts, words and actions. They become constipated, unable to sleep, greatly concerned with their physical condition and uncertain of themselves. Obviously, old age brings out latent neurotic conditions or aggravates existing ones, so that it is not unusual to find some of the commoner symptoms of neurosis, such as anxiety, aggressive selfishness, intermittent depression and morbid preoccupation with bodily functions.

Many elderly psychotics come from the lower socio-economic strata of society. They are poor, badly clothed and housed, and physically debilitated. Their unfortunate circumstances intensify the feelings of apathy and hopelessness brought about by the disease.

Functional depressions often appear abruptly without obvious earlier indications, whereas depressions secondary to brain damage usually appear gradually, with mild early symptoms such as impaired recall for recent events, intellectual deterioration, absent-mindedness and disorientation, poorer personal and social habits, and cruder emotional reactions. Depressions secondary to brain damage also fluctuate, have a more 'superficial' quality, and lessen as the effects of brain disease become more pronounced and dementia supervenes. Sometimes psychiatric illnesses are precipitated by a physical illness which patients had ignored or were unaware of – such as an infection, kidney or heart disease; this can give rise to secondary psychological symptoms which complicate the clinical picture.

Mania is usually mild in later life and much less frequent than the depressive reaction; the rate of recovery is lower. Mania can appear suddenly – the patient becomes over-active and has a feeling of well-being, but no insight. Mania in the elderly and infirm brings an added risk of exhaustion and aggravation of physical illness. It can occur without definite signs of organic impairment or intellectual deterioration.

LATE PARAPHRENIA. Late paraphrenia has been described as a kind of schizophrenia of late onset, in which the main symptom is the delusion of persecution. It is sometimes difficult to distinguish from paranoid depression and organic brain disease.[38,39] The genetic factor is not as prominent as in early schizophrenia. Many patients have a predisposition towards seclusiveness, suspicion and anxiety about people; they are socially isolated, eccentric and difficult to deal with. The personal characteristics of patients with late paraphrenia include quarrelsomeness, religious extremism, egocentricity and lack of affection for others. Jealousy, arrogance and lack of emotional control are also fairly common. The personal qualities and habits which have been effective in coping with problems of adjustment during adult life can become more (or less) appropriate in old age. Women patients outnumber men considerably, and many of these women are either unmarried or living alone for other reasons, though bereavement, as such, seems not to be the precipitating factor in late paraphrenia. It is more likely to be the social upheaval, or possibly the reduction in close social interaction, which follows the loss of a husband, child or close companion.

The usual age of onset is after 60, unlike paranoia, which occurs at an earlier age. Partial or total deafness occurs more frequently than in other psychiatric groups of the same age, but physical health is not usually impaired. Defects of hearing (and of vision in other patients) may contribute to the development of hallucinations. Senile degeneration or cerebral arteriosclerosis in persons with pronounced 'schizoid' dispositions may result in late paraphrenia, especially when sensory impairments and social isolation are also involved. Paranoid delusions are often linked with hallucinatory experiences. Patients feel that radio transmitters are being used to control their thoughts, that people are walking through their rooms, that unseen enemies are threatening them or urging them to act, or that they are being sexually assaulted. The coincidental actions of other people and everyday sounds and events are woven into the delusions. Gradually the delusional beliefs disrupt their ordinary activities, so that they can no longer shop, or walk along the street normally. Finally their behaviour becomes socially unacceptable (because of their accusations, hostility and strangeness) and they are obliged to enter hospital for care and treatment.

When brought face-to-face with other people, late paraphrenics may seem alert and aware of what is going on. They show distress, anxiety and anger when their delusions are touched upon, but their emotions and attitudes are sometimes out of keeping with their professed beliefs. They may, for instance, refer to an alleged sexual assault in a flat matter-of-fact tone of voice, or smile vaguely when talking about the way their neighbours spy upon them.

Electroplexy (ECT) and antidepressant drugs improve some cases; but the general response to such treatment is poor, suggesting that late paraphrenia is not a primary affective disorder. Treatment with tranquillizers controls the condition in some patients – the problem is to get patients to continue taking these drugs after discharge from hospital.

DEMENTIA IN MIDDLE AGE. Dementia in middle age can be a *secondary consequence* of a number of disorders including cerebral vascular disease (with cerebral hypoxia), brain injury, toxic states (such as alcoholism), infection (such as meningitis or syphilis), brain tumour and other conditions. Patients with dementia, therefore, must be examined by a physician since the cause of the dementia may be amenable to treatment. The examination consists of an evaluation of the history of the condition, a physical examination, investigation by means of special tests such as EEG, air studies and lumbar puncture. Psychological tests are used to assess brain damage and intellectual deterioration.

There are also rare psychiatric conditions which may or may not be connected with the normal processes of ageing or with the psychiatric disorders of old age.[40] They are the 'presenile dementias'. Presenile dementia appears between the late forties and early sixties, as a consequence of degenerative disorders in the nervous system which are *not* associated with cerebral tumour, arteriosclerosis or other definite causes. The presenile dementias include: Alzheimer's disease, in which the brain suffers widespread degenerative changes and atrophy, and the patient suffers a gradual but systematic and profound disintegration of his personality; and Pick's disease, in which the degenerative changes and atrophy of the brain are mostly confined to the frontal and temporal areas – the effects are similar to those of Alzheimer's disease, except that there is no impairment of posture or movement, and no hallucinations or delusions. Other very infrequent disorders (involving degenerative changes in the brain and accompanied by various kinds of mental and behavioural abnormalities) include Jakob-Creutzfeldt's disease and Huntington's Chorea. Convulsions appearing for the first time late in life can be symptomatic of cortical atrophy or cerebral tumour. Other kinds of presenile dementia giving rise to cortical atrophy have been described, including that associated with mongolism, but no standard system of classification has yet emerged. In practice the various presenile disorders are rare and difficult to distinguish.

3. CARING FOR PSYCHOGERIATRIC PATIENTS

There are psychological and behavioural aspects to *any* physical illness. But, more particularly in old age, respiratory inadequacy, heart failure, malnutrition and stroke have definite psychological effects, such as confusion and anxiety. About one third of the elderly sick develop psychiatric problems, though only a small percentage need prolonged in-patient treatment; in fact, most people live their lives in reasonable health and vigour and die without having experienced serious psychiatric disorders in later life. More is being done to improve the conditions in which geriatric patients spend their last years, though much still remains to be done. The problem is likely to be a growing one, unless (as seems unlikely) we are able to apply drugs or other forms of preventive medicine to stave off senescence.

Increases in the number of geriatric patients create serious problems; financial and human resources on a large scale are needed in order to deal with them because elderly sick people need a great deal of medical and social care.[41] Different kinds of patient need different kinds of accommodation: some are better off at home or in sheltered housing, others need to be looked after in mental hospitals, in the geriatric units of general hospitals, or in adequately equipped and serviced homes or hostels for old people. The treatment of psychiatric patients and the elderly infirm has been improved in recent years by the development of 'day hospitals' where selected patients can attend during the day for medical or social reasons or as part of their rehabilitation. Such hospitals have a number of advantages – they are flexible, economical in the use of medical resources, 'community oriented' and well suited to the needs of individual patients.[42–45]

The 'demand' for geriatric and psychiatric treatment and care is considerably in excess of the available health and welfare services. The resources for coping with these problems are *relatively* much less than for other kinds of social and medical service. The attitudes of many medical students and practitioners (and the rest of us) tend to lag behind modern developments. Individuals living in the community (rather than the health and welfare services) carry the main burden of ageing. At present the health services deal with the tip of the 'iceberg' of psychogeriatric illness, since only a small proportion of old people with psychiatric disorders are cared for as hospital in-patients or as residents of homes. Perhaps the most effective ways of dealing with the problem would be to improve the facilities for domiciliary care by, for example, payments to kin and for foster-care, maintaining registers of all old people, making greater financial provision for the elderly and, perhaps no less important, raising the standard of health education in the community and changing social attitudes.

Hospital treatment has a number of advantages: the risk of suicide is reduced; the patient can be observed continuously; he can be examined and treated more conveniently and effectively; his family and friends can obtain some relief from an intolerable burden. A frequent cause of referral (of an elderly person to a physician) is the difficulty experienced by the family in looking after him, which has led to emotional stress, loss of sleep, loss of earnings, interpersonal conflicts and other frustrations. Hospital treatment, which brings rest, a change of surroundings and proper food, can lead to fairly rapid recovery. Most patients suffering from an affective psychosis in later life recover, and many are discharged. Some patients recover, but then relapse and are readmitted to hospital; this sequence of events may be repeated.

The effectiveness of out-patient treatment and community care depends to a large extent on such obvious factors as the patient's material resources, his domestic circumstances, local psychiatric facilities, cooperation from the extended family, friends and neighbours, and local voluntary services.[46] Not the least important consideration is the effect that the patient living outside an institution has on the people who have to look after him.

A patient may become confused and disoriented if he is transferred abruptly, and without explanation or support, from his familiar domestic circumstances to the unfamiliar circumstances of a nursing home or hospital.[47] Full explanations and repeated assurances are needed to allay the fears that patients have; a considerable amount of subsequent support and guidance may be necessary to get them settled in and actively participating in the social activities of the hospital or home. Left to themselves, they may just sit and remain withdrawn and apathetic. Some old people need a lot of convincing that they are too ill to live at home. Men, especially, resist the suggestion that they are sick and in need of care and treatment, and women need to be assured that they are not being rejected by the family. For some individuals interest in members of the opposite sex continues to provide an incentive for forming new social relationships.

How can one decide that the benefits derived from transfer to improved physical and social surroundings are not offset by the costs incurred in making the readjustment – especially for vulnerable aged people? They may not survive for as long or as well as they would have if treatment had been limited to the elimination of serious defects in their original environment. The effects of treatment are hard to evaluate. Treatment often cannot be allocated on an experimental basis; nor can one rely simply on clinical impressions of individual cases or even on a comparison of patients before or after treatment. Some recent research into the effects of various sorts of treatment and rehabilitation seems not to have demonstrated substantial or lasting improvements for geriatric patients in general, presumably because the comparisons have been between existing and new treatments rather than between treatment and no treatment.

This is an indication of the severity and extent of the degenerative effects of ageing and of the difficulty in achieving substantial and lasting improvements in functional capacity and well-being.[48-50]

There is a growing awareness of the needs of the elderly, and efforts are being made by hospital staffs and those in residential homes to create optimum physical and social surroundings. The built environment is important, since many patients are unable to climb stairs or walk without support. Many need guidance about wearing glasses and using hearing aids if they are to make the most of their opportunities for entertainment and recreation. Mobility can be improved by treatment of the feet and by physiotherapy; ergonomic considerations and 'environmental geriatrics' can make useful contributions to the design and layout of 'behaviour settings' and to the effectiveness of 'prosthetic' aids and domestic utensils. Accidents and infections have serious consequences for the aged and must be guarded against. Efficient and imaginative nursing care can do much to ease the discomforts of chronic physical illness. The environment and the daily routines should be uncomplicated and satisfying. The more competent patients should be able to leave from time to time to stay with relatives or friends.

The rehabilitation of elderly psychiatric patients who recover from a mental illness requires supervision and subsequent follow-up, since such patients cannot cope with the normal problems of adjustment. At present this is inadequate because of the shortage of money and trained personnel. However, more small residential homes are being established where old people with manageable psychiatric disorders can be helped to make a readjustment. People are becoming more aware of the severity and extent of the disorders of old age, and this is leading to earlier and more effective forms of care and treatment. Wherever possible, elderly psychiatric patients are encouraged to stay active and participate in social activities. The treatment of mental illness in old age is not a once-and-for-all affair. Psychiatric disorders in old age require treatment to be maintained after discharge from hospital. After a period of improvement some patients relapse and need renewed examination and treatment. Follow-up often includes hospital out-patient attendances for the supervision of maintenance treatment. Sometimes special treatments are required, such as physiotherapy or occupational therapy, and it is desirable to have home visits by a social worker.

Preventive psychiatric techniques lie in the future. Present treatment methods for psychogeriatric conditions are largely supportive and palliative. Even so, economies could be secured if it were possible to predict the benefit that any particular patient would get from treatment. For example, certain drugs are effective in reducing the severity and duration of exhausting mental disturbance and may therefore help to prevent the patient from hurting himself and other people. There has not been nearly as much research on the effects of drugs on psychiatric illness in old age as in early adult life. The use of drugs in the treatment of elderly psychiatric patients (and preventively) constitutes an important area of research. These drugs are intended to help re-establish physiological and psychological equilibrium, but the use of drugs in the treatment of elderly people presents difficulties. The effects of drugs are not necessarily the same over a wide age range, hence the behavioural and physiological measures used to assess them must be validated independently for each age group and diagnostic group. Some drugs administered to older patients may elicit unusual reactions – even reversals of effect are not discounted; the side-effects may be different from those seen in younger patients, and the dosage levels may have to be adjusted – as with barbiturates or appetite inhibitors. Individual differences in reaction to drugs are not likely to diminish as age increases, and this makes it difficult to establish reliable norms and base-lines for the assessment of the effects of age in response to drugs. The older person's greater physiological inadequacy adds to the difficulty of assessing the effect of a particular drug. The growing demand for treatment to prevent, retard or ameliorate the adverse effects of ageing is stimulating drug research and sales pressure. But it would be unfortunate, to say the least, if commercial interests were to override scientific and ethical considerations.

4. GERIATRIC CLINICAL PSYCHOLOGY

(a) *Problems and Methods of Psychological Assessment*

Changes in the brain in old age have been thought of in terms of diffuse brain damage – hence the term 'chronic brain syndrome' (CBS). But these changes can also be thought of as the accumulation of a number of specific neurological defects. From this point of view, senile dementia can be characterized as a collection of focal deficits set in a context of more general impairment.[51] Memory impairment, for example, seems to be a consequence of damage or dysfunction in certain parts of the temporal lobes, hippocampus and mammillary bodies. Neurological changes in the hippocampus in senile dementia and normal old age can have adverse effects on memory through their involvement in the limbic system. Loss of short-term learning and memory capacity is conspicuous in senile dementia. It is an amnesic syndrome – greatly in excess of normal memory impairment in later life. It involves the loss of recent memories, an inability to profit from new experience, disorientation – for time, place and circumstance; and confabulation, i.e. ad hoc guesswork, substitutes for a rational account of one's actions. Elderly patients suffering from CBS have poor orientation for time and place even if their sense of personal identity is still intact. They are easily distracted and confused, and likely to misunderstand what they see and hear. Their emotional reactions are exaggerated and tied to momentary circumstances, rather than modulated and kept in perspective. Language impairment affects meaning rather than grammar and vocabulary. Psychomotor and other signs of brain damage, like perseveration and aphasia, can be elicited by neurological tests.

Diagnostic psychological assessment of the elderly consists largely of the assessment of mental status and behavioural competence by means of simple questionnaires or by more systematic psychometric investigation in a medical context (though possibly in a domestic setting). The assessment of feelings and desires is less formal, and is normally done through the intuitive appraisal of expressive behaviour during clinical interviews. More formal methods of assessment, however, are available, for example in relation to the measurement of anxiety and depression. Rating scales, symptom check lists, biographical inventories and other clinical instruments are employed.[52–69] The WAIS was described and discussed in Chapter Six.

There seems to be some need for a critical reappraisal of the aims and methods of psychological assessment in relation to adult ageing, and especially in relation to psychological disorders in late life.[70] Methods of assessment validated on young adults are not necessarily equally valid or appropriate for the old. Furthermore, if adult ageing is the accumulation of various interrelated pathological conditions, then it may not be profitable to think in terms of distinguishable diseases or 'types' of impairment, and more emphasis would have to be given to the assessment of individual cases. Rather than attaching diagnostic labels and prescribing blanket treatments, more emphasis should be given to individualized assessment and treatment programmes, taking into account the *milieu* as well as the person.

Normal ageing, mental disease and brain damage all impair cognitive capacity in both general and specific ways – hence differential diagnosis is frequently difficult and inaccurate. The problem of base rates and risks of misclassification in diagnostic assessment are too well known to need elaboration. They enter into clinical psychology with the elderly as with other kinds of patient. The frequency of misclassification depends upon a variety of factors; there is no fixed rate for a particular test or index.

A mental status questionnaire examines a patient's orientation for time, place and person, his ability to follow simple instructions, and so on. Senile patients are deficient in this kind of general functional competence relative to normal old people. A patient's mental status is usually established at an initial assessment for screening purposes, but may prove useful in connection with diagnosis and prediction. Systematic rating scales are used to assess physical disability, drug effects, motivation (apathy), communication and social behaviour, and so on. The assessment of behavioural competence, however, has to be more narrowly focused, so that specific functions can be assessed directly, for example the patient's ability to manage the activities of daily living or to understand and carry out instructions. Global measures of biological function or intellectual capacity appear not to be particularly useful. Indeed, mental status questionnaires are needed partly because senile patients cannot cope with the ordinary sorts of intelligence test.

New tests of residual cognitive capacity are being devised that may be capable of yielding independent measures at frequent intervals. Such tests might have particular value as sensitive indices of treatment, showing, for example, the effect of a drug or a retraining programme. So far, however, little progress has been made, although the advent of automated psychological testing has provided some useful hardware for research of this sort.[71,72] The idea behind such tests is that a simple non-verbal task, like identifying shapes on a form-board or common objects depicted on cards, can be administered with different but equivalent samples of items on several different occasions. The patient's errors and performance times are recorded and, if the measure is sensitive, they should vary with physical and mental health and in response to treatment.

The author has used the form-board method to demonstrate residual cognitive differences between very deteriorated patients (scoring zero on a mental status questionnaire) and to obtain repeated measures on many occasions. Naturally, difficulties are encountered with regard to cooperation, sensory or motor impairment, comprehension, motivation and so on; all of these affect the reliability and validity of measurements.

Tests of residual cognitive capacity, however, should prove useful to clinical psychologists working with elderly patients by providing base-line measures – with patients acting as their own controls; they avoid some of the difficulties associated with item content, norms, and undue reliance on verbal comprehension. They are intended to be sensitive to small variations in pathology and treatment effects. Their chief asset would be the opportunity to repeat virtually the same measure on successive occasions.[73]

What is needed is a bridge between neuropathology and psychological assessment. Whether this will be achieved by identifying the neurological deficits underlying performance inadequacies on psychological tests, or by constructing psychometric or other instruments to define the behavioural counterparts of neurological deficits, remains to be seen. It seems likely that serial variations and trends in performance as well as 'snapshot' assessments will have diagnostic utility. This implies a need for the construction of tests giving repeated measures which will provide norms for, and record the course of, intellectual deterioration in normal and pathological ageing. At present, we are largely restricted to single assessments which reveal abnormal discrepancies within a patient's cognitive abilities, or between his performance and some standard of comparison, or reveal relative differences between diagnostic groups, but do not reveal the trend in his performance over time or under different treatment conditions.

The disadvantage of intellectual performance as a single behavioural index of the state of the brain is that it is globally impaired by *various* organic and functional conditions. What is required is a set of behavioural indices which are differentially sensitive to focal (specific) neuropathological or psychopathological conditions. Sometimes focal damage can be treated by surgery whereas diffuse brain damage cannot – this is one aspect of diagnostic psychological assessment.

It seems likely that the best behavioural indices of neuropathological states will be revealed by cognitive tests; but quite different methods cannot be ruled out – those of behavioural ecology, for example, the analysis of language or expressive behaviour, biographical analysis, or self-rating of mood and symptoms. Attempts to devise behavioural indices of neurological lesions have not been conspicuously successful, but among the more commonly reported behavioural effects are the following: a reduction in abstraction and generalization; an increase in primitive, literal and concrete forms of cognition; increased perseveration and rigidity of response; a reduction in the ability to translate or codify – to operate with symbols and meanings; increased difficulty in the serial organization of behaviour; a reduction in short-term learning and remembering; increased language impairment; perceptual-motor and visual–spatial disorganization.

It does not seem probable that a substantial bridge between neuropathology and the psychological assessment of behavioural deficits will be established in the near future; but this does not mean that behavioural research can mark time. Attempts should be made to develop theories about the behavioural effects of adult ageing and to show how psychological assessment can be used directly in the validation of treatment. Theories about behaviour and psychological processes can be formulated without reference to neurological conditions or psychiatric diagnosis. For example, explanatory concepts such as interference, consolidation and 'effort after meaning', help to account for the apparent effects of age and disease on learning, remembering and thinking. At present, many psychometric measures of memory confound the mechanisms of attention, primary storage, rehearsal, transfer, interference, retrieval and output. Ideally, one would like to be able to produce, under controlled experimental conditions, the behavioural deficits associated with neuropathological states. In this way, we should gain more insight into brain mechanisms. Clinical psychologists are not likely to provide neuropathologists with useful *behavioural* data, however, until they can specify, and predict or control, the effects of such mechanisms.

The Wechsler digit-span test is a relatively crude measure of memory span. But even more sensitive memory scales are affected by functions over and above those which define memory.[74] Word learning, paired associate learning, probe-digit recognition, and other measures of relatively short-term learning and remembering have their clinical uses. They can be adjusted for sensory or motor impairment and can be made simple enough to test residual capacities.

It would be interesting to examine whether tests capable of providing repeated measurements (of the sort already referred to) could be used to study the extent to which the capacities underlying performance could *respond to demand* by growth i.e. by showing improvement over a number of test occasions. A word-learning test, for example, measures response to demand over a short continuous period of testing; more informative results might be achieved by measuring changes in score over a number of training sessions. This suggestion further emphasizes the need for longitudinal studies over short intervals using standard tests capable of yielding comparable measures on several occasions – although there are serious problems here (see Chapter Eleven). One difficulty is to design tests which can be validated against concurrent or post-mortem neuropathological findings regarding focal damage. Another problem is to construct psychological theories which explain any differential effects of normal ageing, brain damage and mental disease on cognition.

(b) *Possibilities for Psychological Treatment*

Minor psychiatric disorders are sometimes not referred to the general practitioner or not recognized by him for what they are. As with physical ailments, people learn to live with their condition and do not think of themselves as needing treatment. Many elderly people especially are at risk because they are relatively isolated and do not have friends or relatives to encourage them to seek help. Thus preventive or early treatment is not given as it might be, and disturbances respond less well to late treatment. Suicide and attempted suicide, for example, are often associated with neurotic depression and depression provoked by physical illness. Physical illness – to which middle-aged and older people become increasingly liable – creates stress and may provoke a variety of psychological reactions to aggravate the overall situation; surgical disfigurement too may lead to depression, anxiety, loss of self-esteem and social withdrawal.

Counselling procedures suitable for younger people are not necessarily suitable for the elderly. The elderly patient's increased dependence upon others is real, not imaginary, and his environment is genuinely difficult. His intellectual and emotional resources are reduced and he can no longer organize his behaviour adequately. Thus therapeutic procedures need to be adapted to suit the special conditions of neurosis and maladjustment in later life.[75-77] Treatment is limited to handling specific problems over short periods of time, providing guidance and support. Whenever possible, use is made of the patient's long-standing strategies of adjustment, even though they may not be ideal, for example, aggressiveness. The psychotherapist can expect only marginal improvements and frequent relapses, and he may have to establish a relationship with his elderly patient which is more natural (less formal) and more superficial (in the sense of dealing with immediate practical issues) than would be the case with a younger patient. His aim is to alleviate present symptoms rather than to produce lasting changes in the personality. Deep psychotherapy is regarded as difficult, inappropriate and ineffective for elderly neurotic patients. Psychological counselling, on the other hand, can help an older person to solve current interpersonal problems and perhaps to handle disturbing emotions.

Group psychotherapy has beneficial results with some elderly patients; social interaction and discussion obviously differs from that found among groups of younger patients, but the social psychology of group dynamics in relation to ageing has received relatively little attention from experimenters.[78] The apparent increase with age in social conformity may be partly a function of the older subject's diminished confidence in his performance on the experimental task.

Reminiscence – often thought of as more prominent in late

life – does not necessarily signify lack of concern with the present or future, since reminiscence is found at all ages. It can be used as a source of biographical data. Reminiscence in late life has a number of psychological functions. It serves a communicative and an expressive function: that is, it makes explicit – so that others may understand and learn – the ideas and beliefs that form the contents of the old person's experience; and it allows the elderly person to express his feelings, attitudes and values. Reminiscence, through the process of life-review, seems to provide the elderly person with opportunities to re-examine his past life and possibly to reorganize his present activities and attitudes.[79-81] Psychotherapeutic intervention can use reminiscence to improve the process of self-analysis; the elderly person is, as it were, predisposed to free-associate. By helping him to explore the ramifications of his life-review, to resolve the conflicts and contradictions in it, to reassess and reinterpret what has happened, the psychotherapist may improve the older person's image of himself and promote more effective strategies of adjustment.

This method seems particularly appropriate if there is a risk that a patient will lose his sense of personal identity because of relocation or institutionalization. It would also seem to be appropriate in counselling maladjusted people in mid-life who are suffering from some kind of crisis of identity. The institutional environment – physical as well as social – can be arranged so that it helps to improve and maintain a patient's sense of personal identity. The patient's life-review may be shaped by techniques of behaviour modification; that is to say, he can be led, by means of suitable rewards, to express opinions about himself, his past life and present circumstances which are conducive to good adjustment and realistic self-appraisal. There seems to be no reason why behaviour modification and related techniques should not prove useful in the treatment of psychogeriatric patients, if only to supplement pharmacological and psychotherapeutic methods, and to help counteract the effects of disuse.[82-88] Relatively little is known about the effectiveness of behaviour therapy in laboratory or institutional settings (or of 'contingency management' in more natural settings) for the treatment of elderly patients.[89–91] The effects of ageing on mentally retarded adults are difficult to separate out from those of institutionalization and pathology.[92–95] Obviously the *milieu,* and not merely the patient, requires 'treatment' if the patient is to be successfully rehabilitated; hence the need for the selection and training of staff and for good social welfare services. These are long-term treatment measures, however; as psychiatric help is often required urgently, this usually means giving antidepressant drugs or other physical treatment as a first line of defence.

CHAPTER ELEVEN

Methodological Issues in the Study of Human Ageing

1. INTRODUCTION

The material in this chapter is rather specialized and technical, and will be of interest mainly to research workers in gerontology. Readers who find it difficult or of little interest may wish to omit some sections or go directly to the next and final chapter.

Scientific research in social and behavioural gerontology is difficult, for a number of reasons. As we have seen, it is something of a metapsychological puzzle to work out how the process of ageing is to be conceptualized. As a sequence of morphological changes? As a series of gradual quantitative changes on a set of basic dimensions of individual differences? As a complex causal path?

These questions are difficult to answer, partly because it is not clear what is to count as a morphological (structural) change or how it is to be represented, partly because the basic psychological dimensions of individual differences and of age changes are obscure and difficult to measure. Age changes *appear* to be continuous, but may be stepwise and out of phase between individuals, in which case representation by average values would be misleading. In addition, it is necessary to find methods for dealing with empirical data. This gives rise to problems associated with sampling – created by dependence on the cooperation of volunteer subjects and by the selective effects of attrition through death, migration or other cause. There are further difficulties associated with measurement, created by the inadequacies of many psychometric tests. Other problems are associated with the design and administration of experiments.

These so-called 'methodological' problems have been admitted for a long time but are now being widely and vigorously discussed.[1-8] They are not confined to the study of ageing, but are encountered in other areas of research, including developmental psychology, economics, and the social sciences generally.[9-13] Indeed, it could be argued that their importance has been somewhat exaggerated in recent years – perhaps as a reaction to previous neglect of them. Moreover, some of the discussion has become so elaborate and technical that it threatens to hinder consideration of other fundamental issues concerning theory and applications.

Perhaps the best way to deal with this thorny topic is to describe in very simple terms the three basic methods of research and then go on to discuss some of the assumptions and complications. Research investigations follow one of three basic designs: longitudinal, cross-sectional, and mixed.

The *longitudinal,* or *follow-up,* method measures the performance of a sample of subjects at an initial chronological age, and then on one or more subsequent occasions – over shorter or longer intervals. The results are described in graphs or tables, and the appropriate tests are applied to examine whether the 'effects of age' are statistically significant. Contrasting groups of subjects, for example males versus females, or contrasting experimental treatments, such as nutrition or exercise, can be examined for any differential effects of ageing. If several variables are measured, changes in their relationships over time may be of interest, for example blood pressure and psychiatric symptoms.

The *cross-sectional* method measures the performance of two or more comparable samples of subjects at different age levels, at say, 20, 40, and 60 years of age. The method of setting up comparable samples varies, depending on whether they are intended to represent actual age groups or a hypothetical set of populations matched for, say, education, health and intelligence. As with the longitudinal method, contrasting groups or experimental treatments can be examined for any differential effects of ageing. If several variables are measured, their relationships with each other may vary systematically from one age level to another, as in the differential decline of mental abilities.

As shown in Figure 12, the investigator has to decide whether the *average* differences between age groups are statistically and psychologically significant. This is difficult because age differences are sometimes small, and the score distributions for different age groups overlap considerably. Statistical decision theory is needed to solve such problems. Further complications arise if the score distributions are not 'normal', if upper and lower score limits artificially restrict the range of observations, if the units of measurement are not at least 'interval' scale units, and if the scores are obtained from the same subjects on three different occasions.

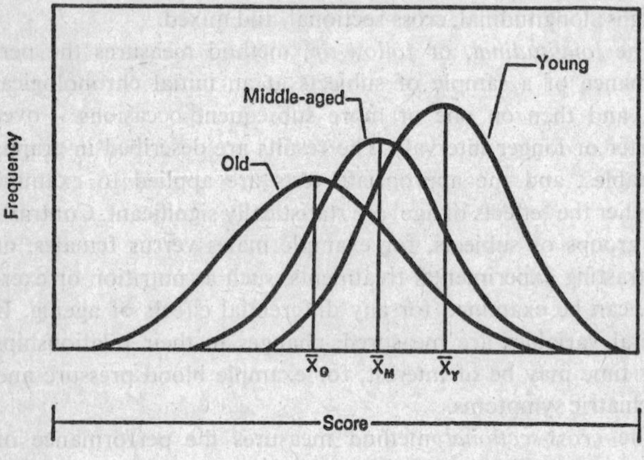

FIGURE 12 Overlapping frequency distributions for three age groups

The mixed or *cross-longitudinal* method measures the performance of several groups (assumed to be comparable) at different initial ages, say 20, 40, and 60 years, as in the cross-sectional method, and then follows up each group with similar measures on one or more subsequent occasions. This method combines the advantages and eliminates some of the disadvantages of the longitudinal and cross-sectional methods, and for this reason it is regarded by some as the ideal method. We shall see, however, that there is no ideal method which will suit all investigations. Experimental design and statistical analysis must conform to the logical, empirical and administrative circumstances governing each particular investigation.

2. ASSUMPTIONS AND COMPLICATIONS

(a) *Age Changes and Age Differences*

The age changes revealed by the longitudinal method are not always the same as those revealed by the cross-sectional method, hence the persisting concern with methodological issues. The mixed method is a convenient way of cross-checking results and testing additional hypotheses.

By general agreement, the term 'age change' is used to refer to the results from longitudinal studies – for the obvious reason that changes in score have been observed for the *same* persons. Similarly, the term 'age difference' is used to refer to the results from cross-sectional studies – because the scores for *different* persons are being compared. This familiar and easy usage is misleading however, because it implies that an observed change or difference is an effect of *age,* when it might be the effect of a secular trend, or an environmental influence, or even an experimental artefact, such as a fallible measure.

Figure 13 represents the hypothetical results obtained by measuring two functions A and B cross-sectionally and longitudinally. Several groups of subjects at different age levels are tested initially and on a second occasion ten years later. The complications arising from sampling errors and measurement errors are ignored. The trend line running through the cross-sectional results for Function A corresponds with the series of lines connecting the initial and follow-up scores for each age group, so the two methods give the same result. The trend line running through the cross-sectional results for Function B, however, does not correspond with the series of lines connecting the initial and follow-up scores obtained by the longitudinal method. The cross-sectional result

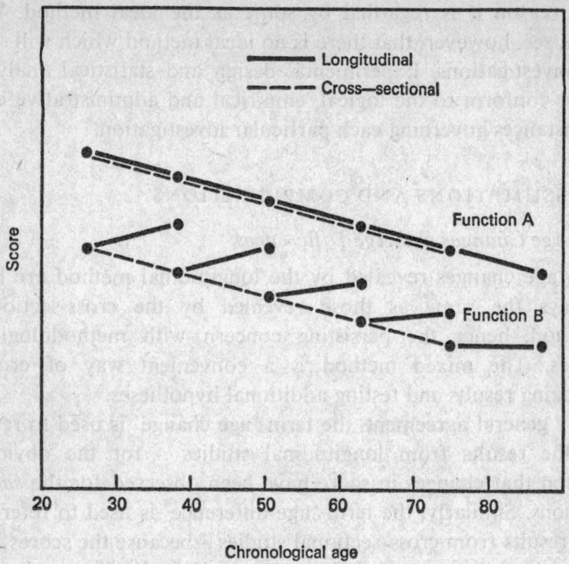

FIGURE 13 Schematic representation of the effects of age on two functions as measured by two methods.

for Function B shows a systematic linear decrease against age, whereas the longitudinal result shows a series of diminishing improvements at successively higher age levels. Such comparisons have been made, for example, for the effects of age on intelligence, hearing and weight. The existence of a discrepancy means that one or the other or both methods are failing to show the effects of *ageing*; and even when no discrepancy occurs, it does not follow that an age effect has been conclusively proven.[14-18] Thus, strictly speaking, the term *age changes* should refer to *changes within* persons which are demonstrably due to the effects of increased age; the term *age differences* should refer to *differences between* persons which are demonstrably due to the effects of increased age. Age effects are not necessarily the same as age-related effects. Some of the reasons why the hypothetical results shown in Figure 13 are not as simple as they appear to be are dealt with in the following sections.

(b) *Cross-Sectional and Longitudinal Analyses with Worked Examples*

Consider a situation in which a variable, X, appears to decline in adult life. How can one investigate the phenomenon and estimate the rate of decline?

CROSS-SECTIONAL. A simple method, as we have seen, is to examine the *differences* between comparable samples of subjects at various adult age levels. This method, however, depends upon a number of conditions which are unlikely to be met, such as the following: that there has been no selective loss through death over the age-range considered; that samples which are truly representative of the 'population' under investigation can be selected and tested at each age level; and that the measure of X is valid, reliable, and equally applicable to all age groups. Even if all these conditions could be met, there still remains a major source of confusion: each age group represents its respective cohort, defined as the people born into the reference population in a specific year, and there may have been systematic secular changes – generation by generation changes – in X, the function under investigation. Such secular changes have taken place over recent generations in height, weight, menarche, physical health, education and possibly intelligence. However, it is not clear to what extent such secular trends bring about equal changes in all or most members of the population, or systematic differential changes, as between men and women, or between different socio-economic classes. Secular effects can interact with age, for example in relation to amount of absence from work.[19]

The relationships between age effects and secular effects can be demonstrated in a fairly simple way by resort to artificial data, as in the examples which follow. These contrived data show that secular changes could produce a shift not only in the average level of X (condition I), but also in the dispersion of scores on X (condition II), as follows.

Cohort born:	*1930*	*1940*	*1950*	
Time of measurement:	*1970*	*1970*	*1970*	*Condition I*
Age at time of measurement:	*40*	*30*	*20*	
Scores on X, n = 5	70	80	85	
	60	70	75	
	50	60	65	
	40	50	55	
	30	40	45	
Mean X:	50	60	65	
Range X:	40	40	40	

Cohort born:	*1930*	*1940*	*1950*	
Time of measurement:	*1970*	*1970*	*1970*	*Condition II*
Age at time of measurement:	*40*	*30*	*20*	
Scores on X, n = 5	70	70	70	
	60	65	67·5	
	50	60	65	
	40	55	62·5	
	30	50	60	
Mean X:	50	60	65	
Range X:	40	20	10	

Under condition I, measured in 1970, X shows an *increase* of 15 points between the cohorts of 1930 and 1950, corresponding to a *decrease* with age between 20 and 40. The same result holds for condition II. However, the dispersion of scores is the same for each cohort under condition I, whereas under condition II it *decreases* generation by generation, or *increases* with age.

Longevity itself shows a secular trend. The average duration of life has been increasing generation by generation, but it has not been increasing equally for all members of a cohort; it has been increasing more for those members with a relatively short life expectation – the upper limit of longevity seems to have remained fixed. It is possible that the average level and distribution of intelligence, and other psychological capacities, are affected by secular trends reflecting the selective effects of social evolution, such as differential fertility rates or assortative mating in relation to intelligence.

If the reader 'experiments' by making up other examples using hypothetical data, he will see that various outcomes are possible, depending upon the assumptions he makes regarding measurement limits, rates of change, interaction effects between two or more variables, errors and so on. The 'experiments' can be further complicated by considering samples comprising sub-samples of subjects differently affected by secular trends or age changes. The reader may thus gain some insight into the different ways of interpreting the results of investigations into the effects of ageing.

The next examples also use artificial data: condition III represents the scores for a Function F in the absence of a secular trend; condition IV represents the scores for a Function C and an increasing secular trend. The hypothetical effect of age on Function C is nil; the hypothetical effect of age on Function F is to reduce the score by 5 points in each successive decade after age 20, as follows:

Cohort born:	*1930*	*1940*	*1950*	
Time of measurement:	*1970*	*1970*	*1970*	
Age at time of measurement:	*40*	*30*	*20*	
Mean score assuming no secular trend:	70	70	70	*Condition III*
Add hypothetical age effect:	−10	−5	0	
Result (for Function F):	60	65	70	
Mean score assuming a secular increase:	50	60	70	*Condition IV*
Add hypothetical nil age effect:	0	0	0	
Result (for Function C):	50	60	70	

If we now compare Funtions F and C with regard to their differences, *and assume no knowledge of the secular trends,* we get the following result:

Age at test:	*20*	*30*	*40*
Mean score on Function C:	70	60	50
" " " " F:	70	65	60
Difference:	0	−5	−10

Both functions appear to decline with age but Function F appears to decline more slowly than Function C, so that the discrepancy between them increases with age. The purpose of this illustration is to show that the apparent differential decline with age of psychological functions need not be entirely caused by the effects of ageing. Indeed, the above illustration has been deviously designed to show a paradoxical effect, as follows. Let Function C represent intellectual attainment; this shows a secular increase and no age decline. Let Function F represent native intelligence; this shows no secular increase and an age decline; but the apparent effect, *assuming no prior knowledge*, is a differential decline with age in C and F, with C, contrary to actual empirical evidence, declining faster than F. An actual increase with age in C (crystallized ability), if combined with an actual secular increase of similar size, could give the impression of no age differences in a cross-sectional study. Similarly, the effect of a small actual secular decrease combined with a small actual decrease with age could give the impression of a substantial decline with age in F (fluid ability).

It is clear that the cross-sectional method of examining age differences could be grossly misleading if secular trends were present. However, any reader not convinced of the description of the differential effects of ageing on intelligence given in an earlier chapter, and based largely on cross-sectional studies, might find it instructive to try to work out the implications of an alternative description which minimizes ageing as an explanatory variable, as in the above example.

LONGITUDINAL. Another way of examining an apparent decline with age in some variable X, we saw, was to examine the *changes* within the same sample of subjects followed up at various adult ages. This method, however, also depends upon a number of conditions which are unlikely to be met, such as the following: that the cohort selected for investigation is fairly typical; that the measures of X are similarly valid and reliable at each age level on successive occasions of testing, and are sequentially independent; and that there is no systematic loss of subjects from the sample throughout the follow-up period. Even if they could be met, there still remains a major source of confusion: the sample is subjected to environmental influences or 'treatment effects' other than those functionally associated with ageing. Changes associated with environmental influence might be associated with cultural evolution, socio-economic conditions, and with environmental health hazards – infectious diseases, pollution, radiation, stress, malnutrition. Little is known about such naturally occurring 'treatment effects' on psychological capacities and behavioural dispositions in adult life, although some aspects of medical statistics take account of analogous effects, for example in rubella, and for thalidomide.

Using simple artificial data again, and assuming no knowledge of the effect of time of measurement (environmental influence), condition V shows a decline of 10 points between the ages of 20 and 40 years, as follows:

Cohort born:	*1930*	*1930*	*1930*	
Time of measurement:	*1950*	*1960*	*1970*	*Condition V*
Age at time of measurement:	*20*	*30*	*40*	
Repeated measures on the same sample, n = 5, k = 3	70	65	60	
	60	55	50	
	50	45	40	
	40	35	30	
	30	25	20	
Mean:	50	45	40	

The natural inclination is to search for an intrinsic age effect which explains the observed scores, but the effect might be contingent upon extrinsic influences, of the sort already mentioned.

(c) *Interdependence of Age, Cohort and Time of Measurement*

BASIC RELATIONSHIPS. Three constraints on the design of an investigation have been distinguished: chronological age, date of birth (cohort), and time of measurement. However, when any two of these are specified, the third is implied. For example, if we specify the ages and dates of birth, the times of measurement are implied. It is possible to use either one age level or several, either one time of measurement or several, and either one cohort with repeated measures on the same subjects or one cohort with measures on independent random samples. Since some combinations (of ages, cohorts and times of measurement) are impossible and others are trivial, only three of the simple designs are of interest, namely those that hold constant one of the variables, as follows:

Several ages:	40	50	60	Fixed cohort
One cohort:	1940	1940	1940	(longitudinal
Several times of				method)
measurement:	1980	1990	2000	
Several ages:	40	50	60	Fixed time of
Several cohorts:	1940	1930	1920	measurement
				(cross-
One time of				sectional
measurement:	1980	1980	1980	method)
One age:	40	40	40	Fixed age
Several cohorts:	1960	1950	1940	(secular
Several times of				method)
measurement:	2000	1990	1980	

These three simple designs can be incorporated and improved upon in a more complex design by taking several values for two of the three variables and letting the values for the third variable be implied – and entered in the cells of the matrix formed by the first two variables. This procedure is illustrated in the worked example in the following section. Note, however, that it is important to draw a distinction between designs which measure effects *within* the same subjects, and those which measure effects *between* subjects; the error term in analysis of variance is usually smaller in the former.

WORKED EXAMPLE. The following complex example uses artificial data. It shows how the effects of age, cohort and time of measurement might combine to produce a given set of measurements of Function X. There are five age levels – 20, 30, 40, 50 and 60 years; five cohorts – 1910, 1920, 1930, 1940 and 1950; and nine measurement dates – by decades from 1930 to 2010. The effect of age on Function X is artificially set to decrease it by 10 every decade from the age of 20; the cohort effect – the secular trend – is set to decrease X by 2 every decade from a zero base-line in 1910; the effect of environmental influence, i.e. time of measurement, is set to increase X by 3 every decade from a zero base-line in 1930. The example assumes an average base-line score for X of 100 for subjects born in 1910 and tested in 1930 at the age of 20, as shown overleaf.

The example is elementary in comparison with the real world – the effects are simple, additive and regular, only one dependent variable, X, is considered, the values of X represent average values, and no random or other error factor is included. In practice, however, even a diligent and well-supported research team would be unlikely to complete such a mammoth investigation. The worked example further simplifies the real world by not taking into account the many sources of confusion to which we have already referred – the selective effects of death, practice effects, unequal measurement validity, and so on.

Table 4 shows the values of X in each cell of the age by co-

TABLE 4. A hypothetical data matrix illustrating the relationships between the effects of age level, cohort date, and time of measurement

Age: effect					
60: —40	72(1970:+12)	73(1980:+15)	74(1990:+18)	75(2000:+21)	76(2010:+24)
50: —30	79(1960:+9)	80(1970:+12)	81(1980:+15)	82(1990:+18)	83(2000:+21)
40: —20	86(1950:+6)	87(1960:+9)	88(1970:+12)	89(1980:+15)	90(1990:+18)
30: —10	93(1940:+3)	94(1950:+6)	95(1960:+9)	96(1970:+12)	97(1980:+15)
20: 0	100(1930:0)	101(1940:+3)	102(1950:+6)	103(1960:+9)	104(1970:+12)
Cohort: effect	1910:0	1920:—2	1930:—4	1940:—6	1950:—8

Note: Score on Function X, and, in brackets, time of measurement:effect

hort matrix; alongside each value of X in brackets is the measurement date and its effect. The cumulative effects are shown for each and every level of the three variables. Observe that the values cannot form a three-dimensional array because they are not independent, as explained above; thus one cannot extract three independent effects. The artificial data in Table 4 form an age by cohort matrix in which five cohorts at ten-year intervals from 1910 are intercepted at five age levels at decade intervals from age 20. Diagonal entries from upper left to lower right represent a single time of measurement, e.g. 1970 or 1980, and thus provide *cross-sectional* comparisons. Vertical entries represent a single cohort date, e.g. 1920 or 1930, and thus provide *longitudinal* comparisons. Horizontal entries represent a single age level, e.g. 30 or 40, and thus provide *secular* comparisons. But – more important – a combination of diagonal and vertical entries represents two or more cohorts at two or more times of measurement, e.g. cohorts 1920 and 1930 each measured in 1960 and 1970, and thus provide *mixed* or *cross-longitudinal* comparisons.

The differences between any two adjacent scores on Function X fall into convenient sets. For example, we can examine the differences between the two cohorts 1910 and 1920 (or any other pair of cohorts) over all age levels from 20 to 60 years, or over all times of measurement from 1940 to 1970 (other times for other pairs of cohorts). Another possibility is to examine the differences between the two age levels 40 and 50 (or any other pairs of ages) over all cohorts from 1910 to 1950, or over all times of measurement from 1960 to 1990 (other times for other age levels). In this way, we can find differences between every pair of adjacent scores: vertically, horizontally, and diagonally. Naturally, a similar design could be used over a narrower age-range, measured perhaps in months. Animal studies, for example, could be used to demonstrate the various relationships over a shorter time span. The differences between adjacent values of X in Table 4 fall into the patterns illustrated below:

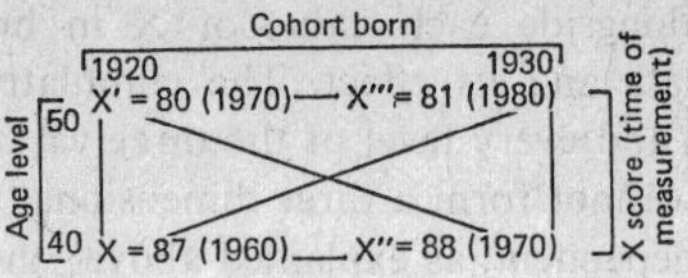

Note that if we had specified age and time of measurement, instead of age and cohort date, the matrix of scores would have been as follows:

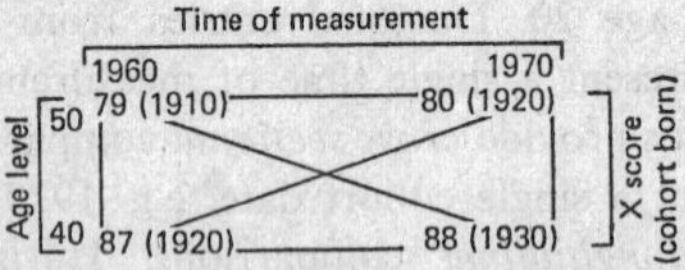

The values of Function X, of course, remain the same, since exactly the same conditions are operating. The four values in the above example correspond to a diagonal tetrad in the original age by cohort matrix, and the differences between the values of Function X are the same, as shown below:

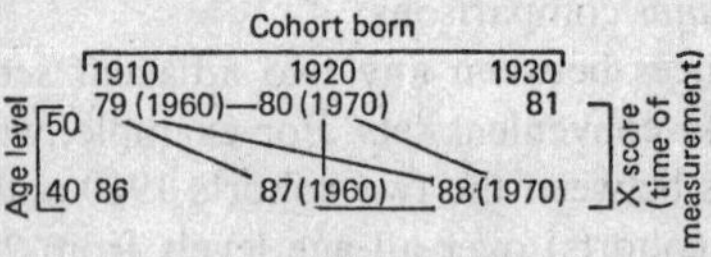

Similarly, if we had specified cohort and time of measurement, the respective values of Function X would remain the same, and so, obviously, would the differences between them.

What we find is that: a longitudinal comparison of one (or more) cohorts over the five age levels yields an average age decrease of 7 points per decade, including varying environmental effects; a secular comparison of one (or more) age levels over the five cohorts yields an average increase of 1 point per decade, including varying environmental effects; a cross-sectional comparison of one (or more) times of measurement over five age levels and five cohorts yields an average combined age and secular decrease of 8 points, including a constant time of measurement effect.

We must now consider whether or to what extent the values

in the matrix for Function X can be analysed in terms of the variables and effects postulated in the compilation of the artificial data, *i.e. assuming no prior knowledge of them.* In other words, how might we interpret the data and isolate the effects in an actual investigation? The *observed* pattern of differences between adjacent values in the matrix can be conveniently represented as follows:

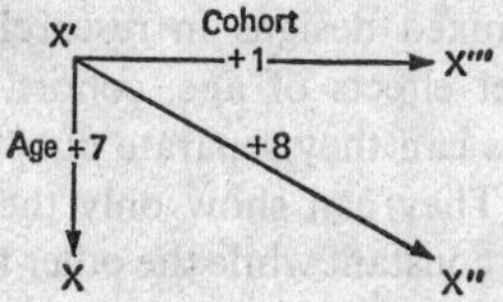

But underlying this surface pattern lies the latent pattern which we arbitrarily arranged as follows: a decrease with age of 10 points per decade from a base-line of 100 at the age of 20; an increase with time of measurement of 3 points per decade from a base-line of 0 in 1930; a secular decrease of 2 points per decade from a base-line of 0 in 1910. This underlying pattern can be represented as follows:

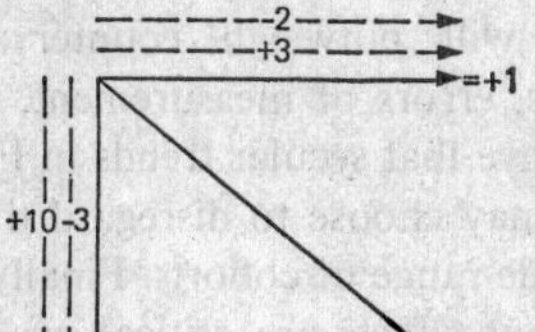

It is obvious that latent effects other than those we have postulated could have produced the same surface relationships. For example:

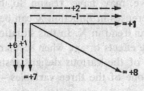

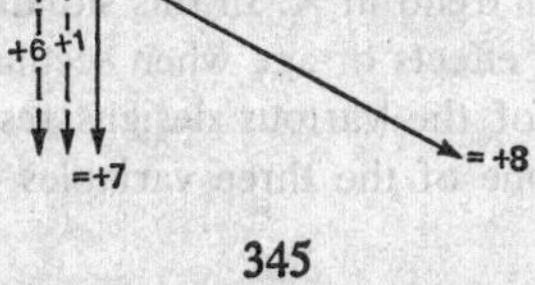

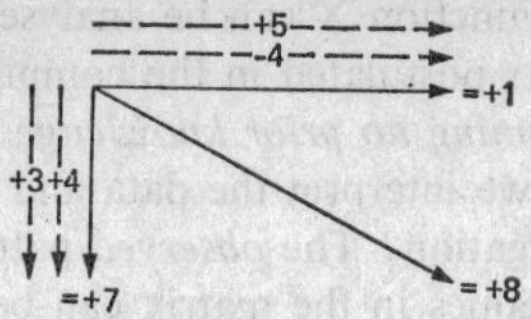

Hence, under some circumstances at least, the cross-sectional, longitudinal, and mixed designs in research in ageing cannot separate out the net effects of age, cohort, and time of measurement, much less can they separate out the sub-components of these variables. They can show only the effects of holding one of the variables constant while the other two vary.

IMPLICATIONS. The question arises as to why one research design rather than another should be preferred. Apart from administrative considerations, such as cost and time, the choice of design depends upon what we are trying to discover and upon what we believe about the phenomenon we are investigating. For example, if we have reason to believe that the net effects of age on Function X are small, then we must examine a wide age range in order to increase the likelihood that the cumulative effect will outweigh countervailing influences, sampling variations, errors of measurement, and so on. If we have reason to believe that secular trends in Function X are nil or small, then we may choose to disregard them and feel free to select from a wide range of cohorts. Finally, if we think that time of measurement effects are critical, we may find it possible to restrict ourselves to a given set of retrospective measurement dates, for example those associated with epidemics, exceptional weather conditions or social disorganization.

Alternatively, we may have reason to believe that the measured age differences in Function X can be largely accounted for by a secular trend in X. In this situation, we obviously wish to look at the effects of age when secular trends are controlled. The logic of the various designs rests upon the idea that the effect of one of the three variables – age, cohort, or time of measurement – can be made negligibly small in comparison with the effects of the other two. These two main effects can then be examined in relation to each other. As we have seen, however, the observed surface measures and their differences cannot be *literally* accounted for in terms of these effects for the simple reason that the effects are compatible with several different interpretations. Exceptions to this general conclusion could occur if there were substantial changes at a critical age level or for a given cohort or at a particular time of test. For then the score surface over a matrix like the one set out in Table 4 would no longer be smooth but would reveal systematic shifts or contour effects at, say, the ages of 45 to 50 in women (reflecting menopausal changes), or at cohorts 1935 to 1940 (reflecting the stressful effects of war on young children) or at a time of testing in 1973 (reflecting local weather conditions). The significance of contour effects in the score surface would naturally depend on the extent to which such effects could be reliably identified, duplicated and attributed to such definite causal factors.

In the complex artificial data matrix shown above, the apparent decline with age in Function X is 8 points per decade when measured by means of a cross-sectional survey of five age levels in 1970. The decline is 7 points per decade, however, when measured by means of a longitudinal follow-up of one cohort over five age levels. In the absence of other information, this discrepancy might be regarded as a secular trend, but if there is independent evidence of a different degree and/or direction of secular trends, then the investigator may be inclined to suspect a countervailing effect of time of measurement.

(d) *The Need for Longitudinal Studies of Ageing*

SEQUENTIAL CHANGES WITHIN SUBJECTS. Longitudinal studies of ageing are essential, even though the method itself does not exclude contaminating variables such as selective sampling and treatment effects, and may need to be verified separately for different cohorts. The description and explanation of changes *within* subjects, and the comparison of patterns of growth or deterioration *between* subjects, defines the essential aim of the longitudinal method.[20,21] How else could one demonstrate, say, the natural history of a disorder of late onset?

Retrospective studies in the absence of adequate data on the function(s) being investigated are not very profitable, except in so far as intensive case studies provide evidence relevant to specific questions about individual persons. Longitudinal studies usually have to be planned, i.e. prospective, if their full value is to be realized; but it is not unusual for a type of longitudinal study to be carried out in a quasi-retrospective fashion – by making observations in the present on subjects for whom similar or relevant observations were made in the past.[22-24] The idea of the data-bank, with its standardized records, is already familiar in commerce and in the medical and social sciences, and could be usefully applied in more behaviourally oriented studies of ageing, for example in relation to psychiatric disorder, longevity, and the maintenance of ability.

Much of the benefit derived from longitudinal studies accrues from the restrictions imposed upon the types of subject selected for investigation, such as gifted adults or twins, and from the restrictions imposed upon the scope of the inquiry, say, intelligence and longevity, the differential decline of abilities, intervening stress and illness. In other words, where longitudinal studies are planned prospectively they are designed to answer specific questions, such as whether changes are more concordant for identical twins than for fraternal twins, or whether a repeated measures study confirms or fails to confirm the cross-sectional finding that brighter people live longer, or that fluid abilities decline more rapidly than crystallized abilities. Other longitudinal studies have been frankly opportunist – an investigator happens to notice that observations made on subjects some time ago could now be repeated or used to throw light on other observations which can now be made. There appear to have been few if any longitudinal studies designed to elucidate typical sequential patterns of ageing (within persons); much less has there been any attempt to develop a taxonomy of age changes.

Most of the administrative and logical problems encountered in longitudinal studies of ageing have already been encountered in longitudinal studies of child development and social change, and to some extent – with reference to statistical procedures – in biomedical studies of treatment effects, economic trends, attitude formation, and other studies of change. Such studies suggest that the main contributions to be made by pre-planned longitudinal studies include: testing the effect of a treatment intervention, comparing the differential ageing of subjects with different initial characteristics and/or undergoing different treatments, and identifying possible 'critical periods' in adult life.

There is no optimum length for a longitudinal study. The starting and finishing ages are indicated by the nature of the problem under investigation: if the suspected ageing process is slow but cumulative, the follow-up period will be long; if critical ages or episodes are hypothesized, for example retirement or the menopause, then the follow-up period will date from shortly before until after these events; and so on. The essential features of a well-organized longitudinal study of ageing are that the observations should be strategically timed to span the process under investigation and to 'catch' the critical phases as they occur.

MORPHOLOGICAL APPROACH TO LONGITUDINAL ANALYSIS. Normally a dimension of individual differences such as introversion or auditory acuity is investigated by comparing the scores of many individuals observed on one occasion. It has been argued that, in a similar way, a developmental or ageing dimension, i.e. sequence, could be investigated by the analysis of longitudinal changes in one or more subjects observed over many occasions. But what are to be the bases of such inter-individual comparisons? Presumably, they will be analogous to sequences like: the course of an illness, a career path, locomotor development, or a series of intellectual stages.

The point is that it is not sufficient merely to describe quantitative age effects on a variety of existing dimensions of individual differences; such dimensions were established to describe static differences between persons – they are analogous to the properties of maps in geography. One map does not reveal how the individual parts of a given territory are changing over time; a series of maps, however, might reveal that changes were taking place – just as a series of cross-sectional studies of the same individuals might reveal that psychological changes were taking place. The problem is to devise suitable concepts to describe the morphological changes (in form or structure) thus observed. Using the analogy of the maps, one might speak of silting, erosion, subsidence and so on, which do not correspond to anything on a map, but help to explain changes over a series of maps. In human ageing, one speaks of the following dimensions of change: senile dementia, social disengagement, compensatory slowing in perceptual motor performance, mid-life revaluation, and so on. These are explanatory, i.e. hypothetical, concepts intended to make sense of the observed changes in behaviour, capacity and experience; they differ from the geographical concepts only in so far as they are less familiar, less well supported by empirical evidence, and less well embedded in a conceptual system or theory.

In behavioural gerontology, frequent references to the relationship between the longitudinal and cross-sectional methods imply that the variables of interest are common to both the psychology of inter-individual differences and intra-individual development or ageing. The cross-sectional method, after all, simply compares individual differences at various age levels. The longitudinal method could be said to eliminate some of the hypotheses that might otherwise account for these differences between individuals. It does not follow, however, that the variables established as dimensions of individual differences are necessarily the ones best suited for the analysis of development and ageing. For example, some of the dimensions of individual differences in personality reveal little in the way of age trends. Hence, it may be desirable to modify our approach by identifying variables or morphological patterns that show age trends, and *then* test whether they have value as dimensions of individual differences, independent of age. Such an approach would require a radical departure from existing methods, and possibly the abandonment of some existing psychometric methods used in studies of ageing.

The measurement and representation of changes or differences over time are preliminary to the consideration of how these changes or differences are connected. That is, they provide evidence relevant to *experimental* issues derived from psychological *theories* about ageing.[25-28] Gerontology should provide more than a mere narrative or chronology of events in adult life. It should show the causal connections between these events and make a kind of 'path analysis' of the psychobiological sequences of events that we refer to as ageing.[29,30] Time, or age itself, although it can be easily identified and measured as a distinct variable seems to be a ghostly influence – it needs to be made substantial by showing that it is really a timetable of events. The processes of ageing are unbroken sequences of events which at present are known only fractionally and intermittently by reference to changes, usually losses, in function relative to an arbitrary base-line, and over relatively arbitrary age periods. Path analysis or causal analysis need make little reference to age or the passage of time, except to establish norms. It could be used, for example, to trace the typical sequences of events which lead to late paraphrenia, suicide, social isolation, or the 'paths' to the ward of a geriatric hospital.[31] One aim is to identify adverse influences leading to increasingly deteriorated morphological states; another aim is to find ways of retarding deterioration, and for renewing or improving functional capacities.

PSYCHOMETRICS AND LONGITUDINAL ANALYSIS. Age changes can be characterized broadly as metric or non-metric. Non-metric, or qualitative, changes are those which can be described but not quantified in any useful way. Metric or quantitative changes are those which can be ordered or measured according to some kind of scale, however simple. Ordinal changes for example refer to characteristics or states which can be identified and located according to their position in a series of similar or related characteristics distributed over time. The scale would have to have some meaning as a psychological or behavioural dimension, like a disease process, self-esteem, or disengagement. Such a series of behavioural characteristics with a fixed order of occurrence might form a Guttman scale (strictly ordinal), but of course there is no point in devising an ordinal scale unless it represents a genuine dimension of change.

Behavioural characteristics measured by means of psychometric tests are frequently treated like physical measurements, although it is well known that ordinal scales do not have all the properties associated with a ratio scale, that is, they lack a true zero and equality of units. It is obvious that the *level* of measurement might affect the plausibility of any argument based on psychometric data. In biometric studies of ageing, physical measurements such as cell count, blood pressure and EEG frequency, make it legitimate to specify the mathematical function that seems to fit a particular pattern of age changes. Psychological measures are less amenable to mathematical treatment. Even biometric studies, however, must face the more general methodological obstacles which have been described above.

A serious disadvantage with psychometric tests is that they may not be applicable, or equally applicable, throughout the whole period of adult life and old age. One reason for this is sheer inconvenience: tests tend to be standardized on readily available samples of subjects, and it is exceptional to find a test which has been standardized on representative samples of subjects at all adult age levels. Even the Wechsler Adult Intelligence Scale – probably the best example – might not qualify if one imposed the kinds of sampling requirements prescribed for social survey work. The consequence is that a test's norms may be in error, particularly at age levels not adequately represented in the standardization sample.

If a test has been validated only for young adults, then there may be changes in the meaning of scores obtained by older subjects. Similarly, medical or psychiatric symptoms and biometric measures may carry a different diagnostic significance depending upon the age of the subject and other relevant conditions. The validation of psychological measures over a wide age range is obviously a major task for descriptive gerontology; perhaps the fact that few social and behavioural gerontologists are pursuing this kind of work reveals a lack of confidence in the usefulness of many psychometric tests.

The considerable duration of adult life coupled with the apparently slow rate of change makes it necessary to devise measures which can be sensibly applied to subjects of widely differing ages, or at least makes it necessary to devise a series of measures, each applicable to a narrow age-range, overlapping the adjacent ages to which other measures in the series are applicable .

Factor analysis approaches the study of development and ageing not only by investigating relationships between psychometric tests administered to different subjects on one occasion but also by investigating relationships between tests for the same subject on many occasions.[32-37] This approach is expected by some to reveal age-related effects on existing dimensions of individual differences and their interrelationships, but the method itself cannot reveal the crucial 'dimensions of ageing' for the simple reason that such notions are theoretical constructs – conjectures – and factor analysis merely provides one sort of evidence for or against them.

3. THE MEASUREMENT OF AGE CHANGES

(a) *Difference Measures*

The measurement of *changes* presents some formidable problems in statistics and psychometrics.[38-42] Ideally, an investigator wishes to repeat many measurements on the same subjects over a long period of time in controlled conditions for several variables; but this is slow and expensive and administratively difficult. Hence, faster and more economical methods are needed to identify the crucial issues.

Some aspects of longitudinal analysis can be explained by considering just two occasions of measurement. Each subject in a sample is tested on two occasions. On the first occasion, an initial measure or pre-test score is obtained. At a later age, a final measure or post-test score is obtained. Let X represent the initial measurement, and Y the final measurement. The difference between them is a measure of the absolute gain or loss in score. Assuming that ageing produces a difference D – often a decrease in score – then: $D = Y - X$. However, the value of $Y - X$ can be positive, negative, or zero. If no change is observed, i.e. if $Y - X = 0$, it does not follow that no change has taken place. Why? Parts of the explanation are as follows.

RELIABILITY. The measures of both X and Y are imperfect, i.e. the observed score X comprises a true measure X_t and a measurement error X_e; similarly $Y = Y_t + Y_e$; and these measurement errors (+ or −) may cancel out a true change. For example,
if $X_t + X_e = 12 - 1 = 11$, and $Y_t + Y_e = 10 + 1 = 11$, then
$D = (Y_t + Y_e) - (X_t + X_e) = (Y_t - X_t) + (Y_e - X_e) = 0$.
Hence, $D = D_t + D_e$, i.e. the observed difference comprises a *true* difference plus an error of measurement, which is, of course, compounded of the two basic errors of measurement Y_e and X_e. The obvious solution to this particular problem is to minimize errors of measurement, i.e. to improve the reliability of the observational methods. Errors of measurement cannot be eliminated altogether, however, and in the social and behavioural sciences, they are typically large. The reliability of D is r_{dd}', and can be calculated as follows:

$$r_{dd}' = \frac{s^2_y r_{yy}' + s^2_x r_{xx}' - 2 s_y s_x r_{xy}}{s^2_y + s^2_x - 2 s_y s_x r_{xy}}$$

The relatively low value of r_{dd}' means that D does not provide a good estimate of the positions of subjects even on an ordinal scale of change. The square of r_{dd}' represents the upper limit of the validity of D as a measure of true change. In correlating D with variables of interest, such as sex or treatment, it is not uncommon to 'correct for attenuation', i.e. to calculate what the correlation would be if unreliability could be eliminated. Where individual items are scored as passed or failed on each of the two occasions, item analysis can be used to improve the D scale as a single measure of change. The problem is complicated, however, because item selection which leads to an improvement in the reliability of D may alter its validity by changing its meaning and reducing its correlations with the original criteria.

SCALING. Score intervals at different regions of a scale of psychological measurement do not signify equal 'amounts' of the variable under investigation. For example, a subject whose score has declined from 80 to 70 has not necessarily deteriorated to the same extent as a subject whose score has declined from 30 to 20. There are broadly three ways of dealing with this issue. The first is to disregard the problem and deal with scores directly (rather than as surface indicators of an underlying function); the second is to standardize the scales – for example by representing initial and final scores in terms of a common distribution; the third is to adopt some other kind of scaling procedure, for example, by treating the differences as relative to the level of score; thus:

$$\text{Relative difference} = \text{Dr} = \frac{Y - X}{\frac{1}{2}(Y + X)}$$

This last sort of transformation can sometimes help to make sense of otherwise uninterpretable data, but does not relieve the investigator of the usual burdens of standardizing his scale of measurement, establishing its reliability and validity, and meeting the assumptions underlying the statistical tests he applies. The indices $\frac{1}{2}(Y + X)$ and $Y - X$ are useful, as we shall see later in connection with the problem of regression effects, because any correlation between them is independent of any correlation between X and Y. The index $\frac{1}{2}(Y + X)$ provides an average estimate of the variable being studied; the index Y – X estimates the rate of change. Such indices – called orthogonal polynomials – can be generalized to comparisons using more than two measures, and used to examine age trends.

VALIDITY. In repeated measurements to test for age changes the measures X and Y are regarded as equivalent; but as they are administered on two widely separated occasions, they may no longer measure the same thing. For example, a measure of extroversion administered at age 30 may correlate reasonably well with external criteria of validity – such as sociability or work performance – but the same measure may not be similarly valid 10 or 20 years later when perhaps a variety of underlying predispositions have been modified in ways which influence the subject's response to the test. Moreover, he may obtain the same score on two widely separated occasions, but for different reasons. Although the burden of proof rests upon the investigator who makes this assertion, it is risky to conclude that the variable of interest has not changed just because the test score has not changed. Although the test provides an operational definition of the concept, this definition does not exhaust the meaning of that concept or free the test from contextual influences. This illustration ignores errors of measurement, and presents a hypothetical situation, but not a fantastic one. Apart from the obvious exceptions, few psychometric measures have been standardized over comparable samples of subjects at different ages; and we cannot just assume that a test is valid to the same extent or in the same way at all age levels.

One way out of this difficulty is to improve the validity of D as a measure of change. But reliability and validity interact and it may prove difficult to determine exactly what it is that a reliable difference measure is measuring. Another way is to design a complex experiment which permits a closer analysis of the factors affecting a subject's responses. For example, a comparison of several sorts of subject examined on a number of occasions by a variety of measures may permit the falsification of some hypotheses which would be tenable as explanations of the results from a simple Y−X comparison.

(b) *Regression Effects*

The phenomenon of statistical regression is best explained by assuming a normal bivariate distribution for correlated measures. The typical situation in a longitudinal study of ageing is to compare the scores of the same sample of subjects on two 'equivalent' measures, X and Y, on two widely separate occasions. If the two measures are reasonably reliable and

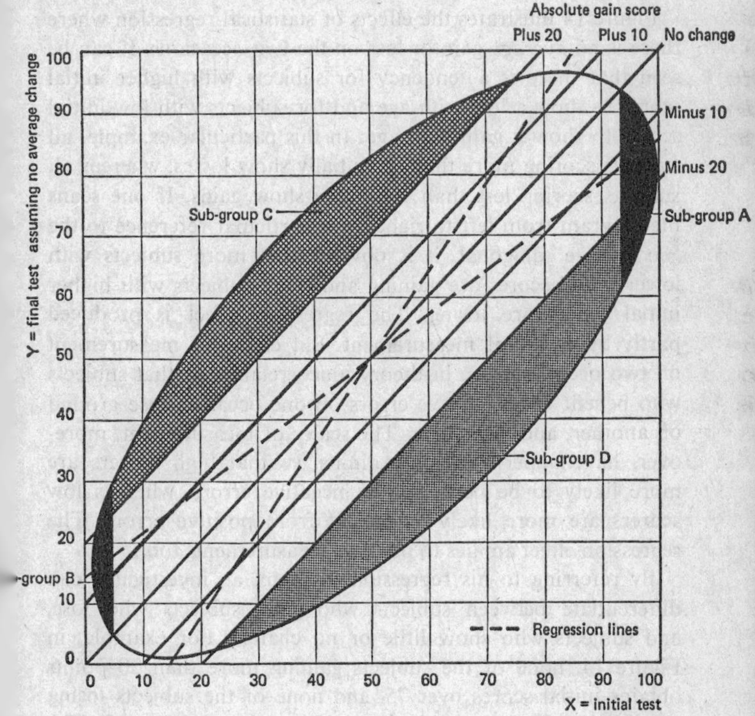

FIGURE 14 The effects of statistical regression. See text for explanation.

similarly valid, then the correlation between them should be high, as would be the case for two parallel forms of a test of intelligence or of extroversion. However, if ageing has differential effects on the subjects, as well as systematic effects on the function or set of functions measured by the tests, as seems likely, then the correlation between the two measures on the two widely-spaced occasions will be substantially less than the reliability coefficient measured by a short-term test–retest or split-half correlation. This effect has been demonstrated in developmental studies, where it can be shown that predictive accuracy diminishes as the time-interval increases.

Figure 14 illustrates the effects of statistical regression where there is no *average* gain or loss on the two occasions. It can be seen that there is a tendency for subjects with higher initial scores to show a loss with age and for subjects with low initial scores to show a gain with age. In this particular example, all subjects scoring more than 95 initially show losses, whereas all subjects scoring less than 5 initially show gains. If one scans the diagram from left to right, with particular reference to the 'no change' diagonal, it is obvious that more subjects with lower initial scores are gaining and more subjects with higher initial scores are losing. The regression effect is produced partly by errors of measurement. But errors of measurement on two occasions are, in theory, uncorrelated, so that subjects who benefit from positive errors on one occasion lose ground on another, and vice versa. The scales of measurement, moreover, have upper and lower limits, so that high scorers are more likely to be penalized by negative errors, whereas low scorers are more likely to benefit from positive errors. The regression effect applies to physical measurements too.

By referring to his regression diagram, an investigator can differentiate between subjects who gain, subjects who lose, and subjects who show little or no change. For example, in Figure 14, none of the subjects gaining more than 20 points obtains initial scores over 75, and none of the subjects losing more than 20 points obtains initial scores under 25. The mean initial score of subjects who gain more than 20 is obviously lower than that of subjects who lose more than 20. Hence, since initial score is associated with gains and losses, it has been used, sometimes erroneously, to help identify the characteristics of subjects whose scores improve with age as compared with those whose scores decline. In general, high initial scorers decline (or gain less), low initial scorers improve (or decline less).

It follows from this last fact that any variable which happens to be correlated with initial score, i.e. with the variable under investigation, will be correlated with gain score. Thus, if there is a sex difference on the initial measure, for example if men on average score higher than women, the rate of decline with age might appear to be faster for men than for women. Regression effects can thus produce spurious results. The effect of an overall decrease in score with age is to alter the values of the gains and losses associated with the diagonal lines on Figure 14. For example, if age brings about a loss of 10 points at all levels, then each diagonal value is reduced by 10 points, and this might further emphasize the appearance of less decline with age among subjects with low initial scores.

Taking account of the fact that age *change* may be negatively correlated with initial score is usually achieved by measuring gains or losses relative to the regression line of final score on initial score. This is the line which makes the best fit to the means of the successive distributions of Y scores for each class of X scores. In other words, if an investigator knows a subject's class score on X, i.e. X_c, and wishes to predict that subject's score on Y, his best estimate is not $\bar{Y}$, the mean of all the Y scores, but $\bar{Y}_c$, i.e., the mean Y score of subjects scoring X_c.

The diagonal lines representing different degrees of *absolute* gains or losses are drawn at 45° through the rectangular bivariate score matrix, whereas the lines representing different degrees of *relative* gains or losses are drawn through or parallel with the regression line of final score on initial score. In the situation represented in Figure 16, i.e. a normal bivariate distribution with no average change from initial score to final

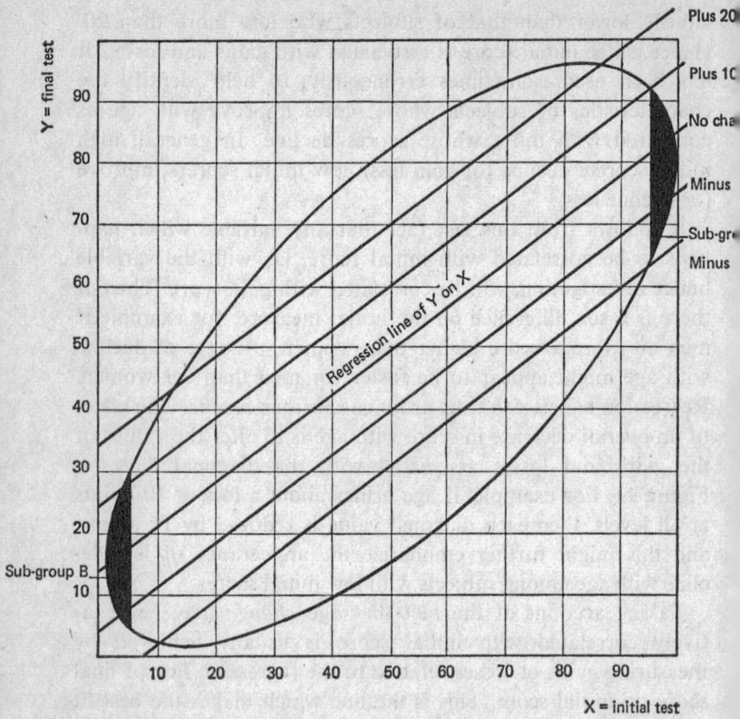

FIGURE 15 The effects of statistical regression. See text for explanation.

score, subjects who score, say, 30 on X can be expected to score 35 on Y, because X and Y are correlated variables, and an *absolute gain* of 5 from an initial level of 30 is normal. Similarly, subjects who score, say, 70 on X, can be expected to score 65 on Y, and an *absolute loss* of 5 from an initial level of 70 is normal. Subjects scoring near the mean on X can be expected to score near the mean on Y. However, if we measure gains and losses *relative to the regression* of Y on X, then scores falling on or near the regression line show little or no change. Thus subjects scoring over 95 on X may show either relative gains or relative losses, as may subjects scoring less than 5; subjects with high relative gains do not tend to have low X scores, and subjects with high relative losses do not tend to have high X scores. In order to show a corrected or relative gain of 10, a subjects with an initial score of 30 has to score about 45 on Y; a subject with an initial score of 70 has to score about 75 on Y to achieve the same relative gain. If the relationship between X and Y is curvilinear or if the frequency distributions are not normal, the situation is further complicated.

It is possible to correlate relative gains or losses with other variables; this is essentially a partial correlation between D and Z with X held constant. Alternatively, X can be thought of as if it were an independent variable which could be experimentally controlled.

The distinction between absolute and relative differences is not that absolute differences are false and relative differences are true, but rather that the meaning of absolute differences, and their apparent relationships with other variables, are obscured and distorted by statistical and metrical artefacts. These must be controlled in longitudinal studies of individual and group differences in the effects of ageing.

The ability to deal with D scores independently of initial level of score means that the relationship between D and other variables can be examined more incisively, even though these other variables are correlated with the variable measured by the initial and final tests. When the time between initial and final tests is fairly long – several years usually in research in human ageing – it is assumed that difference measures will be larger, more reliable, and more easily validated than when the interval is shorter. The various factors making for change have accumulated and consolidated their effects; the incidental and temporary circumstances influencing performance are different on the two occasions; the transfer effects of the initial test, if any, have probably diminished.

Thus, although the statistical complications of measuring changes are inconvenient, there appears to be no reason why changes in adult life should not be measured in the same way as changes during the juvenile period – provided the adult measurements can be made sufficiently valid and reliable. On reflection, however, if present-day findings are any guide, adult changes in behaviour and psychological capacities are generally slow and small relative to changes in the juvenile period (and relative to the discriminating power of many psychological scales of measurement). It is sometimes difficult to demonstrate that an observed age change is statistically significant, much less that it is psychologically significant, since the measurement error is usually large.

In the simplest case, the gain achieved by a treatment can be examined by taking differences relative to the regression line of Y on X, as described above. For example, the functional physiological capacity of two groups of adults – one subjected to a programme of physical exercise, the other taking normal exercise – could be compared. Over a long interval there might be little to choose between the two treatments in terms of the difference between pre-test and post-test. However, if the group subjected to a programme of physical exercise were volunteers, they would probably have initially higher scores on a general measure of physiological capacity. Thus their absolute gain scores would underestimate the effect, while the absolute gain scores of the normal controls would overestimate it. If gain scores were measured relative to the respective regression lines of final on initial test, however, they would almost certainly reveal that the exercised group had gained more than the controls.

Figure 16 illustrates a possible situation. The mean absolute gain for the normal controls is 10; the mean gain for the exercised subjects is also 10. So, superficially, there appears to be no benefit from exercise. However, relative to the common regression line of Y on X, the exercised subjects gain more than the normal controls. If subjects have been assigned at random to two treatment groups, differences in initial score should be negligible.

The ideal post-test or follow-up study is illustrated in Figure 17. Group A and Group B are assumed to be fairly large;

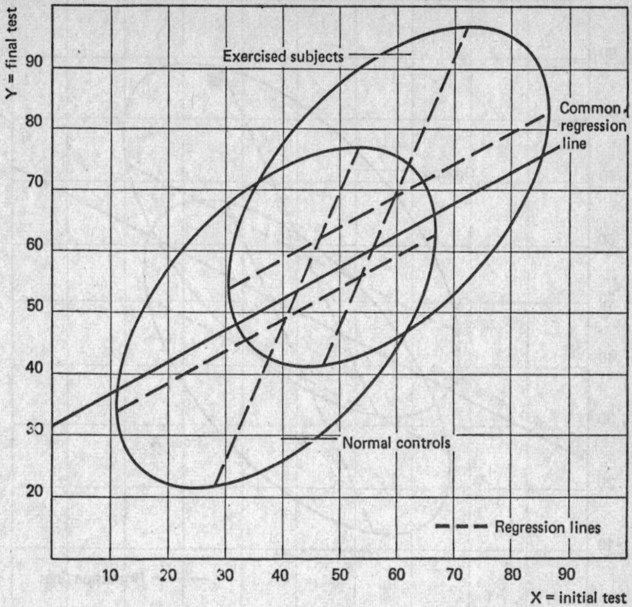

FIGURE 16 The effects of statistical regression. See text for explanation.

they are drawn at random from the same population, so that their means on X, the initial test, are identical or nearly so. The differential effect of treatment B compared with treatment A, for example males versus females, intervening life stresses versus no intervening life stresses, is to raise the post-test scores of Group B. Whereas Group A has an average loss of —10, Group B has an average gain of +10. The relative gain scores, of course, take regression effects into account, but no interaction between treatment and gain is shown, i.e. the difference between Group A and Group B subjects with high initial scores is the same as the difference between Group A and Group B subjects with low initial scores.

Since adult subjects cannot be randomly sampled, and

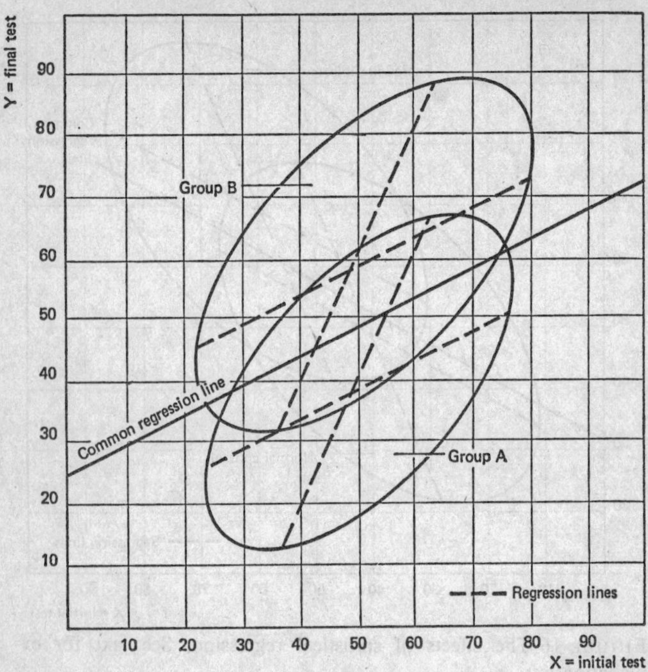

FIGURE 17 The effects of statistical regression. See text for explanation.

chronological age cannot be randomly assigned as a treatment, it is important to identify the kinds of bias produced by volunteer effects and to examine critically the assumption underlying statistical analysis.

4. DISCUSSION

So far we have assumed that errors of measurement on two occasions are uncorrelated. But this assumption may not hold, and ageing may produce systematic bias in measurement error. For example, suppose that, in a test of introversion, measurement errors occur because some items tend to be misconstrued by depressed and anxious subjects – thus leading them to 'appear' more introverted than they 'really' are. If depression and anxiety increase with age, this particular sort of measurement error will increase, creating a spuriously large increase in introversion. Similarly, the tendency to construe test instructions one way or another may change with age – by being taken too literally or forgotten in part; this sort of measurement error then becomes confounded with the validity of the measured age change. It could be argued that the effects are not measurement errors in the technical sense, but sources of invalidity; for all practical purposes, however, they are the same.

The peculiarity of change scores is that the more closely correlated the initial and final scores are, the less reliable the change scores are; in the extreme case they reduce to random errors. But if the initial and final scores are not closely correlated, then, by definition, the final test is measuring something different from the initial test. But if that is the case, what is the change score a measure of? How can one tell whether the subject has changed relative to a stable measure or whether the second test is measuring a different aspect of the subject on the second occasion? The possibility that a follow-up measure is measuring something different from the initial measure seems to be a tenable explanation of the differences sometimes observed between longitudinal and cross-sectional investigations.

This line of reasoning raises a number of problems for the psychometric assessment of age changes and age differences. For example, are the scoring procedures for projective tests valid at different age levels? How does the definition of intelligence change with age? There may be changes in the cognitive level of the subjects, changes in test-taking attitudes, a learning effect, or a sensitization produced by the first occasion of testing, or other changes not formally recognized as sources of variation in the measurements obtained by the test. The idea can be generalized, for example, in the sense that medical and psychiatric symptoms may not have the same diagnostic significance at different ages. If we know that the functional validity of a test is unchanged, we can say the *person* has changed; but if the functional validity of the test changes, how do we become aware of this fact?

The ambiguity arises from the failure to distinguish between the test (the tangible instrument or measurement operation) and its referent (the variable it is said to measure). It should be clear that inter-individual differences and intra-individual changes in performance on a test are not *entirely* accounted for by the function that the test is supposed to measure. Psychological tests are fallible, they are imperfect measures of the functions to which they refer and performance on them is influenced by extraneous factors. Difficulties arise when the referent cannot be conceptualized, measured, or given an evidential basis independently of the test or class of tests used in an investigation. But the lack of adequate evidence of validity is precisely the reason why some psychometric instruments are used. In biology, measurements are usually anchored to well-validated theoretical referents, such as blood pressure and basal metabolic rate, or they are simple descriptions, such as cell counts and EEG records. In sociology, measurements are often relatively simple descriptions (although the information may be obtained indirectly and imperfectly), for example number of kin within 30 minutes travelling time, weekly income, or number of visits to the doctor. In much psychological work, however, the relationship between a test and its referent is often complex and obscure – hence the extensive work carrid out in psychometrics and allied fields.

Many areas of psychology lack the conceptual clarity and orderliness of much of biology, but are no longer restricted to simple descriptive counts. At a descriptive level, absolute psychological changes may be perfectly sensible and useful, for example age changes in reading speed or self-ratings of confidence. But if an investigator wishes to examine the underlying causes and conditions of these psychological changes and relate them to causal variables, then, as we have seen, he can no longer rely upon absolute changes from initial score to subsequent score – because of regression effects and because the explanatory variables may be correlated with the initial levels of measurement. The investigator can establish that changes have taken place independently of initial level, and that these changes are correlated with explanatory variables, but he may find it difficult to separate out changes in the functional validity of the test from psychological or other changes within the subjects.

The measurement of reliable differences between two occasions of measurement is a way of mapping changes in the meaning of standard measuring instruments; that is, it becomes a method of identifying changes in the validity referents over, say, chronological age or intervening environmental influences. Thus differences in the validity of a test for subjects of different ages, which at first sight seem to be a methodological inconvenience, may be seen as a new way of conceptualizing the effects of age.

The effects of initial testing, other than by unobtrusive measures, are likely to be fairly pronounced in studies of psychological change with age. For example, adaptation to the relatively unfamiliar testing situation should be much faster on retest than on the initial test. The natural tendency of older subjects to look back to previous experience to provide a basis for response to a current problem should increase the similarity of behaviour between the two occasions. Hence, repeated measures on the same subjects create sequential dependencies, especially if the time intervals are short; and such time series call for special methods of statistical analysis. More frequent occasions of measurement, by rendering the situation more familiar, should have the effect of stabilizing the performance of older subjects, at least after the first few occasions. The problem of devising scales of measurement suitable for frequent repetition is difficult but not insurmountable.

A repeated-measures longitudinal analysis can be regarded as more than simply another way of analysing trends in individual differences. It is a way of identifying and measuring *dimensions of change* peculiar to development and ageing, i.e. sequential changes associated with groups, treatments, or individuals. If measured age differences in a variable are large, the need for a longitudinal analysis is less, unless there are reasons for supposing that these age differences are spurious. Generally speaking, measured age *changes* – estimated by repeated measures – are sensitive to smaller effects and can be handled more effectively in the design of experiments. Cross-sectional studies of ageing usually require a wide age range and fairly large samples because the spread of individual differences in many behavioural characteristics is large, whereas the changes with age are often relatively small. However, if individual variations are large in respect of the rate or pattern of age changes *within* persons, then large samples may be needed, even in longitudinal studies, to stabilize the average pattern of change. A comparison *between* individuals with respect to patterns of change *within* individuals may not be very meaningful unless the *average* pattern of change for individuals of that sort is known, and unless we know something of the extent of individual differences in patterns of change. Thus, in this respect, the assessment of a pattern of change is no different from the assessment of a static dimension of individual differences. It is well known that there are group and individual differences in growth curves for some functions, and it seems obvious that differences will be found for curves of deterioration too, although at present there is little or no information on this topic.

Part of the difficulty with research in ageing arises as a consequence of the limited opportunities for experimental manipulation of relevant variables such as initial level of performance, or treatment influences between two occasions of measurement. A certain degree of control can be achieved by selection but, for example, it might prove impossible to compare a sex difference among younger subjects with a sex difference among older subjects because of a differential change with age (or time of measurement) in the rates at which men and women volunteer to participate in the investigation. The volunteer effect in research requires detailed examination.[43-47]

The statistical design of some experiments, for example covariance analysis, makes certain assumptions – about equality of variance, randomization, and so on – which are impossible to meet in relation to the investigation of ageing. It should be possible, however, by means of statistical methods like serial and cross-lagged correlation, to examine some long-range causal effects in adult ageing – for example the effects of illness or stress on work output or sleep – especially during periods which might reasonably be expected to show marked changes, such as retirement, bereavement and relocation. Unfortunately, it is not easy to prove conclusively that an observed change was induced by a particular event or condition.

Lehman's work on age and achievement is an interesting example of how valuable research can be done without bothering about the methodological issues we have raised. The logic underlying the effects Lehman obtained was mentioned briefly in Chapter Seven.

Many of the more interesting aspects of social and behavioural gerontology are not amenable to experimental manipulation; there is evidence that psychometric methods which 'probe' the subject under relatively artificial and unfamiliar conditions sometimes fail to obtain measures which reflect the subject's normal state in the ordinary conditions of everyday life, and so fail to provide effective tests of psychological theories. Hence there is much to be said in favour of unobtrusive and quasi-experimental methods in the investigation of ageing. The commonest type of longitudinal study – using the test–re-test method – turns out to be a relatively weak but not completely useless design. It does not take into account the possibility that factors other than ageing might have produced the change: a shift in test validity, incidental experiences unrelated to age, sequential dependency between the tests, sampling bias, and so on. By contrast, a design which establishes a base-line trend and then introduces a treatment (or establishes a base-line prior to the occurrence of a natural event, like a stress) displays an effect which can be compared with the trend for an untreated sample with the same base-line. Naturally, the effect induced by the treatment can only be considered against a background of statistical and theoretical issues like reliability and plausibility.

One attempt to deal with the problem of measuring and explaining change has been to study variations over occasions for the same individual for two or more variables. One expects tests which measure the same thing to co-vary over different occasions and changed conditions. In some circumstances the variation *between conditions* (or occasions) for the same subjects is much greater than the variation *between subjects* for the same condition (or occasion); in other circumstances the situation is reversed. It is widely recognized that both organismic (personal) and environmental (situational) factors need to be taken into account in order to explain a specific performance like a test result.

Thus far, we have discussed change mainly in terms of the difference between two supposedly equivalent measures separated by a wide interval of time. But change or lack of change can be measured over any number of occasions. Ideally, we would like to describe and explain the *continuous* process of change, over the adult lifespan, of all the variables that are of interest to us. In practice we are usually limited to describing and partly explaining intermittent variations or trends in the behaviour of a relatively small sample of subjects, over relatively short intervals of time, on perhaps two or three occasions. The long-range goal, however, is to see whether basic relationships between the surface characteristics shown by psychometric and biometric data can be demonstrated by relating them to chronological age (the time variable), thus revealing characteristic decay curves, successive transformations in structure, and causal pathways for different characteristics and for different times of life. Hence the need for new theories and concepts and for rigorous quantitative methods.

A related topic, which has not been directly discussed, is that of predicting longevity by means of indices related to functional capacity or to social conditions. The multivariate procedures already mentioned are relevant to this particular problem. By means of discriminant analysis for example, longevity can be shown to be related to such causes as smoking, weight and happiness.[48]

CHAPTER TWELVE

Epilogue

We have come a long way, about four thousand years in fact, from man's earliest recorded attempts to prevent or retard the process of ageing to present-day gerontology. We have sampled an extensive scientific literature, finding many causes for dismay, a few for satisfaction and hope. Possibly the most striking aspects of gerontology are the scale and complexity of the subject. The notion that gerontology is a *multi-disciplinary* study should now be abundantly clear.

There is no escaping the fact that the social and behavioural aspects of ageing derive mainly from the degenerative physical changes that take place in the body over time. But social and behavioural gerontology has now reached the point at which research findings can be applied to counter many of the unwelcome and unnecessary consequences of physical ageing.

The main change since 1950 has been a remarkable proliferation of research work – so massive and often so technical that no one individual can hope to master more than a small portion of it. Unfortunately, much of what we have learned consists of detailed, low-level, empirical observations, lacking system and explanation. It is not sufficient merely to observe that certain age changes take place; we need to know *why* they take place. In most areas, theory construction has made little headway, mainly because few social and behavioural scientists engage in this kind of endeavour, but partly because the conceptual and empirical contents of these disciplines do not lend themselves easily to the traditional forms of logic and mathematics. Crude empiricism, however, is no substitute for a well thought-out philosophy of science, which at least indicates the *sorts* of theories that make sense (even if they are subsequently proved incorrect). Explanations at a 'proto-theoretical' level are not entirely lacking: they exist, for example, in relation to the effects of age on skill, creativity and disengagement.

The relationships between juvenile development and adult ageing are not at all clear. In some respects, adult ageing is a natural extension of the juvenile period, but in other respects it is a radical departure from it. The concept of 'ageing' itself is complicated and obscure; we must not assume that concepts and methods suited to the study of juvenile behaviour apply equally well to adult life. It has been argued that adult ageing is mainly a *post-developmental* process. That is to say, the genetic programme of development (unfolding) is largely complete, and subsequent intrinsic changes are the unprogrammed consequences of earlier development.

Gerontology lies at the point of intersection of many disciplines and interests since 'ageing', however defined, is a process of decay found in many living and non-living systems. Multidisciplinary research is particularly important since it is generally agreed that the important intrinsic factors are overlaid and obscured by all sorts of masking and extrinsic factors. We have been concerned with the *combined* effects of intrinsic and extrinsic factors. At present we cannot separate these effects, or distinguish with certainty between 'normal' and 'pathological' ageing.

The rapid rate of research and development in biology makes it unwise to suppose that an 'elixir of life' – or something approaching it – is a fanciful dream lacking substance. We must at least begin to think of what the social and behavioural consequences might be if such a discovery were made. The search for elixirs continues – viper flesh has given way to butylated-hydroxytoluene and other polysyllabic pharmacological preparations; and the preservation of health and vigour in old age and the prolongation of life should not be regarded as impossibilities.

The specific tasks of social and behavioural gerontology are to establish facts and theories about the effects of ageing on the individual and society, and to find ways of preventing or diminishing the adverse consequences of ageing. The first task can be dealt with effectively only by deploying adequate scientific resources, and this depends not only upon political and economic considerations but also upon the interest and enthusiasm of research workers. Compared with its constituent sciences, gerontology attracts few research workers; and many of these do not devote all their research time to the problem of *ageing* – partly because they see little scope for fundamental advances. Research workers in the constituent sciences often see chronological age simply as another – usually minor – source of variation, to be taken care of by statistical or experimental control.

Science is basically concerned with the development of conceptual systems which organize and explain the facts of observation. Gerontology as a basic science, therefore, deals with empirical data only in order to test out theories of ageing. Social and behavioural gerontology is at present largely a descriptive and applied science; it has yet to construct the theories that will give it the conceptual organization characteristic of a basic discipline. The sciences from which it is largely derived – psychology and sociology – have themselves a long way to go in the direction of theory construction.

Methodological difficulties should be viewed as a challenge rather than as another disincentive for research work in human ageing, though it is difficult to see how the numerous administrative, statistical and psychological obstacles can be overcome unless we are ambitious about research in this area. Given resources comparable to those in the natural sciences and technology, research results would be as spectacular – always provided the resources are used by original and diligent scientists.

Opportunities for improving the social welfare of the aged are numerous and much research work is directly stimulated by a concern for human welfare. Gradual but steady improvements in the practical management of ageing, in all its aspects, can be expected as the research findings from social and behavioural gerontology gradually get assimilated into common knowledge through education and popularization. Much more could be done to disseminate the knowledge generated by research. Social and behavioural gerontology should have a prominent place in the education of adults; at present, gerontological research in adult education is minimal. Increased public interest and enlightenment might even be a necessary preliminary to the advancement of gerontology. It would help to bring home to the people concerned the need to keep careful records and statistics so that, in time, research workers can examine data collected over long periods and reach reliable conclusions with regard to accidents, illness, output, and other important matters. Furthermore, public opinion could influence decisions affecting investment in science, education, health and welfare. For example, the United Kingdom should have a number of institutions where multi-disciplinary research work in ageing (pure and applied) could be carried out. University education in biology, medicine, psychology and sociology should include adequate instruction in human ageing, and some university departments in these disciplines should provide facilities for, and encourage post-graduate training and research in, the study of ageing. Schools of medicine should give instruction in geriatrics, and should include geriatric psychiatry as part of the syllabus for training in psychiatry. Departments of social science should at least draw the attention of students to the demographic, sociological and economic aspects of human ageing.

A wider general interest in human ageing should bring in more funds and more research workers. Research grants, fellowships and endowments are needed. The dissemination of scientific and technical information among 'users' should eventually yield practical benefits, as in other fields. Applied social and behavioural gerontology could become a specialized profession. The diversity of problems, methods and interests in gerontology calls for a variety of larger and smaller organizations. The advantages of developing Institutes of Gerontology are: they provide the necessary administrative machinery and resources for continuity in long-term follow-up studies; they are the appropriate agencies for international cooperation; they provide resources for the maintenance of specialized colonies of animals; they incur the benefits (and suffer the costs) of large-scale organizations; they have the resources to maintain adequate libraries, records, archives and all the different kinds of ancillary equipment and personnel necessary for modern research. They could do for adult life and old age what has been done for child development, that is investigate it fully and systematically on a longitudinal basis.

In the U.S.A., a Presidential Council on Aging was set up in 1962; it convenes meetings from time to time to coordinate and improve government activities related to older citizens. In the United Kingdom, as in America, we are moving beyond the general issues of population structure, pensions, health and welfare, towards the identification and alleviation of specific problems faced by individual cases. Such 'problem cases' provide exacting tests of society's willingness or ability to face up to the facts of ageing. This principle applies not only to the more obvious problems in community care – isolation and rehabilitation – but also to less obvious problems in industrial gerontology, such as retraining, ergonomics, and in environmental psychology, such as housing, leisure and consumer behaviour.

A small selection of very recent publications relevant to some of the issues referred to above are listed in the bibliographical notes to this chapter.[1-8]

Ambivalence has been a persistent feature of man's attitudes towards human ageing throughout recorded history. Our present-day ability to retard and ameliorate the process has improved enough to warrant a shift towards the so-called Ciceronian point of view; and there are no longer grounds for destructive pessimism and apathy, especially among people who may have something to contribute to applied gerontology, like teachers, doctors and nurses, administrators, and, of course, social and behavioural scientists. There are advantages in adopting for oneself, and encouraging in others, positive attitudes towards maturity and old age, which means being optimistic and realistic. Such attitudes need to be cultivated *throughout* life.

Although we cannot say that positive social attitudes *necessarily* bring good adjustment in later life, adjustment and a long life are strongly associated with a number of socially desirable personal characteristics including a sense of humour, intelligence, realistic self-appraisal, usefulness, emotional stability and the view that others of one's own age seem somehow older than oneself. Readers who are fortunate enough to possess such enviable personal qualities are likely to be optimistic anyway and will make the most of whatever opportunities lie ahead. Readers who are not so fortunate, and view the prospect with some dismay, can at least try some of the preventive measures which have been indicated. If the cynic asks, 'What are you saving yourself for?', the answer is, 'For the last enemy – old age'.

optimistic and realistic. Well-balanced interests need to be cultivated throughout life.

Although we cannot say that positive social attitudes (or many other good adjustments in later life) adjustment and a long life are strongly associated with a number of socially acceptable personal characteristics including a sense of humour, intelligence, realistic self-appraisal, usefulness, emotional stability, and the [illegible] of one's own are seen to grow older [illegible]. Readers who are fortunate enough to possess such enviable personal qualities are likely to be optimistic anyway and will make the most of whatever opportunities lie ahead. Readers who are not so fortunate and view the prospect with some dismay can at least try some of the preventive measures which have been indicated. If the cynic asks 'What are you saving yourself for?', the answer is 'For the last enemy – old age'.

Bibliographical Notes

CHAPTER ONE

1. Morgan, R. F., 'The adult growth examination: preliminary comparisons of physical aging in adults by sex and race', *Perceptual and Motor Skills*, vol. 27, 1968, pp. 595–9.
2. Dirken, J. M., 'Een voorlopig orrdeel over de maatlat voor de functionele leeftijd' ('A tentative judgement about the yardstick for functional age'), *Mens en Onderneming*, vol. 22, 1968, pp. 342–51.
3. Comfort, A., 'Test-battery to measure ageing-rate i nman', *The Lancet*, 27 December 1969, pp. 1411–15.
4. Boulière, F., *The Assessment of Biological Age in Man*, World Health Organization, Geneva, 1970.
5. *Aging and Human Development*, vol. 3, no. 2, special issue: Normative Aging Study. Part II, 'Functional age', 1972, pp. 143–211.
6. Birren, J. E., 'The psychology of aging in relation to development', in *Relations of Development and Aging*, ed. J. E. Birren, C. C. Thomas, Springfield, 1964, pp. 99–120.
7. Goulet, L. R. and Baltes, P. B. (eds.), *Life-Span Developmental Psychology*, Academic Press, New York, 1970.
8. Nesselroade, J. R. and Reese, H. W., *Life-Span Developmental Psychology: Methodological Issues*, Academic Press, New York, 1972.
9. McCay, C. M., 'Historical Retrospect', in *Problems of Ageing: Biological and Medical Aspects* (2nd edn), ed. E. V. Cowdry, Williams & Wilkins, Baltimore, 1942, pp. 908–16.
10. Fry, M., 'Public oration', in *Old Age in the Modern World* (Report of the Third Congress of the International Association of Gerontology, London, 1954), E. and S. Livingstone Ltd, 1955, pp. 4–14.

CHAPTER TWO

1. Zeman, F. D., 'Old age in ancient Egypt. A contribution to the history of geriatrics', *J. Mt. Sinai Hosp.*, N.Y., vol. 8, 1942, pp. 1161–5.
2. Zeman, F. D., 'The gerontocomia of Gabriele Zerbi. A fifteenth-century manual of hygiene for the aged'. *J. Mt. Sinai Hosp.*, N.Y., vol. 10, 1944, pp. 710–16.

3. Zeman, F. D., 'Life's later years. Studies in the medical history of old age. Part 1: introduction'. *J. Mt. Sinai Hosp.*, N.Y., vol. 11, 1944, pp. 45–52.
4. Zeman, F. D., op. cit., Part 2 not traced.
5. Zeman, F. D., op. cit., 'Part 3: the ancient Hebrews', 1944, pp. 97–104.
6. Zeman, F. D., op. cit., 'Part 4: the contribution of Greek thought', 1944, pp. 224–31.
7. Zeman, F. D., op. cit., 'Part 5: Roman attitudes and opinions', 1945, pp. 300–307.
8. Zeman, F. D., op. cit., 'Part 6: the medicine of Islam (732–1096 A.D.)', 1945, pp. 339–44.
9. Zeman, F. D., op. cit., 'Part 7: the medieval period (1096–1438 A.D.)', 1945, pp. 783–91.
10. Zeman, F. D., op. cit., 'Part 8: the revival of learning (1483–1600 A.D.)', 1945, pp. 833–46.
11. Zeman, F. D., op. cit., 'Part 9: the seventeenth century', 1945, pp. 890–91.
12. Zeman, F. D., op. cit., 'Part 10: the eighteenth century', 1945, pp. 939–53.
13. Zeman, F. D., op. cit., 'Part 11: the nineteenth century', 1947, pp. 241–56.
14. Zeman, F. D., op. cit., 'Part 12: the nineteenth century (continued)', 1950, pp. 308–22.
15. Zeman, F. D., op. cit., 'Part 12: the nineteenth century (concluded)', 1950, pp. 53–68.
16. Grant, R. L., 'Concepts of aging: an historical review', *Perspectives in Biology and Medicine*, vol. VI, 1963, pp. 443–78.
17. Gruman, G. J., 'History of ideas about the prolongation of life', *Transactions of the American Philosophical Society*, vol. 56, Part 9, 1966, pp. 1-102.
18. Onians, R. B., *The Origins of European Thought*, Cambridge University Press, 1951.
19. Blaxland Stubbs, S. G. and Bligh, E. W., *Sixty Centuries of Health and Physick: the Progress of Ideas from Primitive Magic to Modern Medicine*, Sampson Low, Marston & Co. Ltd, 1931.
20. See notes 16 and 17 above.
21. Comfort, A., 'Introductory and historical', in *Ageing. The Biology of Senescence*, Routledge & Kegan Paul, 1964, pp. 1–21.
22. Comfort, A., 'Old age, the last enemy', in *The Process of Ageing*,

New American Library of World Literature, Inc., New York, 1964, pp. 7–20.

23. Bacon, Roger, *The Cure of Old Age and the Preservation of Youth*, T. Flesher, London, 1683.
    See also *The Opus Majus of Roger Bacon*, 1661, translated by R. B. Burke, vol. II, University of Philadelphia Press, 1938, pp. 618–26.
24. Zeman, F. D., 'Life's later years. Studies in the medical history of old age. Part 8: the revival of learning (1483–1600 A.D.)', *J. Mt. Sinai Hosp.*, N.Y., vol. 12, 1945, pp. 836–7.
25. Zeman, F. D., see note 2 above.
26. Zeman, F. D., see note 10 above, p. 840.
27. Bacon, Francis, *History of Life and Death*, printed for William Lee and sold by Thomas Williams and William Place, London, 1658.
28. Burne, R. V. H., 'The treatment of the poor in the 18th century in Chester', *Journal of the Chester and North Wales Architectural, Archaeological and Historical Society*, vol. 52, 1965, pp. 33–48. See also note 12 above.
29. Thoms, W. J., *The Longevity of Man: its Facts and Fictions*, John Murray, 1873.
30. Hobson, W., 'General problems of aging', in *Modern Trends in Geriatrics*, ed. W. Hobson, Butterworth, 1956, pp. 1–21.
31. Bruce, M., *The Coming of the Welfare State* (4th edn), Batsford, 1968.
32. Poor Law Commissioners, *Report from His Majesty's Commissioners for Inquiring Into the Administration and Practical Operation of the Poor Laws*, Fellowes, London, 1834.
33. Booth, C., *The Aged Poor in England and Wales: Condition*, Macmillan, 1894.
34. Royal Commission on the Aged Poor, *Report Vol. 1*, H.M.S.O., 1895.
35. Shanas, E., Townsend, P., Wedderburn, D., Friis, H., Milhøj, P. and Stehouwer, J., *Old People in Three Industrial Societies*, Routledge & Kegan Paul, 1968.
36. Beveridge, W. H., *Social Insurance and Allied Services*, report, H.M.S.O., 1942.
37. Report of the Royal Commission on Population, H.M.S O., 1949.
38. Treasury, *Report of the Committee on the Economic and Financial Problems of the Provision for Old Age*, H.M.S.O., 1954.

39. Galton, F., 'On the anthropometric laboratory at the late International Health Exhibition', *J. Anthropol. Inst.*, vol. 14, 1885, pp. 205–18.
40. Hall, G. S., *Senescence: the Last Half of Life*, Appleton-Century-Crofts, New York, 1923.
41. National Council of Social Service, 26 Bedford Square, London, W.C.1.
   Age Concern (National Old People's Welfare Council), 55 Gower Street, London, W.C.1.
   National Corporation for the Care of Old People, Nuffield Lodge, Richmond Park, London, NW1 4RS.
   Federation of National Old Age Pensions Associations (local associations).
42. Graunt, J., 'Natural and political observations made upon bills of mortality' (1662). Reprinted in *J. Inst. Actuaries*, vol. 90, 1964, pp. 1–61.
43. Kendall, M. G., 'Where shall the history of statistics begin?', in *Studies in the History of Statistics and Probability*, ed. E. S. Pearson and M. G. Kendall, Charles Griffin & Co. Ltd, 1970, pp. 45–6. Reprinted from *Biometrika*, vol. 47, 1960, pp. 447–9.
44. Greenwood, M., 'Medical statistics from Graunt to Farr: Introduction, I The Lives of Petty and Graunt, II Petty's scientific work', op. cit., pp. 47–73. Reprinted from *Biometrika*, vol. 32, 1941, pp. 101–27.
45. Greenwood, M., 'Medical statistics from Graunt to Farr: III The statistical work of Graunt, IV Halley's Life Table, V Guessing the population', op. cit., pp. 74–96. Reprinted from *Biometrika*, vol. 32, 1942, pp. 203–25.
46. Greenwood, M., 'Medical statistics from Graunt to Farr: VI Some English medical statisticians in the eighteenth century, VII Some representative continental demographers of the eighteenth century, VIII Methodological advances, IX The end of an epoch', op. cit., pp. 97–120. Reprinted from *Biometrika*, vol. 33, 1943, pp. 1–24.
47. Benjamin, B. and Haycocks, H. W., *The Analysis of Mortality and Other Actuarial Statistics*, Cambridge University Press, 1970.
48. Gompertz, B., 'On the nature of the function expressive of the law of human mortality; and on a new mode of determining the value of life contingencies', *Philosophical Transactions*, vol. 115, 1825, p. 513. (Cited in note 47 above).
49. Makeham, W. M., 'On the law of mortality', *J. Inst. Actuaries*, vol. 13, p. 325. (Cited in note 47 above.)

50. Thiele, P. N., 'On a mathematical formula to express the rate of mortality throughout the whole of life', *J. Inst. Actuaries*, vol. 16, p. 313. (Cited in note 47 above.)
51. Quetelet, A., *Sur l'Homme et le Développement de ses Facultés*, 2 vols. Bachelier, Paris, 1835.
52. Birren, J. E., 'Principles of research on aging', in *Handbook of Aging and the Individual*, ed. J. E. Birren, University of Chicago Press, 1959, pp. 3–42.
53. Birren, J. E., 'A brief history of the psychology of aging. I and II', *Gerontologist*, vol. 1, 1961, pp. 67–77 and 127–34.
54. Pearson, K., *The Chances of Death*, Edward Arnold, 1892.
55. See note 36 above.
56. General Register Office of England and Wales, and of Scotland, *Census 1951. Great Britain. One Per Cent Sample Tables, Pts I and II*, H.M.S.O., 1952.
57. General Register Office of England and Wales, and of Scotland, *Census, 1961: Medical Tables. Population Tables. Commentary*, H.M.S.O., 1962.
58. Central Statistical Office, *Social Trends*, H.M.S.O., (from no. 1) 1970.
59. In the U.S.A., statistics on ageing are issued by the Administration on Aging, U.S. Department of Health, Education and Welfare, Washington, D.C.
60. See note 47 above.
61. Booth, C. (ed.), *Life and Labour of the People in London*, 4 vols., Macmillan, 1904.
62. See note 33 above.
63. Rowntree, B. S., *Poverty: A Study of Town Life* (2nd edn), Macmillan, 1902.
64. Moser, C. A., 'The evolution of social surveys in Great Britain', in *Survey Methods in Social Investigation*, Heinemann Educational Books, 1958, pp. 18–38.
65. Heron, A. and Chown, S. M., *Age and Function*, J. and A. Churchill Ltd, 1967.
66. Hearnshaw, L. S., *The Psychological and Occupational Aspects of Ageing. Liverpool Researches 1953–1970*, Medical Research Council, Liverpool, 1971.
67. Maxwell, J., 'Intelligence, education and fertility: a comparison between the 1932 and 1947 Scottish surveys', *Journal of Biosocial Science*, vol. 1, 1969, pp. 247–71.

68. Nuffield Foundation, *Old People*, Oxford University Press, 1947.
69. Sheldon, J. H., *The Social Medicine of Old Age: Report of an Enquiry in Wolverhampton*, Oxford University Press, 1948.
70. Various publications on the welfare of the aged have been issued by the National Council of Social Service. See note 41 above.
71. U.K. Ministry of Pensions and National Insurance, *National Insurance Retirement Pensions: Reasons Given for Retiring or Continuing at Work*, H.M.S.O., 1954.
72. Wall, W. D. and Williams, H. L., *Longitudinal Studies and the Social Sciences*, Heinemann, 1970.
73. Cowdry, E. V. (ed.), *Problems of Ageing*, Williams & Wilkins, Baltimore, 1939 (2nd edn 1942).
74. Korenchevsky, V., *Physiological and Pathological Ageing*, ed. G. H. Bourne, S. Karger, New York and Basel, 1961.
75. Comfort, A., *Ageing: the Biology of Senescence*, Routledge & Kegan Paul, 1964.
76. Pressey, S. L., 'The new division on maturity and old age. Its history and potential services', *Amer. Psychologist*, vol. 3, 1948, pp. 107–9.
77. Dorland, W. A. N., *The Age of Mental Virility. An Inquiry into the Records of Achievement of the World's Chief Workers and Thinkers*, Century Co., New York, 1908.
78. Charles, D. C., 'Historical antecedents of life-span developmental psychology', in *Life-Span Developmental Psychology*, ed. L. R. Goulet and P. B. Baltes, Academic Press, New York, 1970, pp. 23–52.
79. Groffman, K. J., 'Life-span developmental psychology in Europe: past and present', op. cit., pp. 53–68.
80. Bromley, D. B., 'Intellectual changes in adult life and old age: a commentary on the assumptions underlying the study of adult intelligence', in *Ageing of the Central Nervous System*, H. M. van Praag, De E. F. Bohn, N.V., Haarlem, 1972, pp. 76–100.
81. *Journal of Gerontology*, published quarterly by the Gerontological Society Inc., Washington, D.C.
82. *The Gerontologist*, published by the Gerontological Society, Inc., Washington, D.C.

    International Directory of Gerontology, prepared by the Gerontological Society, Inc., Bethesda, National Institute of Child Health and Human Development, 1968.
83. *Gerontologia*, Journal of Experimental Biological and Experimental Medical Research on Aging. Two vols. of four numbers each

issued annually, S. Karger, Basel and New York (British agent: J. Wiley & Sons).

84. In recent years, several new journals partly or entirely devoted to the study of ageing have been published:

Human Development, formerly *Vita Humana*, as for Gerontologia (see above). First issue 1958.

Experimental Gerontology, published by Pergamon Press Inc., New York. First issue 1966.

Developmental Psychology, published by the American Psychological Association Inc., Washington, D.C. First issue 1969.

Aging and Human Development, published by Baywood Publishing Co. Inc., Westport, Conn. First issue 1970.

Age and Ageing, the official journal of The British Geriatric Society and of the British Society for Research on Ageing, published by Ballière, Tindall & Cox, London. First issue 1972.

Industrial Gerontology, a publication of the National Institute of Industrial Gerontology, published by The National Council on the Aging, Washington, D.C. (Index issue vol. 11, Autumn 1971.)

Mechanisms of Aging and Development, published by Elsevier Sequoia S.A., Lausanne. First issue 1972.

In addition, a wide variety of scientific journals and publications contain articles on ageing – see *Psychological Abstracts* and other literature abstracts.

85. The social and behavioural aspects of human ageing overlap with those of biology and medicine. Readers are referred to the usual sources for technical information in these two latter areas, but the widely known ones include: *Journal of the American Geriatrics Society*, *Gerontologia Clinica*, and *Geriatrics*.

86. Birren, J. E., 'Psychological aspects of aging', in *Annual Review of Psychology*, vol. 11, ed. P. R. Farnsworth and Q. McNemar, Annual Reviews Inc., Palo Alto, 1960, pp. 161–98.

87. Chown, S. M. and Heron, A., 'Psychological aspects of aging in man', in *Annual Review of Psychology*, vol. 16, ed. P. R. Farnsworth, O. McNemar and Q. McNemar, Annual Reviews, Inc., Palo Alto, 1965, pp. 417–50.

88. Botwinick, J., 'Gero-psychology', in *Annual Review of Psychology*, vol. 21, ed. P. Mussen and M. R. Rosenzweig, Annual Reviews Inc., Stanford, 1970, pp. 239–72.

89. Shock, N. W., *A Classified Bibliography of Gerontology and Geriatrics*, Stanford University Press, 1951.

90. Shock, N. W., *A Classified Bibliography of Gerontology and Geri-*

atrics. Supplement One, 1949–55, Stanford University Press, 1957.

91. Shock, N. W., *A Classified Bibliography of Gerontology and Geriatrics. Supplement Two, 1956–61*, Stanford University Press, 1963.
92. International Association of Gerontology, *Proc. VIIIth Intern. Congress of Gerontology*, International Association of Gerontology, Washington, D.C., 1969. Vol. 1, *Abstracts of Symposia and Lectures;* vol. 2, *Abstracts of Volunteer Papers and Films.*
93. International Association of Gerontology, *Proc. IXth Intern. Congress of Gerontology*, International Association of Gerontology, Kiev, 1972. Vol. 1, *Reports and Introductory Lectures;* vol. 2, *Reports;* vol. 3, *Abstracts.*

    The Main Problems of Soviet Gerontology by Chebotarev, D. F., Mankovsky, N. B., Frolkis, V. V., Mints, A. Ya., Duplenko, Yu. K.

    Materials for IXth Intern. Congress of Gerontologists, International Association of Gerontology, Kiev, 1972.

    English language access to the Soviet literature on ageing can be gained via *Psychological Abstracts*, proceedings of international congresses, occasional surveys of Soviet work, and library translation services.
94. The National Corporation for the Care of Old People, *Old Age. A Register of Social Research, 1964 onwards*, National Corporation for the Care of Old People, 1972.

CHAPTER THREE

1. Korenchevsky, V., *Physiological and Pathological Ageing*, S. Karger, Basel, 1961.
2. Comfort, A., *Ageing: The Biology of Senescence*, Routledge & Kegan Paul, 1964.
3. Goldstein, S., 'The biology of aging', *New England J. Medicine*, vol. 285, 1971, pp. 1120–29.
4. Andrew, W., *The Anatomy of Aging in Man and Mammals*, Heinemann Medical Books, 1971.
5. Kohn, R. R., *Principles of Mammalian Aging*, Prentice-Hall International Inc., 1971.
6. Lind, A. R. and Hellon, R. F., 'Changes in thermoregulatory process in man due to aging', in *Biological Aspects of Aging. Aging Around the World*, ed. N. W. Shock, Columbia University Press, New York, 1962, p. 208.

7. Henschel, A., Cole, M. B. and Lyezkowskyj, O., 'Heat tolerance of elderly persons living in a subtropical climate', *J. Gerontol.*, vol. 23, 1968, pp. 17–22.
8. Kormendy, C. G. and Bender, A. D., 'Experimental modification of the chemistry and biology of the aging process', *J. Pharmaceutical Sciences*, vol. 60, 1971, pp. 167–80.
9. McFarland, R. A., 'Experimental evidence of the relationship between ageing and oxygen want: in search of a theory of ageing', *Ergonomics*, vol. 6, 1963, pp. 339–66.
10. Jacobs, E. A., Winter, P. M., Alvis, H. J. and Small, S. M., 'Hyperoxygenation effect on cognitive functioning in the aged', *New England J. Medicine*, vol. 281, 1969, pp. 753–7.
11. Feinberg, I., Korseko, R. L. and Heller, N., 'E E G sleep patterns as a function of normal and pathological aging of man', *J. Psychiat. Research*, vol. 5, 1967, pp. 107–44.
12. Feinberg, I. and Carlson, V. R., 'Sleep variables as a function of age in man', *Archives Gen. Psychiat.*, vol. 18, 1968, pp. 239–50.
13. Kahn, E. and Fisher, C., 'The sleep characteristics of the aged', *Psychophysiology*, vol. 5, 1968, p. 229.
14. Tune, G. S., 'Sleep and wakefulness in 509 normal human adults', *Brit. J. Med. Psychol.*, vol. 42, 1969, pp. 75–80.
15. Tune, G. S., 'The influence of age and temperament on adult human sleep-wakefulness pattern', *Brit. J. Psychol.*, vol. 60, 1969, pp. 431–41.
16. Webb, W. B. and Swinburne, H., 'An observational study of sleep of the aged', *Perceptual and Motor Skills*, vol. 42, 1971, pp. 895–8.
17. Vogel, F. S., 'The brain and time', in *Behavior and Adaptation in Late Life*, ed. F. W. Busse and F. Pfeiffer, Little, Brown & Co., Boston, 1969, pp. 251–62.
18. Blumenthal, H. T. (ed.), *Interdisciplinary Topics in Gerontology, Vol. 7. The Regulatory Role of the Nervous System in Aging*, S. Karger, Basel, 1970.
19. Dobbing, J., 'Undernutrition and the developing brain', *Amer. J. Diseases of Children*, vol. 120, 1970, pp. 411–15.
20. Rosenzweig, M. R., 'Environmental complexity, cerebral change, and behavior', *Amer. Psychologist*, vol. 21, 1966, pp. 321–32.
21. Altschuler, H., Kleban, M. H., Gold, M., Lawton, M. P. and Miller, M., 'Neurochemical changes in the brain of aged albino rats resulting from avoidance learning', *J. Gerontol.*, vol. 26, 1971, pp. 63–9.

22. Shagass, C. and Schwartz, M., 'Age, personality, and somatosensory cerebral evoked responses', *Science*, vol. 148, 1965, pp. 1359–61.
23. Matousek, M., Volavka, J., Roubicek, J. and Roth, Z., 'EEG frequency analysis related to age in normal adults', *Electroencephalography and Clinical Neurophysiology*, vol. 23, 1967, pp. 162–7.
24. Surwillo, W. W., 'Timing of behavior in senescence and the role of the central nervous system', in *Human Aging and Behavior*, ed. G. A. Talland, Academic Press, New York, 1968, pp. 1–35.
25. Gardner, E., 'Decrease in human neurones with age', *Anatomical Records*, vol. 77, 1940, pp. 529–60.
26. Critchley, M., 'Aging and the nervous system', in *Problems of Ageing* (2nd edn), ed. E. V. Cowdry, Williams & Wilkins, Baltimore, 1942, pp. 518–34.
27. Wright, E. A. and Spink, J. M., 'A study of the loss of nerve cells in relation to age', *Gerontologia*, vol. 3, 1959, pp. 277–87.
28. Bondareff, W., 'Morphology of the aging nervous system', in *Handbook of Aging and the Individual*, ed. J. E. Birren, University of Chicago Press, 1959, pp. 136–72.
29. Satz, P., 'Specific and non-specific effects of brain lesions in man', *J. Abn. Psychol.*, vol. 71, 1966, pp. 165–70.
30. Brody, H., 'Structural changes in the aging nervous system', in *Interdisciplinary Topics in Gerontology, Vol. 7 The Regulatory Role of the Nervous System in Aging*, S. Karger, New York, 1970, pp. 9–21.
31. Tomlinson, B. E., 'Morphological brain changes in non-demented old people', in *Ageing of the Central Nervous System*, ed. H. M. van Praag, De E. F. Bohn, N.V., Haarlem, 1972, pp. 38–57.
32. Levy, P., 'Neurophysiological disturbances associated with psychiatric disorders in old age', op. cit., pp. 141–61.
33. Hicks, L. H. and Birren, J. E., 'Aging, brain damage, and psychomotor slowing', *Psychol. Bull.*, vol. 74, 1970, pp. 377–96.
34. Pavolva, G. A., 'Axosomatic contacts in senile dementia', *Zhurnal Nevropatologii i Psikhiatrii*, vol. 71, 1971, pp. 413–16. (From *Psychol. Abstracts.*)
35. Shmavonian, B. M., Yarmat, A. J. and Cohen, S. I., 'Relationships between the autonomic nervous system in age differences in behavior', in *Behavior, Aging, and the Nervous System*, ed. A. T. Welford and J. E. Birren, C. C. Thomas, Springfield, 1965, pp. 235–58.

36. Davidson, P. O., Payne, R. W. and Sloane, R. B., 'Conditionability and age in human adults', *Psychol. Reports*, vol. 17, 1965, pp. 351–4.
37. Shmavonian, B. M., Miller, L. H. and Cohen, S. I., 'Differences among age and sex groups with respect to cardiovascular conditioning and reactivity', *J. Gerontol.*, vol. 25, 1970, pp. 87–94.
38. Eisdorfer, C., 'Arousal and performance: experiments in verbal learning and a tentative theory', in *Human Aging and Behavior*, ed. G. A. Talland, Academic Press, New York, 1968, pp. 189–216.
39. Eisdorfer, C., 'On the issue of relevance in research', *Gerontologist*, vol. 10, 1970, pp. 5–10.
40. Corso, J. F., 'Sensory processes and age effects in normal adults', *J. Gerontol.*, vol. 26, 1971, pp. 90–105.
41. Wells, C. E. C., 'Central disorders of the special senses in the elderly', *Gerontologia Clinica*, vol. 13, 1971, pp. 329–38.
42. Weale, R. A., *The Ageing Eye*, H. K. Lewis, 1963.
43. Lakowski, R., 'Is the deterioration of colour discrimination with age due to lens or retinal changes?', reprinted from *Tagungs-Bericht der Internationalen Farbtagung*, Dusseldorf, 1961. Teil 2, 'Die Farbe' 11, Nr. 1/6, 1962, pp. 69–86.
44. Burg, A., 'Light sensitivity as related to age and sex', *Perceptual and Motor Skills*, vol. 24, 1967, pp. 1279–88.
45. Burg, A., 'Lateral visual field as related to age and sex', *J. Appl. Psychol.*, vol. 52, 1968, pp. 10–15.
46. Wilson, T. R., 'Flicker fusion frequency, age and intelligence', *Gerontologia*, vol. 7, 1963, pp. 200–208.
47. Farley, F. H., 'The threshold of fusion of paired light flashes as a function of age in normal adults', *J. Genetic Psychol.*, vol. 144, 1969, pp. 143–8.
48. Comalli, P. E., Jr, 'Life-span changes in visual perception', in *Life-Span Developmental Psychology*, ed. L. R. Goulet and P. B. Baltes, Academic Press, New York, 1970, pp. 211–26.
49. Meneghini, K. A. and Leibowitz, H. W., 'Effect of stimulus distance and age on shape constancy', *J. Exp. Psychol.*, vol. 74, 1967, pp. 241–8.
50. Eisner, D. A. and Schaie, K. W., 'Age changes in response to visual illusions from middle to old age', *J. Gerontol.*, vol. 26, 1971, pp. 146–50.
51. Bell, B., Wolf, E. and Bernholz, C. D., 'Depth perception as a function of age', *Aging and Human Dev.*, vol. 3, 1972, pp. 77–81.
52. Fortuin, G. J., 'Age and lighting needs', *Ergonomics*, vol. 6, 1963, pp. 239–45.

53. Bab, W., *The Uses of Psychology in Geriatric Ophthalmology*, C. C. Thomas, Springfield, 1964.
54. Corso, J. F., 'Age and sex differences in pure-tone thresholds: a survey of hearing levels from 18 to 65 years', *American Foundation for the Blind, Research Bulletin*, no. 17, 1968, pp. 141–72.
55. Farrimond, T., 'Visual and auditory performance variations with age: some implications', *Aust. J. Psychol.*, vol. 19, 1967, pp. 193–201.
56. Bergman, M., 'Hearing and aging: implications of recent research findings', *Audiology*, vol. 10, 1971, pp. 164–71.
57. Rees, J. N. and Botwinick, J., 'Detection and decision factors in auditory behavior of the elderly', *J. Gerontol.*, vol. 26, 1971, pp. 133–6.
58. Smith, R. A. and Prather, W. F., 'Phoneme discrimination in older persons under varying signal-to-noise conditions', *Journal of Speech and Hearing Research*, vol. 14, 1971, pp. 630–38.
59. Farrimond, T., 'A test of the ability to lip-read – use of visible cues of speech', *J. Psychol.*, vol. 75, 1962, pp. 477–81.
60. Hinchcliffe, R., 'Aging and sensory thresholds', *J. Gerontol.*, vol. 17, 1962, pp. 45–50.
61. Byrd, E. and Gertman, S., 'Taste sensitivity in aging persons', *Geriatrics*, vol. 14, 1959, pp. 381–4.
62. Cohen, T. and Gitman, L., 'Oral complaints and taste perception in the aged', *J. Gerontol.* vol. 14, 1959, pp. 294–8.
63. See note 39 above.
64. Mumford, J. M., 'Pain perception threshold and adaptation of human teeth', *Archives of Oral Biology*, vol. 10, 1965, pp. 957–68.
65. Clark, W. C., 'Sensory-decision theory analysis of the placebo effect on the criterion for pain and thermal sensitivity (*d'*)', *J. Abn. Psychol.*, vol. 74, 1969, pp. 363–71.
66. Clark, W. C. and Mehl, S., 'A sensory-decision theory analysis of the effect of age and sex on *d'*, various response criteria, and 50% pain threshold', *J. Abn. Psychol.*, vol. 78, 1971, pp. 202–12.
67. Mysak, E. D. and Hanley, T. D., 'Aging processes in speech: pitch and duration characteristics', *J. Gerontol.*, vol. 13, 1958, pp. 309–13.
68. Ryan, W. J., 'Acoustic aspects of the aging voice', *J. Gerontol.* vol. 27, 1972, pp. 265–8.
69. Williams, D., 'The menopause', *Brit. Med. J.* vol. 2, 1971, pp. 208–10.
70. Hamilton, J. B. and Mestler, G. E., 'Mortality and survival: com-

parison of eunuchs with intact men and women in a mentally retarded population', *J. Gerontol.*, vol. 24, 1969, pp. 395–411.
71. Pfeiffer, E., Verwoerdt, A. and Wang, H-S., 'Sexual behavior in aged men and women: I Observation on 254 community volunteers', *Archives Gen. Psychiat.*, vol. 19, 1968, pp. 753–8.
72. Pfeiffer, E., Verwoerdt, A. and Wang, H-S., 'The natural history of sexual behavior in a biologically advantaged group of aged individuals', *J. Gerontol.* vol. 24, 1969, pp. 193–8.
73. Berezin, M. A., 'Sex and old age. A review of the literature', *J. Geriat. Psychiat.*, vol. 2, 1969, pp. 131–49.
74. Felstein, I., *Sex and the Longer Life*, Allen Lane, 1970; Penguin Books, 1974.
75. Jarvik, L. F. and Kato, T., 'Chromosomes and mental changes in octogenarians: preliminary findings', *Brit. J. Psychiat.*, vol. 115, 1969, pp. 1193–4.
76. Jarvik, L. F., 'Human genetics and aging', in *Duke University Council on Aging and Human Development: Proceedings of Seminars 1965–69*, ed. F. C. Jeffers, Center for the Study of Aging and Human Development, Duke University Medical Center, Durham, N.C., 1969, pp. 266–78.
77. Acsádi, G. Y. and Nemeskéri, J., *History of Human Life Span and Mortality*, Akadémiai Kiadó, Budapest, 1970.
78. Retzlaff, E., Fontaine, J., and Furuta, W., 'Effect of daily exercise on life-span of albino rats', *Geriatrics*, vol. 21, 1966, pp. 171–7.
79. Edington, D. W., Cosmas, A. C. and McCafferty, W. B., 'Exercise and longevity: evidence for a threshold age', *J. Gerontol.*, vol. 27, 1972, pp. 341–3.
80. Barry, A. J., Steinmetz, J. R., Page, H. F. and Rodahl, K., 'The effects of physical conditioning on older individuals. II Motor performance and cognitive function', *J. Gerontol.*, vol. 21, 1966, pp. 192–9.
81. Barry, A. J., Webster, C. W. and Daly, J. W., 'Validity and reliability of a multi-stage exercise test for older men and women', *J. Gerontol.*, vol. 24, 1969, pp. 284–91.
82. Wessel, J. A., Small, H., Van Huss, W. D., Heusner, W. W. and Cederquist, D. C., 'Age and physiological responses to exercise in women 20–69 years of age', *J. Gerontol*, vol. 23, 1968, pp. 269–78.
83. Skinner, J. S., 'Exercise, aging and longevity', in *Proc. VIIIth Intern. Congress Gerontology*, vol. 1, International Association of Gerontology, Washington, D.C., 1969, pp. 47–50.
84. de Vries, H. A., 'Physiological effects of an exercise training regi-

men upon men aged 52–88', *J. Gerontol.*, vol. 25, 1970, pp. 325–36.

85. Polednak, A. P. and Damon, A., 'College athletics, longevity, and cause of death', *Human Biology*, vol. 42, 1970, pp. 28–46.
86. Powell, R. R. and Pohndorft, R. H., 'Comparison of adult exercisers on fluid intelligence and selected physiological variables', *Research Quarterly*, vol. 42, 1971, pp. 70–77.
87. Gore, Y., 'Physical activity and ageing – a survey of Soviet literature', in 3 parts, *Gerontologia Clinica*, vol. 14, 1972, pp. 65–9, 70–77 and 78–85.
88. See notes 1 to 5 above.
89. Spiegelman, M., 'The curve of human mortality', in *Duke University Council on Aging and Human Development: Proceedings of Seminars 1965–69*, ed. F. C. Jeffers, Center for the Study of Aging and Human Development, Duke University Medical Center, Durham, N.C., 1969, pp. 286–98.
90. See also bibliographical notes to Chapter Two.
91. Johnson, M. L., 'Self-perception of need amongst the elderly: an analysis of illness behaviour', *Proc. Brit. Soc. of Social and Behavioural Gerontology*, Nottingham, 1972.
92. Comfort, A., 'The prolongation of vigorous life', *Impact of Science on Society*, vol. XX, 1970, pp. 307–19.
93. Petrov, R., 'Organ transplantation: problems and perspectives', *Impact of Science on Society*, vol. XX, 1970, pp. 293–305.
94. Estes, E. H., 'Health experience in the elderly', in *Behavior and Adaptation in Late Life*, ed. E. W. Busse and F. Pfeiffer, Little, Brown & Co., Boston, 1969, pp. 115–28.
95. Blalock, H. M. (ed.), *Causal Models in the Social Sciences*, Macmillan, 1972.
96. Samis, H. V., 'Aging: the loss of temporal organization', *Perspectives in Biology and Medicine*, vol. 12, 1968, pp. 95–102.
97. Busse, E. W., 'Theories of aging', in *Behavior and Adaptation in Late Life*, ed. E. W. Busse and F. Pfeiffer, Little, Brown & Co., Boston, 1969, pp. 11–32.
98. Comfort, A., 'Biological theories of aging', *Human Develop.* vol. 13, 1970, pp. 127–39.
99. See notes 1 to 5 above.
100. Furchtgott, E., 'Radiation as a tool in studies of behavioural age changes', in *Behavior, Aging, and the Nervous System*, ed. A. T. Welford and J. E. Birren, C. C. Thomas, Springfield, 1965, pp. 450–60.

CHAPTER FOUR

1. Tibbitts, C. (ed.), *Handbook of Social Gerontology. Societal Aspects of Aging*, University of Chicago Press, 1960.
2. Burgess, E. W. (ed.), *Aging in Western Societies*, University of Chicago Press, 1960.
3. Kaplan, J. and Aldridge, G. J., *Social Welfare of the Aging*, Columbia University Press, New York, 1962.
4. Tibbitts, C. and Donahue, W. (eds.), *Social and Psychological Aspects of Aging*, Columbia University Press, New York, 1962.
5. Williams, R. H., Tibbitts, C. and Donahue, W. (eds.), *Processes of Aging*, Atherton Press, New York, 1963.
6. Shanas, E., Townsend, P., Wedderburn, D., Friis, H., Milhøj, P. and Stehouwer, J., *Older People in Three Industrial Societies*, Atherton Press, New York, 1968.
7. UNESCO, 'Old Age', *International Journal of Social Science*, vol. XV, no. 3, 1963, pp. 339–465.
8. Townsend, P. and Wedderburn, D., *The Aged in the Welfare State*, Bell, 1965.
9. Rosset, E., *Aging Process of Population* (trans. from Polish edn by H. Infield), Pergamon Press, 1964.
10. Office of Population Censuses and Surveys, *Population projections, 1970–2010*, prepared by Government Actuary, H.M.S.O., 1971.
11. McKinney, J. C. and de Vyver, F. T. (eds.), *Aging and Social Policy*, Appleton-Century-Crofts Inc., New York, 1966.
12. Kreps, J. M., *Lifetime Allocation of Work and Income, Essays in the Economics of Aging*, Duke University Press, Durham, N.C., 1971.
13. National Council on the Aging, Washington, D.C. 'Studies on Problems of Work and Age', *Industrial Gerontology*, vol. 16, 1973, pp. 1-98.
14. Kapnick, P. L., Goodman, J. S. and Cornwell, E. E., 'Political behavior in the aged: some new data', *J. Gerontol.*, vol. 22, 1967, pp. 305–10.
15. Rosow, I., *Social Integration of the Aged*, Free Press, Glencoe, 1967.
16. Benjamin, B., 'Some aspects of model building in the social and environmental fields', in *Social Trends No. 2*, Central Statistical Office, H.M.S.O., 1971 pp. 24–30.
17. Davis, R. W. 'Social influences on the aspiration tendency of older people', *J. Gerontol.*, vol. 22, 1967, pp. 510–16.

18. Kahana, E. and Coe, R. M., 'Dimensions of conformity: a multidisciplinary view', *J. Gerontol.*, vol. 24, 1969, pp. 76–81.
19. Martin, J. D., 'Power, dependence, and the complaints of the elderly: a social exchange perspective', *Aging and Human Dev.*, vol. 2, 1971, pp. 108–12.
20. Klein, R. C., 'Age, sex, and task difficulty as predictors of social conformity', *J. Gerontol.*, vol. 27, 1972, pp. 229–36.
21. Havighurst, R. J., Munnichs, J. M. A., Neugarten, B. L. and Thomae, H., *Adjustment to Retirement: A Cross-National Study*, Royal Vangorcum Ltd, Assen, Netherlands, 1969.
22. Palmore, E., 'Why do people retire?', *Aging and Human Dev.*, vol. 2, 1971, pp. 29–37.
23. Carp, F. M. (ed.), *Retirement*, Behavioral Publications, New York, 1971.
24. Rowe, A. R., 'The retirement of academic scientists', *J. Gerontol.*, vol. 27, 1972, pp. 113–18.
25. Bortner, R. W. and Hultsch, D. F., 'A multivariate analysis of correlates of life satisfaction in adulthood', *J. Gerontol.*, vol. 25, 1970, pp. 41–7.
26. Bromley, D. B., 'An approach to theory construction in the psychology of development and aging', in *Life-Span Developmental Psychology*, ed. L. R. Goulet and P. B. Baltes, Academic Press, New York, 1970, pp. 71–114.
27. Maddox, G. L., 'Themes and issues in sociological theories of human aging', *Human Develop.*, vol. 13, 1970, pp. 17–27.
28. Atchley, R. C., 'Disengagement among professors', *J. Gerontol.*, vol. 26, 1971, pp. 476–80.
29. Townsend, P. and Tunstall, S., 'Isolation, desolation and loneliness', in *Old People in Three Industrial Societies*, by Shanas, E., et al., Routledge & Kegan Paul, 1968, pp. 258–87.
30. Lowenthal, M. F. and Haven, C., 'Interaction and adaptation: intimacy as a critical variable', in *Middle Age and Aging*, ed. B. L. Neugarten, University of Chicago Press, 1968, pp. 390–400.
31. Simmons, L. W., 'Aging in preindustrial societies', in *Handbook of Social Gerontology*, ed. C. Tibbitts, University of Chicago Press, 1960, pp. 62–91.
32. Clarke, M., 'The anthropology of aging: a new area for studies of culture and personality', in *Middle Age and Aging*, ed. B. L. Neugarten, University of Chicago Press, 1968, pp. 433–43.
33. Gutmann, D. L., 'Aging among the Highland Maya: a comparative study', op. cit., pp. 444–52.

34. Harlan, W. H., 'Social status of the aged in three Indian villages', op. cit., pp. 469–75.
35. Maxwell, R. J. and Silverman, P., 'Information and esteem: cultural considerations in the treatment of the aged', *Aging and Human Dev.*, vol. 1, 1970, pp. 361–92.

CHAPTER FIVE

1. Paillat, P. M. and Bunch, M. E. (eds.), *Interdisciplinary Topics in Gerontology, Vol. 6 Age, Work and Automation*, S. Karger, New York, 1970.
2. Stagner, R., 'An industrial psychologist looks at industrial gerontology', *Aging and Human Dev.*, vol. 2, 1971, pp. 29–37.
3. Organization for Economic Co-operation and Development, *International Management Seminar on Job-Redesign and Occupational Training for Older Workers*, O.E.C.D., Manpower and Social Affairs Directorate, Social Affairs Division, Paris, 1964.
4. Murrell, K. F. H., 'Organizational factors *v.* age', in *Ergonomics: Man in his Working Environment*, Chapman & Hall, 1965, pp. 442–51.
5. Snook, S. H., 'The effects of age and physique on continuous-work capacity', *Human Factors*, vol. 13, 1971, pp. 467–79.
6. Belbin, E. and Belbin, R. M., *Problems in Adult Retraining*, Heinemann, 1972.
7. Jamieson, G. H., 'Study of adult learning', *Studies in Adult Education*, vol. 2, 1970, pp. 18–26.
8. Jamieson, G. H., 'Learning and retention: a comparison between programmed and discovery learning at two age levels', *Programmed Learning*, vol. 8, 1971, pp. 34–40.
9. Welford, A. T., *Ageing and Human Skill*, Oxford University Press, 1958.
10. Heron, A. and Chown, S. M., *Age and Function*, J. and A. Churchill Ltd, 1967.
11. Hearnshaw, L. S., *The Psychological and Occupational Aspects of Ageing*. Liverpool Researches 1953–1970, Medical Research Council, Liverpool, 1971.
12. Miles, W. R., 'Measures of certain human abilities throughout the life span', *Proc. National Academy of Science*, vol. 17, 1931, pp. 627–33.
13. Bromley, D. B., 'Age differences in the Porteus Maze Test', in

Proc. VIIth Intern. Congress Gerontology, International Association of Gerontology, San Francisco, 1966, pp. 225–8.
14. Welford, A. T. and Birren, J. E. (eds.), *Behavior, Aging and the Nervous System*, C. C. Thomas, Springfield, 1965.
15. Rabbitt, P., 'Age and the use of structure in transmitted information', in *Human Aging and Behavior*, ed. G. A. Talland, Academic Press, New York, 1968, pp. 75–92.
16. Harwood, E. and Naylor, G. F. K., 'Rates of information-transfer in elderly subjects', *Aust. J. Psychol.*, vol. 21, 1969, pp. 127–36.
17. Daly, J. W., Barry, A. J. and Birkhead, C., 'The physical working capacity of older individuals', *J. Gerontol.*, vol. 23, 1968, pp. 134–9.
18. Salvendy, G. and Pilitsis, J., 'Psychophysiological aspects of paced and unpaced performance as influenced by age', *Ergonomics*, vol. 14, 1971, pp. 703–11.
19. Sofer, C., *Men in Mid-Career*, Cambridge University Press, 1970.
20. Sheppard, H. L. (ed.), *Toward an Industrial Gerontology: An Introduction to a New Field of Applied Research and Service*, Schenkman, Cambridge, Mass., 1970.
21. Heron, A. and Cunningham, C. M., 'The experience of younger and older men in a works reorganization', *Occup. Psychol.*, vol. 36, 1962, pp. 10–14.
22. Wedderburn, D., *White Collar Redundancy*, Cambridge University Press, 1964.
23. Smith, J. M., 'Age and re-employment: a regional study of external mobility', *Occup. Psychol.*, vol. 41, 1967, pp. 239–43.
24. Tune, G. S., 'Sleep and wakefulness in a group of shift workers', *Brit. J. Indust. Med.*, vol. 26, 1969, p. 54.
25. Jamieson, G. H., 'Inspection in the telecommunications industry: a field study of age and other performance variables', *Ergonomics*, vol. 9, 1966, pp. 297–303.
26. Tune, G. S. and Davies, D. R., *Human Vigilance Performance*, Staples Press, 1970.
27. Heron, A. and Chown, S. M., *Ageing and the Semi-Skilled*, Medical Research Council Memo, no. 40, H.M.S.O., 1961.
28. Whitehead, F. E., 'Trends in certificated sickness absence', in *Social Trends No. 2*, Central Statistical Office, H.M.S.O., 1971, pp. 13–23.
29. McFarland, R. A., 'Psychological and behavioral aspects of automobile accidents', *Traffic Safety Research Review*, vol. 12, 1968, pp. 71–80.

30. Planek, T. W. and Fowler, R. C., 'Traffic accident problems and exposure characteristics of the aging driver', *J. Gerontol.*, vol. 26, 1971, pp. 224–30.
31. Wetherick, N. E., 'Changing an established concept: a comparison of the ability of young, middle-aged and old subjects', *Gerontologia*, vol. 11, 1965, pp. 82–95.

CHAPTER SIX

1. Yerkes, R. M., *Psychological Examining in the U.S. Army*, Part III, Ch. 14, Memoirs of the National Academy of Science, Vol. 15, Washington, 1921.
2. Doll, E. A., 'The average mental age of adults', *J. Appl. Psychol.*, vol. 3, 1919, pp. 317–28.
3. Botwinick, J., *Cognitive Processes in Maturity and Old Age*, Springer Publ. Co., New York, 1967.
4. Cassel, R. N., 'Historical review of theories on the nature of intelligence', *Psychology*, vol. 6, 1969, pp. 39–46.
5. Schaie, K. W., 'A reinterpretation of age related changes in cognitive structure and functioning', in *Life-Span Developmental Psychology*, ed. L. R. Goulet and P. B. Baltes, Academic Press, New York, 1970, pp. 485–507.
6. Bromley, D. B., 'Intellectual changes in adult life and old age: a commentary on the assumptions underlying the study of adult intelligence', in *Ageing of the Central Nervous System*, ed. H. M. van Praag, De E. F. Bohn, N.V., Amsterdam, 1972, pp. 76–100.
7. Wechsler, D., *Wechsler Adult Intelligence Scale*, Psychological Corporation, New York, 1955.
8. Wechsler, D., *The Measurement and Appraisal of Adult Intelligence* (4th edn), Baillière, Tindall & Cox, 1958.
   See also Matarazzo, J. D. *Wechsler's Measurement and Appraisal of Adult Intelligence* (5th edn), Williams & Wilkins, Baltimore, 1972.
9. Riegel, K. F., 'Changes in psycholinguistic performances with age', in *Human Aging and Behavior*, ed. G. A. Talland, Academic Press, New York, 1968, pp. 239–79.
10. Arenberg, D., 'Age differences in retroaction', *J. Gerontol.*, vol. 22, 1967, pp. 88–91.
11. Schonfield, D., 'Memory loss with age: acquisition and retrieval', *Psychol. Reports*, vol. 20, 1967, pp. 223–6.

12. Talland, G. A., 'Age and the span of immediate recall', in *Human Aging and Behavior*, ed. G. A. Talland, Academic Press, New York, 1968, pp. 93–129.
13. Craik, F. I. M., 'Short-term memory and the aging process', op. cit., pp. 131–68.
14. Craik, F. I. M., 'Age differences in recognition memory', *Quart. J. Exp. Psychol.*, vol. 23, 1971, pp. 316–23.
15. Peak, D. T., 'A replication study of changes in short-term memory in a group of aging community residents', *J. Gerontol.*, vol. 25, 1970, pp. 316–19.
16. Kausler, D. H., 'Retention – forgetting as a nomological network for developmental research', in *Life-Span Developmental Psychology*, ed. L. R. Goulet and P. B. Baltes, Academic Press, New York, 1970, pp. 305–53.
17. Taub, H. A. and Walker, J. B., 'Short-term memory as a function of age and response interference', *J. Gerontol.*, vol. 25, 1970, pp. 177–83.
18. Monge, R. H. and Hultsch, D. F., 'Paired-associate learning as a function of adult age and the length of the anticipation and inspection intervals', *J. Gerontol.*, vol. 26, 1971, pp. 157–62.
19. Hultsch, D. F., 'Organization and memory in adulthood', *Human Develop.*, vol. 14, 1971, pp. 16–29.
20. Anders, T. R., Fozard, J. L. and Lillyquist, T. D., 'Effects of age upon retrieval from short-term memory', *Develop. Psychol.*, vol. 6, 1972, pp. 214–17.
21. Drachman, D. A. and Leavitt, J., 'Memory impairment in the aged: storage versus retrieval deficit', *J. Exp. Psychol.*, vol. 93, 1972, pp. 302–8.
22. Goulet, L. R., 'New directions for research on aging and retention', *J. Gerontol.*, vol. 27, 1972, pp. 52–60.
23. Warrington, E. K. and Sanders, H. I., 'The fate of old memories', *Quart. J. Exp. Psychol.*, vol. 23, 1971, pp. 432–42.
24. Gilbert, J. G. and Levee, R. T., 'Patterns of declining memory', *J. Gerontol.*, vol. 1, 1971, pp. 70–75.
25. Davies A. D. M., 'Age and memory-for-designs test', *Brit. J. Soc. Clin. Psychol.*, vol. 6, 1967, pp. 228–33.
26. Graham, F. K. and Kendall, B. S., 'Memory-for-designs test: revised general manual', *Perceptual and Motor Skills*, vol. 7, 1970 (Monograph, Suppl. 2).
27. Arenberg, D., 'Concept problem solving in young and old adults', *J. Gerontol.*, vol. 23, 1968, pp. 279–82.

28. Bromley, D. B., 'Studies of intellectual function in relation to age and their significance for professional and managerial functions', in *Interdisciplinary Topics in Gerontology, Vol. 4 Decision Making and Age*, ed. A. T. Welford and J. E. Birren, S. Karger, Basel, 1969, pp. 103–26.
29. Wetherick, N. E., 'The responses of normal adult subjects to the matrices test', *Brit. J. Psychol.*, vol. 57, 1966, pp. 297–300.
30. Raven, J. C., *Progressive Matrices (1938), Sets A, B, C, D and E*, H. K. Lewis, 1938; *Progressive Matrices (1947), Sets A, Ab, B*, H. K. Lewis, 1949; *Guide to the Standard Progressive Matrices, Sets A, B, C, D and E*, H. K. Lewis, 1954.
31. Blumenkrantz, J., Wilkin, W. R. and Tuddenham, R. D., 'Relationships between the progressive matrices and AGCT-3a among older military personnel', *Educ. and Psychol. Measurement*, vol. 28, 1968, pp. 931–5.
32. Raven, J. C., *Guide to Using the Crichton Vocabulary Scale with Progressive Matrices (1947), Sets A, Ab, B*, H. K. Lewis, 1954.
33. Guertin, W. H., Ladd, C. E., Frank, G. H., Rabin, A. I. and Hiester, D., 'Research with the Wechsler Intelligence Scale for Adults: 1960–1965', *Psychol. Bull.*, vol. 66, 1966, pp. 385–409.
34. Guertin, W. H., Ladd, C. E., Frank, G. H., Rabin, A. I. and Hiester, D., 'Research with the Wechsler Intelligence Scales for Adults: 1965–1970', *Psychol. Record*, vol. 21, 1971, pp. 289–339.
35. Wechsler, D., *Wechsler-Bellevue Intelligence Scale, Form 1*, The Psychological Corporation, New York, 1939.
36. Wechsler, D., *The Measurement of Adult Intelligence* (3rd edn), Williams & Wilkins, Baltimore, 1944.
37. Britton, P. G. and Savage, R. D., 'A short form of the WAIS for use with the aged', *Brit. J. Psychiat.*, vol. 112, 1966, pp. 417–18.
38. Levine, N. R., 'Validation of the Quick Test for intelligence screening of the elderly', *Psychol. Reports*, vol. 29, 1971, pp. 167–72.
39. Norman, R. D., 'A revised deterioration formula for the Wechsler Adult Intelligence Scale', *J. Clin. Psychol.*, vol. 22, 1966, pp. 287–94.
40. Tellegen, A. and Briggs, P. F., 'Old wine in new skins: grouping Wechsler subtests into new scales', *J. Consult. Psychol.*, vol. 31, 1967, pp. 499–506.
41. Jannssen, R. H., Welman, A. J. and Colla, P., 'Wechsler-Bellevue test and brain-damaged patients', *Nederlands Tijdschrift voor de Psychologie en haar Grensgebieden*, vol. 24, 1969, pp. 257–66.
42. Gonen, J. Y., 'The use of Wechsler's deterioration quotient in

cases of diffuse and symmetrical cerebral atrophy', *J. Clin. Psychol.*, vol. 26, 1970, pp. 174–7.
43. Bromley, D. B., 'Age differences in conceptual abilities', in *Processes of Aging, Social and Psychological Perspectives*, vol. 1, ed. R. H. Williams, C. Tibbitts and W. Donahue, Atherton Press, New York, 1963, pp. 96–112.
44. Bromley, D. B., 'Age differences in the Porteus Maze Test', in *Proc. VIIth Intern. Congress Gerontology*, International Association of Gerontology, San Francisco, 1966, pp. 225–8.
45. Horn, J. L., 'Organization of data on life-span development of human abilities', in *Life-Span Developmental Psychology*, ed. L. R. Goulet and P. B. Baltes, Academic Press, New York, 1970, pp. 423–66.
46. Bromley, D. B., 'Rank order cluster analysis', *Brit. J. Math. and Stat. Psychol.*, vol. 19, 1966, pp. 105–23.
47. Bilash, I. and Zubek, J. P., 'The effects of age on factorially "pure" mental abilities', *J. Gerontol.*, vol. 15, 1960, pp. 175–82.
48. Horn, J. L. and Cattell, R. B., 'Age differences in primary mental ability factors', *J. Gerontol.*, vol. 21, 1966, pp. 210–20.
49. Savage, R. D. and Britton, P. G., 'The factorial structure of the WAIS in an aged sample', *J. Gerontol.*, vol. 23, 1969, pp. 183–6.
50. Reinert, G., 'Comparative factor analytic studies of intelligence throughout the human life-span', in *Life-Span Developmental Psychology*, ed. L. R. Goulet and P. B. Baltes, Academic Press, New York, 1970, pp. 467–84.
51. Papalia, D. E. 'The status of several conservation abilities across the life-span', *Human Develop.*, vol. 15, 1972, pp. 229–43.
52. Bromley, D. B., 'Age and sex differences in the serial production of creative conceptual responses', *J. Gerontol.*, vol. 22, 1967, pp. 32–42.
53. Heron, A. and Chown, S. M., *Age and Function*, J. and A. Churchill Ltd, 1967.
54. Young, M. L., 'Age and sex differences in problem solving', *J. Gerontol.*, vol. 26, 1971, pp. 330–36.
55. Owens, W. A., 'Age and mental abilities: a second adult follow-up', *J. Educ. Psychol.*, vol. 57, 1966, pp. 311–25.
56. Burns, R. B., 'Age and mental ability: re-testing with thirty-three years interval', *Brit. J. Educ. Psychol.*, vol. 36, 1966, p. 116.
57. Wall, W. D. and Williams, H. L., *Longitudinal Studies and the Social Sciences*, Heinemann, 1970.
58. Hall, E. A., Savage, R. D., Bolton, N., Pidwell, D. M. and Bles-

sed, G., 'Intellect, mental illness, and survival in the aged: a longitudinal investigation', *J. Gerontol.*, vol. 27, 1972, pp. 237–44.

59. Blum, J. E., Jarvik, L. F and Clark, E. T., 'Rate of change on selective tests of intelligence: a twenty-year longitudinal study of aging', *J. Gerontol.*, vol. 25, 1970, pp. 171–6.
60. See notes 5 and 6 above.

CHAPTER SEVEN

1. Lehman, H. C., *Age and Achievement*, Oxford University Press, 1953.
2. Lehman, H. C., 'More about age and achievement', *Gerontologist*, vol. 2, 1962, pp. 141–8.
3. Lehman, H. C., 'The creative production rates of present versus past generations of scientists', *J. Gerontol.*, vol. 17, 1962, pp. 409–17.
4. Lehman, H. C., 'The relationship between chronological age and high level research output in physics and chemistry', *J. Gerontol.*, vol. 19, 1964, pp. 157–64.
5. Lehman, H. C., 'The production of masterworks prior to age 30', *Gerontologist*, vol. 5, 1965, pp. 24–30.
6. Lehman, H. C., 'Young thinkers and memorable creative achievements', *J. Genetic Psychol.*, vol. 105, 1964, pp. 237–55.
7. Lehman, H. C., 'The most creative years of engineers and other technologists', *J. Genetic Psychol.*, vol. 108, 1966, pp. 263–77.
8. Bromley, D. B., 'Some experimental tests of the effect of age on creative intellectual output', *J. Gerontol.*, vol. 11, 1956, pp. 74–82.
9. Bromley, D. B., 'Age and sex differences in the serial production of creative conceptual responses', *J. Gerontol.*, vol. 22, 1967, pp. 32–4.
10. Dennis, W., 'Creative productivity between the ages of 20 and 80 years', in *Middle Age and Aging*, ed. B. L. Neugarten, University of Chicago Press, 1968, pp. 106–14.
11. Taylor, C., 'Age and achievement of noted pianists', *Proc. 77th Annual Conv. of Amer. Psychol. Assocn*, vol. 4, 1969, pp. 745–6.
12. Committee on Higher Education, *Higher Education, Appendix Three: Teachers in Higher Education*, H.M.S.O., 1963.

CHAPTER EIGHT

1. Loughmiller, G. C., Ellison, D. L., Taylor, C. W. and Price, P. B., 'Predicting career performance of physicians using the biographical inventory approach', *Proc. 78th Annual Conv. of Amer. Psychol. Assocn*, vol. 5, 1970, pp. 153–4.
2. Pearson, J. S., Swenson, W. M. and Rome, H. P., 'Age and sex differences related to MMPI response frequency in 25,000 medical patients', *Amer. J. Psychiat.*, vol. 121, 1965, pp. 988–95.
3. Thumin, F. J., 'MMPI profiles as a function of chronological age', *Psychol. Reports*, vol. 22, 1968, pp. 479–82.
4. Britton, P. G. and Savage, R. D., 'The factorial structure of the Minnesota Multiphasic Personality Inventory from an aged sample', *J. Genetic Psychol.*, vol. 114, 1969, pp. 13–17.
5. Bolton, N. and Savage, R. D., 'Neuroticism and extraversion in elderly normal subjects and psychiatric patients: some normative data', *Brit. J. Psychiat.*, vol. 118, 1971, pp. 473–4.
6. Rosen, J. L. and Neugarten, B. L., 'Ego functions in the middle and later years: a thematic apperception study of normal adults', *J. Gerontol.*, vol. 15, 1960, pp. 62–7.
7. Carp, F. M., 'The applicability of an empirical scoring standard for a sentence completion test administered to two age groups', *J. Gerontol.*, vol. 22, 1967, pp. 301–7.
8. Smith, J. M., 'Age differences in achievement motivation', *Brit. J. Soc. Clin. Psychol.*, vol. 9, 1970, pp. 175–6.
9. Katz, S., 'Progress in development of the index of ADL', *Gerontologist*, vol. 19, 1970, pp. 20–30.
10. Kogan, N. and Shelton, F. C., 'Beliefs about "old people": a comparative study of older and younger samples', *J. Genetic Psychol.*, vol. 100, 1962, pp. 93–111.
11. Aaronson, B. S., 'Personality stereotypes of aging', *J. Gerontol.*, vol. 21, 1966, pp. 458–62.
12. Palmore, E., 'Attitudes toward aging as shown by humor', *Gerontologist*, vol. 11, 1971, pp. 181–6.
13. Neugarten, B. L., 'Adult personality: toward a psychology of the life cycle', in *Middle Age and Aging*, ed. B. L. Neugarten, University of Chicago Press, 1968, pp. 137–47.
14. Neugarten, B. L., 'Dynamics of transition of middle age to old age. Adaptation and the life cycle', *J. Geriat. Psychiat.*, vol. 4, 1970, pp. 71–87.

15. Parkes, C. M., 'Psycho-social transitions: a field for study', *Social Science and Medicine*, vol. 5, 1971, pp. 101–15.
16. Kuhlen, R. G., 'Developmental changes in motivation during the adult years', in *Middle Age and Aging*, ed. B. L. Neugarten, University of Chicago Press, 1968, pp. 115–36.
17. Carp, F. M., 'Attitudes of old persons towards themselves and others', *J. Gerontol.*, vol. 22, 1967, pp. 308–12.
18. Botwinick, J., 'Age differences in self-ratings of confidence', *Psychol. Reports*, vol. 27, 1970, pp. 865–6.
19. Vroom, V. H. and Pahl, B., 'Relationship between age and risk taking among managers', *J. Appl. Psychol.*, vol. 55, 1971, pp. 388–405.
20. Erikson, E. H., 'Generativity and ego integrity', in *Middle Age and Aging*, ed. B. L. Neugarten, University of Chicago Press, 1968, pp. 85–8.
21. Pressey, S. L. and Pressey, A. D., 'Two insiders' searchings for best life in old age', *Gerontologist*, vol. 6, 1966, pp. 14–16.
22. Havighurst, R. J., 'How does it feel to grow old?', *Gerontologist*, vol. 6, 1966, pp. 130–31.
23. Neugarten, B. L. (ed.), *Middle Age and Aging*, University of Chicago Press, 1968.
24. Field, J. G., *The Health of Middle Aged Men. A Research Contribution to a Campaign*, prepared for The Health Education Council, Behavioural Science Consultants Ltd, 1970.
25. Sofer, C., 'The career as a personal experience', in *Men in Mid-Career*, Cambridge University Press, 1970, pp. 39–70.
26. Pineo, P. C., 'Disenchantment in the later years of marriage', in *Middle Age and Aging*, ed. B. L. Neugarten, University of Chicago Press, 1968, pp. 258–62.
27. Segal, B. E., 'Suicide and middle age', *Sociological Symposium*, vol. 3, 1969, pp. 131–40.
28. Eisenstadt, S. N., *From Generation to Generation: Age Groups and the Social Structure*, Free Press of Glencoe, New York, 1956.
29. Troll, L. E., 'Issues in the study of generations', *Aging and Human Dev.*, vol. 1, 1970, pp. 199–218.
30. Reichard, S., Livson, F. and Peterson, P. G., *Aging and Personality: A Study of Eighty-Seven Older Men*, John Wiley, New York, 1962.
31. Oden, M. H., 'The fulfillment of promise: 40-year follow-up of the Terman gifted group', *Genetic Psychol. Monographs*, vol. 77, 1968, pp. 3–93.

32. Sander, F. M. and Greenberg, H. R., 'A proverbial excursion: on the hazards of administering proverbs to test the capacity to abstract', *Psychiat. Quart.*, vol. 42, 1968, pp. 696–7.
33. Neugarten, B. L., 'The awareness of middle age', in *Middle Age and Aging*, ed. B. L. Neugarten, University of Chicago Press, 1968, pp. 93–8.
34. Chown, S. M. 'Age and the rigidities', *J. Gerontol.*, vol. 16, 1961, pp. 353–62.
35. Edwards, A. E. and Wine, D. B., 'Personality changes with age: their dependency on concomitant intellectual decline', *J. Gerontol.*, vol. 18, 1963, pp. 182–4.

CHAPTER NINE

1. Feifel, H. (ed.), *The Meaning of Death*, McGraw-Hill, 1959.
2. Glaser, B. G. and Strauss, A. L., *Awareness of Dying*, Aldine, Chicago, 1965.
3. Fulton, R. (ed.), *Death and Identity*, John Wiley, 1965.
4. Munnichs, J. M. A., *Old Age and Finitude, A Contribution to Psychogerontology*, S. Karger, Basel, 1966.
5. Hinton, J., *Dying* (2nd edn), Penguin Books, 1972.
6. Kubler-Ross, E., *On Death and Dying*, Macmillan Co., New York, 1969.
7. Brim, O. G., Freeman, H. E., Levine, S. and Scotch, N. A. (eds.), *The Dying Patient*, Russell Sage Foundation, New York, 1970.
8. U.S. Dept of Health, Education and Welfare, Public Health Service, National Institute of Child Health and Human Development, *Selected Bibliography on Death and Dying*, U.S. Govt Printing Office, Washington, D.C., 1970.
9. Grollman, E. A., *Talking About Death: A Dialogue Between Parent and Child*, Beacon Press, Boston, 1970.
10. Parkes, C. M., *Bereavement: Studies of Grief in Adult Life*, Tavistock Publications, 1972.
11. Kastenbaum, R. and Aisenberg, R. B., *Psychology of Death*, Springer Publ. Co., New York, 1972.
12. Beecher, H. K. and Dorr, H. I., 'The new definition of death: some opposing views', *Int. J. Clin. Pharmacol., Therapy and Toxicol.*, vol. 5, 1971, pp. 120–24.
13. Gorer, G., *Death, Grief and Mourning*, Cresset Press, 1965.
14. Glaser, B. G. and Strauss, A. L., 'Temporal aspects of dying as a

non-scheduled status passage', in *Middle Age and Aging*, ed. B. L. Neugarten, University of Chicago Press, 1968, pp. 520–30.
15. Beaty, N. L., *The Craft of Dying: A Study in the Literary Tradition of Ars Moriendi in England*, Yale University Press, New Haven, 1970.
16. Cartwright, A., Hockey, L. and Anderson, J. L., *Life Before Death*, Routledge & Kegan Paul, 1973.
17. Meerloo, J. A. M., 'Het sterven bij bejaarden: Discussie van preadvies over euthanasia' ('Dying in the aged and euthanasia'), *Nederlands Tijdschrift voor Gerontologie*, vol. 2, 1971, pp. 302–5.
18. Ley, P. and Hopkinson, G., *Communicating with the Patient*, Staples Press, 1967.
19. Hinton, J., 'Assessing the views of the dying', *Social Science and Medicine*, vol. 5, 1971, pp. 37–43.
20. Kazza, D. S. and Vickers, R., 'Geriatric staff attitudes toward death', *J. Amer. Geriatrics Soc.*, vol. 16, 1968, pp. 1364–71.
21. Golub, S. and Reznikoff, M., 'Attitudes toward death: a comparison of nursing students and graduate nurses', *Nursing Research*, vol. 20, 1971, pp. 503–8.
22. Cramond, W. A., 'Psychotherapy of the dying patient', *Brit. Med. J.*, vol. 3, 1970, pp. 389–93.
23. See note 10 above.
24. Ellison, D. L., 'Alienation and the will to live', *J. Gerontol.*, vol. 24, 1969, pp. 361–7.
25. Cannon, W. B., '"Voodoo" death', *Amer. Anthropologist*, vol. 44, 1942, pp. 169–81.
26. Weisman, A. D. and Kastenbaum, R., *The Psychological Autopsy: A Study of the Terminal Phase of Life*, Behavioral Publications Inc., New York, 1968.
27. Feifel, H., 'Older persons look at death', *Geriatrics*, vol. 11, 1956, pp. 127–30.
28. Roberts, J. L., Kimsey, L. R., Logan, D. L. and Shaw, G., 'How aged in nursing homes view dying and death', *Geriatrics*, vol. 25, 1970, pp. 115–19.
29. Averill, J. R., 'Grief: Its nature and significance', *Psychol. Bull.*, vol. 70, 1968, pp. 721–48.
30. Clayton, P. J., Demarais, L. and Winokur, G., 'A study of normal bereavement', *Amer. J. Psychiat.*, vol. 125, 1968, pp. 168–78.
31. Schneidman, E. S., 'Orientations towards death: a vital aspect of the study of lives', *Internat. J. Psychiatry*, vol. 2, 1968, pp. 167–88.

32. Feifel, H., 'Attitudes towards death: a psychological perspective', *J. Consult. and Clin. Psychol.*, vol. 33, 1969, pp. 292–5.
33. Maddison, D. and Viola, A., 'The health of widows in the year following bereavement', *J. Psychosomatic Research*, vol. 12, 1968, pp. 297–306.
34. Parkes, C. M., Benjamin, B. and Fitzgerald, R. G., 'Broken heart: a statistical study of increased mortality among widowers', *Brit. Med. J.*, vol. 1, 1969, pp. 740–43.
35. Parkes, C. M., 'The first year of bereavement: a longitudinal study of the reaction of London widows to the death of their husbands', *Psychiatry*, vol. 33, 1970, pp. 444–67.
36. Clayton, P. J., Kalikes, J. A. and Maurice, W. L., 'The bereavement of the widowed', *Diseases of the Nervous System*, vol. 32, 1971, pp. 597–604.

CHAPTER TEN

1. Mayer-Gross, W., Slater, E. and Roth, M., *Clinical Psychiatry* (3rd edn), Ballière, Tindall & Cox, 1969.
2. Busse, F. W. and Pfeiffer, F. 'Functional psychiatric disorders', in *Behavior and Adaptation in Late Life*, ed. F. W. Busse and F. Pfeiffer, Little, Brown & Co., Boston, 1969, pp. 183–235.
3. Wang, H-S., 'Organic brain syndromes', op. cit., pp. 263–87.
4. Zung, W. W. K., 'Depression in the normal adult population', *Psychosomatics*, vol. 12, 1971, pp. 164–7.
5. Hare, E. H., Price, J. S. and Slater, E. T. O., 'The age-distribution of schizophrenia and neurosis: findings in a national sample', *Brit. J. Psychiat.*, vol. 119, 1971, pp. 445–8.
6. Turner, B. F., Tobin, S. S. and Lieberman, M. A., 'Personality traits as predictors of institutional adaptation among the aged', *J. Gerontol.*, vol. 27, 1972, pp. 61–8.
7. Kay, D. W. K., Garside, R. F., Roy, J. R. and Beamish, P., '"Endogenous" and "neurotic" syndromes of depression: a 5- to 7-year follow-up of 104 cases', *Brit. J. Psychiat.*, vol. 115, 1969, pp. 389–99.
8. Bergmann, K., 'The neuroses of old age', in *Recent Developments in Psychogeriatrics*, ed. D. W. K. Kay and A. Walk, Headley Brothers Ltd., Ashford, Kent, 1971, pp. 39–50.
9. Crisp, A. H. and Priest, R. G., 'Psychoneurotic profiles in middle age', *Brit. J. Psychiat.*, vol. 119, 1971, pp. 385–92.

10. Kellner, R., *Family Ill-Health: An Investigation in General Practice*, Tavistock Publications, 1963.
11. Rahe, R. H., McKean, J. D. and Arthur, R. J., 'A longitudinal study of life-change and illness patterns', *J. Psychosomatic Research*, vol. 10, 1967, pp. 355–66.
12. Hays, D. S. and Wisotsky, M., 'The aged offender: a review of the literature and two current studies from the New York State Division of Parole', *J. Amer. Geriatrics Soc.*, vol. 17, 1969, pp. 1064–73.
13. Epstein, J. C., Mills, C. and Simon, A., 'Anti-social behavior of the elderly', *Comprehensive Psychiatry*, vol. 11, 1970, pp. 36–42.
14. Allersma, J., 'Ouderdom en criminaliteit' ('Criminality in old age'), *Nederlands Tijdschrift voor Gerontologie*, vol. 2, 1971, pp. 285–93.
15. Horrocks, J. E. and Mussman, M. C., 'Middlescence: age-related stress periods during adult years', *Genet. Psychol. Monograph*, vol. 82, 1970, p. 119.
16. Kay, D. W. K. and Bergmann, K., 'Physical disability and mental health in old age', *J. Psychosomatic Research*, vol. 10, 1966, pp. 3–12.
17. Blundell, E., 'A psychological study of the effects of surgery on eighty-six elderly patients', *Brit. J. Soc. and Clin. Psychol.*, vol. 6, 1967, pp. 297–303.
18. Anderson, W. F., 'The inter-relationship between physical and mental disease in the elderly', in *Recent Developments in Psychogeriatrics*, ed. D. W. K. Kay and A. Walk, Headley Brothers Ltd, Ashford, Kent, 1971, pp. 19–24.
19. Greger, J., 'Somatische und psychosoziale Faktoren im Vorfeld psychischer Ekrankungen des höheren Lebensalters' ('Somatic and psychosocial factors in the time immediately before psychiatric illnesses of the older age groups'), *Psychiatria Clinica*, vol. 4, 1971, pp. 159–77.
20. Barraclough, B. M., 'Suicide in the elderly', in *Recent Developments in Psychogeriatrics*, ed. D. W. K. Kay and A. Walk, Headley Brothers Ltd., Ashford, Kent, 1971, pp. 87–97.
21. McCulloch, J. W. and Philip, A. E., *Suicidal Behaviour*, Pergamon Press, 1972.
22. Lester, D., *Why People Kill Themselves*, C. C. Thomas, Springfield, 1972.
23. General Register Office, *The Registrar General's Statistical Review of England and Wales*, Medical Tables, H.M.S.O., 1969.
24. See note 10 above.
25. Kay, D. W. K., Beamish, P. and Roth, M., 'Old age mental dis-

orders in Newcastle upon Tyne. Part I: A Study of Prevalence; Part II: A Study of Possible Social and Medical Causes; Part III: A Factorial Study of Medical, Psychiatric and Social Characteristics', *Brit. J. Psychiat.*, vol. 110, 1964, pp. 146–58 and 668–82; vol. 111, 1965, pp. 939–46.

26. Åkesson, H. O., 'A population study of senile and arteriosclerotic psychoses', *Human Heredity*, vol. 19, 1969, pp. 546–66.
27. Corsellis, J. A. N., *Mental Illness and the Ageing Brain*, Maudsley Monograph No. 9, Oxford University Press, 1962.
28. Blessed, G., Tomlinson, B. E. and Roth, M., 'The association between quantitative measures of dementia and of degenerative changes in the cerebral grey matter of elderly subjects', *Brit. J. Psychiat.*, vol. 114, 1968, pp. 797–811.
29. Blumenthal, H. T., *The Regulatory Role of the Nervous System in Aging*, S. Karger, Basel, 1970.
30. Roth, M., 'Classification and aetiology in mental disorders of old age: some recent developments', in *Recent Developments in Psychogeriatrics*, ed. D. W. K. Kay and A. Walk, Headley Brothers Ltd, Ashford, Kent, 1971, pp. 1–18.
31. Post, F., *The Clinical Psychiatry of Late Life*, Pergamon Press, 1965.
32. Post, F., 'Schizo-affective symptomatology in late life', *Brit. J. Psychiat.*, vol. 118, 1971, pp. 437–55.
33. Muller, C. and Ciompi, L. (eds.), *Senile Dementia*, H. Huber, Bern, Switzerland, 1968.
34. McDonald, C., 'Clinical heterogeneity in senile dementia', *Brit. J. Psychiat.*, vol. 115, 1969, pp. 267–71.
35. Alexander, D. A., '"Senile dementia": a changing perspective', *Brit. J. Psychiat.*, vol. 121, 1972, pp. 207–14.
36. Neilsen, J., 'Chromosomes in senile, presenile and arteriosclerotic dementia', *J. Gerontol.*, vol. 25, 1970, pp. 312–15.
37. Kay, D. W. K. Garside, R. F., Beamish, P. and Roy, J. R., 'Endogenous and neurotic syndromes of depression: a factor analytic study of 104 cases: clinical features', *Brit. J. Psychiat.*, vol. 115, 1969, pp. 377–88.
38. Post, F., *Persistent Persecutory States of the Elderly*, Pergamon Press, 1966.
39. Herbert, M. E. and Jacobson, S., 'Late paraphrenia', *Brit. J. Psychiat.*, vol. 113, 1967, pp. 461–9.
40. Salmon, J. H., 'Senile and pre-senile dementia', *Geriatrics*, vol. 24, 1969, pp. 67–72.

41. Isaacs, B., 'Studies of illness and death in the elderly in Glasgow. Part One: Survival of the unfittest; a survey of geriatric patients in Glasgow; Part Two: Life before dying', *Scottish Health Service Studies*, No. 17, Scottish Home and Health Department, Edinburgh, 1971.
42. Felstein, I., *Later Life: Geriatrics Today and Tomorrow*, Penguin Books, 1969.
43. Anderson, W. F., *Practical Management of the Elderly*, F. A. Davis, Philadelphia, 1971.
44. Kay, D. W. K., and Walk, A. (eds.), *Recent Developments in Psychogeriatrics*, Headley Brothers Ltd., Ashford, Kent, 1971.
45. Brody, E., 'Long-term care for the elderly: optimums, options and opportunities', *J. Amer. Geriatrics Soc.*, vol. 19, 1971, pp. 482–94.
46. Consumers' Association, *Arrangements for Old Age*, Consumers' Association, 1969.
47. Markus, E., Blenkner, M., Bloom, M. and Downs, T., 'The impact of relocation upon mortality rates of institutionalized aged persons', *J. Gerontol.*, vol. 26, 1971, pp. 537–41.
48. Rosenkranz, H. W. and Pihlblad, C. T., 'Measuring the health of the elderly', *J. Gerontol.*, vol. 25, 1970, pp. 129–33.
49. Brody, E. M., Kleban, M. H., Lawton, M. P. and Silverman, H. A., 'Excess disabilities of mentally impaired aged: impact of individualized treatment', *Gerontologist*, vol. 11, 1971, pp. 124–33.
50. Kleban, M. H. and Brody, E. M., 'Prediction of improvement in mentally impaired aged: personality ratings by social workers', *J. Gerontol.*, vol. 27, 1972, pp. 69–76.
51. Williams, M., 'Geriatric patients', in *The Psychological Assessment of Mental and Physical Handicaps*, ed. P. Mittler, Methuen, 1970, pp. 319–39.
52. Kendrick, D. C. and Post, F., 'Differences in cognitive status between healthy, psychiatrically ill, and diffusely brain-damaged elderly subjects', *Brit. J. Psychiat.*, vol. 113, 1967, pp. 75–81.
53. Bolton, N., Savage, R. D. and Roth, M., 'The Modified Word Learning Test and the aged psychiatric patient', *Brit. J. Psychiat.*, vol. 113, 1967, pp. 9–40.
54. Lishman, W. A., 'Amnesic syndromes and their neuropathology', in *Recent Developments in Psychogeriatrics*, ed. D. W. K. Kay and A. Walk, Headley Brothers Ltd, Ashford, Kent, 1971, pp. 25–38.
55. Irving, G., Robinson, R. A. and McAdam, W., 'The validity of some cognitive tests in the diagnosis of dementia', *Brit. J. Psychiat.*, vol. 117, 1970, pp. 149–56.

56. Savage, R. D., 'Psychometric assessment and clinical diagnosis in the aged', in *Recent Developments in Psychogeriatrics*, ed. D. W. K. Kay and A. Walk, Headley Brothers Ltd, Ashford, Kent, 1971, pp. 51–61.
57. Post, F., 'The diagnostic process', op. cit., pp. 63–73.
58. Wilson, L. A. and Brass, W., 'Brief assessment of the mental state in geriatric domiciliary practice: the usefulness of the mental status questionnaire', *Age and Ageing*, vol. 2, 1973, pp. 92–101.
59. Hodkinson, H. M., 'Evaluation of a mental test score for assessment of mental impairment in the elderly', *Age and Ageing*, vol. 1, 1972, pp. 233–8.
60. Gilmore, A. J. J., 'Personality in the elderly: problems in methodology', *Age and Ageing*, vol. 1, 1972, pp. 227–32.
61. Howell, S. C., et al., 'A Symposium on the Assessment of Functions of the Aging Adult', in 5 parts, *Gerontologist*, vol. 10, 1970, pp. 18–52.
62. Meer, B. and Baker, J. A., 'The Stockton Geriatric Rating Scale', *J. Gerontol.*, vol. 21, 1966, pp. 392–403.
63. King, M. and Krag, C. L., 'The use of the Stockton Geriatric Rating Scale in evaluating large groups of chronically ill geriatric patients in a psychiatric hospital', *California Mental Health Research Digest*, vol. 5, 1967, pp. 163–4.
64. Spitzer, R. L., Fleiss, J. L., Endicott, J. and Cohen, J., 'Mental status schedule: properties of factor-analytically derived scales', *Archives Gen. Psychiat.*, vol. 16, 1967, pp. 479–93.
65. Savage, R. D. and Britton, P. G., 'A short scale for the assessment of mental health in the community aged', *Brit. J. Psychiat.*, vol. 113, 1967, pp. 521–3.
66. Gurel, L., Linn, M. W. and Linn, B. S., 'Physical and mental impairment-of-function evaluation in the aged: the PAMIE scale', *J. Gerontol.*, vol. 27, 1972, pp. 83–90.
67. Apfeldorf, M. and Hunley, P. J., 'The adjective check list applied to older institutionalized men', *J. Personality Assessment*, vol. 35, 1971, pp. 457–62.
68. Yoshino, H., 'Characteristics of word association in some samples of the aged', ex. 'Tohoku Psychologica Folia', tom XXV, fasc. 3–4, 1967, pp. 115–23.
69. Bevans, H. G., 'Development of experimental method assessing attention, learning and recall in geriatric patients', in *Ageing of the Central Nervous System*, ed. H. M. van Praag, De E. F. Bohn, N.V., Haarlem, 1972, pp. 123–40.

70. Lawton, M. P., 'Gerontology in clinical psychology, and vice-versa', *Aging and Human Dev.*, vol. 1, 1970, pp. 147–59.

71. Gedye, J. L. and Miller, E., 'Developments in automated testing systems', in *The Psychological Assessment of Mental and Physical Handicaps*, ed. P. Mittler, Methuen, 1970, pp. 735–60.

72. Brierley, H., 'A fully automated intellectual test', *Brit. J. Soc. Clin. Psychol.*, vol. 10, 1971, pp. 286–8.

73. Lehmann, H. E. and Kral, V. A., 'Psychological tests: practice effects on geriatric patients', *Geriatrics*, vol. 23, 1968, pp. 160–63.

74. Alexander, D. A., 'The application of the Graham-Kendall Memory-for-Designs Test to elderly normal and psychiatric groups', *Brit. J. Soc. Clin. Psychol.*, vol. 9, 1970, pp. 85–6.

75. Rechtschaffen, A., 'Psychotherapy with geriatric patients: a review of the literature', *J. Gerontol.*, vol. 14, 1959, pp. 73–84.

76. Wolff, K., 'Individual psychotherapy with geriatric patients', *Psychosomatics*, vol. 12, 1971, pp. 89–93.

77. Meerloo, J. A. M., 'Ervaringen met psychotherapie boj bejaarden' ('Psychotherapy with the aged'), *Nederlands Tijdschrift voor Gerontologie*, vol. 2, 1971, pp. 160–69.

78. Kubie, S. H. and Landau, G., *Group Work with the Aged*, International Universities Press, 1969.

79. Butler, R. N., 'The life review: an interpretation of reminiscence in the aged', in *Middle Age and Aging*, ed. B. L. Neugarten, University of Chicago Press, 1968, pp. 486–96.

80. Lewis, C. N., 'Reminiscing and self-concept in old age', *J. Gerontol.*, vol. 26, 1971, pp. 240–43.

81. Havighurst, R. J. and Glasser, R., 'An exploratory study of reminiscence', *J. Gerontol.*, vol. 27, 1972, pp. 245–53.

82. Meichenbaum, D. H., 'Training of the aged in the verbal control of behaviour', in *Proc. IXth Intern. Congress of Gerontology*, International Association of Gerontology, Kiev, 1972, p. 361.

83. Cohen, D., 'Research problems and concepts in the study of aging: assessment and behavior modification', *Gerontologist*, vol. 7, 1967, pp. 13–19.

84. Cautela J. R. 'A classical conditioning approach to the development and modification of behavior in the aged', *Gerontologist*, vol. 9, 1969, pp. 109–13.

85. Libb, J. W. and Clements, C. B., 'Token reinforcement in an exercise program for hospitalized geriatric patients', *Perceptual and Motor Skills*, vol. 28, 1969, pp. 957–8.

86. Richman, L., 'Sensory training for geriatric patients', *Amer. J. Occup. Therapy*, vol. 23, 1969, pp. 254–7.
87. Leow C. A. and Silverstone, B. M., 'A program of intensified stimulation and response facilitation for the senile aged', *Gerontologist*, vol. 11, 1971, pp. 341–7.
88. Baltes, P. B. (ed.) et al., Symposium on 'Psychological Intervention in Old Age', *Gerontologist*, vol. 13, 1973, pp. 4–38.
89. Lindsley, O. R., 'Geriatric behavioral prosthetics', in *New Thoughts on Old Age*, ed. R. Kastenbaum, Springer Publ. Co., New York, 1964, pp. 41–60.
90. Mueller, D. J. and Atlas, L., 'Resocialization of regressed elderly residents: a behavioral management approach', *J. Gerontol.*, vol. 27, 1972, pp. 390–92.
91. Pastalan, L. A., and Carson, D. H. (eds), *Spatial Behavior of Older People*, Ann Arbor: University of Michigan, 1970.
92. McCulloch, T. L., 'The retarded child grows up: psychological aspects of aging', *Amer. J. Mental Deficiency*, vol. 62, 1957, pp. 201–8.
93. Baller, W. R., Charles, D. C. and Miller, E. L., 'Mid-life attainment of the mentally retarded: a longitudinal study', *Genetic Psychol. Monographs*, vol. 75, 1967, pp. 235–329.
94. Francis, S. H., 'Behavior of low-grade institutionalized mongoloids: changes with age', *Amer. J. Mental Deficiency*, vol. 75, 1970, pp. 92–101.
95. Elam, L. H. and Blumenthal, H. T., 'Aging in the mentally retarded' in *Interdisciplinary Topics in Gerontology, Vol. 7 The Regulatory Role of the Nervous System in Aging*, ed. H. T. Blumenthal, S. Karger, New York, 1970, pp. 87–117.

CHAPTER ELEVEN

1. Schaie, K. W., 'Age changes and age differences', *Gerontologist*, vol. 7, 1967, pp. 128–32.
2. Riegel, K. F., Riegel, R. M. and Meyer, G., 'Socio-psychological factors of aging: a cohort-sequential analysis', *Human Develop.*, vol. 10, 1967, pp. 27–56.
3. Baltes, P. B., 'Longitudinal and cross-sectional sequences in the study of age and generation effects', *Human Develop.*, vol. 11, 1968, pp. 145–71.
4. Goulet, L. R. and Baltes, P. B. (eds.), *Life-span Developmental Psychology*, Academic Press, New York, 1970.

5. Wohlwill, J. F., 'The age variable in psychological research' *Psychol. Review*, vol. 77, 1970, pp. 49–64.
6. Nesselroade, J. R., Schaie, K. W. and Baltes, P. B., 'Ontogenetic and generational components of structural and quantitative change in adult behavior', *J. Gerontol.*, vol. 27, 1972, pp. 222–8.
7. Riegel, K. F. and Riegel, R. M., 'Development, drop, and death', *Develop. Psychol.*, vol. 6, 1972, pp. 306–19.
8. Nesselroade, J. R. and Reese, H. W. (eds.), *Lifespan Developmental Psychology: Methodological Issues*, Academic Press, New York, 1972.
9. Bloom, B. S., *Stability and Change in Human Characteristics*, John Wiley, New York, 1964.
10. Harris, C. W. (ed.), *Problems in Measuring Change*, University of Wisconsin Press, Madison, 1967.
11. Goldstein, H., 'Longitudinal studies and the measurement of change', *Statistician*, vol. 18, 1968, pp. 93–117.
12. Wall, W. D. and Williams, H. L., *Longitudinal Studies and the Social Sciences*, Heinemann, 1970.
13. Murray, J. R., Wiley, D. E. and Wolfe, R. G., 'New statistical techniques for evaluating longitudinal models', *Human Develop.*, vol. 14, 1971, pp. 142–8.
14. Kuhlen, R. G., 'Age and intelligence: the significance of cultural change in longitudinal vs cross-sectional findings', *Vita Humana*, vol. 6, 1963, pp. 113–24.
15. Damon, A., 'Discrepancies between findings of longitudinal and cross-sectional studies in adult life: physique and physiology', *Human Develop.*, vol. 8, 1965, pp. 16–22.
16. Schaie, K. W. and Strother, C. R., 'The effects of time and cohort differences on the interpretation of age changes in cognitive behavior', *Multivariate Behavioral Research*, vol. 3, 1968, pp. 259–94.
17. Schaie, K. W. and Strother, C. R., 'A cross-sequential study of age changes in cognitive behavior', *Psychol. Bull.*, vol. 70, 1968, pp. 671–80.
18. Davies, A. D. M., 'The effects of age, sex, and occupation on selected psychological and physical variables: some preliminary results of a longitudinal survey', in *Ageing of the Central Nervous System: Biological and Psychological Aspects*, ed. H. M. van Praag, De E. F. Bohn, N.V., Amsterdam, 1972, pp. 101–22.
19. Whitehead, F. E., 'Trends in certificated sickness absence', in *Social Trends, No. 2*, Central Statistical Office, H.M.S.O., 1971, pp. 13–23.

20. Oldham, P. D., 'A note on the analysis of repeated measurements of the same subjects', *J. Chronic Diseases*, vol. 15, 1962, pp. 969–77.
21. Sussman, M. B., 'Use of longitudinal designs in studies of long-term illness: some advantages and limitations', *Gerontologist*, vol. 4, 1964, pp. 25–9.
22. Burns, R. B., 'Age and mental ability: re-testing with thirty-three years' interval' (thesis abstract), *Brit. J. Educ. Psychol.*, vol. 36, 1966, p. 116.
23. Blum, J. E., Jarvik, L. F. and Clark, E. T., 'Rate of change on selective tests of intelligence: a twenty-year longitudinal study of aging', *J. Gerontol.*, vol. 25, 1970, pp. 171–6.
24. See notes 4, 6, 7, 12, 14, 17 and 18 above.
25. Birren, J. E., 'Toward an experimental psychology of aging', *Amer. Psychologist*, vol. 25, 1970, pp. 124–35.
26. Baltes, P. B. and Goulet, L. R., 'Exploration of developmental variables by manipulation and simulation of age differences in behavior', *Human Develop.*, vol. 14, 1971, pp. 149–70.
27. Bromley, D. B., 'An approach to theory construction in the psychology of development and aging', in *Life-Span Developmental Psychology*, ed. L. R. Goulet and P. B. Baltes, Academic Press, New York, 1970, pp. 71–114.
28. Reese, H. W. and Overton, W. F., 'Models of development and theories of development', op. cit., pp. 115–45.
29. Blalock, H. M., *Theory Construction*, Prentice-Hall Inc., Englewood Cliffs, N.J., 1969.
30. Blalock, H. M. (ed.), *Causal Models in the Social Sciences*, Macmillan, 1972.
31. Lowenthal, M. F., *Lives in Distress: The Paths of the Elderly to the Psychiatric Ward*, Basic Books Inc., New York, 1964.
32. Cattell, R. B., 'The data box: its ordering of total resources in terms of possible relational systems', in *Handbook of Multivariate Experimental Psychology*, ed. R. B. Cattell, Rand McNally, Chicago, 1966, pp. 67–128.
33. Cattell, R. B., 'The structuring of change by P-technique and incremental R-technique', in *Problems in Measuring Change*, ed. C. W. Harris, University of Wisconsin Press, Madison, 1967, pp. 167–98.
34. Cattell, R. B., 'Comparing factor trait and state scores across ages and cultures', *J. Gerontol.*, vol. 24, 1969, pp. 348–60.
35. Baltes, P. B. and Nesselroade, J. R., 'Multivariate longitudinal and cross-sectional sequences for analyzing ontogenetic and genera-

tional change: a methodological note', *Develop. Psychol.*, vol. 2, 1970, pp. 163–8.

36. Nesselroade, J. R., 'Application of multivariate strategies to problems of measuring and structuring long-term change', in *Life-Span Developmental Psychology*, ed. L. R. Goulet and P. B. Baltes, Academic Press, New York, 1970, pp. 193–207.
37. Corballis, M. C. and Traub, R. E., 'Longitudinal factor analysis', *Psychometrika*, vol. 35, 1970, pp. 79–98.
38. Bereiter, C., 'Some persisting dilemmas in the measurement of change', in *Problems in Measuring Change*, ed. C. W. Harris, University of Wisconsin Press, Madison, 1967, pp. 3–20.
39. Lord, F. M., 'Elementary models for measuring change', op. cit., pp. 21–38.
40. Webster, H. and Bereiter, C., 'The reliability of changes measured by mental test scores', op. cit., pp. 39–59.
41. Cronbach, L. J. and Furby, L., 'How should we measure "change" – or should we?', *Psychol. Bull.*, vol. 74, 1970, pp. 68–80.
42. Werts, C. E. and Linn, R. L., 'Problems with inferring treatment effects from repeated measures', *Educ. and Psychol. Measurement*, vol. 31, 1971, pp. 857–66.
43. Rose, C. H., 'Representatives of volunteer subjects in a longitudinal aging study', *Human Develop.*, vol. 8, 1965, pp. 152–6.
44. Tune, G. S., 'A note on differences between cooperative and non-cooperative volunteer subjects', *Brit. J. Soc. Clin. Psychol.*, vol. 7, 1968, pp. 229–30.
45. Tune, G. S., 'A further note on the differences between cooperative and non-cooperative volunteer subjects', *Brit. J. Soc. Clin. Psychol.*, vol. 8, 1969, pp. 183–4.
46. Schultz, D. P., 'The human subject in psychological research', *Psychol. Bull.*, vol. 72, 1969, pp. 214–28.
47. Slater, R., 'Characteristics of cooperation in a volunteer panel', *Brit. J. Soc. Clin. Psychol.*, vol. 9, 1970, pp. 371–2.
48. Rose, C. L. and Bell, B., *Predicting Longevity: Methodology and Critique*, D. C. Heath & Co., Lexington, 1972.

CHAPTER TWELVE

1. Palmore, E. (ed.), *Normal Aging*, Duke University Press, Durham, N.C., 1970.
2. Eisdorfer, C. and Lawton, M. P. (eds.), *The Psychology of Adult*

Development and Aging, Amer. Psychol. Association, Washington, D.C., 1973.
3. Goldberg, E. M., *Helping the Aged. A Field Experiment in Social Work*. Allen & Unwin, 1970.
4. White House Conference on Aging, 1971, *Towards a National Policy on Aging. Final Report* (2 vols.), U.S. Govt Printing Office, Washington, D.C., 1972.
5. Granick, S. and Patterson, R. D., *Human Aging II. An Eleven-Year Follow-Up Biomedical and Behavioral Study*, U.S. Dept of Health, Education and Welfare, Nat. Inst. Mental Health, Section on Mental Health of the Aging, Rockville, Maryland, 1971.
6. Britton, J. H. and Britton, J. O., *Personality Changes in Aging: A Longitudinal Study of Community Residents*, Springer Publ. Co., New York, 1972.
7. Birren, J. E. et al., 'Research, demonstration and training: issues and methodology in social gerontology', *Gerontologist*, vol. 12, 1972, pp. 49–83.
8. Kalish, R. A. (ed.), *The Dependencies of Old People*, Institute of Gerontology, Ann Arbor: University of Michigan, 1969.

Index of Names

Index of Subjects

MORE ABOUT PENGUINS AND PELICANS

Penguinews, which appears every month, contains details of all the new books issued by Penguins as they are published. From time to time it is supplemented by *Penguins in Print*, which is a complete list of all titles available. (There are some five thousand of these.)

A specimen copy of *Penguinews* will be sent to you free on request. For a year's issues (including the complete lists) please send 50p if you live in the British Isles, or 75p if you live elsewhere. Just write to Dept EP, Penguin Books Ltd, Harmondsworth, Middlesex, enclosing a cheque or postal order, and your name will be added to the mailing list.

In the U.S.A.: For a complete list of books available from Penguin in the United States write to Dept CS, Penguin Books Inc., 7110 Ambassador Road, Baltimore, Maryland 21207.

In Canada: For a complete list of books available from Penguin in Canada write to Penguin Books Canada Ltd, 41 Steelcase Road West, Markham, Ontario.

THE PSYCHOLOGY OF COMMUNICATION

George A. Miller

George Miller (who is Co-director of the Centre for Cognitive Studies at Harvard and whose book, *Psychology: The Science of Mental Life*, has already been published in Pelicans) discusses, in these seven essays, information and memory; the limits to the human capacity for processing information; psychical research; psycholinguistics; computers and cognition; and, finally, his own intellectual hobby, Project Grammarama, an attempt to investigate how people learn the grammatical rules underlying artificial languages.

Amused and amusing in expression, these essays are united by a concern for problems at the intersection of scientific psychology and communication theory.

'Beatifully written . . . It provides a rare insight into a world that is usually hidden from the layman' – *Economist*

'A remarkable achievement. He explains desperately abstruse ideas in elegant metaphor and jaunty simile' – *Evening News*

'An authoritative guide to an exciting field' – *The Times Literary Supplement*

THE PSYCHOLOGY OF CHILDHOOD AND ADOLESCENCE

C. I. Sandstrom

In this concise study of the processes of growing up Professor Sandstrom has produced a book which, although it is perfectly suited to the initial needs of university students and teachers in training, will appeal almost as much to parents and ordinary readers. His text covers the whole story of human physical and mental growth from conception to puberty.

Outlining the scope and history of developmental psychology, Professor Sandstrom goes on to detail the stages of growth in the womb, during the months after birth, and (year by year) up to the age of ten. There follow chapters on physical development, learning and perception, motivation, language and thought, intelligence, the emotions, social adjustment, and personality. The special conditions of puberty and of schooling are handled in the final chapters.

Throughout this masterly study the author necessarily refers to 'norms of development': these neatly represent the average stages of growing up, but (as Professor Mace comments in his introduction) they must only be applied to individual children with caution.

THE PSYCHOLOGY OF MORAL BEHAVIOUR

Derek Wright

It is by no means true that a sheltered 'moral' upbringing, with lots of early nights and Sunday school, produces the most honest guilt-free people: neither is altruism the most helpful of qualities.

In *The Psychology of Moral Behaviour* Derek Wright, of the Department of Psychology at the University of Leicester, introduces the reader to the psychological study of moral behaviour, and in particular to the empirical approach within it. The author takes various theoretical perspectives and examines the following subjects in the light of them.

Why some people find it easier to resist temptation than others, and the psychological effects of doing something wrong; what kinds of adult behaviour induce what kinds of behaviour in children; delinquency; altruism; moral insight and ideology; different types of character; religion; education and morality.

The author emphasizes the difficulty of discussing this subject without being biased by personal beliefs, e.g. Western moral ideas, and sets out to do so along the strictest scientific lines.

THE PSYCHOLOGY OF THINKING

Robert Thomson

Ever since Aristotle defined man as a 'rational animal' psychologists have attempted to show how it is that men have a capacity for thinking about themselves and their environment, which other animals have not managed to achieve. In recent years an increased interest has been shown by psychologists in the problem of describing and explaining the nature of thought. Indeed, one distinguished psychologist has said that the central problem for psychology today is the problem of thought. Not only does this book report some of the recent studies on thinking: it also attempts to evaluate the achievements and limitations of the work which has been carried out. It serves also as a general introduction to several branches of psychological inquiry; it discusses such varied topics as the intelligent behaviour of animals; the formation of a repertory of basic concepts by children; the direct experimental investigation of adult thought processes; the role of learning operations; and imaginative thinking in aesthetic and scientific work.